Asian/Oceanian Historical Dictionaries
Edited by Jon Woronoff

Asia

1. *Vietnam,* by William J. Duiker. 1989
2. *Bangladesh,* by Craig Baxter and Syedur Rahman, second edition. 1989
3. *Pakistan,* by Shahid Javed Burki. 1991
4. *Jordan,* by Peter Gubser. 1991
5. *Afghanistan,* by Ludwig W. Adamec. 1991
6. *Laos,* by Martin Stuart-Fox and Mary Kooyman. 1992
7. *Singapore,* by K. Mulliner and Lian The-Mulliner. 1991
8. *Israel,* by Bernard Reich. 1992
9. *Indonesia,* by Robert Cribb. 1992
10. *Hong Kong and Macau,* by Elfed Vaughan Roberts, Sum Ngai Ling, and Peter Bradshaw. 1992
11. *Korea,* by Andrew C. Nahm. 1993
12. *Taiwan,* by John F. Copper. 1993
13. *Malaysia,* by Amarjit Kaur. 1993
14. *Saudi Arabia,* by J. E. Peterson. 1993
15. *Myanmar,* by Jan Bečka. 1995
16. *Iran,* by John H. Lorentz. 1995
17. *Yemen,* by Robert D. Burrowes. 1995
18. *Thailand,* by May Kyi Win and Harold Smith. 1995
19. *Mongolia,* by Alan J. K. Sanders. 1996
20. *India,* by Surjit Mansingh. 1996
21. *Gulf Arab States,* by Malcolm C. Peck. 1996
22. *Syria,* by David Commins. 1996
23. *Palestine,* by Nafez Y. Nazzal and Laila A. Nazzal. 1997
24. *Philippines,* by Artemio R. Guillermo and May Kyi Win. 1997

Oceania

1. *Australia,* by James C. Docherty. 1992.
2. *Polynesia,* by Robert D. Craig. 1993.
3. *Guam and Micronesia,* by William Wuerch and Dirk Ballendorf. 1994.
4. *Papua New Guinea,* by Ann Turner. 1994.
5. *New Zealand,* by Keith Jackson and Alan McRobie. 1996

New Combined Series

25. *Brunei Darussalam,* by D. S. Ranjit Singh and Jatswan S. Sidhu. 1997
26. *Sri Lanka,* by S. W. R. de A. Samarsinghe and Vidyamali Samarsinghe. 1997
27. *Vietnam,* 2nd ed., by William J. Duiker. 1997
28. *People's Republic of China: 1949–1997,* by Lawrence R. Sullivan, with the assistance of Nancy Hearst. 1997
29. *Afghanistan,* 2nd ed., by Ludwig W. Adamec. 1997
30. *Lebanon,* by As'ad AbuKhalil. 1998

Historical Dictionary of Lebanon

As'ad AbuKhalil

Asian Historical Dictionaries, No. 30

The Scarecrow Press, Inc.
Lanham, Md., & London
1998

SCARECROW PRESS, INC.

Published in the United States of America
by Scarecrow Press, Inc.
4720 Boston Way
Lanham, Maryland 20706

British Library Cataloguing in Publication Information Available

Library of Congress Cataloging-in-Publication Data

AbuKhalil, As'ad.
Historical dictionary of Lebanon / As'ad AbuKhalil.
p. cm. — (Asian historical dictionaries ; no. 30)
Includes bibliographical references (p.).
ISBN 0-8108-3395-6 (cloth : alk. paper)
1. Lebanon—History—Dictionaries. I. Title. II. Series.
DS80.9.A28 1998
956.92'003—dc21 97-26849
CIP

ISBN 0-8108-3395-6 (cloth : alk. paper)

™ The paper used in this publication meets the minimum requirements of American National Standard for Information Sciences—Permanence of Paper for Printed Library Materials, ANSI Z39.48-1984.
Manufactured in the United States of America.

To the memory of my father, Iḥsān AbūKhalīl
to my mother, Jingol ʻAlāyilī

to Ihāb Al-Mudawwar
(who was killed before reaching his target,
figuratively and literally)

and to Maria

That light in his eyes has certainly died,
No heroisms will rescue him,
Not even the humiliation of prayer.

Khalīl Ḥāwī

Contents

Editor's Foreword

During the 1950s and 1960s, Lebanon appeared to be an oasis of peace and prosperity in an otherwise tumultuous Middle East. Then, during the 1970s and into the 1980s, it slid into what was called a civil war but which was, in reality, more like a free-for-all among constantly fragmenting groups that allied with, or fought against, one another and also allied with, or resisted, various outside powers. The situation was, for most observers, incomprehensible. However, it is considerably more understandable after examining Lebanon's twisted history and divided allegiances. That the once-reputed oasis of peace and prosperity was largely a mirage is obvious. Whether the nation and its economy can be patched together in a semblance of harmony and well-being remains uncertain. But it will be easier to assess the future after shedding a few illusions.

The purpose of this *Historical Dictionary of Lebanon* is thus twofold: to provide essential information in order to grasp the realities of an exceedingly complex country and, in passing, to dispel some myths and illusions. This is done with an emphasis on the former, although the frankness of the presentation consistently recalls the latter. The dictionary includes entries on significant persons, parties, and groups across the political spectrum as well as non-political figures who have contributed to Lebanese society and culture. Other entries deal with important political, economic, social, religious, and ethnic institutions. Dramatic events, including coups and civil wars, naturally receive extensive coverage, as does an amazingly lively press. Those who wish to know more about any of these should consult the bibliography.

Lebanon's situation has always been controversial. Any differences of opinion could obviously be glossed over or hidden under cliches and generalities. We are fortunate that the author has most emphatically not taken this easy way out. As'ad AbuKhalil was born and grew up in Lebanon. His knowledge of the country is solid. But it was certainly easier for him to explain the inexplicable to outsiders after residing in the United States, where he continued his studies and began teaching. At present, he is an associate professor of political science at California

State University, Stanislaus, and research fellow at the Center for Middle Eastern Studies at the University of California, Berkeley. He lectured and wrote extensively before taking on this work, arguably one of the most difficult volumes in the series.

Jon Woronoff
Series Editor

Acknowledgments

It was Michael C. Hudson who recommended me as the writer for this book. For that, and much more, I am grateful to him. Michael Hudson and Hanna Batatu were the direct reasons behind my decision to come to the United States to complete my doctoral studies in political science. I was fortunate to work under both of them. Michael Hudson in addition served as my dissertation advisor. His 1968 book *The Precarious Republic* was a source of intellectual inspiration for me long before I ever met him.

I also mention with gratitude Rashid Khalidi, my first political science advisor and mentor. I was fortunate in being able to take every course that Rashid taught at the American University of Beirut, where he served as my master's thesis advisor. Another Lebanon specialist, Augustus Richard Norton, has been supportive of my work; his personal and professional kindness toward me is much appreciated. The editor of the series, Jon Woronoff, has been very patient with me throughout this process. He was prompt in answering my seemingly unending questions. And I am grateful for his superb editing, which honed the style and improved the form of the presentation of this volume.

Gordon S. Adams of the Survey Methods Program at the University of California, Berkeley, was of invaluable help to me at a moment of panic when computer-related problems seemed to paralyze me, as was Larry Giventer, my colleague at California State University, Stanislaus, who hired me. Brian Duff, of the Department of Nuclear Physics at the University of California, Berkeley (not to be confused with Brian Duff of the Department of Political Science) claims that he also was of assistance; although that is disputed, he skillfully managed to get his name into these acknowledgments. Bob Wright, the computer specialist at CSU, Stanislaus, has been tremendously helpful and patient over the years—and with this special project, in particular. Steve Hughes, the chairperson of my department, has been consistently supportive of my work ever since I stepped foot on the campus of CSU, Stanislaus. Lana Jones, our department secretary, has the unenviable task of dealing with the eccentricities and egos of the department faculty; I wish to express my many thanks to her.

Many of my friends have been helpful in locating materials (including Za'tar) for me; I wish to thank Linā Shammā' and Rabī' 'Arīḍī. My close friend from childhood days, Amthal Ismā'īl, has shared with me years of irreverent conversations and arguments on Lebanese affairs, and so has my friend in American exile, Imād al-Hajj. Julie Reuben, of the Interlibrary Loan Department at CSU, Stanislaus, has put up with my complicated requests. Furthermore, Naji Tueni (Marketing Manager of An-Nahār Newspaper) provided key information about dates when I needed them. And my friend Tara-Lynn Schendel ensured the consistent accuracy of all French words. While it is customary to note the assistance of people and institutions in this section, I wish to single out those who did not help. The Lebanese Embassy in Washington, D.C. promised to provide some information but did not, and the Lebanon desk officer at the U.S. Department of State, Victor Hertado, did not return my phone calls.

Finally, some more personal notes. My ex-wife (and permanent friend) Kathy C. Spillman, with whom I spent ten formative years of my life and who is a Middle East specialist in her own right, deserves my thanks for sharing with me a passion for Middle East studies and much more. I learned from her things American, Middle Eastern, and human. I dedicate this book to the memory of my father, Iḥsān AbūKhalīl, who was unrestrained in his support for my work despite our deep political, ideological, cultural, economic, and social disagreements, and to my brilliant mother, Jingol 'Alāyilī who instilled the love of books in me at an early age. I also dedicate this book to the eternal love of my life, Maria R. Rosales, whose impact on my life has been, and will forever be, immeasurable.

Note on Transliteration

While I believe in respecting the expressive forms and flavor of the language that one uses, I am not pleased with the standard forms of English transliteration of Arabic, especially since Arabic words have been consistently corrupted in Western usages. I favor the form of transliteration once used by the Near East Division of the Library of Congress. For this volume, I have tried to be faithful to the classical form of Arabic and when using the Lebanese dialect tried to give the classical rendition of the words. My transliteration is close to that used by the International Journal of Middle East Studies, although I use ḍh for *ḍha'* (instead of z) and ah for *ta' marbūṭah*. I distinguish between Shamsi and Qamarī letters, to remain consistent with Arabic pronunciation of words, although al- was ignored for the purposes of alphabetization of entries. Thus, at-Turk, Niqūlā will be found under t, not a. *Shaddah*, the emphasized letter in Arabic, was always reflected in transliteration. I have violated the rules of transliteration for four common names that have been so popularized in the Western press: Nasser, instead of Nāṣir (although I kept 'Abdul-Nasser as the full last name of the man); Gemayyel, instead of al-Jumayyil; Al-Jahiz, instead of Al-Jāḥiḍh; and Gibran, instead of Jubrān (except for Jubrān Khalīl Jubrān).

Abbreviations and Acronyms

AMAL	*Afwāj al-Muqāwamah al-Lubnāniyyah*
AUB	American University of Beirut
DFLP	Democratic Front for the Liberation of Palestine
IDF	Israeli Defense Forces
IRFID	Institut de Recherche et de Formation en vue du Développement
LCP	Lebanese Communist Party
LF	Lebanese Forces
LNM	Lebanese National Movement
MEA	Middle East Airlines
PFLP	Popular Front for the Liberation of Palestine
PLO	Palestine Liberation Organization
SAIS	School of Advanced International Studies
SSNP	Syrian Social National Party
U.N.	United Nations
UNIFIL	United Nations Interim Force in Lebanon
UNRWA	United Nations Relief and Works Agency
U.S.	United States
USSR	Union of Soviet Socialist Republics

Chronology

2800 B.C.	Canaanite occupation of Sidon and Tyre.
1315	Egyptian occupation of the Phoenician coast.
1200	Phoenician expansion toward the sea.
814	Carthage founded.
738	Assyrian occupation of Tyre.
681	Destruction of Sidon.
539	Phoenician alliance with Persia.
332	Alexander the Great occupies and destroys Tyre.
A.D. 195	Incorporation of Mount Lebanon into the Roman Empire.
551	Major earthquakes hit Lebanon.
555	Beirut destroyed by an earthquake.
636	Arab armies enter the al-Biqā‘ valley.
644	Fall of Tripoli.
738	Arab conquest of the Lebanese coast.
763	Tannukhians settle in Lebanon.
781	Emergence of the Qaysi-Yemeni conflict.
872	Formation of the Tannukhian dynasty.
901	Qaramatian control of the area.
969	Fatimid control of Lebanon.
1030	Druze arrival in Lebanon.
1110	Crusaders' occupation of Beirut.
1124	Crusaders' occupation of Tyre.
1156	Earthquakes hit Lebanon.
1167	Nūr ad-Dīn attacks ‘Akkār and threatens Beirut.
1179	Marj ‘Uyūn battle between Salaḥ ad-Dīn and the crusaders.
1291	Mamluk armies capture Tyre.
1440	Shihabis settle in Wādī At-Taym.
1516	Battle of Marj Dābiq. Ottoman control of Lebanon.
1590	Fakhr ad-Dīn II captures princedom.
1613	Exile of Fakhr ad-Dīn II.
1618	Return of Fakhr ad-Dīn II.

1623	Battle of Majdal ʻAnjar between Ottoman and local armies.
1635	Fakhr ad-Dīn II surrenders and is executed.
1664	Earthquake damages Roman temple in Baʻalbak.
1711	Battle of ʻAyn Dārah and the victory of the Qaysis.
1750	Earthquake hits Baʻalbak. Rise of Yazbaki-Jumblati feud.
1806	Construction of Bayt ad-Dīn palace.
1810	Prince Bashīr II aids Egyptian campaign against Wahhabis.
1811	Prince Bashīr II invites Aleppo Druze to settle in Lebanon.
1820	Prince Bashīr II steps down.
1821	Prince Bashīr II returns to power.
1825	Revolt of Bashīr Jumblāṭ against Prince Bashīr II.
1831	Egyptian occupation of Bilād ash-Shām.
1838	Egyptian suppression of Druze uprising.
1840	End of Egyptian rule in Lebanon.
1841	Sectarian warfare in Lebanon.
1843	Beginning of double *Qa'immaqamate* system.
1845	Intensification of sectarian strife.
1850	Death of Prince Bashīr II.
1859	Peasant revolt. Rise of Ṭānyus Shāhīn.
1860	Sectarian civil war in Lebanon.
1861	*Mutasarrifate* system.
1866	Revolt of Yusuf Karam.
1915	End of *mutasarrifate* system. Execution of independence advocates.
1916	Execution of more opponents of Turkish rule.
1918	End of Ottoman era.
1920	Declaration of Greater Lebanon and beginning of the French Mandate.
1926	Lebanon declared a republic. Constitution adopted.
1932	Suspension of constitution.
1933	Conference of "coast." Muslims demand unity with Syria.
1943	Lebanon gains independence.
1945	Lebanon joins League of Arab States.
1946	Evacuation of French troops from Lebanon.
1947	Bishārah al-Khūrī's term renewed.
1949	Armistice between Lebanon and Israel. Execution of Anṭūn Saʻādah.
1951	Assassination of Riyāḍ aṣ-Ṣulḥ.
1952	Resignation of Bishārah al-Khūrī. Election of Kamīl Shamʻūn to presidency.
1956	Arab summit in Beirut.

1958	Civil war. Deployment of U.S. troops. Election of Fu'ād Shihāb to the presidency.
1961	Aborted coup d'état by Syrian Social National Party.
1964	Bank of Lebanon founded. Charles Ḥilū elected to presidency.
1968	Israeli air raid against Beirut International Airport (December 28).
1969	Rashīd Karāmī protests army's role (April 24). Governmental crisis and rise of right-wing militias. Cairo agreement signed (November 3).
1970	Election of Sulymān Franjiyyah to presidency.
1973	Clashes between Lebanese Army troops and Palestine Liberation Organization forces (May). Melkart Agreement signed (May 17).
1974	President Sulaymān Franjiyyah addresses U.N. General Assembly on behalf of League of Arab States (November 14).
1975	Ma'rūf Sa'd assassinated (February 28). Massacre at 'Ayn ar-Rummānah (April 13). Beginning of the Lebanese civil war.
1976	Split in army. Ilyās Sarkīs elected to presidency (May 8). Syrian troops (officially) enter Lebanon (May 31). Arab summit in Riyāḍ and Cairo (October 17–18). Creation of Arab Deterrent Forces (October 25–26).
1977	Assassination of Kamāl Jumblāṭ (March 16).
1978	Israeli invasion of Lebanon (March 14). U.N. Security Council Resolution 425 passed (March 19). Assassination of Toni Franjiyyah (June 13). Clashes between Syrian troops and right-wing militias (June–October). "Disappearance" of Imām Mūsā aṣ-Ṣadr (August 31).
1979	Clashes between Phalangist forces and Sham'un's militia.
1980	Lebanese Forces defeat Tigers (July 7). Increased Israeli support for Bashīr Gemayyel.
1981	Israel shoots down two Syrian helicopters (April 28). Syria deploys SAM missiles in the al-Biqā' valley (April 29). Israeli-Palestinian cease-fire reached (July 24). Lebanese Forces leave Zaḥlah.
1982	Large-scale Israeli invasion of Lebanon begins (June 6). Siege of Beirut (June 11). Evacuation of Palestine Liberation Organization troops from Lebanon (August 21–September 3). Assassination of president elect Bashīr Gemayyel (September 14). Ṣabrā and Shātīlā massacres (September 16–18). Amīn Gemayyel succeeds his brother (September 21).

1983 Bombing of U.S. embassy in Lebanon (April 18). Lebanon and Israel sign May 17 Agreement (May 17). Syria forces Yāsir ‘Arafāt out of Tripoli (June 24). Suicide bombing of U.S. and French military targets in Lebanon (October 13). Geneva reconciliation meeting held (October 31–November 4).

1984 Withdrawal of U.S. forces from Lebanon (February). Shi‘ite militia in control of West Beirut (February 6). Second reconciliation meeting held in Lausanne, Switzerland (March 12–20).

1985 Eruption of War of the Camps between Amal forces and Palestinians in the camps (May 19). Tripartite Agreement signed in Damascus (December 28).

1986 Samīr Ja‘ja‘ launches war against Elie Ḥubayqah's forces and seizes control of Lebanese Forces (January 15).

1987 Assassination of Rashīd Karāmī (June 1).

1988 End of Amīn Gemayyel's term and the resulting split in government (September 22). Clashes erupt between Amal and Ḥizbullah.

1989 General Michel ‘Awn launches war of liberation (March 14). Assassination of Muftī Hasan Khālid (May 16). Aṭ-Ṭā'if Accords adopted by Lebanese deputies (October 22). Election of Rene Mu‘awwaḍ to presidency (November 5). Assassination of Mu‘awwaḍ (November 22). Ilyās Hrāwī elected president (November 25).

1990 General ‘Awn launches offensive against the Lebanese Forces (January 31). Syrian troops defeat ‘Awn's forces (October 13), and Ilyās Hrāwī's government establishes control over Lebanese territory (except for Israeli-occupied south Lebanon). Assassination of Dānī Sham‘ūn (October 21).

1991 Signing of Treaty of Brotherhood, Cooperation, and Coordination between Lebanon and Syria (May 22).

1992 Popular demonstrations and labor protests lead to fall of government of ‘Umar Karāmī (May 6). First parliamentary election since 1972 (August–September). Rafīq Ḥarīrī appointed prime minister (October 30).

1993 Oslo Accords between Israel and the Palestine Liberation Organization signed in Washington, D.C. (September 13). Bombing of the Phalangist Party office (December 20). Clashes between Islamic Resistance forces and Israeli Defense Forces in Lebanon.

1994 Bombing of church in Zūq Mikhā'īl (February 27). Dissolution of Lebanese Forces (March 23). Arrest of Samīr

Ja'Ja' (April 24). Naturalization of some 130,000 new citizens (June 21). Rafīq Ḥarīrī resigns (December 1) but is persuaded by Syria to stay in office.

1995 Government troops prevent labor unions from demonstrating (July 19). Constitution amended to allow President Hrāwī to serve three years beyond his term (October 19).

1996 Beirut Stock Exchange resumes trading (January 22). French president Jacques Chirac visits Lebanon (April 4–6). Beginning of Israeli invasion of Lebanon, code named Grapes of Wrath (April 12). Qana massacre (April 18). Ḥarīrī and Nabīh Birrī are victors in parliamentary elections (August 18–September 15).

1997 Pope visits Lebanon. The Revolt of the Hungry (July 4). U.S. government lifts ban on travel to Lebanon (August).

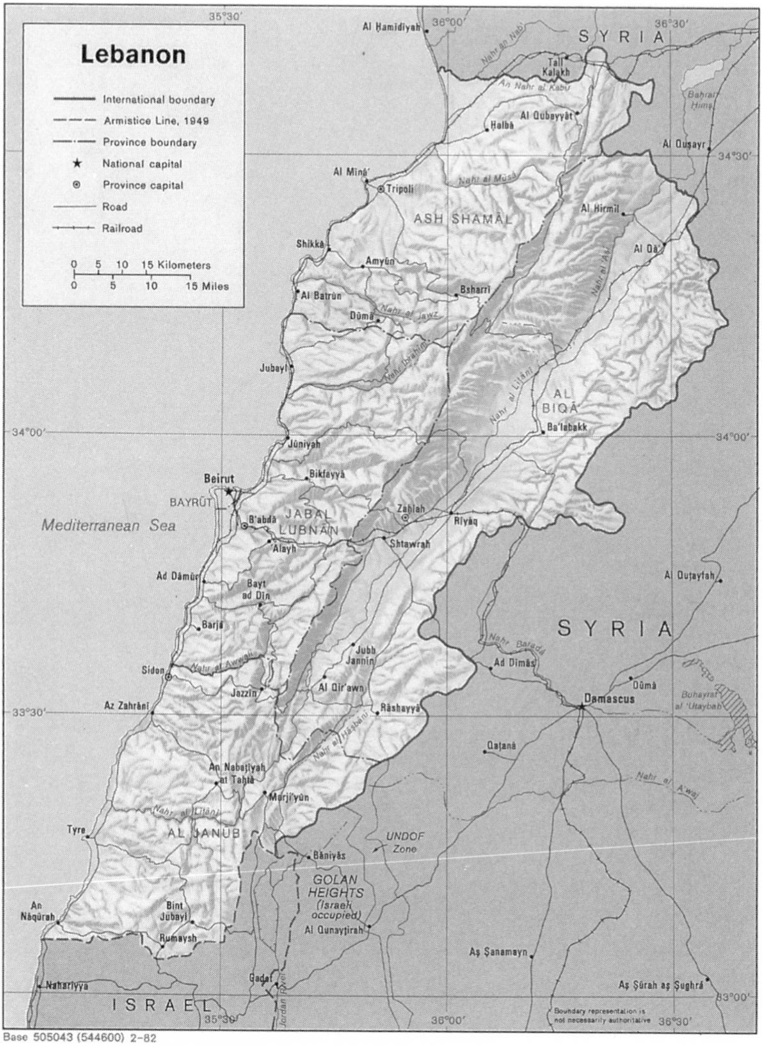

Base 505043 (544600) 2-82

Beirut

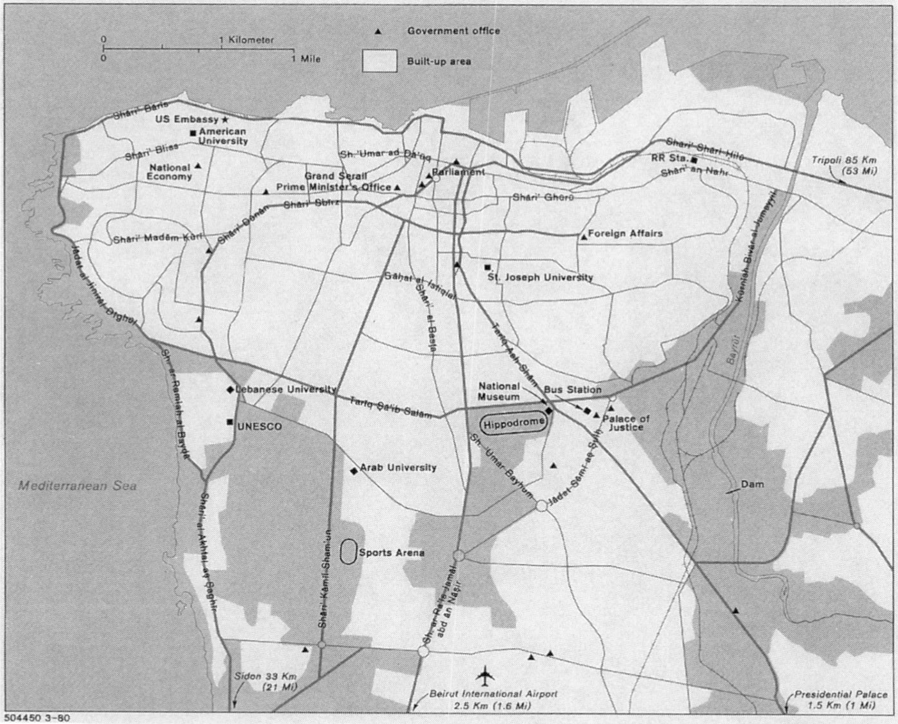

504450 3-80

Introduction

The study of Lebanon has attracted a number of Western and Arab scholars over the years. The democratic political system of pre-war Lebanon was in contrast to the military regimes in much of the rest of the region. The pro-Western orientation of many Lebanese political leaders distanced Lebanon from its Arab environment and insulated it from responsibilities for the Arab-Israeli conflict. The openness and prosperity of pre-war Lebanon were often exaggerated, probably because most scholars focused their attention on the capital city of Beirut. The outbreak of civil war in 1975 dashed the hopes of those who saw Lebanon as a model for communal coexistence. The war surprised only those who denied the political salience of the deep divisions in Lebanese society. It also marginalized for two decades the role of Lebanon in Arab affairs.

Lebanese existence in history is in dispute among historians. Lebanese ultranationalists, who have dominated the official historiography of the country, claim that Lebanon has been in continued existence for over 5000 years and that the present-day country is no more than an extension of the ancient Phoenician kingdom(s). In reality, Lebanon is a modern phenomenon; it can be traced to 1920, when the French government proclaimed a "Greater Lebanon" in response to intense lobbying by Lebanese Christians. Not that Lebanon has no history; but the political existence of an entity called "Lebanon" is not ancient. Claims of Phoenician roots and extensions serve only propaganda purposes and do not answer crucial questions about the nature of the Lebanese national problem. Identification with ancient symbols and motifs has been used to counter claims of Arab identification and has left Lebanon with a split national identity.

Location and Physical Setting

This small but strategically located country has long served as a link between the Arab world and the Mediterranean world. It consists of some 130 miles of coastline on the Mediterranean Sea and comprises, with its mountains, some 4,000 square miles. It has been part of the Eastern Arab world, or the Levant, for much of its recent history. Its physical location has had an impact on its socio-cultural history; immigrants—especially members of minority sects—have sought refuge in Lebanon, with its political security, abundant water, and fertile soil. Its relative isolation has allowed various sectarian groups to survive with their cultures intact.

There are four geographical regions in Lebanon. The narrow coastal plain is the site of the major cities because of its access to the sea. This region is the historical homeland of the Phoenician peoples. The coastal mountain range consists of the historical Mount of Lebanon, which rises sharply from the coastal plains and extends along the Mediterranean coast. The highest peaks of the mountain are southeast of Tripoli. East of Mount Lebanon is the central plateau of al-Biqāʿ valley, which was known in ancient times as the Coelosyria. It is separated from the Jordan valley by hills. It is more than 70 miles in length but no more than eight miles in width. East of al-Biqāʿ valley is the interior mountain range, known as the Anti-Lebanon Mountains, and its southern extension, known as Mount Hermon, covering the eastern border between Lebanon and Syria. The region has been subject to earthquakes; Beirut has been devastated several times in its long history. The last severe earthquake hit South Lebanon in 1956.

Population

The last official census of the Lebanese population was conducted in 1932. The government has considered the distribution of the population along sectarian lines a state secret that could potentially destabilize the country. To avoid any alteration of the delicate distribution of power along sectarian lines, which has been historically to the advantage of the Christians, the government has resisted demands to conduct a new comprehensive census, which would certainly prove that the Muslims now constitute the majority of the population.

According to the most recent official census, conducted by the Ministry of Social Affairs (which does not provide information on sectarian distribution) the Lebanese population was 3,118,828 as of October 1996. The figure excludes Palestinian refugees in Lebanon, whose estimate has been in dispute for years. The population was distributed as follows in the six governorates: 13.1 percent in Beirut; 36.8 percent in Mount Lebanon; 12.9 percent in al-Biqāʿ; 21.6 percent in North Lebanon; 9.1 percent in South Lebanon; and 6.6 percent in Nabaṭiyyah. Age distribution of the population was as follows: 29.2 percent less than 15 years; 63.8 percent, 15–64 years; 6.9 percent, 65 years or more. The average family size was 4.7. In North Lebanon it is 5.3; it is 5.0 in al-Biqāʿ; 4.9 in South Lebanon; 4.6 in Nabaṭiyyah; 4.4 in Mount Lebanon; and 4.1 in Beirut.

The sectarian composition of the Lebanese population has been an explosive political problem ever since the Lebanese Republic was structured along sectarian lines. Political rewards and economic spoils have been distributed according to a sectarian formula that privileged Christians, who constituted the majority of the population in the 1932 census (which measured the demographic weight of each of the confessional communities). Aware of the increased weight of the Muslims, Christian leaders have insisted that Lebanese emigrants be counted in any future census. Most of the emigrants have been Christians, although more Muslims have left Lebanon since the outbreak of the civil war. It is estimated that, since 1975, hundred of thousands of Lebanese have settled temporarily or permanently outside of Lebanon.

The effects of the war on the Lebanese population have been drastic; as Lebanese were constantly fleeing sites of war and bloodshed, and as families were avoiding sectarian killing and massacres, villages and cities assumed a more purely sectarian composition. Communities were less and less mixed, and inter-sectarian marriages and neighborhoods decreased. Lebanon lost tens of thousands of its citizens to the war; the Lebanese government estimates that some 19,085 people were killed in the Israeli invasion of 1982. The restoration of government control and the extension of state authority have been gradually restoring civil life and public order to Lebanese society. It is unclear how the Lebanese will cope with demands of national integration and social interaction.

Culture and Language

Lebanese culture been influenced by historical interactions with the West and the East. The Arab East has shaped Lebanese culture more, however, especially since the seventh century, when Islam conquered Syria (including present-day Lebanon). Arabic was quickly adopted by the local population, replacing Aramaic even as the language for religious ritual among Maronite sects. Throughout the Arab world, written Arabic adheres to the rules and manner of classical Arabic, the Arabic of the holy Qur'ān. Spoken Arabic refers to the local dialect of the Arabic language, which also includes some non-Arabic words, mostly from Aramaic and Turkish. Arabic is the official language of Lebanon and all official documents are printed and published in that language. Arabic is sometimes used as the criterion of membership for the League of Arab States.

Other languages are also used; Armenian is spoken by Armenians, Kurdish by Kurds. Furthermore, French and English are widely understood among the elites. While French has been the favored language of high society, English has quickly gained ground. In the computer age, English has marginalized other languages. Also, English is the language of instruction at the American University of Beirut, which has made English a feature of what is considered a prestigious education.

One cannot speak specifically about a Lebanese culture, perhaps because the culture of Lebanon has been part of the larger Arab and regional culture. Lebanon has always served as a bridge among cultural influences and trends. Moreover, Lebanon has actively participated in the formation of cultural trends. Lebanese writers led the renaissance among Arabs in the nineteenth century. Buṭrus al-Bustānī, Naṣīf al-Yāzijī, Ibrāhīm al-Yāzijī, and Aḥmad Fāris Ash-Shidyāq were all notable figures in the cultural revival movement of the Arab world in the last two centuries, which has solidified Lebanon's ties with the Arab world.

Lebanon's role in the culture of the region was also enhanced when the country emerged as the most open and democratic country of the Arab world. The Lebanese press became a voice for the entire region before the war, as other Arab countries purchased a share in the Lebanese press. Inter-Arab war was fought on Lebanese territory. The most gifted and famous writers of the region bought space in the pages of Lebanese newspapers.

Ethnicity

Ethnically speaking, the Lebanese are indistinguishable from the peoples of the eastern Mediterranean. They are undoubtedly a mixed population, reflecting centuries of population movement and foreign occupation. It is not uncommon to see in Lebanon people with blonde hair and light-colored eyes, reflecting perhaps the legacy of the Crusades. While Arabness is not an ethnicity but a cultural identity, some ardent Arab nationalists, in Lebanon and elsewhere, talk about Arabness in racial and ethnic terms to elevate the descendants of Muḥammad. Paradoxically, Lebanese nationalists also speak about the Lebanese people in racial terms, claiming that the Lebanese are "pure" descendants of the Phoenician peoples, whom they view as separate from the ancient residents of the region, including—ironically—the Canaanites. For the statistical purposes of the American Census Bureau, Arab people (of Asia and North Africa) are listed as Caucasian.

Religion

Lebanon, it is often remarked, is more shaped by religion than by any other single factor. This observation, however, ignores the distinctive features of the Lebanese sectarian problem. In other words, sectarian membership and identification are not acts of religious worship but characteristics of narrow political identification. The Lebanese are likely to identify with, in addition to their family, their religions. The strong ties of religion in Lebanon are not unrelated to the special system of sectarianism that divided political powers and governmental posts according to the sectarian distribution of the population. Furthermore, the absence of secular personal status laws in Lebanon forced citizens to view themselves as members of a sect, first and foremost. As if to underline this membership, Lebanese identity cards, which are carried by people everywhere, identify the individual by sect.

Lebanon has attracted members of all the religions of the region, if not the world. Muslims, Christians, Jews, and Druzes have coexisted in Lebanon for centuries. Historical feuding and conflict, however, have marred the communal experience of Druzes and Maronites, who dominated Mount Lebanon. Other sects have on occasion sided with one party or another, depending on communal benefits and sectarian alliances. Unlike all other Arab states and Israel, Lebanon does not identify itself with one religion. Lebanon has no state religion. But Islam and Christianity are the main religions; and although the country is supposed to be based on neutrality of the state on matters of religious preference, Christian and Muslim ecclesiastical authorities enjoy tremendous power as the government uses them to obtain political legitimacy. Druzes, who have played important roles in Lebanese history, have also been treated with respect by the government, and they have been adequately represented in governmental appointments and cabinet formations. The Jews lived in Lebanon as a tolerated member of Lebanese communal families until 1967, when popular hostility to Israel often expressed itself in anti-Jewish terms.

Historical Profile

Historically, the area that is known as Lebanon today has been inhabited by people since ancient times. The name "Lebanon" was associated with the mountains and its cedars, both of which are mentioned in the Bible. Many peoples and civilizations have passed through Lebanon and have left their imprint on its people, which derive from a marriage of different peoples and races, not unlike population characteristics in other parts of the Arab world. Lebanese, both on the official and popular levels, created a mythical version of the role of Phoenicians in history to facilitate the invention of a Lebanese national community. This community was to be seen as unlike any other community in the region, characterized by genius and adventure.

ANCIENT AND MEDIEVAL TIMES

While Lebanese ancient roots are subject to imaginary national speculation, it is certain that the area that is Lebanon has been settled since ancient times. The Phoenicians, however, did not create a glorious civilization and did not form one nation. They were, instead, divided into several city-kingdoms, and their divisions allowed external powers, primarily Egypt, to control them. Lebanese poet Sa'īd 'Aql still maintains that the roots of Western civilization can be traced back to Phoenician "civilization," although the claim that the Phoenicians invented the alphabet is disputed. Ironically, *Black Athena*, a recent book by Cornell University professor Martin Bernal (2 vols., 1989 and 1991) seems to confirm that the role of the Phoenicians may have been belittled by scholars, who elevated the contributions of European people at the expense of the contributions of Africans and Asians. It is probable that the Phoenicians learned from neighboring peoples. They excelled in commerce, perhaps because their coastlands did not allow for the formation of an agricultural economy.

Lebanon's cedarwood and pine were prized by its neighbors. The exploitation of Lebanon's forests, almost totally extinct today, was a common feature of ancient foreign rule of the country. Lebanon was subject to foreign occupations and external influences. People belonging to various sects and ethnicities settled in its mountainous region. The last and most lasting impact on Lebanon was caused by the Arab-Islamic conquest of the seventh century. Muslims settled in the country, and Arabization, as a cultural and linguistic trend, began affecting various facets of its culture. The Arab-Islamic conquest also treated Lebanon not as a separate entity but as part of that region historically known as Bilād ash-Shām, or lands of Shām. Shām was a term applied by early Arabs to refer to natural (or geographic) Syria. Some legends about local (Lebanese) resistance to Arabization were also invented; the role of the Maronites during the Crusades has been used to underline the ostensible pro-Western orientation of the Lebanese people. It is true that some Maronites actively helped the invading crusaders, but others identified with the Arabs. The crusaders, after all, did not value local Christians and protested mild theological and ritual differences.

OTTOMAN RULE

Ottoman rule began early in the 16th century and continued the long process of the Islamization of the region. Lebanon did not enjoy an independent status in the Ottoman Empire, although individual rulers (like Fakhr ad-Dīn II) made some attempts at gaining local power. Those attempts, however, were not motivated by Lebanese national sentiments but by classical power calculations. The presence of rival sects in the country, especially the Druzes and Maronites in the mountain region, fa-

Muslims was necessary; and he was adamant about increasing the powers of the presidency. The state budget also reflected his strong regional and sectarian bias in favor of the Christian heartland. In 1973, Prime Minister Ṣā'ib Salām resigned because his orders to dismiss the commander-in-chief of the army were ignored by Franjiyyah. The events of 1973 were similar to the 1905 rehearsal of revolution in Russia, as Lenin called it. The story of the civil war is retold in the body of the dictionary but some remarks here are in order.

The civil war changed Lebanon forever, leaving a lasting impact on its inhabitants and their political culture. Political violence was used on a massive scale and was perpetrated with a ferocity and savagery that was extreme even by the horrific standards of war in this century. Some quarter of a million Lebanese were killed or injured, and hundreds of thousands were displaced. The civil war fully integrated Lebanon into the regional political system and eliminated the possibility of Lebanese insulation from Arab-Israeli affairs. Lebanese will debate for a long time the causes of the civil war; many still refuse to blame the Lebanese themselves, opting instead for the popular conspiracy theories that fault one external player or another. Many Lebanese are still convinced that the war was the result of a master plan designed and implemented by Henry Kissinger, aimed at the unique prosperity and "democracy" of pre-war Lebanon.

The civil war inaugurated the end of Lebanese sovereignty and the beginning of a deadly competition between Israel and Syria over control of Lebanon. Syria was clearly victorious; its allies are deeply rooted in the Lebanese political system and history, while Israel relies on a militia of irregulars who follow Israel's line in Israeli-occupied South Lebanon. Syria's dominance was briefly interrupted during the Israeli era that followed the Israeli invasion of 1982; but it did not last for long, despite American military and political support for the regime of Amīn Gemayyel.

Ilyās Sarkīs managed the civil war after his election to the presidency in 1976, but he had little power and constantly threatened to resign. He navigated between the various warring factions, trying to appease them without any success. He was clearly sympathetic to the Lebanese right-wing camp, especially after heavy Syrian bombardment of East Beirut in 1978. The warring factions ruled the country, and Sarkīs had to satisfy himself with ruling the vicinity of the presidential palace, no more.

The Sarkīs era ended with the Israeli invasion of 1982, which intended to install pro-Israeli militia leader Bashīr Gemayyel as president. He was assassinated before he could assume his presidential authority and was succeeded by his brother Amīn Gemayyel, another militia leader who rose from the ranks of the Lebanese Phalanges Party (which was founded by the father of the two Gemayyels, Pierre Gemayyel). The administration of Amīn Gemayyel was dependent on U.S. promises that ignored the Syrian agenda in Lebanon. Both Muslim and leftist critics saw him as provocative. A coalition of Syrian, Palestinian, and Lebanese forces succeeded in a relatively short period of time in expelling Gemayyel's forces from predominantly Muslim areas. When Gemayyel could not create a peaceful climate for the selection of a successor, he installed his Maronite commander-in-chief of the army as interim president.

General Michel 'Awn saw himself as the savior of Lebanon, and many Christians agreed with that designation. He, however, left himself with few political allies, with the exception of the Iraqi regime of Ṣaddām Ḥusayn. He launched a war of national liberation in 1989, which caused a lot of damage to the infrastructure of the country. Syria ended 'Awn's rule in 1990, when the world was occupied with the Gulf War and support for 'Awn was at a minimum. The end of 'Awn was ostensibly the end of the civil war, although it is yet to be determined whether Lebanon's deadly civil war is really over.

Post Civil War

The administration of president Ilyās Hrāwī has been asserting that the war is officially and completely ended. Militias are said to be disbanded and the process of construction begun in earnest. The optimism of the government is not unjustified; many vestiges of the civil war have been eliminated. Some militias have been dissolved and integrated into the Lebanese army. Prime Minister Rafīq Ḥarīrī has restored confidence in Lebanon, although his promises of economic recovery have not materialized. Many investors are skeptical, and immigrant Lebanese capital is still invested abroad. Furthermore, the existence of armed groups clashes with the goal of restoring the sole legitimate authority of the Lebanese armed forces. The Party of God, for example, retains an armed presence in South Lebanon in the name of liberating it from Israeli occupation. Even the Lebanese government recognizes the right of groups to engage in armed resistance against Israeli occupation.

Nevertheless, many worrisome factors remain. Israel refuses to evacuate South Lebanon and rejects United Nations Security Council resolutions pertaining to its illegal presence in the country. Furthermore, Israel continues to arm and finance ruthless gangs of armed men in areas under its control. This militia does not recognize the legitimacy of the Lebanese government, favoring instead the patronage of the Israeli army. There are also underground armed groups throughout Lebanon, which the Lebanese government does not want to deal with at this stage of its delicate political experience.

The Syrian presence in Lebanon also poses challenges for the government. Syria still enjoys supreme political and military influence in the country, and Lebanese officials are reluctant to criticize Syrian policy in Lebanon. In the absence of progress in the Syrian-Israeli talks, Syria is more eager to keep its dominance in Lebanon. The Lebanese government, similarly, does not object to Syrian interests in Lebanon as long as the world continues to ignore the Israeli occupation of South Lebanon. Lebanon needs the regional stature of Syria to remind the world of the longevity of its sovereignty problem in the south.

Rafīq Ḥarīrī has embarked on an ambitious reconstruction plan. Downtown Beirut is soon to resume its pre-war status as the city center, after years of hosting the warring factions' most bitter wars. Critics object to Ḥarīrī's plans, claiming that he is not reforming the Lebanese economy but merely reviving the service sectors at the expense of its industrial and agricultural sectors. They also doubt that Ḥarīrī has the interests of the poor and dispossessed at heart. Yet, people recognize that Ḥarīrī has brought vitality and dynamism to Lebanese political life, despite his desire to restrain freedom of information. His plan for the organization of the media is certain to consolidate sectarian monopoly over the distribution of information.

Lebanon's most important achievement has been the parliamentary elections of 1992 and 1996. The 1992 elections cannot be taken seriously, because the Christian boycott undermined the credibility and legitimacy of the elected. Furthermore, elections take place in a political environment that does not tolerate criticism of Syrian policies in Lebanon. The 1996 election was marred by fraud and other irregularities, but voting turnout was higher, and more Christian parties, organizations, and personalities agreed to participate. Deputy Buṭrus Ḥarb, for example, won with a high margin despite Syrian efforts against him. The restoration of Lebanese parliamentary life signals Lebanon's commitment to partial democracy in a region dominated by authoritarian regimes.

Finally, it is debated whether the civil war will ever resume; arguments can be made on both sides. The causes of the civil war were deeply rooted in the system of sectarian bias, and that system has not been replaced. It was merely reformed to accommodate Muslim demands. It will not be surprising, then, if armed conflict erupts again in Lebanon.

THE DICTIONARY

-A-

‘ABBŪD, MĀRŪN (1886–1962). A writer and educator, he was born in ‘Ayn Kifā‘ and educated in Beirut (q.v.). He practiced journalism but spent most of his life as director at the National School in ‘Alayy, which was founded in the last century by Buṭrus al-Bustānī (q.v.). Early in his career, he edited the magazine *Ar-Rawḍah*, and in 1907 he edited *An-Naṣīr*. In 1909 he founded the newspaper *Al-Ḥikmah* which only ceased publication in World War I. He held municipal posts in his region and was immensely popular. He resigned from the National School in 1957 and founded his own school in ‘Alayy, where he taught until 1962.

His writings were noted for their satirical wit. He was often compared to the famous al-Jahiz but he lacked al-Jahiz’ depth. He wrote correct Arabic (q.v.) in simplified form, angering linguistic fanatics by incorporating into his novels dialogues in colloquial Arabic. He contributed literary criticism to a variety of publications and reviewed books for the Lebanese press, criticizing sharply what he did not like. He was contemptuous of the Christian clerical class in Lebanon, and he named his son Muḥammad (unusual for Christians) in defiance. His novels are read by school students throughout Lebanon to this day.

‘ABDUH, JŪNĪ (1940–). An intelligence chief, he was born in Ḥaifa, but his family moved to Lebanon (q.v.) in 1946 where they obtained Lebanese citizenship. He joined the military academy in 1958. In 1965 he joined the Deuxième Bureau (q.v.), when it was the most powerful government apparatus in the country. He met most Lebanese politicians through this sensitive position. In 1968 he was assigned as an aide to commander-in-chief of the army Emile al-Bustānī. In 1975, while in retirement, he volunteered to serve in the intelligence apparatus of the Lebanese Phalanges Party (q.v.) under the direct command of Bashīr Gemayyel (q.v.). He did not last long in his post, although he maintained ties with Gemayyel.

'Abduh reached the highest echelons of power in 1977, when Shihabi president Ilyās Sarkīs (q.v.) placed him in charge of the Deuxième Bureau, to the displeasure of Syrian officials who knew of his association with Bashīr Gemayyel. In his new role, he began plotting for Bashīr's presidential campaign, introducing Bashīr to Muslim and Palestinian personalities in order to improve his image. 'Abduh also worked hard to smooth relations between Sarkīs and the Lebanese Forces (q.v.). It is believed that he was behind American support for Bashīr, despite deep suspicions about Bashīr on the part of American diplomats in Beirut. He served as a mediator between the Israeli army command and the Lebanese army and state during the 1982 Israeli invasion (q.v.) of Lebanon. In the administration of Amīn Gemayyel (q.v.) he was appointed ambassador in West Germany, where he quietly established an alliance with future prime minister Rafīq Ḥarīrī (q.v.). His name is often mentioned as a presidential candidate.

'ABDUL-NASSER, JAMĀL (1918–1970). This famous Arab leader played an important political role in Lebanese affairs. His nationalization of the Suez Canal in 1956 propelled him to a pan-Arab leadership level never achieved afterward. He saw his mission as Arab unity. Lebanese Muslims responded positively to his message, and his popularity was such that all Muslim candidates for parliament had their pictures taken with him. His ambassador to Lebanon was one of the most important politicians in the country, often approached by eager politicians who wanted Nasser's approval and blessing. The 1958 civil war (q.v.) pitted forces loyal to pro-Western president Kamīl Sham'ūn (q.v.) against forces sympathetic to Nasser. Nasser understood the delicate social balance in Lebanon and did not press the country to join the United Arab Republic. His interest in Lebanese affairs declined after 1958, because he trusted the leadership of General Fu'ād Shihāb (q.v.) and his successor, Charles Ḥilū (q.v.). Many political parties in Lebanon are dedicated to his memory and ideology. While he was popular among some Christians, right-wing forces in Lebanon were unhappy about his intervention in Lebanese internal affairs.

ABELLĀ, ALBERT (1921–). He was born in Jizzīn and received a secondary education. He is one of the wealthiest businessmen in Lebanon, with business ventures in Lebanon, the Arab world, Europe, and the United States. He is chairman and general manager of Alberat Abela S.A.L.

***ABḤĀTH, al-*.** This leading scholarly journal, published by the American University of Beirut (q.v.), was founded in 1948. It prints articles by university professors and proceedings of academic conferences held at the university.

ABĪ AL-LAM', FĀRŪQ (1934–). A politician, he was born in Beirut (q.v.) to a princely family that converted to Christianity from Druzism (q.v.). He was educated in Beirut and received a law degree from St. Joseph University (q.v.). He practiced law until 1977, when Ilyās Sarkīs (q.v.), a close friend, appointed him director-general of the Directorate of Public Security. He cooperated closely with the Lebanese Forces (q.v.) and resisted issuing work permits to Palestinians. He was appointed ambassador to France in 1982, resigning this post in 1987. He became a vocal advocate of General Michel 'Awn (q.v.), especially after the latter's exile in France.

ABKĀRYUS, ISKANDAR YA'QŪB. A writer, he was born early in the 19th century in Beirut (q.v.) and was educated at the National College in 'Alayy, before completing his studies at the American University of Beirut (q.v.). He is of Armenian (q.v.) descent. He was part of the 19th century revival of Arabic (q.v.) literature. He visited Europe and returned to work at the pioneering journal *Al-Jinān* (q.v.). He settled in Egypt in 1874 and died in Beirut in 1885. He is known for his book on 19th-century civil strife in Lebanon, which has been translated into English.

ABŪ 'AḌAL, GEORGE (1920–). An industrialist, he was born in Beirut and educated at St. Joseph University (q.v.). He is one of the wealthy Lebanese who funded the electoral campaigns of Kamīl Sham'ūn (q.v.) and, later, of Sulaymān Franjiyyah (q.v.). He is chairperson of George Abū 'Aḍal and Company and owns the Lebanese weekly *al-Usbū' al-'Arabī,* which has never achieved commercial success. He was sent by Sulaymān Franjiyyah on diplomatic missions to African countries, where he had business interests.

ABŪ MĀḌĪ, ILIYYĀ (1889–1957). A poet, he was born in al-Muḥaydithah in al-Matn region and emigrated to Egypt in 1901, where he worked in commerce. He returned to Lebanon in 1912 before emigrating to the United States (q.v.). He published in several Arabic magazines in the United States, including *Al-Ḥurriyyah* and *Al-Fatāh.* From 1918 to 1928 he edited the journal *Mir'āt Al-Gharb* (Mirror of the West). In 1929 he produced the magazine *As-Samīr,* which he later turned into a daily newspaper. He is celebrated in Lebanon for his traditional poetry, which rejects innovative tendencies in Arabic (q.v.) literature. Among his books are *Al-Jadāwil* and *Al-Khamā'il.* His son recently donated his father's personal library to the Lebanese state.

ABŪ NĀḌIR, FU'ĀD (1956–). A militia leader, he was born in Ba'albak (q.v.). His mother is Pierre Gemayyel's (q.v.) daughter. He studied in East Beirut (q.v.) before being accepted to the Medical School at the American University of Beirut (AUB) (q.v.). He was briefly kidnapped by Nasser's Forces (q.v.). His studies at AUB were interrupted, and he completed his medical studies at St. Joseph University (q.v.). He started his political activities in the Lebanese Phalanges Party (q.v.) in 1970, although he only became a card-carrying member in 1974. He joined the special forces that Bashīr Gemayyel (q.v.) formed during the war and known by his initials. He fought on different fronts and was injured twice, in 1975 and 1983. He became chief-of-staff of the Lebanese Forces (q.v.) in 1982 and a commander in 1984. His brief tenure was characterized by unwavering loyalty to his uncle, Amīn Gemayyel (q.v.), and for that he was soon ousted. He has not been heard of in recent years, perhaps the Gemayyel name is not as popular as it once was.

ABŪ SHABAKAH, ILYĀS (1903–1947). A poet, he was born in the United States (q.v.) and grew up in Lebanon (q.v.). He never finished his formal education and began writing early in his life for various newspapers and magazines, including *Al-Jumhūr, Al-Bayān, Al-Makshūf, Al-Ma'raḍ*, and *Ṣawt Al-Aḥrār*. He translated French novels into Arabic (q.v.) and composed romantic poetry. He is best known as a sensitive poet who championed the poor. His love poetry is intense and original. His books include *Ghalwā', Afā'ī Al-Firdaws,* and *Ilā Al-Abad*. He is remembered as a pioneer of the romantic school of expression in Arabic. The Lebanese government commemorated the 50th anniversary of his death in 1997.

ABŪ SHAHLĀ, MICHEL (1898–1959). A journalist, he was born in Beirut (q.v.) and completed his secondary education. He wrote poetry at an early age but is known for his journalistic work. He co-founded in 1925 (with Mishel Zakkūr) the magazine *Al-Ma'raḍ*, which attracted young writers and poets like Ilyās Abū Shabakah. In 1936, he founded the *Al-Jumhūr,* a literary and political magazine. A book of his poetry was published after his death.

ABŪ SHAQRĀ, MUḤAMMAD (1910–1991). He was born in 'Amāṭūr and received a secondary education. In 1948, he was selected as shaykh al-'aql (q.v.) for the Jumblati Druzes (q.v.), the highest official religious post in the Druze community. He was closely associated with Kamāl Jumblāṭ (q.v.); the death of the Yazbaki Druze shaykh al-'aql before the war allowed him to monopolize the Druze religious leadership during the crucial years of civil strife.

ABŪ SULAYMĀN, SHĀKIR (1927–). He was born in Beirut (q.v.) and was educated in law studies at St. Joseph University (q.v.). For years, he headed the Maronite League (q.v.), which comprised right-wing Maronite (q.v.) professionals. He was a member of the Lebanese Front (q.v.) and often played the role of mediator between feuding Maronite factions. He failed to win a seat in the 1996 parliamentary election.

ACTION PARTY. *SEE* SOCIALIST CHRISTIAN DEMOCRATIC PARTY.

'AḌHM, ṢĀDIQ JALĀL al-. A scholar and polemicist, he was born to one of the wealthiest notable families of Syria (q.v.). He studied at the American University of Beirut (q.v.) and later received a Ph.D. in philosophy from Yale University, where he wrote a dissertation on the German philosopher Immanuel Kant. He joined the Syrian Social National Party (q.v.) in his youth but later was disillusioned with its ideology. He advocated Marxism-Leninism, although he never officially joined any political party. He was closely associated with Nāyif Ḥawātimah of the Democratic Front for the Liberation of Palestine and helped the leaders of the DFLP formulate their programs. Al-'Aḍhm taught philosophy at the American University of Beirut but was fired in the late 1960s for his extreme leftist views and for his criticisms of the administration.

He caused a political scandal in 1969 when he published his book *Naqd Al-Fikr Ad-Dīnī* (Critique of Religious Thought). He was condemned by the religious establishment and was put on trial for insulting Islam. Lebanon's best lawyers took up his defense, and he was acquitted. He remained in Lebanon writing political polemics and influencing generations of Arab radicals. Al-'Adḍhm was one of the first Arab thinkers to include in his self-critical approach criticisms of religion, Jamāl 'Abdul-Nasser (q.v.), and the Arab patriarchal system. He left Lebanon after the 1975–76 civil war (q.v.) and taught philosophy at Damascus University. He has lectured widely in the United States (q.v.) and was a visiting professor at Princeton University in the early 1990s.

ADĪB, al-. This monthly magazine, founded in 1942 by Albert Adīb, was a popular literary publication that avoided the controversies of narrow partisan affiliations and attracted writers and poets from around the Arab world. Muḥsin Mahdī (currently professor at Harvard University) and 'Abdullah Al-'Alāylī (q.v.) wrote for it.

ADONIS (1930–). This is the pen name of Syrian-born poet-critic 'Alī Aḥmad Sa'īd. He was born in Latakia, Syria, moving later to Lebanon.

He obtained a degree in Arabic (q.v.) literature from Damascus University and later received a Ph.D. in Arabic from St. Joseph University (q.v.). His dissertation was later published in four volumes under the title *Ath-Thābit wa-l-Mutaḥawwil* (The Constant and the Dynamic). He settled in Lebanon 1956 and obtained Lebanese citizenship. He co-founded in 1957 with Yūsuf al-Khāl (q.v.) the magazine *Shiʻr* (q.v.), which introduced free verse to the Arab world. He is the author of several volumes of poetry and literary criticism. He was a sympathizer with the Syrian Social National Party (q.v.) in his youth but later charted an independent political course. He founded the critical magazine *Mawāqif* (q.v.) in 1968. Adonis does not have a mass readership but is appreciated by academics, critics, and Westerners who have read his poetry in translation. In the 1980s, Adonis took up residence in Paris. His name is often mentioned as a candidate for the Nobel Prize in literature.

ʻAFLAQ, MICHEL (1910–1989). This Syrian Greek Orthodox (q.v.) left an impact on contemporary Arab politics. He is one of the founders of the Arab Socialist Baʻth Party (q.v.), along with his comrade Ṣalāḥ ad-Dīn al-Bīṭār. He was a romantic nationalist who never defined his ideological vision beyond poetic expressions of a desire for Arab unity and Arab socialism. He spent many of his years in the cafes of Beirut, discussing and theorizing. Lebanese publishing houses printed his collected speeches and propagated his message. The Baʻth Party in Lebanon never gained power although individual Baʻthists have served in parliament. ʻAflaq died in Iraq, where he had lived a quiet life under the sponsorship of Ṣaddām Ḥusayn's regime. *See also* Arab Socialist Baʻth Party.

AGRICULTURE. The Lebanese soil has been used agriculturally for centuries in the al-Biqāʻ valley (q.v.), the mountains, and the coastal plain. Farmers grow a variety of crops: tobacco, citrus, bananas, figs, olives, fruits, and vegetables. Ḥashīsh is also cultivated in the al-Biqāʻ, although the Lebanese government, under pressure from the United States (q.v.), has been eliminating these illegal fields. Yet, in recent years, some Syrian and Lebanese army officers have been profiting from the trade. One member of parliament was recently arrested and tried for drug trafficking. Wines have also been produced in the country.

Lebanese land is one-fourth cultivable, but the Lebanese government has not regarded the agriculture sector of the economy as a high priority. Farmers receive little aid from the state although much of the work force (23 percent of the labor force in 1985), before the war, was involved in agriculture. Irrigation plans have been designed but not implemented, especially in South Lebanon. On the contrary, new reconstruction plans are aimed at the service sectors of the economy, with emphasis on conference centers, hotels, casinos, and banking. With such little attention paid to agriculture, Lebanon must still import some of its food needs.

AḤRĀR, al-. This newspaper was founded in 1922 by Jubrān Tuwaynī (q.v.), among others. Tuwaynī later sold the paper, and it was published under the name *Ṣawt Al-Aḥrār*. It was purchased by the pro-Iraqi Arab Socialist Ba'th Party (q.v.) in the 1960s, but the National Liberal Party (q.v.) took control of it during the war, and it became a daily mouthpiece of the party. It never had a mass circulation.

AIDS. The first registered case of the AIDS virus in Lebanon was reported in 1984. The first two Lebanese who were infected with the virus were men who lived for years in the United States. The number of reported cases increased over the years: two in 1985, two in 1986, nine in 1987, 22 in 1988, 23 in 1989, 33 in 1990, 21 in 1991, 19 in 1992, and 104 in 1993. Many cases were not reported because patients feared the stigma—of both the disease and homosexuality (q.v.)—with which the virus is closely associated in the minds of many Lebanese.

The Ministry of Health did not respond to the cases; only in 1988 did it issue a statement about its plan for dealing with disease. In 1990, the ministry formed a special department to fight the spread of the virus; by 1990, several organizations dedicated to the treatment of AIDS and the education of the public about its prevention were already in existence. Even the Lebanese Red Cross, which avoided the issue for years, began a public awareness program. Despite these efforts, many patients prefer, if they can afford it, to seek treatment abroad to avoid social stigma to them and to their families.

AKHṬAL AṢ-ṢAGHĪR, AL. *SEE* KHŪRĪ, BISHĀRAH 'ABDULLAH AL.

'ALAMUD-DĪN, NAJĪB (1909–1996). An airline executive, he was born in Ba'aqlīn to a wealthy Druze (q.v.) family and educated at the American University of Beirut (q.v.) and at the University College of the Southwest of England at Exeter, where he received his degree in engineering. He taught mathematics before accepting an offer from the Jordanian government to work in the public sector in the fields of education and economics. In 1940, he held the position of secretary-general of the Jordanian cabinet. He returned to Beirut in 1942 and founded his own company, Near East Resources. He was associated for most of his life with Lebanon's official airline, Middle East

Airlines (MEA). He was general manager of MEA between 1952 and 1956 and served as the chairman of its board from 1956 until 1977, when he resigned. He improved and expanded the company, which was once the best airline carrier in the Middle East region. He held several ministerial positions in his life, beginning in 1965 when he was appointed minister of tourism. He moved to London at the beginning of the 1975 civil war (q.v.), where he died.

'ALAWITE SECT. Several thousand 'Alawites are scattered throughout Northern Lebanon. 'Alawites have assumed more political significance since the rise to power of the 'Alawite faction of Ḥāfiḍh al-Asad within the Arab Socialist Ba'th Party (q.v.). The 'Alawites are also known as the Nusayris because of their concentration in the Nusayriyyah Mountains in northwestern Syria (q.v.). 'Alawites were not considered Shi'ite (q.v.) Muslims until Imām Mūsā aṣ-Ṣadr (q.v.) declared the 'Alawite sect a branch of Shi'ite Islam in the 1970s. The 'Alawites of Lebanon were able, thanks to Syrian political support, to achieve a guarantee of two parliamentary seats in 1992. The leadership of the community is closely aligned with Syria (q.v.).

'ALĀYLĪ, 'ABDULLĀH al- (1910–1996). He was one of the most distinguished linguists in the Arab world, with a reputation that extends far beyond Lebanon. He was born in Beirut (q.v.) to a Sunni family and exhibited signs of genius at an early age. He was one of the youngest graduates of Al-Azhar University, the premier institute of Islamic education in the world, although he was more interested in philology than in theology. His first book was on the roots of Arabic (q.v.) words and is still considered a classic. He was involved in leftist politics, which ruined his chances for a high religious post in Lebanon. He helped found the Progressive Socialist Party (q.v.) with Kamāl Jumblāṭ (q.v.) but he was soon disillusioned with the experiment, especially as the party took an increasingly sectarian cast over the years. He was one of the rare thinkers to criticize Jamāl 'Abdul-Nasser (q.v.) before the 1967 war.

His books deal with Arab nationalism, the famed classic poet al-Ma'arrī, Muḥammad's first wife (Khadījah), and the Ḥusayn ('Alī's son). He often called for Sunni-Shi'ite (qq.v.) solidarity and believed that Islam is not opposed to civil marriages. In the late 1970s, he was attacked by the religious establishment for producing a book, titled *Ayna Al-Khaṭa'* (Where Is the Error?), that presented a progressive and socialist interpretation of Islam. The book is still banned in a number of Arab states. The Lebanese publishing house Dar al-Jadīd in Beirut has been reissuing all of his books. He continued to write and give interviews in his last years.

ALEXANDRIA PROTOCOL. This agreement was signed in 1945 by the Arab states that founded the League of Arab States. It included an appendix that affirmed Lebanon's full independence and sovereignty. The Lebanese delegation insisted on this qualification because they feared that the idea of Arab solidarity might jeopardize the sovereignty of Lebanon. The protocol was a fulfillment of the terms of the National Pact (q.v.), wherein Muslims pledged not to seek unity with any Arab state.

ALWIYAT AṢ-ṢADR. *SEE* BRIGADES OF AṢ-ṢADR.

AMAL MOVEMENT *(Ḥarakat Amal)*. The original name of this important political movement was *Ḥarakat al-Maḥrūmīn* (Movement of the Disinherited). After 1978 the movement became known by the acronym of its military arm, *Afwāj al-Muqāwamah al-Lubnāniyyah* (Detachments of Lebanese Resistance): AMAL. Amal also means "hope" in Arabic. The history of this relatively new organization is closely associated with the role of its founder Imām Mūsā aṣ-Ṣadr (q.v.). Aṣ-Ṣadr came to Lebanon in 1959 from Iran and began to organize the Shi'ite community, which was—and is—the poorest community in Lebanon. Aṣ-Ṣadr wanted to expand the political role of the Shi'ites and to bring about economic improvement in their lives. Israeli bombardment of predominantly Shi'ite South Lebanon in the 1960s radicalized the community further and allowed Palestinian organizations to recruit from its ranks. Aṣ-Ṣadr called on the Lebanese state to take up the cause of the Shi'ites and to protect their villages from Israeli raids.

In 1969 aṣ-Ṣadr's religious and political leadership was boosted when he was elected chairman of the Higher Islamic Shi'ite Council, which he had helped create with the help of Ṣabrī Ḥamādī (q.v.). The council was founded to press for a separate Shi'ite agenda and, more important, to separate the Shi'ite agenda in Lebanon from the general Islamic agenda, which was championed by the traditional Sunni (q.v.) elite. Aṣ-Ṣadr did not seek to align his movement with traditional Shi'ite leaders, because he accused many of them, especially Kāmil al-As'ad (q.v.), of ignoring the grievances of the community. In the 1972 election, Aṣ-Ṣadr lobbied against individuals closely aligned with established state interests. The popularity of Lebanese and Palestinian leftist organizations among southern Lebanese convinced aṣ-Ṣadr that armed struggle was an acceptable weapon of retaliation against Israeli bombing raids. Further, armed political organizations commanded the respect and allegiance of thousands of Shi'ites. With Syrian and Fatḥ (qq.v.) help, aṣ-Ṣadr founded his movement, which became part of the political equation when the 1975 civil war (q.v.) broke out.

The civil war was not beneficial to aṣ-Ṣadr's leadership or to Amal; most Shiʿites were still members of Lebanese and Palestinian nationalist and leftist organizations. Amal was not radical enough for a community composed largely of angry youths. The relatively small size of the movement was exposed in 1976 when the alliance of the Lebanese National Movement (q.v.) and the Palestine Liberation Organization (q.v.) ejected Amal members from areas under its control due to Amal's support for Syrian military intervention in Lebanon. From 1976 onward, the movement never wavered in its support for the Syrian role in Lebanon, and aṣ-Ṣadr's role was marginalized until his mysterious "disappearance" in the wake of—or during—an official visit to Libya (q.v.) in 1978. His disappearance boosted his cause and his movement at a time of great disillusionment among the Shiʿites.

The Palestine Liberation Organization (PLO) (q.v.) and its Lebanese leftist allies were no more popular, and Shiʿite radicals began to express their resentment in religious terms. The leadership of the movement passed to deputy Ḥusayn al-Ḥusaynī (q.v.). A power struggle put Nabīh Birrī (q.v.) at the helm of the movement in 1980, and he has ever since been the single most important Shiʿite political figure in Lebanese politics. Birrī distanced the movement from the PLO and solidified the alliance with Syria.

The 1982 Israeli invasion (q.v.) of Lebanon caused a split within the movement when Ḥusayn al-Mūsawī and others left the movement in protest against Birrī's "moderate" tendencies. Birrī succeeded over the years in ridding the movement of most serious rivals and filling all the important posts with reliable allies. In 1987, the movement launched a war against the Palestinians (q.v.) in the refugee camps of Lebanon, which dragged on for three years. The movement's prominence profited from Birrī's enhanced prestige. Birrī became a minister in 1984 and was elected speaker of parliament (the highest Shiʿite slot in government) in 1992.

The Amal movement was disarmed along with other militias, with the exception of the Party of God (q.v.), during the first administration (1989–1995) of Ilyās Hrāwī (q.v.). Nevertheless, members of the movement in South Lebanon, where the Lebanese government has but a token presence, remain armed. It had four parliamentary seats in the 1992 parliament, and its list won overwhelmingly in the South in the 1996 parliamentary election, in which Amal and Ḥizbullāh unified their list. *See also* Aṣ-Ṣadr, Imām Mūsā, and Birrī, Nabīh.

AMERICAN UNIVERSITY OF BEIRUT (AUB). This university was established by American missionaries as the Syrian Protestant College in 1866. It soon emerged as the leading educational institution in the region and was renamed the American University of Beirut. The university influenced the cultural awakening in the Arab world. In the first few years, teaching was conducted in Arabic (q.v.) but it later changed to English, which remains the language of instruction. It founded a medical school which produced physicians who work in the entire Arab world. The university also established the American University Hospital, which renders medical services to people from around the region. A board of trustees has authority over the university, which is incorporated under the laws of the state of New York. The university has faculties of arts and sciences, medicine, architecture, public health, and agriculture.

The university awards bachelor's and master's degrees in most fields. Some programs also offer doctorate degrees. The quality of teaching has declined over the years, especially with the flight of foreign professors during the 1975 civil war (q.v.). Furthermore, militias have influenced hiring and imposed unqualified professors on the faculty. The civil war had a deep impact on the quality of its education, and the university was forced to open a branch of the university in East Beirut (q.v.) under pressure from the Lebanese Forces (LF) (q.v.). Many professors were threatened, some were killed, and others were kidnapped. In 1984, its president, Malcolm Kerr, was assassinated by unknown gunmen. The LF wanted the university to retain the East Beirut branch, known as the Off-Campus Program, even after the unification of East and West Beirut (qq.v.). The university, however, rejected the pressure and successfully unified both branches in a relatively short period of time.

The challenge of the university, however, is not only in raising the quality of education but also in offering its important services to larger segments of the population. Since its inception, AUB has catered to rich upper-class families. Its high tuition fees excluded poor students, despite scholarships. A large percentage of the cultural, political, business, and scientific elite of the Arab world are graduates of AUB. In 1991–92, it had 4,885 students.

AMĪN, 'ABDALLĀH al- (1946–). This pro-Syrian Party leader was born to a Shi'ite (q.v.) family in Ṣuwwān, South Lebanon. He studied Arabic (q.v.) literature and received his degree from the Beirut Arab University (q.v.). He started his political activism within the Arab Socialist Ba'th Party (q.v.) in 1965, where he quickly became a member of the Regional Command. He became secretary-general of the party in the 1980s, a position owed more to Syrian political influence in Lebanon than to charismatic leadership qualities on his part. He was appointed minister in 1990 and has been a member of successive cabinets. He won a seat in the 1992 elections. He lacks an independent power base, but is one of the most influential politicians in Lebanon because of his consistent loyalty to Syria (q.v.).

AMĪN, IBRĀHĪM AL. *SEE* SAYYID, IBRĀHĪM AMĪN AS-.

'ĀMMIYYAH. Meaning "commune," this Arabic word was used in the 19th century to refer to peasant communal takeovers of lands in Mount Lebanon. There are suggestions that this could have been one of the first influences of the French Revolution in Lebanon. These takeovers of the estates of large landowners triggered aggressive responses from the political elite, who promoted sectarian conflict.

ANBĀ', al-. A magazine founded in 1951 by Kamāl Jumblāṭ (q.v.) and edited by Edmond Na'īm, it was the official mouthpiece of the Progressive Socialist Party (q.v.). Its publication has been irregular over the years.

ANṢĀR. This small village is 37 kilometers from Nabaṭiyyah (q.v.). Its meaning is "partisans." After the Israeli invasion of 1982 (q.v.), the village was chosen by occupation forces as a site for a prison camp that housed, at one point, more than 5,000 prisoners.

ANṬILYĀS COMMUNE. This *'āmmiyyah* (q.v.), the first of its kind, was founded in 1820 when peasants revolted against the rule of Bashīr II (q.v.), protesting tax increases. It is considered the first recognizable class uprising in Lebanese history.

ANṬŪN, FARAḤ (1874–1922). This gifted thinker was born in Tripoli (q.v.). He worked briefly in commerce before teaching in local schools. He headed the Orthodox School in Tripoli and embarked on a long process of self-education. He was influenced by many Western thinkers, namely Rousseau, Renan, Tolstoy, and Bernard Shaw. As a social reformer, he criticized established opinions on religion and politics. He immigrated to Egypt in 1897 and founded *Al-Jāmi'ah,* a unique journal that combined journalism with scholarship. He lived briefly in the United States (q.v.), where he tried unsuccessfully to continue publication of his journal. He also wrote for the daily *Al-Ahālī*. He was a prolific writer, writing and translating plays, novels, and historical and scholarly works. He had a famous debate on secularism and Islam with Muḥammad 'Abduh. He wrote a celebrated philosophical work on Ibn Rushd, which remains a classic.

'AQL, SA'ĪD (1912–). A poet and controversial literary and political figure, nobody has done more than he has to promote myths about

Lebanon and its history. He only received a secondary education but excels in the Arabic language and taught Arabic (q.v.) for years at a variety of schools and institutes. He is a champion of a brand of Lebanese ultranationalism that contains ideas of ethnocentrism. He traces all modern civilizations and scientific discoveries to "the ancient Lebanese civilization," referring to the Phoenicians, and he traces the ethnic origins of the great men of poetry, government, philosophy, and science to Lebanese families. He advocates writing "the Lebanese language" (the colloquial form of Arabic spoken in Lebanon) in the Roman script. Although he produced his best work in the classical Arabic language, he has recently been writing in this spoken form of the language. An ultranationalist, 'Aql has been an ardent opponent of any Arab presence in Lebanon, especially Palestinians. He is associated ideologically with one of the most extreme right-wing parties in Lebanon, the Guardians of the Cedars (q.v.). In 1962, he founded the Sa'īd 'Aql Prize, which awarded a monetary sum to a talented Lebanese. 'Aql suspended the prize during the war. During the war, he published extremist publications during the war and supported the ties between Israel (q.v.) and the Lebanese Forces (q.v.). He is widely considered a Lebanese patriot and a non-sectarian politician.

ARAB DEMOCRATIC PARTY (*Al-Ḥizb al-'Arabī al-Dimuqrāṭī*). The origins of this pro-Syrian and 'Alawite-oriented party can be traced back to 1975, when 'Alī 'Īd (q.v.), a local 'Alawite (q.v.) leader from the Tripoli area who headed a small organization called *Ḥarakat al-Shabāb al-'Alawī* (Movement of the 'Alawite Youths), founded the Confrontation Front along with a Sunni deputy Ṭalāl al-Mir'abī and Shi'ite activist Suhayl Ḥamādī. The Confrontation Front, closely aligned with the Syrian army and intelligence in Lebanon, benefited from the close political and sectarian ties between 'Īd and key officials in Damascus. The front's militia was nicknamed the Pink Panthers, and its fighters were notorious for their thuggery. They were associated in the public mind with acts of murder, rape, and extortion. The front's name was changed in the mid-1980s to the Arab Democratic Party. 'Alī 'Īd was appointed deputy in 1991. He won a seat in the 1992 election but failed to win a seat in the 1996 election.

ARAB DETERRENT FORCE (*Quwwāt ar-Rad' al-'Arabiyyah*). The League of Arab States, in an effort to end the 1975 civil war (q.v.), agreed in 1976 during the Riyaḍ Conference (q.v.) to form a peacekeeping force that comprised Syria (q.v.), Saudi Arabia, Libya (qq.v.), and Kuwait. The Syrian troops, however, dominated the force, and the other Arab troops withdrew. The Syrian army remains entrenched in Lebanon, although in 1982 the Lebanese government requested its withdrawal. The Syrian army did not need the cover of the Arab Deterrent Force because its presence in Lebanon was supported by the ruling elite. The force does not exist anymore.

ARAB SOCIALIST BA'TH PARTY ***(Ḥizb al-Ba'th al-'Arabī al-Ishtirākī).*** This party emerged as an active player in radical Lebanese politics in the 1950s. The Ba'thists, a growing opposition force in the country, were included in the broad front of "progressive and nationalist" organizations headed by Kamāl Jumblāṭ (q.v.). The founding congress of Lebanese Ba'thists was held in 1956, and a local leadership for this Arab-wide party was elected.

The party suffered from various schisms, which split the organization primarily into pro-Syrian and pro-Iraqi factions. The split between the two factions was formally established in 1964, when supporters of the "radical" Iraqi faction met in Beirut (q.v.) and elected a provisional national command, which drew the support of some leading Lebanese Ba'thists, although it was opposed by party founder Michel 'Aflaq (q.v.). After the 1966 coup in Syria (q.v.), the Ba'th party in Lebanon became almost entirely dominated by pro-Iraqi activists. Nevertheless, the proximity of Syria guaranteed the continued existence of a small faction with allegiance to Damascus.

In the 1972 parliamentary election, the pro-Iraqi Ba'thist leader, 'Abdul-Majīd ar-Rāfi'ī (q.v.), was elected to a seat representing Tripoli (q.v.). Another pro-Iraqi Ba'thist sympathizer, 'Alī al-Khalīl, was elected to parliament from Tyre (q.v.). The Ba'th was very active in South Lebanon and utilized generous Iraqi aid for its activities and propaganda. Many newspapers and magazines in Lebanon espoused its political line. The party, like the pro-Syrian party (which adds the word *munadhdhamat* [organization] to the full name of the Ba'th party to distinguish itself from the pro-Iraqi version of the party using the same name) participated in combat during the 1975 civil war (q.v.).

The pro-Iraqi faction suffered a setback in 1976—from which it never recovered—in the wake of the Syrian military intervention in Lebanon, which ushered in an era of Syrian political and military domination of the country. The Syrian army forced pro-Iraqi Ba'thists either to flee abroad or to go underground. Some chose to live under the rule of right-wing militias, especially in the late 1970s and early 1980s. Some leading members of the party were assassinated. Ar-Rāfi'ī, who heads the pro-Iraqi faction, still resides abroad. The small pro-Syrian faction benefits from Syrian influence in Lebanon and was awarded key appointments in the administration. In 1991, 'Abdullāh al-Amīn (q.v.), then leader of the party, was appointed to parliament along with two other leading members. In the 1992 elections, the party won two seats.

ARAB SOCIALIST UNION ***(Al-Ittiḥād al-Ishtirākī al-'Arabī).*** Several small, Sunni(q.v.)-oriented organizations used this name, all agreeing on allegiance to Jamāl 'Abdul-Nasser's (q.v.) legacy but disagreeing on everything else. The main organization by this name, formed in 1975, was headed by 'Umar Ḥarb, Ḥasan Shalḥah, and 'Abdul-Raḥīm Murād (q.v.), the last of whom was appointed to parliament in 1991. The efforts of Libya (q.v.), the main patron of Nasserist groups in Lebanon, to unite all Nasserists in Lebanon failed over the years. This organization benefited from Libyan aid and initiated social programs in al-Biqā' valley (q.v.). It was a member of the Lebanese National Movement (q.v.) during the 1975 civil war (q.v.).

The union held a general congress in 1979, which developed an organizational structure but failed to expand membership. Its ties to Libya were not broken, although Libyan financial aid declined in the 1980s and 1990s. One leader of the movement, Ḥasan Ṣabrā, left in the early 1980s and founded the weekly magazine *al-Shirā',* which broke the story of the Iran-Contra scandal. The aforementioned Murād won a parliamentary seat in the 1992 election. In 1996 Ḥarb and Murād split the movement into two separate organizations.

ARAB SOCIALIST UNION (THE NASSERIST ORGANIZATION) ***(Al-Ittiḥād al-Ishtirākī at-'Arabī [al-Tanḍhīm An-Nāṣirī]).*** This group split from the main Arab Socialist Union (q.v.) in 1976, led by Munīr al-Ṣayyād. It was confined to the Sunni (q.v.) quarter of 'Ayn al-Muraysah in Beirut (q.v.). It disappeared from public view after 1982, although Ṣayyād himself ran for parliament and lost in 1992.

ARABIC. This is the official language in Lebanon. The Arabic language is a distinguishing characteristic of the Arab people, although a local dialect is spoken in most Arab countries. The colloquial Arabic of Lebanon contains loan words from Turkish, Persian, and Aramaic. Although Arabic is spoken by all Lebanese, some ultranationalists in the country take pride in what they consider the "Lebanese language," which is no more than the local dialect of Arabic.

'ARAFĀT, YĀSIR (1929–). Chairman of the Palestine Liberation Organization (PLO), was born in Jerusalem in 1929. This famous Palestinian figure played an important role in Arab politics since the Fatḥ Movement (q.v.) was founded in the late 1950s. After he completed his engineering degree in Cairo, he established a business in Kuwait, where he helped found the Fatḥ movement. 'Arafāt later abandoned his engineering pursuits and devoted his energies full-time to Palestinian activism. 'Arafāt's role in Lebanese politics started before 1970, when the Jordanian regime forced the PLO out of Jordan, following the infamous Black September massacres. 'Arafāt used the Lebanese arena to publicize his Fatḥ movement. He cooperated with the Arab nationalist newspaper *Al-Muḥarrir* (q.v.) to introduce his views and the views of Fatḥ leaders to the larger Arab world. After 1970, the PLO was established in Beirut, and the 1975 civil war (q.v.) allowed 'Arafāt to exercise his authority over an important Arab country. While he was supposed to be in alliance with the Lebanese allies he often acted as the ultimate decision maker in West Beirut (q.v.). His ties to Lebanon were mostly severed after the expulsion of his forces from Beirut in the wake of the 1982 Israeli invasion (q.v.).

'ARAQ. This major alcoholic Lebanese beverage is made from anise and grape. It is consumed with food, especially in the mountain region. It is colorless, but when water is added it changes to milky white.

'ARĪḌAH, MAY (1925–). This socialite's name evokes images of prewar social life in Lebanon. She was married to a famous industrialist-businessman, and her name is closely associated with the Ba'albak (q.v.) International Festival, which she helped found and headed from 1968 until 1975. She was also a board member of the National Music Institute (q.v.). Like many rich Lebanese, she settled in Europe during the 1975 civil war (q.v.). In 1997, she revived the Ba'albak Festival for the first time since 1975.

ARMENIAN ORTHODOX CHRISTIANS. Also known as the Gregorian church; it was organized in the third century and became autocephalous as a national church in the fourth century. In the sixth century, it modified the formulations of the Council of Chalcedon of 451 that confirmed the dual nature of Christ in one person. Instead, the Gregorian Church adopted a form of monophysitism that believes in the single divine nature of Christ, different from the belief of the Copts and the Syrian Orthodox. The Armenian Orthodox Church has five patriarchs, of whom the Catholic of Etchmiadizin in Armenia is the most revered. It also has an Armenian liturgy.

ARMENIAN SECRET ARMY FOR THE LIBERATION OF ARMENIA. This small, secret organization, founded in 1975, has built networks of support worldwide. It views its actions in the context of revenge for the massacre of Armenians (q.v.) early in this century. Its members are ultraleftist Armenian activists who believe that the Turkish government stands in the way of Armenian liberation. It mounted an international campaign of violence against Turkish interests. The party strongly believes in "armed struggle," a euphemism for terrorism, as far as the Turkish government is concerned. Some of its attacks against

Turkish targets took place on Lebanese soil, where members received training and indoctrination from Lebanese and Palestinian leftist organizations. In 1980, the party began publishing its own newspaper. The 1982 Israeli invasion (q.v.) of Lebanon (q.v.) deprived the organization of the climate of freedom of action for international leftism.

ARMENIANS. The Armenians in Lebanon were refugees who fled Turkey during and after World War I following the genocide of their people. They reside in Beirut (q.v.) and its northern suburbs as well as in ‘Anjar in al-Biqā‘ valley (q.v.). They are admired for their craftsmanship and for their diligence, characteristics that have enabled them to gain prominent social positions. Politically, they advocate compromise and moderation and tend to avoid controversies and extremism; they have regularly served in parliaments and cabinets. Even during the civil war of 1975 to 1990 (q.v.), the Armenians, as a community, remained on good terms with all sides. *See also* Dasnah Party; Hunchak Party; Ramgavar Party.

ARMY OF ARAB LEBANON. This name was chosen by a Muslim group of officers and soldiers who defected in 1975 from the Lebanese Army (q.v.), accusing its Maronite (q.v.) leadership of collaborating with Maronite right-wing militias and of plotting the extermination of the Palestinian resistance in Lebanon. The army was supported by the Fatḥ (q.v.) movement within the Palestine Liberation Organization (PLO) (q.v.), and in 1976 it overran the military barracks controlled by the Lebanese Army (q.v.) in West Beirut (q.v.), South Lebanon, and al-Biqā‘ valley (q.v.). The army's role came to an end in the spring and early summer of 1976, when its forces (along with PLO forces and forces of the Lebanese National Movement, q.v.) clashed with the Syrian army, when it intervened on the side of right-wing militias in 1976. Its leader, Aḥmad al-Khaṭīb, was arrested by the Syrians and jailed for a couple of years. He refrained from any political activity upon his release. Al-Khaṭīb was considered a hero by some and a traitor by others.

ARSALĀN FAMILY. It is the leading family of the Yazbaki family confederation among the Druzes (q.v.). It has been a leader among the Druzes for centuries and competes with the Jumblāṭ family (q.v.) over leadership within the community. Its leadership is now assumed by Prince Ṭalāl Arsalān (q.v.), who inherited the position from his father, Majīd (q.v.), and who has been trying, with Syrian encouragement, to revive the role of his family.

ARSALĀN, MAJĪD (1904–1983). He was the leader of the princely Arsalān family and the head of the Yazbaki family confederation in

Lebanon. He was uneducated and was often ridiculed in Lebanon for his lack of intelligence and sophistication. He stated in press interviews that beating a woman was acceptable. He claimed, without any evidence, that he was a war hero from the 1948 war, in which Lebanon played no significant role. He continuously represented the 'Alayy region in parliament and was closely aligned with the political machine of former president Kamīl Sham'ūn (q.v.), which explains why he was marginalized during the 1975 civil war (q.v.). He held numerous ministerial positions, not because of his qualifications but because he was subservient to the Maronite (q.v.) political establishment. He often insisted on heading the Ministry of Defense. He never was able to compete with his sophisticated and highly educated Druze (q.v.) rival, Kamāl Jumblāṭ (q.v.). Upon his death in 1983, his two sons (Ṭalāl (q.v.) and Fayṣal) fought for the leadership position of the family. Ṭalāl eventually won. He was elected to parliament in 1992 and again in 1996. Fayṣal lost both times.

ARSALĀN, SHAKĪB (1869–1946). A pan-Arab thinker, he was born to a traditional leading (princely) Druze (q.v.) family. He was a local governor under Ottoman rule but joined the cause of Arab nationalist emancipation after World War I. He moved to Europe in the 1920s, where he organized and edited the Arab nationalist weekly *La Nation Arabe*. He established contacts with Zionist leaders. He later adopted Islamic ideas, and is still remembered as a leading thinker of Arab nationalism. A committee has been founded to honor him and to republish all his works.

ARSALĀN, ṬALĀL (1963–). A Druze (q.v.) leader, he is the youngest son of Majīd Arsalān (q.v.) and his wife Khawlah. He was educated in Shuwayfāt and received a degree in political science from George Washington University in Washington, D.C. He won the power struggle within his family upon the death of his father due to the backing he received from his shrewd mother. Ṭalāl has solidified his ties with the Syrian (q.v.) regime (and with the sons of Ḥāfiḍh al-Asad, specifically) and with the Franjiyyah family, through his friendship with Sulaymān Franjiyyah Jr. (q.v.). He first served as minister in 1990 and has since served regularly. Ṭalāl is the key rival of Walīd Jumblāṭ (q.v.) for the leadership of the Druze community. He was elected to parliament in 1992 and 1996, although Walīd Jumblāṭ gained far more electoral power in the latter election. Relations between Ṭalāl and Walīd Jumblāṭ have improved following several meetings in 1996.

ARTICLE 95. This article of the constitution (q.v.) of Lebanon injected a controversial principle of sectarianism into the Lebanese political system by juridically affirming a sectarian basis for the distribution of political powers in Lebanon: "As a provisional measure, and for the sake of concord and justice, the sects shall be represented equitably in public posts and in the formation of the cabinet without causing harm to the interests of the state." The article as amended in 1990 promises the ultimate elimination of political sectarianism but it preserves the sectarian composition of the cabinet and the grade A posts in government and their equivalent. *See also* Constitution.

ARTISANAT LIBANAIS. This company was founded by the wife of Emile Iddī (q.v.) in 1937 to encourage Lebanese handicrafts. It specializes in high-quality products that are in demand by tourists and immigrants. It houses a collection of traditional clothing, embroidery, daggers, and paper knives. Its prices are high, and there is no evidence that all its proceeds go to village workers who supply the *Artisanat* with the fruit of their labor.

ARZ AR-RAB. *SEE* CEDARS OF LEBANON.

AS'AD, KĀMIL al- (1929–). A Shi'ite (q.v.) leader, he was one of the most influential politicians in post-independence Lebanon. He was born in Beirut (q.v.) to an established *za'īm* (q.v.) family. His father, Aḥmad, was known for his monopolization of political representation in South Lebanon: it was said that a stick could have been elected on Aḥmad's parliamentary list. Kāmil received his law degree from St. Joseph University (q.v.). He was known for his indulgence in earthly pleasures and for his contempt of the very Shi'ite peasants he ostensibly represented. Unlike his father, Kāmil was notorious for his arrogance and public outbursts against his staff and constituency. He entered the Lebanese parliament in 1953 and was elected speaker of parliament in 1964. He often competed for that highest Shi'ite post with his brother-in-law, Ṣabrī Ḥamādī (q.v.), who was favored during the Fu'ād Shihāb (q.v.) era. He held several ministerial positions but was never famous for hard work or attention to the job. In the 1960s, Kāmil was active in the parliamentary bloc of *al-Wasaṭ* (Center), which included among its members future president Sulaymān Franjiyyah (q.v.). This bloc worked to bring an end to Shihabism, especially for resurrecting the class of *zu'amā'*, which Shihāb wanted to weaken. When the left began mobilizing Shi'ites, he founded the Democratic Socialist Party (q.v.), but it was never taken seriously.

The election of Franjiyyah guaranteed al-As'ad a reign as speaker from 1971 until the end of Franjiyyah's term. After Franjiyyah was out of office, al-As'ad held onto the speakership until 1984, when the political map of Lebanon was radically altered against him, since his political career is tied to the contemporary history of the Shi‘ite political movement in Lebanon. The emergence of radical leftist parties among the Shi‘ites and the success of Imām Mūsā aṣ-Ṣadr (q.v.) among South Lebanese Shi‘ites are related to popular antipathy to al-As‘ad and his traditional leadership of the Shi‘ite masses. Al-As‘ad did not receive average citizens, as most *za‘īms* did—and still do; and he limits the role of *wāsiṭah* (q.v.), being too impatient to fulfill his obligations as an elected political boss toward his constituency. He was also known for spending months in Europe away from his electoral home base in the South, which he visited only infrequently. The leftist newspaper *As-Safīr* (q.v.), carried a picture of him playing tennis at the height of the 1975 civil war (q.v.).

Al-As‘ad stayed in his job because he won the trust of the Syrian political leadership. All that changed in 1982 in the wake of the Israeli invasion (q.v.), when al-As‘ad suddenly reversed himself, stating that presidential elections would take place while Israeli troops remained in Lebanon. It was reported at the time that al-As‘ad received large sums of money from the campaign of Bashīr Gemayyel (q.v.). The Syrian government never forgave him. He lost the speakership in 1984 and retired to France, where he stayed until the early 1990s. He returned to Lebanon when parliamentary elections were announced. He ran and lost resoundingly, along with all other members of his list. He blamed his defeat on irregularities, but his popularity was clearly at an all-time low. His performance was even worse in the 1996 election.

‘AṢFŪRIYYAH. This is a site just outside Beirut (q.v.) where a hospital for the mentally ill was constructed by a German in 1897. It housed patients from the entire region but was not known for its professional or humane treatment of its patients. Mental patients are often beaten and abused.

ASHQAR, NIḌĀL. This daughter of Syrian Social National Party (SSNP) (q.v.) leader Asad al-Ashqar was born in Dīk al-Miḥdī. She studied at the Royal Academy of Dramatic Art in London and established herself as the leading theatrical performer in Lebanon and the Arab world. She has been an enthusiastic supporter of the SSNP and of the left in general. She also performed in many Lebanese and Arab television serials. She was known for her daring performances before the 1975 civil war (q.v.). Her husband, Fu’ād Na‘īm, was director of Lebanese TV before his dismissal by the government in 1996.

ASĪR, YŪSUF al- (1815–1890). A writer, he was born in Sidon (q.v.), where he studied the Qur’ān and the Arabic (q.v.) language. He went to Damascus for further study and later spent seven years in Egypt studying at Al-Azhar University. He returned to Lebanon to serve as a judge in Tripoli (q.v.) but was soon recalled by the government in Istanbul to edit its publications. He also taught Arabic. He eventually fled the cold climate and settled in Beirut (q.v.) where he wrote for a variety of publications. He assisted Buṭrus al-Bustānī (q.v.) in the translation of the Bible. Al-Asīr was among those who taught Cornelius Van Dyck (q.v.) Arabic, and a friendship developed between the two men, which explains why an Islamic scholar assisted Christian missionaries in their translation of the Bible. He was one of the most notable Muslims to be associated with the cultural revival of the 19th century. He wrote several books, some of which are compilations of his articles. He founded and edited the newspaper *Thamarat Al-Funūn* in 1875, thought to be the first newspaper in Lebanon published by a Muslim. He also wrote a commentary on the Ottoman Code, which was published after his death.

ASSYRIAN CHURCH. The Assyrians are the remnants of the Nestorian Church that emerged with the Christological controversies in the fifth century. The Nestorians, who have a Syriac liturgy, stressed that Christ consisted of two separate persons, one human and one divine. Their doctrine was condemned by the Council of Ephesus in 431 A.D. The Assyrian community in Lebanon expresses national solidarity with the Assyrians of Iraq, many of whom hope for the creation of a separate state in northern Iraq. Thousands of Assyrians have emigrated from Lebanon and Iraq to the United States, where they produce nationalist literature.

AUDIT BUREAU. The bureau was founded in 1959 as an administrative-judicial board. Its mission is to monitor public funds and their expenditure. Under its jurisdiction fall state administration, large municipalities, municipalities designated by the cabinet, public firms, and societies and institutions partly funded by the state. The existence of this bureau has not in any way resolved the massive corruption of the Lebanese administration. Members of the board are appointed by the president and the council of ministers; reasons for appointments are often sectarian or political.

‘AWN, MICHEL (1935–). He was born to a Maronite (q.v.) family of modest socio-economic level. He joined the Lebanese Army (q.v.), becoming a lieutenant-colonel in 1975. He fought alongside the right-wing coalition of militias against the Palestine Liberation Organization and its Lebanese allies. He was appointed commander-in-chief of the Lebanese Army (q.v.) by President Amīn Gemayyel (q.v.). In 1988, when the country could not agree on Gemayyel's successor, Gemayyel (to prevent the government from passing into Muslim hands) appointed 'Awn as interim prime minister. No Muslim minister agreed to join 'Awn's cabinet, and the country was split into two governments, one headed by 'Awn in East Beirut (q.v.), and the other headed by Salīm al-Ḥuṣṣ (q.v.) in West Beirut. A year after his appointment, with Iraqi aid, 'Awn launched a "war of liberation" against the Syrian presence in Lebanon. He rejected the aṭ-Ṭā'if Accords (q.v.) in 1989, which were intended to end the 1975–90 Lebanese civil war (q.v.). He also launched a war against the Lebanese Forces (q.v.) in 1990. His brief tenure ended in October 1990, when Syrian troops attacked his headquarters and forced him to flee to the French Embassy in Beirut. According to an agreement with the French government, 'Awn was allowed to leave the country safely with his family to a place outside of Paris. His influence in Lebanon was not eliminated, and he continues to make political statements and declarations from exile. In 1996, 'Awn formed an alliance with Amīn Gemayyel and Dūrī Sham'ūn to protest Syrian dominance in Lebanon. In 1996, he was one of the founders of an opposition alliance called the National Grouping (q.v.).

AWRĀQ LUBNĀNIYYAH. This weekly journal was published by historian Yūsuf Ibrāhīm Yazbak between 1952 and 1958. It contained copies of historical documents, archival correspondence, and various unpublished material on Lebanese history. An effort was made, however, to avoid publishing any documents that revealed the historical roots of sectarianism in Lebanon. The entire collection was reissued in the 1990s in Beirut (q.v.).

'AWWĀD, TAWFĪQ YŪSUF (1911–?). A writer and diplomat, he was born in Bḥirṣāf and educated in Beirut (q.v.). He began his journalistic career early in his life, writing for a variety of weekly magazines and daily newspapers and later became assistant editor of *An-Nahār* (q.v.). He earned a degree in law from Damascus University in 1934. He was sympathetic with the Lebanese Phalanges Party (q.v.) for a while but abandoned party activity in the 1940s when he joined the diplomatic service. He served in many foreign capitals but was known for his commercially successful novels. The most famous of his books are *Aṣ-Ṣabiyy Al-A'raj* (1936), *Qamīṣ Aṣ-Ṣūf* (1937), and *Ar-Raghīf* (1938). He died when a shell fell on his house during the 1975–90 civil war (q.v.).

'AYN AR-RUMMĀNAH MASSACRE. This refers to the murder of the passengers on a Palestinian bus by Lebanese Phalangist (q.v.) forces on April 13, 1975, in the predominantly Christian neighborhood of 'Ayn ar-Rummānah. The massacre is considered by some the spark of the 1975 civil war (q.v.). Phalangist sources claimed that they ambushed the bus in revenge for the earlier killing of four Phalangist gunmen. The bus was carrying Palestinian civilians returning from a Palestinian rally of the Popular Front for the Liberation of Palestine-General Command.

'AYN WARAQAH. The first secular school in Lebanon was established in 'Ayn Waraqah in 1787, when the monastery of St. Anthony at 'Ayn Waraqah in Kisrawān was converted into a clerical seminary. Two years later it was turned into a semi-secular school. The monastery itself had been established by Khayrallāh Isṭifān in 1690.

'AZQŪL, KARĪM (1914–). A diplomat, he was born in Rashayyā and educated at St. Joseph University (q.v.), the Sorbonne, and the University of Munich, where he received his Ph.D. in philosophy. He taught at the American University of Beirut (q.v.) before taking on the assignment of chief delegate of Lebanon to the United Nations (1950–54). He then held a key post at the Lebanese Foreign Ministry before returning to his post at the United Nations, where he stayed until 1957. He held numerous diplomatic positions in Africa and Asia before returning to Lebanon in 1966. He taught at the Beirut University College (later renamed Lebanese American University, q.v.) and the Lebanese University (q.v.). He is the author of several books and articles, notably *Al-'Aql fī-l-Islām* (Reason in Islam).

-B-

BA'ABDĀ. In October 1969, during the administration of Charles Ḥilū (q.v.), the Lebanese presidency was officially moved to Ba'abdā, outside of Beirut (q.v.) where a presidential palace was built. It has served since then as the seat of the Lebanese presidency, with some interruptions. In 1976, the palace received direct hits, forcing Sulaymān Franjiyyah (q.v.) to relocate his offices to Zūq, under right-wing militia control. In October 1990, when Syrian troops bombed the palace to force Michel 'Awn (q.v.) to surrender his presidential claim, the Arab Gulf regimes donated money to rebuild the palace. It is now again the headquarters of the Lebanese president.

BA'ALBAK. This ancient temple-city is famous for its archeological treasures from the Roman period. It is located between Mount Lebanon and the Anti-Lebanon Mountains. In the 1960s, the Lebanese government inaugurated the tradition of the Ba'albak International Festival, which attracted artists and performers from around the world, and Ba'albak became a major tourist center. After the 1975–90 civil war (q.v.), the city lost its main source of revenue and was subject to militia rule. This predominantly Shi'ite (q.v.) city was a center for Islamic fundamentalism in the 1980s and 1990s. The Lebanese government has decided to renew the Ba'albak Festival. *See also* 'Ariḍah, May.

BA'ALBAK INTERNATIONAL FESTIVAL. *SEE* BA'ALBAK.

BA'ALBAKĪ, MUḤAMMAD (1921–). A journalist and dean of the Lebanese Press Syndicate, he was educated in Arabic (q.v.) literature at the American University of Beirut (q.v.). He taught Arabic at various schools in the 1940s. He founded and managed the newspaper *Ṣadā Lubnān* (1951–1985). He joined the Syrian Social National Party (SSNP) (q.v.) and was arrested, along with all other key leaders of the SSNP, in the wake of its failed coup attempt in 1961. He has taken a pro-Syrian, pro-Arab political line but remains on good terms with most Lebanese factions.

BĀBĀ, KĀMIL al- (1905–1991). He was born in Sidon (q.v.) and began his career as an Arabic (q.v.) calligrapher at an early age. He was trained in this art by his father, Salīm al-Bābā, who was a teacher at the Sulṭāniyyah School. He later received training from the official calligrapher of the Egyptian monarch Fu'ād I. He worked from his office in downtown Beirut (q.v.) until the beginning of the civil war in 1975 (q.v.). Al-Bābā's art is displayed on the covers of many books and in government documents. His main work was for the Lebanese Republic, although he also did work for other Arab governments. He taught calligraphy and trained his son Mukhtār to follow in his footsteps. He wrote a book on the "spirit of Arabic calligraphy," and his art was displayed in numerous exhibits. He traveled to Saudi Arabia (q.v.) during the war and died there.

BABIKIAN, KHATCHIQ (1922–). A parliamentarian, he is perhaps the most famous Armenian (q.v.) in Lebanon (q.v.). He has been designated as the preferred representative of the Armenian community in Lebanese cabinets, in large measure due to his superb command of the Arabic (q.v.) language. He was educated at St. Joseph University (q.v.) and the University of London. He practiced law, was elected to parliament in 1957, and became a minister in 1960. He was known for his moderation but was closest politically to Kamīl Sham'ūn (q.v.). His impressive linguistic skills made him a popular choice to represent Lebanese parliamentarians in international conferences. He was elected to parliament in the 1992 election.

BADRĀN, ALEXANDRĀ. *SEE* NŪR AL-HUDĀ.

BAGHĀ'. *SEE* PROSTITUTION.

BAHA'I SECT. This is the name of a 19th century movement that developed into a religion. Although the teachings of the faith are accommodationist and peaceful, the community has been persecuted because it split off from Shi'ite (q.v.) Islam and accepted the prophecy of a man who came after Muhammad, in clear violation of Islam, which considers Muhammad the seal of all Prophets. There are some 400,000 Baha'is in Iran but only hundreds in Lebanon.

BAKHSHĪSH. This refers to the practice of bribery used by citizens to expedite governmental transactions. It may also be used to obtain access to a high government official.

BARAKĀT, ANTOINE. This Lebanese Army (q.v.) officer was not pleased with the level of support given by the army to the right-wing militias, and he left with his men and weapons to join the right-wing militias in the 1975–76 phase of the civil war (q.v.). He believed that the Lebanese Army should not hide its support for the Lebanese Forces (q.v.). His role was criticized, and he was sent to Washington, D.C., as military attaché.

BAṢBŪṢ, ALFRED AND JOSEPH. These brothers are the most famous sculptors in Lebanon. They were born in Roshānā in Lebanon and educated at the Lebanese Academy of Fine Arts. Their works are exhibited in many governmental buildings.

BASHĪR II THE SHIHABI (1767–1840). A ruler and mythical figure, he was born in Ghazīr in Kisrawān to the Shihabi family dynasty, which succeeded the Ma'nid dynasty. Historians still argue over his religious faith. Some say he was born a Sunni Muslim (q.v.) but later converted to the Maronite (q.v.) faith. Others suggest he may have been a Druze (q.v.). It is almost certain that he died a Maronite.

He grew up in the Burj al-Barājinah neighborhood outside of Beirut (q.v.). He may have received some education at the hands of monks. He returned to Bayt ad-Dīn (q.v.), where he managed an estate he had inherited. He assumed the princedom of the Shihabi dynasty in 1788. His seizure of power was not widely accepted and fellow princes within the family, supported by leaders of the Nakad Druze family, tried to unseat him. He was ousted in 1793, despite support from Al-Jazzār, who had sponsored him. He later assumed his previous position and exacted revenge on his Nakad enemies. He was unseated again for supporting Al-Jazzār when confronted by the French expedition, and he left for Egypt.

He returned to rulership following the death of Al-Jazzār. Between 1804 and 1819, Bashīr II consolidated his government and extended his authority over parts of what is today Lebanon (q.v.). After killing many of his enemies, he did not feel safe in the government seat at Dayr Al-Qamar, and he relocated to Bayt Ad-Dīn, where he built a magnificent palace, designed by European architects. It remains today a tourist site, open to visitors and managed by the Lebanese government. Prior to the Egyptian occupation (1831–1840) of Syria and Lebanon, Bashīr II acted ruthlessly against a Druze rebellion and had Bashīr Jumblāṭ, the ultimate Druze leader, strangled. The Druzes never forgave the prince for this crime.

Under Egyptian rule, Bashīr II acted hesitantly, wanting to please Muḥammad 'Alī (the Egyptian ruler) without openly defying the Ottoman Porte. But he was ordered to be subservient to Egyptian rule in the course of the occupation. When rebellions broke out against Egyptian rule, Bashīr II loyally provided assistance. But what caused Bashīr II and the region the most harm, and eventually undermined the Egyptian presence, was the heavy demands on the prince to conscript citizens. Bashīr II also participated in Egyptian campaigns to disarm the Druzes of the Shuf. In 1840, a revolt spread against the rule of Bashīr II, and he was sent into exile in Malta.

BA'TH PARTY. *SEE* ARAB SOCIALIST BA'TH PARTY.

BAYDAS, YŪSUF. *SEE* INTRA BANK CRASH.

BAYHUM, MUḤAMMAD JAMĪL (1887–1978). This writer and reformer was born in Beirut (q.v.) to a wealthy and notable family. He studied at the Uthmāniyyah School before attending French missionary schools. In 1928, he earned a doctoral degree in law from the University of Paris. He worked in commerce while following closely political developments in the region. He represented Beirut in the 1919 conference in Saudi Arabia (q.v.), which requested full Arab independence and opposed the annexation of Beirut to the new state of Lebanon (q.v.).

In 1923 he asked the French government to annex Beirut to Syria (q.v.). He also joined the Iṣlāḥ Party in Syria and campaigned for Arabic (q.v.) to be the official language of Lebanon. In 1929, he was appointed a member of the Scientific Academy. In 1943, he and others founded the Al-Kutlah Al-Islāmiyyah to highlight Islamic demands and to improve the educational standards of Muslims in Lebanon. He was also a founder of the Lebanese Anti-Zionist League and championed the Palestinian cause throughout his life. He was a rare male voice advocating gender equality and wrote a book in 1921 on women in law and history, one of the first serious treatments of the oppression of women in the region. His support for women's rights did not waver over the years, and he was against imitating Western ways. His most famous book deals with the causes of the decline of the Ottoman Empire, the first volume of which was published in 1925.

BAYT AD-DĪN (BTIDDĪN). This is the site (near Dayr al-Qamar) on which Bashīr II (q.v.) built his famous palace in 1806. He later moved his seat of government there. It was visited by travelers, including Lamartine. It has been a tourist attraction for decades.

BEIRUT. The largest city and capital of Lebanon also serves as the center of the *muḥāfaḍhah* of Beirut. Its population was estimated at 407,403 in 1996. The name is probably derived from the old Semitic languages and refers to pine trees. It has been inhabited for thousands of years; the name is found in old Egyptian inscriptions. The location of ancient Beirut, however, has changed; some maintain it was on the site of present-day Bayt Mirī outside of the capital. Under Arab rule, Beirut was part of the *Jund* (province) of Damascus. The status of Beirut changed under Ottoman administration: it was first part of the Iyalat of Damascus but was later incorporated into the Iyalat of Ṣaydā (Sidon, q.v.). It attained some commercial, political, and economic significance in the 19th century, when a new *wilāyat* (district) of Beirut was formed, and the port became prosperous. Its main inhabitants were originally Sunnis (q.v.) and non-Maronite Christians, but it houses today all the sects of Lebanon.

For much of the modern history of Lebanon, Beirut served as an important political, financial, and cultural center for the Arab world. Its relatively open political climate, in contrast to the closed and oppressive conditions in neighboring Arab countries, attracted regional figures. Its press reflected not only local Lebanese political diversity but also Arab internal conflicts. Newspapers were bought and sold on behalf of Arab investors and governments, while local banks benefited from Arab capital fleeing socialist experiments. Oil wealth was at least partly responsible for the pre-war prosperity of Beirut. This wealth, however, was deceptive; it masked the acute social and economic disparities of the population. The city was, after all, surrounded by poverty belts (q.v.), or the impoverished suburbs of Beirut. The modernity of the city was often contrasted with the traditionalism of the suburbs.

After 1975, the image of Beirut was radically transformed. It was the main site of the 1975–90 civil war (q.v.), during which its downtown area was almost totally destroyed. It will take years, according to government estimates, before reconstruction plans for Beirut are completed. The government of Rafīq Ḥarīrī (q.v.) has initiated ambitious plans for the total reconstruction and development of Beirut. Critics, however, say that the plans will destroy the traditional style and restore the service economy to its primacy at the expense of other productive sectors.

BEIRUT ARAB UNIVERSITY. It was founded in 1960 and is affiliated with Alexandria University of Egypt, which administers it and is involved in administrative appointments. Eighty-five percent of its students are citizens of Arab countries, primarily from Gulf countries. It does not require students to attend classes and it has accepted more students than it could accommodate. The quality of its teaching is considered low, and its graduates are not favored in employment. It has faculties of law, letters, commerce, architecture, engineering, sciences, and pharmacy. Because of the lax requirements, many militia men registered at the university during the 1975–90 civil war (q.v.). The sight of armed students was common on campus. It operates on a very small budget and has an extremely low ratio of personal computers to students: 1:287. Prime minister Rafīq Ḥarīrī (q.v.) is a graduate of this university, but he more actively supports the American University of Beirut (q.v.). In 1991–92, it had 28,617 students.

BEIRUT INTERNATIONAL AIRPORT. The first airport, established in the neighborhood of Bīr Ḥasan during the French Mandate (q.v.), was later turned into a military airport. The current airport was established in 1954. It was one of the busiest airports in the region in the 1960s and 1970s. On December 28, 1968, Israeli commandos bombed a fleet of civilian airliners in the airport to punish the Lebanese government for an earlier attack by a Palestinian group on an Israeli plane in Athens. The 1975–90 civil war (q.v.) caused a lot of destruction and damage to the airport's buildings and tarmac. It was closed down for long periods at different stages of the war. It is now undergoing major extensions and improvements.

BEIRUT UNIVERSITY COLLEGE. *SEE* LEBANESE AMERICAN UNIVERSITY.

BIQĀ' VALLEY al-. This term describes both a natural and a political region. It denotes the fertile valley between the Mount Lebanon and Anti-Lebanon ranges. Al-Biqā' is also the name of an administrative unit, the *muḥāfaḍhah* (q.v.). Its major cities are Ba'albak (q.v.) and Zaḥlah (q.v.).

BIRRĪ, NABĪH (1938–). This speaker of parliament was born to a Lebanese emigrant family in Sierra Leone. He studied in Tibnīn in

South Lebanon before moving to Beirut (q.v.) to receive a law degree from the Lebanese University (q.v.). He was active in politics during his student days but came to prominence in the late 1970s when the "disappearance" of Imām Mūsā aṣ-Ṣadr (q.v.) thrust this leader of the Amal Movement (q.v.) to the forefront of the Lebanese political arena. He clashed with Ḥusayn al-Ḥusaynī (q.v.) when the latter headed the movement immediately after the "disappearance" of aṣ-Ṣadr. Birrī first assumed the presidency of Amal in 1980 and went on to become the most influential Shi'ite (q.v.) leader in Lebanon.

His relatively sudden emergence was not entirely the product of his own vision or charismatic qualities; he appeared on the political scene at a most opportune time. Traditional Shi'ite leaders, especially Kāmil al-As'ad (q.v.), were discredited, and the "disappearance" of aṣ-Ṣadr left a vacuum in the Shi'ite political arena. Furthermore, the Syrian regime was looking for a reliable ally. Birrī had established himself as the most reliable ally of Syria (q.v.) in the whole of Lebanon. His tenure, however, at the helm of the Amal Movement was far from smooth, and he had to deal with a variety of splintering factions. Ḥusayn al-Musawī left the movement in 1982 to form the Islamic Amal Movement (q.v.), and Ḥusayn al-Ḥusaynī, one of the founders of Amal, severed his ties with the movement following the ascent of Birrī.

Birrī's challenges also came from the outside. In 1982 the Party of God (q.v.) became an important factor in Shi'ite politics and put pressure on him to take less compromising stances. In 1985, Birrī, whether out of his own volition or at the behest of the Syrian regime, launched a savage war against Palestinian refugee camps in Lebanon. The War of the Camps (q.v.), cost Birrī men and political capital and he was seen, rightly or wrongly, as doing Syria's bidding. The Party of God benefited from Amal's distraction and built up its cells and bases. The relations between the two groups soured, and a war erupted pitting brother against brother and cousin against cousin, all members of the families of the small Shi'ite world in the southern suburbs of Beirut.

The establishment of state control over most of Lebanese territory helped Birrī in his quest to transform Amal from a militia into a political force. He has not succeeded, however, in transforming the movement into a modern political party. In the 1992 election, he headed the "liberation list," the largest bloc in the parliament. His election to the speakership in 1992 allowed him to improve his ties to Christian groups in Lebanon. His relations with Prime Minister Rafīq Ḥarīrī (q.v.) have not been free of tension although they collaborated in achieving victory in the 1996 parliamentary election. *See also* Amal.

BISH'ALĀNĪ, ANṬŪN al- (1827–1856). This man from Ṣālīmā is believed to be the first Lebanese to settle in the United States (q.v.). He settled in Boston in 1854 and died in New York City in 1856. Historian Philip Ḥittī has researched his background for his book *The Syrians in America* (1924).

BKIRKĪ. In 1790, a monastery here was designated as the official seat of the top Maronite (q.v.) religious leader. The summer seat is in Dimān. Bkirkī often hosts crucial meetings of top Maronite leaders. During the 1975–90 civil war (q.v.), militia and party leaders frequently gathered there for consultation.

BLACK SATURDAY. This is the common name for the December 6, 1975, day of killing. It was planned by Bashīr Gemayyel (q.v.) and executed by his loyal men. In response to the discovery of the bodies of four Lebanese Phalangist (q.v.) men, Gemayyel ordered the random killing of Muslims and Palestinians (q.v.) in East Beirut (q.v.). Estimates range from 200 to 300 civilians killed. That day expedited the flight of Muslims and Palestinians from East Beirut. At the time of the killing, Pierre Gemayyel (q.v.) was, coincidentally, in Damascus trying to improve his party's image among Arab governments.

BLOC OF INDEPENDENT MARONITE DEPUTIES (*Tajammu' An-Nuwwāb al-Mawārinah al-Mustaqillīn*). This parliamentary bloc was founded in 1979 by Buṭrus Ḥarb (q.v.) and other Maronite (q.v.) deputies who wanted to chart a political course independent of the hegemony of Bashīr Gemayyel (q.v.), who was emerging as the undisputed warlord of East Beirut (q.v.) and the Christian heartland. It helped reconcile the warring factions and personalities. Its role, however, was restricted to parliament and did not extend to the battlefronts.

BRIBERY. *SEE BAKHSHĪSH.*

BRIGADES OF AṢ-ṢADR (*Alwiyat aṣ-Ṣadr*). This organization was born after 1978, when Imām Mūsā aṣ-Ṣadr (q.v.) "disappeared" while on an official visit to Libya (q.v.). It claimed responsibility for various violent acts, including hijacking, aimed at Libyan interests. It is believed to be out of existence.

BROWN, DEAN. He was appointed special envoy to Lebanon (q.v.) by U.S. President Gerald Ford in March 1976. He mediated between the warring factions, but the war continued anyway. He was accused by Sulaymān Franjiyyah (q.v.) of offering American logistical help to secure the evacuation of all Christians from Lebanon. There is no evidence that Brown made such an offer. Brown was later critical of Maronite (q.v.) intransigence and developed a high regard for Kamāl Jumblāṭ (q.v.).

BSHĀMŪN GOVERNMENT. This brief Lebanese government was proclaimed in Bshāmūn (20 kilometers south of Beirut, q.v.) upon the arrest of the country's leaders in November 1943, when the French government tried to thwart Lebanese independence efforts. It comprised those Lebanese leaders who were not captured by the French. It was headed by Ḥabīb Abī Shahlā and included, among others, Majīd Arsalān (q.v.) and Ṣabrī Ḥamādī (q.v.).

BTIDDĪN. *SEE* BAYT AD-DĪN.

BUSTĀNĪ, BUṬRUS al- (1819–1883). The history of Arab renaissance is almost centered on the efforts of this scholar and educator. He was born to a Christian family from Dibbiyyah in Shūf, where he studied Arabic (q.v.) and Syriac. His teachers spotted his genius and advised him to pursue more education at the famous 'Ayn Waraqah (q.v.) school, the only school in Lebanon with extended education programs. He studied there for 10 years, acquiring scientific knowledge in addition to Latin and Italian. He settled in Beirut (q.v.), where he came into contact with the American missionaries who were establishing the Syrian Protestant College (later renamed American University of Beirut, q.v.), and he was asked to teach at the college. He also converted to Protestantism and was responsible for the 1848 translation of the Bible into Arabic; this is referred to as "the American translation," because he worked on it with American missionaries.

In the wake of the civil war of 1860 (q.v.), he founded a journal, *Nafīr Sūryā* (q.v), that published groundbreaking articles about national unity and patriotism. He also began the first Arabic encyclopedia (later volumes were completed after his death). He founded the journal *Al-Jinān* (q.v.). In 1863, he founded the National School in 'Alayy, which remains one of the best secondary schools in Lebanon. His books included dictionaries (still used to this day), arithmetic texts, an interpretation of Diwān al-Mutanabbī, and a commercial guide. He was one of the first voices in the East to call for the improvement of the status of women. Al-Bustānī was one of the few thinkers to have transcended sectarian loyalties and partisanship at a time of sectarian civil strife.

BUSTĀNĪ, FU'ĀD AFRĀM al- (1906–1995). This university president was born in Dayr al-Qamar and educated at St. Joseph University (q.v.). He specialized in Oriental studies and was a student of Louis Cheikho (q.v.) and Henry Lammens. His approach to Middle East studies followed the classical Orientalist studies of Lammens. He had contempt for the Muslims and their civilization, although he admired classical Arabic (q.v.) literature. He wrote many books and articles on Arabic literature but did very little original research. He was president of the Lebanese University (q.v.) from its inception until 1970.

Al-Bustānī always believed in Lebanon as a Christian homeland and regarded the Arab-Islamic civilization as an inferior culture that burdened Lebanese history and harmed its Christians. The 1975 civil war (q.v.) suddenly cast him into an overtly political role: he became an enthusiastic member of the Lebanese Front (q.v.) and championed the cause of the Lebanese Forces (q.v.). Al-Bustānī, who came from a famous literary family that produced a number of writers and poets, inherited from Buṭrus al-Bustānī (q.v.) the task of completing a comprehensive Arabic encyclopedia, *Dā'irat Al-Ma'ārif*. He was also the author of a widely used dictionary of Arabic for students.

BUSTĀNĪ, MYRNĀ al- (1939–). A businesswoman, she is the first woman ever to hold a parliamentary seat in Lebanon. She was born to a wealthy father, the self-made businessman, Emile al-Bustānī. She received a degree in psychology from St. Joseph University (q.v.), and was unexpectedly thrust onto the political scene when her father died in a plane crash in 1963. She filled his parliamentary seat until the end of the term in 1964. She was never comfortable in the political arena and was later known as a socialite and fundraiser. Myrnā managed the famed Hotel Al-Bustān in Bayt Mirī, one of the most luxurious hotels in Lebanon and one of the few such hotels to continue to function throughout the 1975–90 civil war (q.v.). She lived in France for a while during the civil war.

BUSTĀNĪ, SULAYMĀN al- (1856–1925). A politician and scholar, he was born to the traditionally literary family of al-Bustānī. He received his education at Buṭrus al-Bustānī's (q.v.) National School, where he studied Arabic (q.v.), French, and English. He taught various subjects before practicing journalism. He also taught in Iraq and visited the United States, Europe, and many Arab countries. Sulaymān mastered ancient Greek and translated, in poetry form, Homer's *Iliad*. The translation is considered too literal, but he is praised for his labor. In 1908 he was elected to the Ottoman representative council and was assigned diplomatic tasks. He was appointed minister in 1913.

BUṬRUS, FU'ĀD (1918–). This Greek Orthodox (q.v.) politician was born in Beirut (q.v.) and educated at St. Joseph University (q.v.), where he obtained a law degree. He was a lawyer and a judge before he was recruited to a ministry in 1960. Buṭrus won a parliamentary seat in the same year and later served as deputy speaker of parliament. This Fu'ād Shihāb (q.v.) sympathizer was known for his seriousness and hard work. In 1976, his former Shihabi comrade Ilyās Sarkīs (q.v.) appointed him vice-chair of the Council of Ministers and minister of foreign affairs. His tenure in that post was characterized by extreme skill, especially since Lebanon was under the rule of a variety of militias and foreign armies. He maintained good relations with the Syrian (q.v.) regime without becoming subservient to Damascus. The end of Sarkīs' term brought an abrupt end to Buṭrus' political services. He usually avoided the squabbles of Lebanese sectarian leaders and is often asked by the media to analyze regional and international affairs.

BUWAYZ, FĀRIS (1955–). He was born in Beirut (q.v.), the son of a respected parliamentarian belonging to the National Bloc Party (q.v.), and was educated at St. Joseph University (q.v.), where he earned his degree in law. He has operated his own law office since graduation in 1978. He first appeared on the Lebanese political scene in 1989, when President Ilyās Hrāwī (q.v.), his father-in-law, appointed him as his special advisor with the task of responding in public to any political attack against Hrāwī. He became foreign minister in 1990 and continues in that post. Buwayz was elected to parliament in 1992, although he had reservations about the status of Christians during the preparations for the elections. He harbors presidential aspirations and has maintained close ties to Syria (q.v.). He tries, to no avail, to distance himself from the regime of his father-in-law. He won a seat in the 1996 parliamentary election.

BYBLOS. This is the ancient name of the present-day city of Jubayl. By 4000 B.C., it was already a well-established city and became a center for the Chalcolithic culture for the next thousand years. Byblos was also a center of international trade. In the third millennium, the city and the entire coast of what is today Lebanon were settled by the Canaanites, or Phoenicians, as the Lebanese refer to them.

BYZANTINE RITE. *SEE* GREEK ORTHODOX CHRISTIANS.

-C-

CAIRO AGREEMENT. This secret agreement between the command of the Lebanese Army (q.v.) (with the knowledge of the president and prime minister of Lebanon) and the Palestine Liberation Organization (PLO) was signed on November 2, 1969, and was named after the location of the signing. The government of Jamāl 'Abdul-Nasser (q.v.) intervened to mediate between the Lebanese government and the PLO following a series of clashes between the two sides. The agreement allowed the PLO to operate militarily out of Lebanon, although it stipulated that its activities should be coordinated with the Lebanese Army command. The Lebanese parliament was asked to vote on the agreement without seeing its contents. Only Raymond Iddī (q.v.) protested against an agreement that was kept secret from the elected representatives of the people. The terms of the agreement were affirmed in the Melkart Agreement (q.v.) in 1973.

For the PLO, the Cairo Agreement was a juridical recognition of its military role in Lebanon. For the Lebanese right-wing movement, the agreement was an unacceptable surrender of Lebanese sovereignty. It became a target of denunciation by right-wing militias after 1975, and was blamed for the 1975 civil war (q.v.) (by those who wished to blame the Palestinians for all of Lebanon's problems). In 1987, the Lebanese parliament voted to abrogate the agreement.

CAIRO CONFERENCE. The October 1976 Arab summit conference in Cairo was convened to endorse the resolutions of the Riyāḍ Conference (q.v.), which ostensibly ended the 1975 Lebanese civil war (q.v.).

CANAANITES. This is the name of the first inhabitants of Lebanon in 3000 B.C. *See also* Phoenicians.

CATHOLIC PRESS. Following the example of American Protestant missionaries, who built schools and founded an Arabic printing press, Roman Catholic missionaries also founded schools and established a press, the Catholic Press, in 1847. In 1853, it was printing with movable type. By the early 1900s, it was the leading Arabic press in the region. It was famous for the quality of its books and its style of production. Famed scholar Louis Cheikho (q.v.) published many of his works through this press. It remains in existence today.

CEDARS OF LEBANON. The ancient cedars of Lebanon have been designated a national symbol: their image is emblazoned on the Lebanese flag, and the cedar is the official emblem of the republic. National myths and legends are tied to the *arz ar-Rab* (Cedars of God). Some of them are said to be centuries old, although their ages are often exaggerated. Cedars are seen as a special gift to a special people in a special land; biblical references to cedars are thought to give Lebanese Christians a special place.

CENSORSHIP. The constitution (q.v.) of Lebanon guarantees a variety of freedoms commonly associated with democratic systems. Yet, the practice of the Lebanese government over the years contradicts the promises made in the constitution. The constitution, of course, mentions "interests of state," which allows the government, any government, to declare any politically unacceptable view as "dangerous to state interests."

Long before the 1975 civil war (q.v.), when Lebanon was hailed by its officials and others as an oasis of democracy in an unstable region, the state censored books, articles, tapes, speeches, and leaflets on political grounds. Censorship is managed by a specialized government agency, the Department of Public Security. Newspapers were closed down if they committed any of the following offenses: "undermining the dignity of the president; harming the honor of the president; harming of authorities; harming the prestige of public authorities; harming the powers of public authorities; disturbing the general order; disturbing the public peace and security; arousing public opinion; misleading public opinion; hurting the sovereignty of the state; causing disturbance to general comfort; and harming general morals."

During the war, the list of those who could impose censorship was, of course, greatly expanded. Bombs were planted at the offices of critical newspapers, and writers and scholars were assassinated to punish them for their writings. The new rejuvenated Lebanese state is now returning to the censorship methods of the old democratic system. Books have been banned because the state deems them harmful to its interests or to the interests of the Syrian (q.v.) government. This is not to say that criticism of the government is not tolerated but there are limits that journalists do not normally cross, unless they live abroad and are not worried about their friends and relatives back home.

CENSUS. The government conducted the last census in the modern history of Lebanon in 1932. Successive governments, in an attempt to please Christian public opinion, have resisted conducting another census because it is widely assumed that Muslims today outnumber Christians. The 1932 census, the results of which are not universally accepted, revealed that the Maronites (q.v.) constituted the single largest sect in the country (29 percent) and that Christians, as a group, constituted 53.7 percent of the population of Lebanon. Muslims, however, have enjoyed higher birth rates than Christians and they were assumed to constitute the majority of the population long before the 1975 civil war (q.v.). Unclassified American estimates of the sectarian demographics in Lebanon show the Shi'ites (q.v.) to be by far the single largest sect in the country (38 percent). The significance of the 1932 census lies in its use by the French as the foundation and arithmetic formula for the distribution of political power on a sectarian basis. Some Christians demand the inclusion of Lebanese emigrants from around the world in any future census. It is not likely that a census will be conducted soon, given its explosive political implications.

CHEIKHO, LOUIS (SHAYKHŪ, LUWĪS) (1859–1928). A scholar and publisher, he was born in Mardin in Turkey and received his education in Jesuit schools. He studied Greek, Latin, French, and philosophy in France. Upon his return to Beirut (q.v.), he was appointed a teacher of Arabic (q.v.) at St. Joseph University (q.v.). He became an accomplished Orientalist, mastering the details of the Arabic language. In 1898, he founded the scholarly journal *Al-Mashriq* (q.v.). Cheikho also published previously unpublished manuscripts on Arabic literature and Christian history. His work played a part in the literary revival of the region. He wrote numerous textbooks to facilitate the teaching of Arabic, some of which are still used today. He also published research on Christian poets and writers who lived and worked in the Arab-Islamic civilization, a massive work that is criticized for exaggerating the number of Christians among the Arab poets. Cheikho was a partisan, believing in the superiority of Christians over Muslims, and was unable to separate his roles as a Jesuit priest and a scholar. His book against Freemasonry is still used by Christian churches in the East to battle this movement. The Catholic Press (q.v.) benefited from Cheikho's knowledge and education and produced his painstaking research. He published a chrestomathy of Arabic literature that has rarely been out of print. Cheikho fought bitterly with Protestant writers and other social reformers, whom he accused of corrupting youth.

CHĪḤĀ, MICHEL (1891–1954). A businessman and politician, he was born in Beirut (q.v.) where he received his education. He earned a degree from St. Joseph University (q.v.) and did some graduate work in London. He fled Turkish rule in 1915 and settled in Egypt, where he earned a law degree. He was appointed a deputy from Beirut (q.v.) in 1925 and was one of the main drafters of the constitution (q.v.) in the following year. Chīḥā founded the newspaper *Le Jour* (q.v.) in 1934 and wrote for French publications. He was a wealthy businessman and strongly believed that the Lebanese economy should be based on the free enterprise system. He was a passionate polemicist against Zionism, because he saw in the Jewish state a potential competitor of Lebanon. To Chīḥā, Lebanon should return to the way it was under the French. *See also* Grand Liban.

CIVIL WAR OF 1860. This describes the turmoil in Mount Lebanon between 1858 and 1860. A rebellion of Maronite (q.v.) peasants against Maronite feudal leaders degenerated into a civil war that pitted Druzes (q.v.) against Christians. It led to European intervention, which brought about the political-administrative arrangement for Mount Lebanon known as the *Règlement Organique* (q.v.).

CIVIL WAR OF 1958. The administration of Kamīl Sham'ūn (q.v.) was characterized by a strong identification with Western anticommunism. Sham'ūn, hoping to obtain American aid, emphasized his conservative, capitalist credentials and repressed leftist groups in Lebanon. The mood in Lebanon and the Arab world was intensely anti-Western, especially following the invasion of Egypt in 1956 by France, Britain, and Israel in the wake of the nationalization of the Suez Canal. Sham'ūn's foreign minister, Charles Mālik, was a strong anticommunist rightist who understood Lebanon as a Christian nation. During the early phase of the cold war, Mālik was in demand as a speaker in the United States. He was a popular pamphleteer against Marxist ideologies and in favor of Christian capitalism. The formation of the United Arab Republic heightened Arab nationalism in Lebanon. Lebanese Muslims did not necessarily want to join the new union, which did not last long, but they wanted Lebanese foreign policy to be less antagonistic to Jamāl 'Abdul-Nasser (q.v.). They were also unhappy with the pro-Western orientations of Sham'ūn, because the West was seen as responsible for Israeli (q.v.) actions in the region.

The actual beginning of the civil war is usually marked by the assassination in May 1958 of the journalist Nasīb al-Matnī (q.v.), who was bitterly opposed to Sham'ūn. This brought on nationwide riots and demonstrations protesting the involvement of Sham'ūn's regime in the assassination. Adding to popular resentment was the widely circulating news that Sham'ūn was working toward the amendment of the constitution (q.v.) to allow himself to serve another term in the presidency. To quash the rebellion, Sham'ūn relied on right-wing militias because the commander-in-chief of the Lebanese Army, Fu'ād Shihāb (qq.v.), refused to allow his troops to be used in what he considered an internal political matter. Sham'ūn, however, was insistent that the events in Lebanon were manipulated from the outside by Egypt and the communist world. He was in a weak position because many Maronite (q.v.) leaders, including the Maronite patriarch, were not on his side. Most of the fighting, in the Shūf, was light by the standards of the ferocious civil war of 1975 (q.v.). In July 1958, American marines landed in Beirut (q.v.), partly alarmed at the events in Iraq, where a revolution had just eliminated a pro-Western monarchy. Fu'ād Shihāb emerged as the consensus candidate, receiving, miraculously, both Egyptian and American support. In Lebanon, the events of 1958 are called *thawrah* (revolution).

CIVIL WAR OF 1975–1990. There is no agreement among scholars and researchers on what ignited this civil war, known as the Lebanese Civil War. Some go back to the 19th century and trace it to Druze-Maronite (qq.v.) strife, while others insist it was the direct result of French control over Lebanon in 1920. However, the strike of the fishermen in Sidon (q.v.) in February 1975 could be considered the episode that triggered the outbreak of hostilities and the subsequent collapse of the republic.

The beginning dealt with a specific issue: the attempt by former president Kamīl Sham'ūn (q.v.) to monopolize for his newly created company fishing rights along the coast of Lebanon. The fishermen were outraged and pleaded for support and sympathy from all Lebanese. The Lebanese National Movement (q.v.) was desperately looking for an issue around which it could galvanize the nation, and in the fishermen's plight it found it. Demonstrations and national strikes were announced and public opinion was mobilized.

During one demonstration in Sidon a sniper, probably working for the Lebanese Army (q.v.), killed a popular Nasserist figure in the city, Ma'rūf Sa'd (q.v.). He was known for his opposition to the government and for his support of the Palestinians in Lebanon (q.v.). He had accused the government of fraud in 1972 when he lost the parliamentary election. The events in Sidon were initially contained, but the government was increasingly losing control of the situation, and right-wing militias were already stationed in key posts in East Beirut (q.v.). The crisis exploded in April 1975, when a massacre at 'Ayn ar-Rummānah (q.v.) was perpetrated by the Lebanese Phalanges Party (q.v.) militia. A bus carrying Palestinians returning from a rally was ambushed by party gunmen. The party claimed that unknown gunmen had shot at Pierre Gemayyel's (q.v.) bodyguards. This signaled, for most Lebanese, the official beginning of the Lebanese civil war.

The war initially pitted Maronite-oriented, right-wing militias (comprising most notably the Lebanese Phalanges Party and the National Liberal Party, q.v.) against the leftist, Muslim-oriented militias (that were grouped together in the Lebanese National Movement) supported by the Palestine Liberation Organization (PLO). The military confrontation produced a heated, and seemingly unending, political debate on whether the Lebanese Army, which was led by a right-wing Maronite commander serving a president who had his own right-wing militia, should be deployed to end the fighting. The opinions of most Muslims and leftists was against any use of the army, which was regarded as anti-Palestinian, while most right-wingers called for the immediate deployment of the army to crack down on the PLO and its Lebanese allies.

The characterization of the combatants obscures the nature of the conflict. For many Lebanese, the civil war is seen as the product of a conspiracy hatched by outsiders jealous of "Lebanese democracy and prosperity." Many leaders in Lebanon, on the left and the right, swear that Henry Kissinger (q.v.) personally planned and executed it. But the civil war should be viewed as a multidimensional conflict that was, at its root, classic civil strife, with the domestic parties determining the course but rarely the outcome of the fighting. With the exception of Israel (q.v.) in 1982, external parties have been insistent over the course of Lebanese history on preventing the Lebanese from proceeding unrestrained in their civil strife. To be sure, had the Lebanese been allowed to continue the fighting without external restraints, some sects in Lebanon would probably have been exterminated. This is not to say that the external parties themselves, notably Syria (q.v.), Iraq, Iran, and Israel, have not contributed to the intensification of the conflict whenever it suited their interests. After all, these states had their proxy militias operating in Lebanon.

The roots of the civil war center on issues related to domestic Lebanese politics and to Lebanese foreign policy. The system of sectarian distribution of power, sponsored by France (q.v.) in 1920, led to increasing frustration among Muslims, who grew demographically but not politically. The Lebanese political system continued in 1975 to assume that the figures of the 1932 census (q.v.), which showed the Maronites to be the largest sect in the country, had not changed, although it was widely known that the Shi'ites (q.v.) had long since become the largest sect. The ceremonial post of speaker of parliament was reserved for a Shi'ite while the presidency was reserved for a Maronite, and the prime ministership was reserved for a Sunni (q.v.). The Shi'ites were also, in general, poorer than other sects in Lebanon, although all sects in the country, including the Maronites (contrary to popular belief) have their poor people. To add to their misery, the Shi'ites predominated in South Lebanon, which became in the 1960s an arena for Israeli-Palestinian conflict. The Lebanese state, which always avoided provoking Israel, simply abandoned South Lebanon. Many of the residents of the South migrated to Beirut (q.v.) to live in the suburbs, which are known in the Lebanese popular lexicon as "poverty belts" (q.v.). Young Shi'ite migrants, insulated from the prosperity of pre-war Beirut, became the rank-and-file of many Lebanese and Palestinian organizations.

The Sunnis had their grievances, too. The office of prime minister was marginalized by the strong presidency of Sulaymān Franjiyyah (q.v.) and presidents before him. Since 1973, when prime minister Ṣā'ib Salām (q.v.) could not fire the commander-in-chief of the army after an Israeli commando raid in Beirut which targeted three high-ranking PLO officials, the issue of the powers of the prime minister emerged as a symbol of the sectarian-political imbalance in the country. Socio-economic dissatisfaction plus political resentment generated instability in the political system.

The presence of Palestinians in Lebanon was another thorny issue. The Lebanese state decided to crack down on the Palestinian armed presence in Lebanon, while right-wing militias were being armed and financed by the Lebanese Army with the active involvement of the president. Many leftists and Muslims wanted the state to support the Palestinians and to send the army to protect South Lebanon from Israeli raids. The PLO, on the other hand, was tempted to take advantage of the Lebanese domestic turmoil; it wanted to shore up support for its cause among the Lebanese people and to undermine the military power of the Lebanese Army, which had for long harassed Palestinians in Lebanon.

The first phase of the Lebanese civil war (1975–76) did not end the war; it merely brought to a temporary halt internal fighting due to regional and international intervention. When it was becoming clear that the PLO and the Lebanese National Movement were about to overrun the predominantly Christian area, Syria intervened militarily and, with Israeli, American, and French diplomatic support, fought the Palestinians and their Lebanese allies. For a while, the fighting stopped, although South Lebanon, as always, continued to serve as an arena for the Israeli-Palestinian conflict. Furthermore, the militias, which were present all over the country and belonged to every imaginable ideology, were not disarmed but, rather, strengthened. By 1978, Syrian relations with Maronite-oriented parties, which earlier were grateful to the Syrian forces for saving them from certain defeat, worsened, and the rise of Bashīr Gemayyel (q.v.) as head of the Lebanese Forces (q.v.) brought a change in the course of the civil war. Israel became a close ally of the Lebanese Forces; the Syrian regime sponsored the leftist-Palestinian coalition. The Israeli invasion of 1978 (q.v.) aimed at ending any military presence in South Lebanon except that of the pro-Israeli militia. The international community eventually forced Israel southward, and the United Nations Interim Force in Lebanon (q.v.) was deployed to pacify the region. But Israel continued to occupy a part of South Lebanon, calling that strip of land "the security zone." Israeli intervention in Lebanon, with a Likud government in power, increased in earnest.

The civil war took another radical turn in 1982, when Israel invaded Lebanon, but this time the Israeli forces reached Beirut itself. Israel took advantage of the deteriorating security situation in the country and expected that Lebanese popular resentment against the PLO, due to misconduct by its members, would provide a positive climate for its all-out military intervention. Israel wanted to achieve three goals: first, to expel all PLO forces from Lebanon; second, to end Syrian influence in Lebanon; third, to install Bashīr Gemayyel as president of the republic. The invasion claimed the lives of some 20,000 Lebanese and Palestinians. Israel succeeded in influencing the presidential election: Bashīr was elected president, although he was assassinated a few days later. His assassination was the pretext that pro-Israeli militias in Lebanon gave for the massacre of Palestinian (and some Lebanese) civilians in the Ṣabrā and Shātīlā (q.v.) refugee camps. Bashīr was replaced by his brother, Amīn (q.v.) who supported the signing of an Israeli-Lebanese peace treaty in May 1983. He also invited U.S. forces, present as members of a multinational force ostensibly dispatched to protect Palestinian civilians, to join on his side in the escalating civil war.

Lebanese opposition coupled with Syrian rejection of the pro-Israeli, pro-American orientations of Amīn Gemayyel resulted in the resumption of the all-out civil war, which characterized his entire administration. In fact, his administration may have intensified the scale and duration of the civil war by committing the state and its resources against one side of the civil war. He relied too much on the American administration of Ronald Reagan for help. In the summer of 1983, a new version of the civil war erupted in the mountains of Lebanon, which had been spared much of the agony of war up to that time, between Druzes and Maronite forces, reviving images from 19th century Lebanon. In West Beirut (q.v.), a mini-civil war erupted between the various militias vying for hegemony in that small area. Fundamentalism was more and more the ideology of choice among Sunnis and Shi'ites.

When Amīn Gemayyel's term came to an end in the summer of 1988, he appointed the Maronite commander-in-chief of the army, Michel 'Awn (q.v.), as interim president. His appointment was rejected by many Lebanese, and 'Awn soon launched his "war of national liberation," first against Syrian troops in Lebanon and soon after against the Maronite-dominated Lebanese Forces. His shells, however, fell on innocent Lebanese. The end of the civil war began in October 1989, when Lebanese deputies met in the city of aṭ-Ṭā'if in Saudi Arabia and endorsed a package of internal, constitutional reforms. The aṭ-Ṭā'if Accords (q.v.), however, could not be implemented immediately. General 'Awn was still holed up in the presidential palace in Ba'abdā (q.v.), and many Christians sympathized with his message of defiance.

The aṭ-Ṭā'if Accords were subsequently implemented in the wake of 'Awn's defeat in October 1990, when Syrian troops attacked his headquarters and forced him to seek refuge in France. Ilyās Hrāwī (q.v.) was elected president in 1989, and the territorial integrity of

Lebanon has been partially restored, although Israel still occupies a strip in South Lebanon and Syria still has great political and military influence in Lebanon. The question of whether the civil war has ended depends on the ability of the government to monopolize coercive powers in the country. That condition is far from being achieved. *See also* War Conditions.

COMMITTEE FOR LEBANESE WOMEN'S RIGHTS. In 1946, a group of Lebanese feminist women met to establish an organization that would focus on women's rights without relying on the political promises of male politicians. The founders included Thurayyā ʻAdrah, Mary Ṣaʻb, Georgette ʻAkkāwī, and Mary Iddī. In 1947, the committee announced its goals and internal rules. This first feminist organization dedicated purely to women's rights has held numerous conferences in which the status of women in Lebanon has been discussed. The political climate in Lebanon has put pressure on the committee to incorporate into its declarations political statements dealing with issues of national reconciliation and the liberation of occupied lands. In 1981, the committee presented the Charter of the Rights of Lebanese Women, in which proposals were made to improve the legal, political, social, and economic status of women. The committee played a humanitarian role during the 1975–90 civil war (q.v.), providing assistance to poor and displaced women. *See also* Feminism.

COMMUNE. *SEE* ʻĀMMIYYAH.

COMMUNIST ACTION ORGANIZATION (***Munaḏhḏhamat al-ʻAmal ash-Shuyūʻī***). This second most important communist party in Lebanon was born in May 1971 as a radical alternative to the Lebanese Communist Party (LCP) (q.v.) but later moderated its stance, becoming indistinguishable ideologically from the LCP. The organization was created as a result of the merger in 1969 of the Organization of Lebanese Socialists (which split off from the Movement of Arab Nationalists, q.v.) and the Organization of Socialist Lebanon (a splinter group of the Arab Socialist Baʻth Party, q.v.). It was headed by Muḥsin Ibrāhīm, whose leftist criticisms of George Ḥabash led to the collapse of the Movement of Arab Nationalists. Ibrāhīm, one of the most skillful and effective pamphleteers and polemicists in the Arab world, came to dominate the organization. The Organization of Socialist Lebanon provided the new party with cadres experienced in the recruitment of students and teachers. Yet, the effectiveness of the movement was marred from the beginning by a series of defections and splits.

The organization purged its ranks and introduced more Leninist centralism. The fortunes of this relatively small party benefited from Ibrāhīm's close ties to Kamāl Jumblāṭ (q.v.), who promoted Ibrāhīm in national leftist circles and beyond. By 1975 the organization forged an alliance with the LCP and participated in combat during the 1975–90 civil war (q.v.). Yāsir 'Arafāt (q.v.) provided the party with weapons and financial assistance. After 1982, Ibrāhīm was one of the few remaining allies of the Palestine Liberation Organization in Lebanese politics. In more recent years, the relations of the Communist Action Organization with the LCP worsened, and its role in Lebanese politics was marginalized.

CONSERVATOIRE. *SEE* NATIONAL MUSIC INSTITUTE.

CONSTITUTION. When the League of Nations recognized the French role in Lebanon following World War I, the French government appointed a commission in 1925 to prepare the draft of a constitution. By 1926, the commission had completed its task and in May the Representative Council, a constituent assembly of Lebanese politicians, adopted the draft constitution. A French representative was present throughout the proceedings to ensure that the wishes of France (q.v.) were met. He had the power to veto any modification of the draft, and he also had full control of the agenda. The Lebanese often credit Michel Chīḥā (q.v.) for "writing" the constitution, but his role is widely exaggerated.

Amendments to the constitution may be initiated by the president of the republic or by a resolution of at least 10 members of the chamber of deputies. The chamber, by a two-thirds majority, can recommend the amendment. The most significant amendments to the constitution were promulgated in 1943, when all references to the French Mandate (q.v.) were expunged and Arabic (q.v.) was designated the official language.

The constitution, modeled after the French Third Republic, stresses freedom and equality, although with some limitations. All Lebanese are guaranteed freedom of speech, assembly, and association "within the limits established by law." There are also provisions for freedom of conscience and the free exercise of worship, as long as the dignity of the country's religions and the public order are not affected.

The 1975 civil war (q.v.) did not alter the contents of the constitution until aṭ-Ṭā'if Accords (q.v.) of 1989, which became constitutional law in 1990. This brought about substantial changes in the constitution. Michel 'Awn (q.v.) and his supporters objected to those changes and warned against the loss of Christian power. A preamble was added to the body of the constitution in which Lebanon was defined—for the first time—as Arab in "identity and belonging." It also promised the elimination of "political sectarianism," not to be equated with secularization. It merely implies that a new arithmetic formula for the distribution of powers on a sectarian basis is required to achieve national accord. No more will the Muslims be satisfied with an inferior political status, as had been the case since independence.

To that end, the reforms slightly diminished the powers of the president and increased the power of the Council of Ministers. More important, Article 95 (q.v.) of the constitution was revised; it now reads: "the Chamber of Deputies, which is elected on the basis of equity between Christians and Muslims, shall take the appropriate measures to achieve the elimination of political sectarianism according to a phased plan. It shall also form a national body presided over by the president, and comprising—in addition to the speaker of parliament and the chairperson of the Council of Ministers—social, intellectual, and political personalities. The body's mission is to study and plan those methods that can eliminate sectarianism, and present them to the Council of Ministers and Chamber of Deputies, and to follow up the implementation of the phased plan. In the transitional period: A) the sects shall be represented equitably in the formation of cabinets; B) the formula of sectarian representation shall be eliminated and merit and specialization shall govern appointments in public posts, the judiciary, military and security institutions, and public and mixed institutions according to the needs of national reconciliation with the exception of Grade A posts or their equivalent. Posts at this level shall be on the basis of fifty-fifty between Muslims and Christians without reserving any post to any sect while adhering to the principles of qualification and merit."

The constitution has also sometimes been amended to allow for the renewal of the term of a president. Thus, the constitution was amended in 1949 to allow Bishārah al-Khūrī (q.v.) to serve for another term and in 1995 to allow Ilyās Hrāwī (q.v.) to serve three years beyond his expired first term.

CONSTITUTIONAL BLOC (***Al-Kutlah al-Waṭaniyyah***). This obsolete organization exists only in name. It was founded in 1936 by Bishārah al-Khūrī (q.v.) and his supporters, who demanded Lebanese independence from France (q.v.) and the restoration of Lebanese constitutional life. Al-Khūrī was elected first president of independent Lebanon, and his bloc became one of the most influential political arms of any *za'īm* (q.v.) in Lebanon. The bloc continued to play a role in Lebanese politics until the 1960s. Although it has been completely marginalized by events, Bishārah's son, Khalīl (q.v.), who has lived in France since the beginning of the 1975 civil war (q.v.), still considers himself leader of the party.

CORNICHE. This refers to a wide street in the coastal area of Beirut (q.v.). The U.S. (q.v.) Embassy was located there, although after the 1983 bombing of the embassy it was relocated into East Beirut (q.v.). The corniche was widened under the government of Rafīq Ḥarīrī (q.v.) and illegal vendors were evicted from its sidewalks.

COUNCIL FOR RECONSTRUCTION AND DEVELOPMENT. This council was created by the Lebanese government during the administration of Ilyās Sarkīs (q.v.) in 1977. It was prematurely believed that the 1975 civil war (q.v.) was over, and the government wanted to help in the reconstruction efforts in the country. The council's work was hampered until 1991, when militias were disbanded and the Lebanese government was able to establish control over much of Lebanon's territory, notwithstanding the presence of Syrian (q.v.) and Israeli (q.v.) troops. The council's first president was economist Muḥammad 'Aṭallah.

COUNCIL OF THE SOUTH. *SEE* MAJLIS AL-JUNŪB.

COUP D'ÉTAT. *SEE INQILĀB.*

COURSE (***AN-NAHJ***). This parliamentary (and extraparliamentary) bloc supported the policies of Fu'ād Shihāb (q.v.) in the 1960s and 1970s. It has no political role in present-day Lebanon.

CROTALE MISSILES. Commander-in-chief Emile al-Bustānī, who served under President Charles Ḥilū (q.v.), ordered the purchase of highly ineffective Crotale missiles from France (q.v.) with the provision that a business partner of his would be awarded a commission. In 1972, the regime of Sulaymān Franjiyyah (q.v.) was eager to investigate the corruption of the Shihābi apparatus but was deterred by the fear that such exposure of military corruption could weaken the effectiveness of the military apparatus. The scandal was never fully investigated.

CURRENCY. The Lebanese monetary unit is the Lebanese pound (*līrah*) which is divided into 100 piasters. The value of the *līrah* in relation to the U.S. dollar plummeted in the 1980s; at the beginning of 1998, $1 was equivalent to 1500 *līrah*. The appointment of Rafīq Ḥarīrī (q.v.) as prime minister in 1992 put an end to the continuous decline of the *līrah*.

-D-

DABBĀS, CHARLES (?–1935). Lebanese history textbooks mention him as the first president of Lebanon, although he held the presidency during the era of the French Mandate (q.v.). He was born in Damascus and finished his education in Jesuit schools. He earned a law degree from the University of Paris and married a French woman. He later wrote for a French newspaper in Lebanon before leaving the country in World War I as a proponent of independence. He strongly opposed Arab unity and saw Lebanon as a homeland for Christians. He was appointed to a senior position in the Ministry of Justice and helped to organize the courts and to create the Bar Association. He was chosen by the French in May 1926 to be Lebanon's first president after the adoption of the constitution (q.v.). He was Greek Orthodox (q.v.) and it is said that France (q.v.) did not want to further alienate Muslims, already unhappy with the creation of a Lebanese entity apart from the Arab world, by selecting a Maronite (q.v.) person. Dabbās was reelected in 1929 for three more years. In 1932, he was appointed president by the French high commissioner after he suspended the constitution and dissolved the parliament. He resigned in 1934 and was elected deputy. He died in Paris.

***DABBŪR, ad-*.** This magazine, devoted to caricatures and the lighter side of politics, was first published in 1923 by Yūsuf Mikarzil. It ceased publication for years only to reemerge in the 1970s as a magazine of caricatures and explicit pictures of women. It did not last long.

ḌĀHIR, MIKHĀ'ĪL ad- (1928–). This Maronite politician was born in Qubayyāt in ʻAkkār and was educated in Tripoli (q.v.) and at St. Joseph University (q.v.), where he earned a degree in law. He was a famous lawyer before running for public office in 1964 and 1968. He lost these elections but won a parliamentary seat in the 1972 election. Ḍāhir has been a staunch believer in the mission of the Lebanese Army (q.v.), perhaps because a large number of the rank-and-file of the army hails from ʻAkkār. Ḍāhir supported the Lebanese Forces (q.v.) but with reservations, and he kept his channels open to all other groups in Lebanon. He reluctantly voted for both Bashīr and Amīn Gemayyel (qq.v.) in 1982. In the 1980s, Ḍāhir's relations with the Lebanese Forces under Samīr Ja'ja' (q.v.) worsened because Ḍāhir supported the 1985 Tripartite Agreement (q.v.). In 1988, his name was mentioned by U.S. official Richard Murphy as a compromise presidential candidate, but the Lebanese Forces vetoed this choice. Ḍāhir has come much closer to the Syrian (q.v.) regime, and he won in the 1992 and 1996 elections. He has held several ministerial positions over the years.

DALLŪL, MUḤSIN (1930–). A politician, he was born in al-Biqāʻ valley (q.v.) to a Shiʻite (q.v.) family. He studied in Zaḥlah (q.v.) and earned a degree from St. Joseph University (q.v.) in Beirut (q.v.). He taught Arabic (q.v.) in secondary schools and started a career in journalism in the 1960s. He was initially a writer on softer aspects of politics, interviewing politicians about their personal lives. He became close to Druze (q.v.) leader Kamāl Jumblāṭ (q.v.) and quickly emerged as one of his closest confidantes. He assumed leadership positions within the Progressive Socialist Party (q.v.) and was its deputy president in 1988. He later had a falling-out with Walīd Jumblāṭ (q.v.) and developed a reputation as Syria's (q.v.) obedient client in Lebanon. He was rewarded in 1989 with a ministerial position. He won a seat in both the 1992 and 1996 parliamentary elections, and has held several ministerial positions. He is a brother-in-law of Rafīq Ḥarīrī (q.v.).

DASHNAK PARTY. This party was founded in 1890 in Tiflis in Russia to call attention to the conditions of Armenians (q.v.) living under Ottoman rule. The party began on a revolutionary course but later moderated its stance. The Lebanese Dashnak Party also disagreed with the socialist ideology of the mother party. As one of the three main Armenian parties in Lebanon, it stands for the free enterprise system and was affiliated, perhaps due to the thousands of Armenians in East Beirut (q.v.), with the right-wing militias during the 1975–90 civil war (q.v.). Membership is exclusively Armenian, and its leadership is indistinguishable from the Armenian political and economic elite. Most Armenian deputies and ministers have been either members of or sympathizers with this party. It won four seats in the 1992 parliamentary elections.

DĀWŪD PASHA. An Ottoman governor, Dāwūd Pasha was born in Istanbul in 1812 (some sources say 1816, and others say 1818) into an Armenian (q.v.) Catholic family. He received his education at a French school and attended a French college in Vienna, where he earned a law degree. He wrote a book on Western jurisprudence and was known as a doctor of law. He served as consul-general in Vienna and later in administrative posts in Istanbul, first as director of publications and later as director of post and telegraph services. His French education brought him into French circles in Istanbul. He was the first *mutaṣarrif* (q.v.) in Lebanon after the 1861 Mutaṣarrifiyyah (q.v.) order was designed for Lebanon by the Great Powers and the Ottoman Empire. Before he began his mission in Lebanon, he was promoted to the rank of minister and was the highest-ranking Christian working for the Ottoman government. He was known for improving tax collection in Lebanon and for establishing several public schools. He also founded a school for the Druzes (Dāwūdiyyah School) in an attempt to win their favor after the end of the Maronite-Druze (q.v.) armed conflict. His mission was abruptly ended in 1868, when he became embroiled in domestic Lebanese politics, even aspiring to extend the boundaries of the Mutaṣarrifiyyah.

DEMOCRATIC PARTY ***(Al-Ḥizb Ad-Dīmūqrāṭī).*** This party was founded in 1970 by Joseph Mughayzil and other intellectuals who wanted a new political force outside the framework of sectarian politics. The party did not have a coherent ideology, although it was committed to the secularization of society and government. Although one of its leaders, Emile Bīṭār, was appointed minister in 1973, it did not have an impact on Lebanese political life. The civil war of 1975 (q.v.) completely marginalized the party.

DEMOCRATIC SOCIALIST PARTY ***(Al-Ḥizb al-Dīmūqrāṭī al-Ishtirākī).*** This is not really a party but a vehicle for the followers of traditional *za'īm* (q.v.) Kāmil al-As'ad (q.v.), who held the speakership of parliament from 1970 to 1984. Al-As'ad, alarmed by the growing popularity of leftist organizations among Shi'ites (q.v.) in the late 1960s and early 1970s, organized his own followers under the fashionable socialist banner, despite his strong right-wing views and upper class status, to compete with the left and with the Amal movement (q.v.) of Imām Mūsā aṣ-Ṣadr (q.v.). He also, as was common at the time, formed his own militia. His power influenced many Shi'ites to join the party. His political journey came to an end in 1982, when he supported right-wing candidate Bashīr Gemayyel (q.v.). Syria (q.v.) and the Shi'ites never forgave him for this decision, and he lost the election for speaker in 1984 and relocated to Europe. Just before the 1992 election, he returned to Lebanon to run for parliament. His entire list lost. The role of his party is minimal; he lost the election again in 1996, when Nabīh Birrī (q.v.), his main rival, scored an electoral success in the whole of South Lebanon and al-Biqā' (q.v.).

DEUXIÈME BUREAU. This term refers to the Lebanese Army's (q.v.) G2, or intelligence agency. This arm of the army was the most important apparatus of government during the administrations of Fu'ād Shihāb and Charles Ḥilū (qq.v.). Shihāb distrusted Lebanese politicians and relied on this mutli-sectarian apparatus to report to him on various political, social, and economic issues. The bureau was also notorious for its treatment of the Palestinians in Lebanon (q.v.), imposing a rule of terror in the refugee camps and restricting leftist or pro-Palestinian political activity in the country. Members of the Bureau, being in charge of licensing firearms, were feared all over Lebanon. The bureau also observed elections and rendered services to pro-Shihāb candidates. Its influence was diminished under Sulaymān

Franjiyyah (q.v.), who dismissed Shihāb's men. The bureau was revived under Amīn Gemayyel (q.v.), and the rejuvenation of the Lebanese Army under Ilyās Hrāwī (q.v.) also strengthened the bureau.

DIMASHQIYYAH, JULIA ṬU'MAH (1880–1954). This writer was born in Al-Mukhtārah (q.v.) and studied in Sidon (q.v.). She later went to Shuwayfat school to study education. She taught school in Syria (q.v.), Palestine, and Lebanon (q.v.). She married a Sunni (q.v.) even though it was quite uncommon, if not outright condemnable, for a woman to marry outside her faith. She founded a charitable woman's organization called *Jāmi'at As-Sayyidāt* (League of Ladies) in 1917. Its members met at her house once a month to coordinate philanthropic activities. In 1921, Dimashqiyyah founded the magazine *Al-Mar'ah Al-Jadīdah* (New Woman), considered the first serious women's magazine in the East. She wrote a regular column titled, "To the Women of My Country," in which she addressed issues relating to women. This magazine lasted for seven years. Her articles also appeared in many other publications.

DIRĀSĀT 'ARABIYYAH. One of the earliest modern scholarly journals, it was founded in 1964 by pro-Iraqi Ba'thist Bashīr Dā'ūq as a regular monthly platform for radical scholars. Many leaders of the Palestine Liberation Organization wrote for the journal, which was widely read in the Arab academic community. It expressed the first self-criticism in the wake of the 1967 defeat. Ṣādiq Jalāl al-'Aḏhm (q.v.) and Al-'Afīf al-Akhḍar also helped the radical debate in that era through their articles in the journal.

DISPLACED PEOPLE (*Al-Muhajjarūn*). There are at least 500,000 Lebanese people who were forcefully evicted from their homes or who left out of fear for their lives due to intense sectarian hatred and killing. Many were temporarily housed in schools, churches, hotels, and public spaces. A special ministry was created to care for their needs and to ensure their return to their homes, although it is highly unlikely that most of them will return to what are in many cases deserted villages and destroyed neighborhoods.

DOG RIVER (Nahr Al-Kalb). This refers to a spot north of Beirut (q.v.) where successive military dynasties have registered their achievements on monuments of stone. It contains inscriptions in Egyptian, Assyrian, Babylonian, Greek, Latin, French, English, and Arabic. The last monument was dedicated by the Lebanese government to note the evacuation of the last French soldiers from Lebanon in 1946.

DOUBLE QA'IMMAQAMATE. The political-administrative system in place in Mount Lebanon between 1843 and 1958, it followed the demise of the Shihabi dynasty and the collapse of the emirate system. Metternich proposed the plan to divide Mount Lebanon into two regions: a northern district would be administered by a Maronite (q.v.) *qā'immaqām* and a southern district administered by a Druze (q.v.) *qā'immaqām*. In 1845, in the wake of sectarian fighting, consultative councils were formed, to assist each *qā'immaqām*. They did not last, because members of the "opposite" sect resided in the "wrong" district and served as easy prey in times of sectarian tensions.

DRUZE SECT. More than half of Lebanese Druzes reside in rural areas, especially the Shūf, al-Matn, Ḥāṣbayyā, and Rāshayyā regions. Urban Druzes live in Beirut and its suburbs in confessionally marked and confessionally mixed neighborhoods. The Druze elite consists of large landowning families. The religion of the Druzes is regarded as an offshoot of the Isma'ili sect (q.v.). They call themselves unitarians but outsiders call them Druzes, after a historic figure, Darazi. The leadership of the Druze community in Lebanon has traditionally been shared by two familial confederations: the Jumblāṭ family (q.v.) and the Yazbaki family. The community has preserved its cultural separateness by being closely knit socially and by closing the faith to outsiders since the 11th century. They constitute about 7 percent of the Lebanese population. The religious leadership of the community is held by a *shaykh al-'aql* (q.v.). Following the death of Muḥammad Abū Shaqrā (q.v.), the political leadership of the community could not agree on a successor. Shaykh Bahjat Ghayth serves as an interim *shaykh al-'aql*.

DUWAYHĪ, ISṬIFĀN (1630–1704). A historian, he was born in Ihdin (q.v.) to a Maronite (q.v.) family and went to Rome to study at the Maronite College in Rome (q.v.). He assumed the patriarchate in 1670 and wrote several books dealing with the history of the community.

-E-

EAGLES OF AL-BIQĀ' (*Nusūr al-Biqā'*). This small, obscure organization was formed by 'Alī Ḥamādī, the son of the late Shi'ite (q.v.) *za'īm* (q.v.) Ṣabrī Ḥamādī (q.v.), who held the speakership of parliament for most of the 1960s. But Ḥamādī was competing with other nationalist and leftist militias in the al-Biqā' valley (q.v.) region, and when the party failed to attract any substantial following, the family went into political eclipse. Ṣabrī's son Rāshid Ḥamādī ran for parliament in 1996 but lost.

EAST BEIRUT. This refers to that section of the city that was under the control of the Phalanges-led coalition of forces since 1975. Bashīr Gemayyel (q.v.) was the supreme ruler in this section until 1982, when he was assassinated. Very few non-Christians were allowed to reside there. Lebanese Phalanges Party (q.v.) forces forced Shi'ites and Palestinians (qq.v.) out of the district in 1975–76. Beirut (q.v.) was reunited in October 1992 when the government of Ilyās Hrāwī (q.v.) established control over both sections of the city.

EASTERN ORTHODOX CHURCH. *SEE* GREEK ORTHODOX CHRISTIANS.

EDUCATION. Lebanon, along with the Palestinian people, has the highest literacy rate in the Arab world (estimated at 80 percent in the mid-1980s). This figure, however, obscures disparities across sects and regions. In general, Christians have higher literacy rates than Muslims; Shi'ites (q.v.) have the lowest rates among the sects. The 1975–90 civil war (q.v.) resulted in the deterioration of educational standards; students were graduating but with very little education. State exams were regularly canceled, and special certificates of passing were given to all students regardless of performance. Some students were more active in combat than in classes, and there was little control of the student body. Further, many schools were occupied either by displaced people or by militias. The flight of foreign teachers and the admission of students without exams also contributed to the decline in academic standards.

There are three kinds of schools in Lebanon: public, private tuition-free, and private fee-based. Private tuition-free schools are available only at the preprimary and primary levels and are under the control of philanthropic organizations, usually religious orders. The distribution of public schools in Lebanon is uneven. The Beirut (q.v.) area has only 12.9 percent of the country's schools, while a large number of Lebanon's private fee-based schools are located in the Greater Beirut area.

Five years of primary education are mandatory and free to Lebanese children. No certification is awarded at the end of the primary level. At the end of the fifth grade, the student qualifies for admission to the four-year intermediate cycle or to the seven-year secondary cycle. The secondary academic track offers concentrations in philosophy, mathematics, and experimental sciences. The choice of the track depends on one's choice of a future university major. The secondary academic level ends with the awarding of a Baccalaureate II degree, an admission requirement to all institutions of higher learning. One can also obtain a degree from the more than 150 technical and vocational institutes in Lebanon. Most of them, especially those offering computer learning, are concentrated in Beirut, a hardship in remote areas of the country.

University education was introduced to Lebanon in the 19th century by Christian missionaries. The American University of Beirut and St. Joseph University (qq.v.) were both founded in the last century and attracted students from throughout the region. The Lebanese University (q.v.) was founded in the 1950s by the Lebanese government to respond to the educational needs of students who could not afford the costs of private universities. Lebanese American University (q.v.) (formerly Beirut University College) was founded in the 19th century as a small institution for women. It later developed into a four-year, co-ed university. There are many other private universities in Lebanon, and sectarian tensions are often mirrored in school curricula.

-F-

FAḌLALLĀH, SHAYKH MUḤAMMAD ḤUSAYN (1939–). He has emerged as one of the most influential Shi'ite (q.v.) leaders in Lebanon, his rise to prominence coinciding with the dramatic rise of Islamic fundamentalism in Lebanon in the wake of the 1982 Israeli invasion (q.v.) of Lebanon. He descends from a notable family in South Lebanon (an uncle on his mother's side served in government). Faḍlallāh was born and educated in Najaf, where his father, 'Abdul-Ra'ūf, was a religious teacher. He received the traditional Shi'ite religious education but was also attracted to classical Arabic (q.v.) literature. Faḍlallāh was close to Islamic fundamentalist activists and joined them in their conflict against communism, which was once strong in Iraq.

Faḍlallāh returned to Lebanon in the late 1960s and settled in the lower class neighborhood of an-Nab'ah in the suburbs of East Beirut (q.v.). He founded a society to promote Islamic values and solidarity and was alarmed at the appeal of leftism and nationalism among Shi'ites. He was driven from his home during the 1975 civil war (q.v.), as were all other Shi'ites, as part of the 1975–76 sectarian cleansing that the Lebanese Phalanges Party (q.v.) executed in areas under its control. Faḍlallāh was not close to Imām Mūsā aṣ-Ṣadr (q.v.), whom he viewed with suspicion because he was "promoted by Maronite circles as a star."

Faḍlallāh's role during the 1975–76 phase of the civil war was minimal, although he was close to the Iraqi Islamic-oriented Ad-Da'wah Party in Lebanon. He was sympathetic to the Iranian revolution and supported Khumayni's concept of *wilāyat al-faqīh* (guardianship of the theologian). Faḍlallāh became an international figure in the wake of anti-American violence in Lebanon, following the Israeli invasion and the deployment of U.S. marines in the country. His name was linked by Western media to suicide bombings, although he denied any responsibility. He also denies being the "spiritual guide" of the Party of God (q.v.), although he is believed to have influence with party members and leaders. In 1985, Faḍlallāh survived an attack against his life when a massive car bomb, reportedly planted by the U.S. intelligence network, and which killed dozens of his neighbors, missed him. He remains widely respected and continues to write on Islamic affairs. His most famous book is *Al-Islām wa Manṭiq al-Quwwah* (Islam and the Logic of Force). His interviews and press articles have been published in book form.

FAKHR AD-DĪN II (the Ma'nid) (1585–1635). This ruler and national symbol (for some Lebanese) was born to the ruling Ma'nid dynasty in the southern district of Mount Lebanon. He was a Druze (q.v.) who attended prayer with Muslims, perhaps in an act of dissimulation to broaden his political appeal. The career of this local prince took a sharp turn when rulers in Tuscany, hoping to establish a foothold in Syria (q.v.), encouraged Fakhr Ad-Dīn II to seek a confrontation with the Ottoman government. He succeeded in his endeavors and was able to expand his province into Syria. When Ottoman armies began their offensive against the prince, he sought refuge in Tuscany and pleaded for military support. He returned to his province and faced increasing challenge from his former masters. He was defeated in 1633—captured, humiliated, and chained. He was taken to Istanbul, where he was strangled to death.

The significance of this ruler is exaggerated in Lebanese history textbooks. Lebanese historians, keen on proving the historical continuity of the Lebanese political entity, point to Fakhr Ad-Dīn and his enclave as an early manifestation of Lebanese nationalism. Yet, the area under Fakhr Ad-Dīn was not referred to as "Lebanon" during his time but as Jabal Ad-Durūz (Mountain of the Druzes). No mention is made in official Lebanese historiography of his weakness or of his subservience to foreign rule. Many Druzes in Lebanon blame him for the decline of their fortunes, because he bolstered the power of Maronite (q.v.) landlords. He also encouraged the Maronites to inhabit Kisrawān, which had been inhabited by Shi'ites (q.v.).

FĀKHŪRĪ, 'UMAR (1896–1946). A writer, he was born in Beirut (q.v.), where he finished his secondary education. He started but did not complete law studies at St. Joseph University (q.v.). He was active against the tyranny of the Turkish government during World War I and was invited by the government of Prince Faysal in Damascus to edit the official publication of that government, known as *Al-'Āṣimah*. After the war, he left for France (q.v.) where he obtained a law degree. He returned to Lebanon in 1923, practiced law, and worked in the government's estates' department. His writings were influenced by French romantic literature. He was sympathetic to leftist causes and was attacked by his enemies for his communist sympathies, although he probably was not a card-carrying member of the Lebanese Communist Party (q.v.).

FAMILY. The family, the primary social unit in Lebanon, permeates the life of the individual in all of its phases, and family relationships are at the core of Lebanese financial, political, and social life. To a large extent, the Lebanese political system has been a system of family representation; individuals rarely achieve electoral victory in isolation from family politics. A small number of *zu'amā' (s. za'īm,* q.v.) families monopolize political representation and compete for power and prestige. Businesses are run by fathers and sons (rarely by daughters, although exceptions occur). In the personal sphere, the patriarch (the father) and the mother dominate the decision making process for their children. The family tries to control the children's lives, especially the daughters', because it is obsessed with family name and status.

The traditional form is the three-generation, patrilineal, extended family, though they all rarely live under the same roof anymore, except in rural areas. The family commands the primary loyalty (a 1959 study found that loyalty to the family ranked first among Muslims and Christians). Family is emphasized in political literature; the motto of the Lebanese Phalanges Party (q.v.) is: "God, the Fatherland, and the Family." In the 1960 parliament, almost a quarter of the deputies "inherited" their seats from older members of the family (fathers and uncles). And in the 1972 parliament, Amīn Gemayyel (q.v.), for example, served with his father, Pierre Gemayyel (q.v.), after inheriting the seat of his uncle, Maurice Gemayyel (q.v.).

FAR'AWN, HENRĪ (1905–1993). This parliamentarian was born in Beirut (q.v.) to a wealthy Greek Catholic family and was educated in Beirut. Like most Lebanese politicians of the pre-independence period, he obtained a law degree from a French school (University of Lyons). He was a deputy in 1927, 1943, 1947, and 1951. He served as foreign minister between 1946 and 1947. He was a key architect of Lebanon's Arab policy and advocated a limited role for the country in the League of Arab States. He served once again as foreign minister in 1955 and was a minister in 1968. He was president of several companies and banks, including the Beirut Port Company and Pharaon and Shiha Bank. His large collection of Islamic arts and manuscripts was on display in his Beirut mansion. He was murdered by his bodyguard under mysterious circumstances.

FARRŪKH, MUṢṬAFĀ (1902–1957). This artist and painter was born in Beirut (q.v.) and received his secondary education there. His first drawing was published in *Al-Muṣawwar* when he was 10 years old. He spent four years in Rome studying art and then traveled to France (q.v.) and Spain to study their art collections. He returned to Lebanon (q.v.) in 1932 and had his first exhibit at the American University of Beirut (q.v.). His art work is familiar to most Lebanese because his illustrations are found on thousands of book covers and textbooks. His specialty was the portrayal of Lebanese village life.

FARRŪKH, ʻUMAR (1906–1987). A scholar and educator, he was born in Beirut (q.v.) to a Sunni (q.v.) family. He studied at the school affiliated with the American University of Beirut (AUB) (q.v.) and received a bachelor of arts degree from AUB in 1928. He taught at several schools before attending German universities, earning a Ph.D. in Islamic studies in 1937. He never taught at AUB due to his strong denunciation of Christian missionaries and their impact on the local culture, but he taught at several Arab universities and from 1960 until his death taught full-time at Beirut Arab University (q.v.). He wrote many textbooks and books on Islamic philosophy and literature, many of which are still used in schools throughout Lebanon. He was a teacher at al-Maqāṣid (q.v.) schools and helped design their curricula. His scholarly interests did not prevent him from being politically active. He was a bitter foe of Christian Westernization in Lebanon.

FATḤ MOVEMENT. This stands for the reverse acronym—in Arabic—of the National Palestinian Liberation Movement, the name of the strongest element of the Palestine Liberation Organization (PLO). It was founded in the late 1950s by Yāsir ʻArafāt (q.v.), Khālid al-Ḥasan, Abū Jihād, and others. There is no agreement among the founders on the date of its establishment, perhaps because it was set up informally before it was announced to the world. In the 1960s, Fatḥ organized the refugee camp Palestinians in Lebanon (q.v.); it succeeded because it remained ideologically ambiguous and concentrated on the fight against Israel, calling for self-reliance and independent Palestinian decision making. Many of its leaders resided in Beirut (q.v.) prior to the 1982 Israeli invasion (q.v.), when Israel forced the PLO out of the country. Lebanon provided Fatḥ with enormous media resources, which proved crucial for the Palestinian cause. Nevertheless, the concentration of many of the leaders in Beirut facilitated Israeli assassination campaigns against top PLO leaders. Muḥammad Yūsuf an-Najjār, Saʻd Ṣāyil, Kamāl ʻUdwān, Abū Ḥasan Salāmah, among many others, were all killed by Israeli agents in Lebanon. During the 1975–1982 period, Fatḥ operated as an independent government within Lebanon and imposed its will on other PLO organizations.

FAWWĀZ, ZAYNAB (1846–1914). This feminist and writer was born to a Lebanese Shi'ite (q.v.) family in Tibnīn in South Lebanon. A wealthy woman admired Fawwāz's intelligence when she was very young and taught her reading and writing; she soon memorized the whole Qur'ān. After two failed marriages, she left Lebanon for Egypt. She became famous as a prose writer for several newspapers and magazines and for the literary gatherings she held in her home. She called for the universal education of women and opposed restricting the career choices of women. She was known for holding literary gatherings in her residences, whether in Egypt or Syria. A collection of her articles was published by Jurjī Bāz.

FAYRŪZ (ḤADDĀD, NUHĀD) (1934–). She is by far the most famous singer and performer in Lebanon and probably in the Arab world since the death of Egyptian singer Um Kulthūm. Fayrūz was born to a poor Christian family in Beirut (q.v.) and had received a secondary education before she was "discovered" by musician Ḥalīm ar-Rūmī who named her Fayrūz (Arabic for "turquoise"). She sang first in the 1950s, over the Near East Radio. Her first nationally famous song was "'Itāb," which she performed in 1950. It was written by her future husband. Her fame was augmented when she married 'Āṣī ar-Raḥbānī in 1955. 'Āṣī and his brother Manṣūr (the ar-Raḥbānī brothers, q.v.) devoted their musical and literary talents to composing songs for Fayrūz. She performed frequently at the Ba'albak (q.v.) International Festival from the 1950s through the 1970s. She has toured and performed around the world and has appeared in several feature films, though her acting was not on the same level with her singing. Fayrūz remained neutral during the 1975–90 civil war (q.v.) and maintained her residence in West Beirut (q.v.), refusing lucrative offers to reside outside the country. She has recently collaborated with her son Ziyād, who has also established a musical reputation. She keeps a low profile and rarely grants press interviews.

FEBRUARY 6, 1984. This date (after which a movement was named) marks the end of Amīn Gemayyel's (q.v.) control over most Muslim areas of Lebanon (q.v.). A revolt by opposition groups, headed by the Amal Movement (q.v.) and the Progressive Socialist Party (q.v.) evicted government troops from West Beirut (q.v.). It was a watershed in Amīn Gemayyel's relations with the United States because it exposed his unpopularity to the world. It also forced Gemayyel to reconcile with the Syrian (q.v.) regime.

FEMINISM. The involvement of women in Lebanese political and social life has been obscured by literature, which very rarely explored the roles and status of females. The subject has been written about in Arabic (q.v.) but the scholarly literature rarely mentions it. Women's involvement in Lebanese political life was observed at the end of World War I. Women were traditionally involved in philanthropic organizations, and their exclusion from political life was assumed and accepted by men. Women did not obediently accept these restrictions; in 1919, feminist leader Ibtihāj Qaddūrah submitted a petition to the King-Crane Commission (an American-led mission sent after World War I to inquire about the aspirations of the people of the region) expressing Lebanese women's support for full independence. In 1939, she wrote to the president of the republic in her capacity as head of the Lebanese Women's Union, demanding full gender equality asking for full political rights for women.

In 1952, Qaddūrah united the Lebanese Women's Union and the League of Lebanese Women into one unified organization, the Lebanese Women's Council. The emphasis then was centered on the question of political rights, perhaps reflecting the upper-class status of feminist organizations at the time. Voting rights were granted to women in 1952. The government at first restricted the right to women with an elementary school education but women's protests forced it to lift the restriction that same year. Women were appointed to municipal councils before their participation in the 1953 parliamentary election. In this election, Emily Fāris Ibrāhīm (q.v.) became the first woman to run for parliament. She withdrew, but her chance of success was minimal, with Lebanese political life dominated by males dismissive of women's political role. Myrnā al-Bustānī (q.v.) was the first woman to win a parliamentary seat (in 1963, following the death of her father). In the 1992 elections, three women won, all of whom are pledged to advance women's rights in Lebanon. Even the First Lady of Lebanon, Munā Hrāwī, paid lip service to the cause, although her actual support is superficial.

Lebanese male politicians are not the only obstacle to women's emancipation; the influence and power of the clerical establishments of all sects probably pose the greatest obstacle to gender equality. Lebanese clerics also oppose the secularization of personal status laws, because they benefit from the obligatory religious personal status laws, which are imposed on everyone, regardless of whether the person is religious or not. Thus, sexist laws embedded in the three religions are imposed on the Lebanese family (q.v.) and society. Furthermore, Lebanese law discriminates against women. Registration of real estate, for example, specifically refers to male witnesses, and commercial laws deprive married women of their right to engage in certain businesses. In general, feminist organizations object to the equation between children and women in some aspects of the law. The

1975 civil war (q.v.) marginalized the feminist struggle because militia leaders regarded demands for gender equality as irrelevant at a time of "national struggle." The leadership of parties on both right and left are similar in their all-male composition. The struggle of Lebanese women continues, and the addition of three female members of parliament does not necessarily solve the problem.

FERTILE CRESCENT (***Al-Hilāl Al-Khaṣīb***). This unscientific term is used to refer to countries east of the Mediterranean and north of the Arabian peninsula. It includes Lebanon, Syria (qq.v.), Jordan, and Palestine. It has been used in Syrian Social National Party (q.v.) literature to refer to their goal of a united Greater Syria (q.v.) (with Cyprus serving as the star of the crescent).

FGHĀLĪ, AS'AD AL-KHŪRĪ. *SEE* SHUḤRŪR AL-WĀDĪ.

FGHĀLĪ, JEANNETTE. *SEE* ṢABĀḤ.

FITYĀN 'ALĪ. *SEE* YOUTHS OF 'ALĪ.

FORCES OF MARADAH (***Quwwāt al-Maradah***). This is not a political party but a militia of the Franjiyyah family of the Zghartā-Ihdin region. It can be traced to the Zghartā Liberation Army, which was founded in 1968 by Sulaymān Franjiyyah (q.v.), who supplied arms to the militia from the warehouses of the Lebanese Army (q.v.) when he was elected president. The Zghartā Liberation Army was renamed *Liwā' al-Maradah* (Brigade of al-Maradah); the name al-Maradah (q.v.) was borrowed from the historical, and mostly mythical, Mount Lebanon (q.v.) fighters. The brigade participated actively in the 1975 civil war (q.v.) on the Tripoli (q.v.) front against Lebanese and Palestinian militias. Its role was marginalized within the Maronite-(q.v.) oriented right-wing coalition of militias when Bashīr Gemayyel (q.v.) came to dominate the scene. After the conflict between the Lebanese Forces (q.v.) and the Franjiyyah family in 1978, Toni Franjiyyah (q.v.) (Sulaymān's eldest son and head of the brigade) was assassinated by forces loyal to Gemayyel. In the 1980s, Toni's teenage son, Sulaymān Jr. (q.v.), wrested control of the brigade from his uncle Robert and renamed the militia the Forces of al-Maradah. Sulaymān Jr. was elected to parliament in 1992.

FRANCE. This country, which was instrumental in creating Lebanon (q.v.) as an entity, had relations with the Maronites (q.v.) long before Lebanon was founded as a state. The relations were then founded on a purely religious basis: France wanted a foothold in the Middle East when the Ottoman Empire began showing signs of weakness and disintegration. Relations between France and Lebanon, however, were solidified in this century when France created the Republic of Lebanon in 1920 and responded to Maronite national aspirations for the creation of a Christian homeland. During the French Mandate (q.v.), many Maronite politicians, like Emile Iddī (q.v.), were so satisfied with the French political, military, and cultural presence that they did not favor independence, believing that it might increase the Muslim share in power and lead to closer ties between Lebanon and the Arab world.

The French role during the mandate and the suppression of independence sentiments did not strain the relations between independent Lebanon and France; the Lebanese political elite almost entirely favored French cultural and political influences. Lebanese deputies would constantly consult French legal experts about certain articles of the Lebanese constitution (q.v.) and their interpretations. Relations between France and Lebanon were made more intimate during the administration of Charles Ḥilū (q.v.), who strongly believed that Lebanon should be made in France's image. He prided himself on his knowledge of the French language, and his visits to Paris meant much to him, as he recounts in his memoirs.

The stance of Charles de Gaulle after 1967, when he halted shipments of arms to Israel, was widely appreciated in the Arab world. France's image in the Arab world also benefited from its antipathy to the United States (q.v.). The French role during the 1975 civil war (q.v.) was minimal, despite desperate attempts by various French presidents to mediate between the warring factions. The 1995 election of Jacques Chirac to the presidency in France revived some Maronite Lebanese hopes of greater involvement by France in Lebanese affairs. But Lebanon has changed; the closest personal friend of Chirac in Lebanon is not a Christian, but the Sunni (q.v.) Prime Minister Rafīq Ḥarīrī (q.v.), who welcomed Chirac to Beirut (q.v.) in 1995.

FRANCO-LEBANESE TREATY. This treaty regulated relations between the French Mandate (q.v.) government and the Lebanese government (and is similar to the Franco-Syrian treaty of September 1936). It was passed by the Lebanese parliament on November 13, 1936. According to its terms, Lebanon (q.v.) was an independent country and was recommended for admission to the League of Nations. Lebanon pledged to serve as France's (q.v.) ally in peace and war. The Lebanese Army (q.v.) was to be restructured under strict French supervision, and France would continue to retain political and diplomatic privileges. There were other technical details, including issues relating to currencies, foreign institutions, and rights of foreigners. An annex was added to guarantee a "fair" representation of sects, which later amounted to what was known as the 6–6 formula, between Christians and Muslims. Muslim public opinion was opposed to the treaty because it confirmed the entity of Lebanon and denied the Muslims the dream of Syrian (or Arab) unity.

FRANCO PASHA (1814–1873). This *mutaṣarrif* (q.v.) was born in Istanbul to a Greek Catholic family. He was trained in Ottoman administration at an early age and learned several languages. His knowledge and training served him well later, when he assumed the position of chief secretary for foreign affairs. His experience included an official trip to Syria in 1860. Awarded the rank of vizier, he was appointed *mutaṣarrif* in 1868. He died in 1873 before the end of his 10-year term. He was generally well-liked by his subjects, although his separation of western al-Biqā' (q.v.) was unpopular with some.

FRANJIYYAH, ḤAMĪD (1907–1981). This parliamentarian and diplomat was a brother of Sulaymān Franjiyyah (q.v.). He was born in Zghartā and educated at St. Joseph University (q.v.). He was a regular member of parliament starting in the 1930s, and was often a foreign minister. He represented Lebanon (q.v.) in the Arab negotiations that led to the formation of the League of Arab States. He is credited with insisting on Lebanon's full independence and sovereignty. He was considered a moderate Maronite (q.v.) with a pro-Arab perspective. He ran for president in 1952 and was a serious presidential nominee during his political life. His active political life came to a sudden halt in 1957, when he suffered a debilitating stroke. His two sons, Samīr and Qabalān, were active in politics. Samīr was a leftist intellectual in the 1970s and ran unsuccessfully for parliament in 1996.

FRANJIYYAH, SULAYMĀN (1910–1992). His name immediately reminds the Lebanese people of the 1975 civil war (q.v.), perhaps because it erupted under his presidency. This uneducated Maronite (q.v.) hailed from one of the most prominent (i.e., of long-term wealth) families in North Lebanon. He was born in Ihdin (q.v.) and was known as his brother's (Ḥamīd Franjiyyah, q.v.) chief campaign aide and manager. Ḥamīd was a highly regarded lawyer and was often mentioned as a likely president of the country. Sulaymān entered political life only after Ḥamīd suffered a debilitating stroke in 1957. Shortly afterward, Sulaymān engaged in a bitter feud with a rival Maronite family, and reports were that he was responsible for the massacre of worshippers in a church in Mizyārah. During the 1958 civil war (q.v.), he was on good terms with both sides. He fled to Syria (q.v.) to avoid prosecution for the Mizyārah massacre. In Syria, Sulaymān struck up a friendship with the family of Ḥāfiḍh al-Asad, which later proved beneficial to his political career. From 1960 on, Sulaymān was a member of parliament and frequently a minister. He was minister of the interior in 1968 and was praised for overseeing what was regarded as an honest election.

He was known as a passionate patriot and, following clashes between army troops and Palestine Liberation Organization forces in 1969, wrote an editorial for *an-Nahār* (q.v.) titled: "My Country Is Always Right." He was a leading member of the parliamentary coalition called *al-Wasaṭ* (the Center), which comprised key politicians who wanted to end the Shihabi era. Franjiyyah was elected president in 1970, with the promise that the Lebanese would not need to lock their doors anymore. He began his administration with a useful alliance with famous Sunni (q.v.) politician Ṣā'ib Salām (q.v.), whom he appointed prime minister. He ended the Shihabi era and brought many of his regional cronies and relatives into office with him. His few years in office witnessed a rise in leftist opposition and in the PLO's influence in Lebanon (q.v.). Many Lebanese wanted the Lebanese government to aid the Palestinian resistance in its struggle against Israel. Franjiyyah was alarmed at the growth of the PLO's power and instructed the Lebanese Army (q.v.) to arm and train Maronite right-wing militias, including his own militia, which was headed by his son Toni (q.v.). In 1973, his relations with Salām soured when the Lebanese Army failed to respond to an Israeli raid on Beirut (q.v.). Salām wanted Franjiyyah to dismiss his commander-in-chief of the army, Iskandar Ghānim (q.v.).

The beginning of Lebanon's slide into civil war had begun, and the cabinet faced enormous political, social, and economic challenges. When the war broke out, Franjiyyah was clearly identified as the guide of the right-wing coalition, and demands for his resignation increased. His closeness to Ḥāfiḍh al-Asad allowed the right-wing coalition to improve ties with the Syrian regime, which was also concerned about the radical tide in the country. The presidential palace was bombed, and he was forced to relocate to temporary headquarters in East Beirut (q.v.).

In early 1976, he presented a reform proposal (known as the "constitutional document"), drafted in consultation with the Syrian government, that attempted to increase the Muslim share in the distribution of power. After leaving office, Franjiyyah retired to his hometown of Ihdin, while remaining within the boundaries of the Lebanese Front (q.v.). His relations with the Lebanese Phalanges Party (q.v.) deteriorated when it tried to establish cells in areas under his control. It is also reported that he objected to the alliance with Israel.

In 1978, Toni was assassinated, which began a bitter and bloody feud between the Franjiyyah family and the Lebanese Front. This feud strengthened Sulaymān's relations with Syria and he was miraculously allowed into the Muslim camp as a friend of the Arab cause. In 1983, he joined Rashīd Karāmī (q.v.) and Walīd Jumblāṭ (q.v.) in the National Salvation Front, which was founded to unseat Amīn Gemayyel (q.v.). In his last years, Franjiyyah expressed a desire to return to the presidency. *See also* Sniffing Dogs Incident.

FRANJIYYAH, SULAYMĀN, Jr. (1964–). This government minister and Maronite (q.v.) leader is the grandson of Sulaymān Franjiyyah (q.v.) and son of Toni Franjiyyah (q.v.). During the 1978 attack against his father's home, he was staying with his grandfather, with whom he was close. He did not receive much education and was known as a tough in his youth. He married at an early age and assumed political responsibilities in his teens. In the 1980s, he wrested control of the Forces of al-Maradah (q.v.) from his uncle Robert, who was considered a weak politician. He was first appointed minister in 1990 and has held ministerial posts ever since. After the dissolution of militias in 1991, he transformed his militia into a semi-political party, although it was in truth no more than a family political vehicle. He was elected to parliament in the 1992 election and is considered one of the most powerful Maronite leaders in Lebanon (q.v.). He inherited close ties to the al-Asad family in Damascus and is close to Bashshār al-Asad, son of Ḥāfiḍh al-Asad. Sulaymān easily won a seat in the 1996 election.

FRANJIYYAH, TONI (1941–1978). This son of Sulaymān Franjiyyah (q.v.) was destined, as his father's heir, to play an important role in Lebanese political life. He was born in Zghartā and received some secondary education in Tripoli (q.v.). He was a founder of the Social Cultural Club in Zghartā, which was intended to recruit young men to his cause of family leadership. He won a seat in parliament in 1972, when his father was president and emerged as a key parliamentary leader due to his father's influence. Toni served as a minister during the presidency of his father and was accused by his critics of enriching himself from commissions. He formed a militia (the Forces of al-Maradah, q.v.) that was outfitted from the Lebanese Army's (q.v.) warehouses while his father was president. His militia participated in the war against Muslim-leftist militias in Tripoli (q.v.). He joined the right-wing coalition during the 1975 civil war (q.v.) but clashed with Bashīr Gemayyel (q.v.). They disagreed over who should own the revenues from illegal taxation and over the right of the Lebanese Forces (q.v.) to compete with Franjiyyah's political movement in the north. Toni was killed in a night raid on his home. He was succeeded by his son, Sulaymān Jr. (q.v.), in the leadership of the family and the militia.

FREM, FĀDĪ (1953–). This former commander of the Lebanese Forces (LF) (q.v.) was born in Beirut (q.v.) and educated at the American University of Beirut (q.v.), Texas A&M University, and the Harvard Graduate School of Business. He was an engineer by training but headed the intelligence apparatus of the Lebanese Forces for one year (1978–79). He was chief-of-staff of the LF between 1980 and 1982 and its commander between 1982 and 1984. After he was deposed, he retired from political life and concentrated on his business ventures. He has been chairman of Enterprise Holding since 1987.

FRENCH MANDATE. The Supreme Council at the peace conference held at the end of World War I established mandate rule over all territories formerly subject to Turkish or German rule. Not all of those territories were to have the same kind of governmental arrangement. Former German colonies in Africa and the Far East were populated by "backward" people and were to be governed with the assumption that it would be a long time before they were ready for self-rule. Lebanon (q.v.), fell into an area between that category and full independent status. The council assigned France (q.v.) the responsibility for establishing a mandate system in Lebanon to prepare its people for full independence at some future time. The League of Nations later endorsed those plans. The French Mandate period extended from the end of World War I until 1943, although all French troops did not withdraw until 1946.

FURAYḤAH, SA'ĪD (1921–1978). A journalist, he was born in Beirut (q.v.) and grew up an orphan and went to work in his brother's barber shop. He received no formal education but secretly read while working for his brother. His journalistic career began in Aleppo, when he wrote for *Ar-Rāṣid* and *At-Taqaddum* and was a correspondent for newspapers in Beirut and Damascus. He later returned to Beirut, where he wrote for *Al-Aḥrār* (q.v.), *Aṣ-Ṣaḥāfī At-Tā'ih* (q.v.), and *Al-Ḥadīth*. In the mid-1940s Furayḥah founded *Aṣ-Ṣayyād* (q.v.), which remains a widely read weekly. Furayḥah's journalistic style was geared to readers with short attention spans: his magazine avoided long analytical pieces and included many political cartoons; his style was simple, even simplistic—long on description and short on analysis. He was a staunch Arab nationalist who favored Jamāl 'Abdul-Nasser (q.v.) in Arab politics. *Aṣ-Ṣayyād* was transformed in the 1960s into the media and publishing empire, Dār Aṣ-Ṣayyād. Furayḥah's most successful venture, however, was the entertainment magazine *Ash-Shabakah* (q.v.), which pictured scantily clad female Arab stars on its covers. His publishing house is now run by his two sons and daughter.

-G-

GEMAYYEL, AMĪN (1942–). Lebanon's president in the 1980s, he is the eldest son of Pierre Gemayyel (q.v.). Amīn was known as more moderate in comparison to his brother, Bashīr Gemayyel (q.v.). He was educated in Beirut (q.v.) and received a law degree from St. Joseph University (q.v.). As a student, he was active in the Lebanese Phalanges Party (q.v.). He was elected to parliament in 1970 in a by-election following the death of his uncle; he was also elected in 1972. He belonged to a faction within the Phalanges Party that called for improved ties with the Arab world and for strategic coexistence with the Muslims of Lebanon. He rose to prominence during the 1975 civil war (q.v.) and was active on several fronts, along with Bashīr. Amīn's power base was in North Matn, and he stayed close to his followers. In 1975–76, he became a hardliner, believing that war against the Palestinians in Lebanon (q.v.) was necessary and supporting sectarian cleansing in East Beirut (q.v.). In the late 1970s, he established good ties with the Syrian (q.v.) regime and worked to bridge the gap between his party and the Palestine Liberation Organization. His role, however, was insignificant compared with that of his brother, who monopolized the decision making process in East Beirut until his death.

Amīn was elected president unexpectedly, when Bashīr was assassinated weeks after his election to the presidency in the wake of the Israeli invasion of 1982 (q.v.). Amīn's term in office was characterized by an intensification of the civil war and an increase of United States (q.v.) influence in Lebanon. Amīn believed that Ronald Reagan would not allow the opposition to undermine his own regime, and he neglected Lebanon's official relations with Syria, hoping that Syria would not recover from the consequences of the 1982 Israeli invasion of Lebanon. He began in 1983 negotiations with Israel that led to the May 17 Agreement (q.v.), which was abrogated by the Lebanese government in 1984 and its parliament in 1987. When American forces left Lebanon in 1984, Amīn was forced to deal with the opposition. He attended the Lausanne and Geneva Conferences (qq.v.) for national reconciliation. These efforts, however, failed and the war resumed. Amīn rejected Syrian-inspired reform proposals because he did not want to undermine his Christian power base. He was constantly criticized by the Lebanese Forces (q.v.) for not doing enough to help Christian militias. Minutes before the expiration of his term, Amīn surprised the Lebanese people by appointing Michel 'Awn (q.v.) as interim prime minister, in effect the acting head of state. Amīn soon left Lebanon for France (q.v.), where he resides now. He travels around the world to meet with sympathizers of the Lebanese

Phalanges Party. He still accuses Syria of compromising Lebanese sovereignty by intervening in Lebanon's internal affairs.

GEMAYYEL, BASHĪR (1947–1982). A president-elect and militia leader, this Maronite (q.v.) militia leader was the most extremist politician ever elected president of Lebanon (q.v.). Usually, Lebanese candidates for the presidency require a degree of Muslim support, but Bashīr was elected in the presence of the Israeli army in Lebanon in the wake of its 1982 invasion (q.v.). Bashīr studied at St. Joseph University (q.v.) where he was heavily engaged in student politics within the Lebanese Phalanges Party (q.v.) and participated in physical confrontations between right-wing and left-wing students in the 1960s. Bashīr was involved in the training of students and their recruitment into the Phalanges militia. He was particularly bitter about the rising political and military power of the Palestinians in Lebanon (q.v.) and disagreed with the "moderate" policy of his father, Pierre Gemayyel (q.v.), and other Phalangist leaders.

Bashīr quickly assumed military responsibilities during the 1975 civil war (q.v.) and formed his own brigade within the Phalangist militia. He became head of the military apparatus of the Phalanges Party in 1976, when previous leader William Ḥāwī died under mysterious circumstances. Bashīr was present at the various fronts that pitted Phalangist forces against Palestinian forces and called for the elimination of the Palestinian presence in East Beirut (q.v.). His goals were accomplished by the end of the 1975–76 phase of the civil war. Bashīr was not enthusiastic about the brief alliance between the Syrian regime and the Lebanese Front (q.v.); he was aligned, instead, with Israel (q.v.) and was certain that his goals could not be achieved without direct Israeli military and political support. Bashīr succeeded in unifying—by force and bloodshed—all right-wing militias under his own command when he founded the Lebanese Forces (q.v.), which was to have complete hegemony. When Toni Franjiyyah (q.v.) tried to assert his own leadership in his own region, Bashīr sent a hit squad that massacred him and his family. He also eliminated the Tigers militia of the National Liberal Party (q.v.) when Dānī Sham'ūn posed a political threat to his monopoly of power in the region. East Beirut was under his control and Bashīr was the undisputed lord of the entire Christian heartland. Not even his father could challenge him, and he was not on speaking terms with his brother, Amīn (q.v.), for many years. Bashīr engaged in a bitter military confrontation with Syrian troops, achieving their withdrawal from predominantly Christian areas.

The emergence of the Israeli right in Israel under Menachem Begin and Ariel Sharon facilitated Bashīr's aims. The Israeli invasion of 1982 allowed Bashīr to present himself as a candidate for president.

With Israeli tanks surrounding a military barrack that served as a location for the parliament, Bashīr was elected even though most Muslim deputies boycotted the session. Weeks later, on September 14, 1982, Bashīr was killed in a bombing of the Phalangist headquarters aimed at him. A member of the Syrian Social National Party (q.v.) was accused of the killing, but he was later released from jail. The Ṣabrā and Shātīlā massacres (q.v.) followed his assassination. He is still remembered by some Christian supporters as the lost hope of Lebanon. His wife, Solange, heads a foundation in his name, which has published all of his statements and press interviews.

GEMAYYEL, MAURICE (1907–1970). A politician, he was born in Egypt and earned a law degree in Paris. He practiced law in Beirut (q.v.). He was elected to parliament in 1960, 1964, and 1968, and appointed minister in 1960. He was a cousin and brother-in-law of Pierre Gemayyel (q.v.). He was a politburo member of the Lebanese Phalanges Party (q.v.) but was known for his relatively moderate views, emphasizing the need for national planning and social reforms. His enthusiasm for a strategic and technical vision of the future earned the nickname *al-Akhwat* (the idiot) among his colleagues. He died in 1970 and was succeeded in his seat by his nephew, Amīn Gemayyel (q.v.).

GEMAYYEL, PIERRE (1905–1984). This right-wing party leader and ardent ultranationalist left his imprint on Lebanese ideological and political life. He was born in al-Manṣūrah in Egypt and moved to Lebanon to pursue his studies, obtaining a degree in pharmacy in 1936. An accomplished athlete, Pierre was impressed with German nationalism and youth movements while part of the Lebanese delegation to the 1936 Olympic Games. He founded the Lebanese Phalanges Party (q.v.) upon his return and attracted a group of French-educated Christian intellectuals. The party's ideology stressed Lebanese nationalism with an emphasis on the Christian character of the country. Pierre wanted his party to be a paramilitary organization but was foiled in this attempt by the French. He reluctantly and belatedly joined the independence movement, although he was sympathetic to the pro-French movement of Emile Iddī (q.v.).

Pierre Gemayyel came to national prominence after the 1958 civil war (q.v.), when he led the anti-Nasser forces, by serving in the cabinet formed after the crisis was resolved. Pierre was identified with an ultra-Lebanese, sectarian, Christian perspective and failed to win support among Muslims. But he did not need Muslim support for his electoral success. It is often suggested that Fu'ād Shihāb (q.v.) was responsible for boosting Gemayyel to hurt Raymond Iddī (q.v.), a vocal critic of Shihabism. In the 1960s, Pierre was one of the three Maronite (q.v.) leaders of the Tripartite Alliance, which also included Kamīl Sham'ūn (q.v.) and Raymond Iddī. Gemayyel also worked on developing a disciplined militia, receiving help from the Lebanese Army (q.v.), which shared his antipathy to the Palestinians.

Lebanese sovereignty was his professed goal, to which he saw the Palestinians as posing the greatest threat. He did not believe he had any domestic opposition, and analyzed Lebanese and Arab events only through the prism of "the communist conspiracy," which was popular during the cold war. He scorned Lebanon's ties to the Arab world, wanting to insulate Lebanon from the consequences of the Arab-Israeli conflict. During the 1975–90 civil war (q.v.), he was a major figure in the right-wing war command coalition, known as the Lebanese Front (q.v.), although he was overshadowed by his own son, the more militant Bashīr (q.v.), who was more friendly toward Israel (q.v.). Pierre saw two of his sons elected president before his death; he himself was a presidential candidate in pre-war Lebanon. The Phalanges Party never recovered from the loss of its founder; it is now split into several rival factions. *See also* Lebanese Phalanges Party.

GENERAL UNION OF LABOR. This largest union confederation in Lebanon was formed in 1970, when the nine trade unions of Lebanon united. The unity of its leadership, which comprises Lebanese from different sects, mainly blue-collar workers, was not affected by the 1975 civil war (q.v.). The union was one of the few organizations that did not splinter along sectarian lines during the civil war. In the years preceding the war, it had a successful battle against inflation and corruption in the country. Its national strike in May 1992 brought down the government of 'Umar Karāmī (q.v.), which led the Lebanese government to appoint Syria's (q.v.) loyal client in Lebanon, 'Abdallāh al-Amīn (q.v.), as minister of labor, apparently to intimidate labor leaders. In 1997, the government of Rafīq Ḥarīrī (q.v.) forced the elected secretary-general of the union, Ilyās Abū Rizq, out of his leadership position and installed a subservient replacement.

GENEVA CONFERENCE. This conference on national reconciliation was held in Geneva from October 31 to November 4, 1983. It was attended by the majority of Lebanon's political bosses in addition to Syrian officials under the guidance of 'Abdul-Ḥalīm Khaddām (q.v.). While the results were inconclusive, they included an abrogation of the May 17 Agreement (q.v.) and agreement on constitutional and political reforms. Amīn Gemayyel (q.v.) convened the conference to restore credibility and legitimacy to his government. *See also* Lausanne Conference.

GEORGES-PICOT, FRANCOIS. This Frenchman was appointed France's (q.v.) high commissioner in the Levant (q.v.) in 1917, in which capacity he wielded great power in the state. An avenue commemorates his name in Beirut (q.v.). *See also* French Mandate.

GHANDŪR FACTORY STRIKE. This labor strike at two of the Ghandūr factories in Beirut (q.v.) occurred in November 1972. This chocolate and biscuit company is one of the oldest of its kind in the country and is owned by the wealthy Sunni (q.v.) Ghandūr family. The strike, which called for basic improvements in working conditions, led to the intervention of forces of the security services; strikers were shot at, and two of them killed. Many others were arrested. These events exacerbated social and political tensions in the country.

GHĀNIM, ISKANDAR (1913–). He was one of the most controversial commanders-in-chief of the Lebanese Army (q.v.) in its entire history. He was born in Ṣaghbīn in al-Biqā' (q.v.), and was educated in the 1930s at the Military Academy in Ḥumṣ. He held several commanding posts, with a specialty in the artillery. He was military attache in Washington, D.C. (1966–67), where he established ties with American officials. Upon his return, he was appointed commander of the Beirut (q.v.) region, before his retirement in 1969. When his friend Sulaymān Franjiyyah (q.v.) assumed the presidency, he recalled Ghānim to service in 1971, as commander-in-chief. Ghānim was fiercely loyal to Franjiyyah. In 1973, when Prime Minister Ṣā'ib Salām (q.v.) asked for Ghānim's resignation as a punishment for Lebanese Army incompetence in dealing with an Israeli commando raid that killed three Palestine Liberation Organization officials in a Beirut neighborhood, he refused and was backed by the president. He remained in his post until his resignation in 1975. His son, Robert, was elected to the parliament in 1992 and 1996. *See also* Civil War of 1975–90.

***GHURABĀ'*.** Literally, it means "strangers" or "aliens" and was used during the 1975 civil war (q.v.) by right-wing militias and their supporters to refer to all Palestinians in Lebanon (q.v.). The right-wing establishment held that Lebanon would return to normalcy only when all Palestinians were expelled from Lebanon.

GIBRĀN, KHALĪL (JUBRĀN KHALĪL JUBRĀN) (1883–1931). The Lebanese people are very proud of this Lebanese writer and poet. He was born in Bshirrī in North Lebanon and several years later moved to the United States (q.v.) with his sisters. He is famous in the Western world for his book *The Prophet,* which has been translated into many languages. He is known in the Arab world for his tremendous contributions to the modern usage of the Arabic (q.v.) language. He ignored the rigid structures of classical Arabic poetry and called, instead, for free artistic expression. In his writing, he was less a thinker than a dreamer. He was anti-conformist in other spheres, too, being opposed to the dominance of the clerical establishment and calling for the modernization of the Arab region (without copying Western models and ways).

His writings in Arabic and English celebrated individual freedom and warned against sectarianism and class oppression. He was opposed to narrow nationalism, despite efforts by contemporary Lebanese to turn him into a vulgar Lebanese nationalist. His attacks against the religious establishment earned him the wrath of the elders of the Christian church in Lebanon, some of whom did not want to allow him a Christian burial in his birthplace. After his death, the Lebanese treated him as their cultural icon, although Jubrān viewed himself as a Syrian Arab. His most important contribution to Arabic literature lies in his formation in the United States of a literary society known as *Ar-Rābiṭah al-Qalamiyyah* (Pen's League), which played an important role in the cultural and literary revival of the Arab world. Many contemporary writers imitate his style. A committee was founded in Bshirrī to manage his estate and administer a museum dedicated to his memory. *See also* Nu'aymah, Mikhā'īl.

GRAND LIBAN. Meaning "Greater Lebanon," it was the term used by some Lebanese and by the French to refer to the expansion of the Lebanese entity beyond the boundaries of the old Mutasarrifiyyah (q.v.), following the demise of the Ottoman Empire. Its boundaries coincide with the present-day boundaries of Lebanon. The State of Greater Lebanon was proclaimed in September 1920 by the French high commissioner in Beirut (q.v.). *See also* France; French Mandate.

GREATER LEBANON. *SEE* GRAND LIBAN.

GREATER SYRIA. This refers to the goal of Syrian nationalists, especially advocates of the Syrian Social National Party (q.v.), to unify Lebanon, Syria (qq.v.), Jordan, and Palestine into one country. They maintain that geographic Syria, as the area of the Fertile Crescent (q.v.) was known, should be established as a nation-state. This goal, however, is quite unpopular in Lebanon.

GREEK CATHOLIC CHRISTIANS. This second largest Uniate community in Lebanon emerged as a distinct group in the early 18th century, when it split from the Greek Orthodox (q.v.) Church.

Although they fully accept Catholic doctrines as defined by the Vatican, they have generally remained close to the Greek Orthodox, using Arabic (q.v.) and following the Byzantine Rite. In Lebanon (q.v.), when one speaks of Catholics, one is referring to this group, not to Roman Catholics or Maronites (qq.v.). The highest official of the church since 1930 has been the patriarch of Antioch, who resides in ‘Ayn Trāz. Members of this sect live primarily in the central and eastern parts of the country, dispersed among many villages. They are concentrated in Beirut, Zaḥlah, and the suburbs of Sidon (qq.v.). They have a relatively higher educational level than members of other sects. Proud of their Arabic heritage, they have espoused an open attitude toward Arab nationalism. They constitute no more than 3 percent of the population.

GREEK ORTHODOX CHRISTIANS. The Greek Orthodox, who constitute no more than 5 percent of Lebanon’s population, adhere to the Eastern Orthodox Church, a group of autocephalous churches using the Byzantine Rite. These churches grew out of the four Eastern patriarchates (Jerusalem, Antioch, Alexandria, and Constantinople), which beginning in the fifth century diverged from the Western patriarchate of Rome over the nature of Christ. The final split took place in 906. From that time, with the exception of a brief period of reunion in the 15th century, the Eastern Orthodox Church has continued to reject the claim of the Roman patriarchate to universal supremacy and also the concept of papal infallibility. Doctrinally, the main point at issue between the Eastern and Western Churches is that of the procession of the Holy Spirit. There are also divergences in ritual and discipline. The community is less dominated by large landowners than the Maronites (q.v.). In present-day Lebanon, the Greek Orthodox have become increasingly urbanized and form a major part of the commercial and professional class of Beirut (q.v.) and other cities, but many also live in the southeast, the Shūf mountains, and the north, near Tripoli (q.v.). They tend to be highly educated and are known for their pan-Arab orientation.

GREEK ORTHODOX CHURCH. *SEE* GREEK ORTHODOX CHRISTIANS.

GREEN LINE. This refers to the no-man’s-land between East and West Beirut (qq.v.) that came about during the 1975 civil war (q.v.). The line, which designates the streets and neighborhoods that separated the two sections of Beirut (q.v.), was eliminated in 1990 when the Lebanese Army (q.v.), supported by Syrian (q.v.) troops, extended its authority to the entire capital.

GREGORIAN CHRISTIANS. *SEE* ARMENIAN ORTHODOX CHRISTIANS

GROUPING OF THE POPULAR COMMITTEES AND LEAGUES (*Tajammu' al-Lijān wa-l-Rawābiṭ ash-Sha'biyyah*). This small group split from the Arab Socialist Ba'th Party (q.v.) in the wake of the 1967 Arab defeat, which led to ideological and political turmoil in the region. It believed in the primacy of grassroots organizations, in contrast to the theorizing of Ba'thist ideologues. The grouping had an insignificant role in the 1975–90 Lebanese civil war (q.v.), although it was affiliated with the Lebanese National Movement (q.v.). Its leader, Bishārah Mirhij, was elected to parliament in 1992 and held ministerial positions in the administration of Ilyās Hrāwī (q.v.). He was reelected in 1996 on the list of Prime Minister Rafīq Ḥarīrī (q.v.).

GUARDIANS OF THE CEDARS (*Ḥizb Ḥurrās al-Arz*). One of the most extreme right-wing parties in Lebanon, the Guardians of the Cedars was established in 1975, when it issued Communique No. 1 denouncing advocates of the partition of Lebanon (q.v.). It called for—and practiced—the killing of Palestinians in Lebanon (q.v.) and worked for the breaking of Lebanon's Arab ties and for a "strategic" alliance with Israel (q.v.). The party was close to the Front of the Guardians of the Cedars, which has not been heard of since the 1975–76 phase of the civil war (q.v.). The party received money and weapons from Israel, and its leader, Abū Arz (code name for Ityān Ṣaqr), was one of the first Lebanese militia leaders to be publicly photographed with Israeli leaders. Its fighters gained a reputation for savagery and ruthlessness during the civil war. The party was incorporated within the command of the Lebanese Forces (q.v.) under the leadership of Bashīr Gemayyel (q.v.). Lately, it has added the designation *Ḥarakat al-Qawmiyyah al-Lubnāniyyah* (Movement of Lebanese Nationalism) to its name. The party suffered a setback in October 1990 when the Syrian army and Lebanese government troops forced Michel 'Awn (q.v.) out of power. Abū Arz suffered an unspecified injury and was forced to seek refuge in Israeli-occupied South Lebanon. The Lebanese state has issued warrants for his arrest.

-H-

ḤABASHĪ GROUP al-. This small Sunni (q.v.) fundamentalist group, also called the Society of Islamic Philanthropic Projects (*Jam'iyyat al-Mashārī' al-Khayriyyah al-Islāmiyyah*), has been growing in recent years. It has been centered in the Burj Abī Ḥaydar mosque in West Beirut (q.v.) and is headed by an eccentric former *muftī* (q.v.) from

Ethiopia, known as "al-Ḥabashī," or "the Abyssinian." This secret organization has been gaining in popularity since one of its leaders, 'Adnān Ṭarābulsī, was elected to parliament in 1992.

ḤADDĀD, NUHĀD. *SEE* FAYRŪZ.

ḤADDĀD, SA'D (1937–1984). This controversial renegade Lebanese Army (q.v.) officer was born in Marj 'Uyūn in South Lebanon. A Christian, he joined the army in the 1960s and rose to the rank of major in 1976, when, while serving in the command of South Lebanon, he established a political and military alliance with Israel (q.v.). Ḥaddād and Israel shared a hatred of the Palestinians (q.v.) and used the Israeli-occupied strip in the border area to launch attacks against the Palestine Liberation Organization forces in South Lebanon. Israel showered praise and weapons on this obscure major and presented him to the international media as a Lebanese patriot who represented Lebanese public opinion. In reality, the Lebanese considered him a traitor, and right-wing forces dissociated themselves from him, at least publicly.

Ḥaddād helped Israeli forces in 1978, when they occupied South Lebanon before they were forced to withdraw by the international community. Israel retained a strip along the border and put Ḥaddād in charge. It also trained and financed his forces, which were no longer under army command. Under Israeli instructions, Ḥaddād established the South Lebanon Army (q.v.), which was intended to put a Lebanese face on the Israeli military presence in South Lebanon. It numbered some 2,000 men, mostly Christians but including a small number of Shi'ites (q.v.) who were lured by the attractive salaries. Ḥaddād failed to expand his army, which was regarded as Israel's army in Lebanon. His troops often clashed with the United Nations Interim Force in Lebanon (q.v.). Ḥaddād was dismissed from the army and retaliated by declaring his own entity, Free Lebanon. He collaborated with the Israeli forces in 1982 during the Israeli invasion (q.v.) of Lebanon. He died in 1984 and was succeeded in the command of the South Lebanon Army by General Antoine Laḥd.

ḤADDĀD, WADĪ' (1941–). This presidential advisor was born in 'Ayn Dārā, near 'Alayy and was educated at the American University of Beirut (AUB) (q.v.) and the University of Wisconsin, Madison, where he earned a Ph.D. in education in 1968. He returned to Lebanon, where he taught at AUB until 1972 when he became director-general of the government-run Center for Education Research and Development. In 1976, he worked at the World Bank in Washington, D.C., and returned to Lebanon in 1982 to serve as national security advisor to Amīn

Gemayyel (q.v.). He was known as a hard-liner who favored an alliance with Israel and the United States (qq.v.) at the expense of Lebanon's ties with its Arab neighbors. He published a book on Lebanon titled *Lebanon: The Politics of Revolving Doors*. He has now withdrawn from public life.

***ḤADĪQAT AL-AKHBĀR*.** This journal, first published in 1858, was founded and edited by Khalīl al-Khūrī (q.v.). It is considered the first political journal to be published in the Ottoman Empire outside of Istanbul. It advocated universal education and the promotion of industry and agriculture. It was partly funded by a Beirut notable, Mikhā'īl Mudawwar (q.v.). In 1860, it was transformed into an official publication of the Ottoman government, and the editor was salaried from Istanbul. It ceased publication in 1911.

ḤĀFIḌH, AMĪN al- (1926–). This parliamentarian, prime minister, and professor of political science was first elected a deputy from Tripoli (q.v.) in 1960. He was born in Tripoli and educated in Tripoli and Cairo. He served in consecutive parliaments ever since, thanks to support from Rashīd Karāmī (q.v.). He was known mostly for his work in international affairs and held the chairmanship of the committee on foreign affairs in parliament for years. Al-Ḥāfiḍh was appointed prime minister in 1973 by Sulaymān Franjiyyah (q.v.), which led Karāmī to sever ties with him. Al-Ḥāfiḍh pursues moderate policies and has enjoyed respect among various sects and groups. He has been consistently supportive of the Palestine Liberation Organization (PLO) in Lebanon and his wife, Laylā 'Usayrān (q.v.), is a friend of top PLO leaders. He was elected in the 1992 election and still serves as chairman of the Foreign Relations Committee.

HAIGAZIAN UNIVERSITY. This predominantly Armenian (q.v.) university offers religious and secular education, with faculties in Armenian studies; economics and management; languages, letters, and human sciences; science; and social sciences.

ḤAJJ, KAMĀL YŪSUF al- (1917–1976). This thinker and scholar was born to a Lebanese Maronite (q.v.) family in Morocco, and studied in Lebanon, Syria, (qq.v.) and Egypt. He was trained in Arabic calligraphy at an early age. He finished his secondary school at Jesuit schools and received a degree in Arabic literature from the American University of Beirut (q.v.) in 1946. In 1950 he received his Ph.D. in philosophy from the Sorbonne. He taught philosophy at St. Joseph University (q.v.) but resigned in 1952 over his insistence on teaching in Arabic. He started teaching at the Lebanese University (q.v.) in 1952, the year it was founded. Between 1953 and 1957 he headed the cultural section of the Ministry of Education. He later headed the Philosophy Department at the Lebanese University and was appointed acting dean in 1969 and 1971. He was murdered in 1976. He was a strict Lebanese nationalist. Among his writings is a book titled *Falsafat Al-Mithāq Al-Waṭanī* (The Philosophy of the National Pact), which appeared in 1961. It argues that sectarianism is beneficial to Lebanon as the only glue that holds the nation together.

ḤAJJ, UNSĪ al- (1937–). A prominent poet and cultural critic, he was born in South Lebanon, where his father worked for the leading Lebanese daily *An-Nahār* (q.v.). He received his secondary education in Beirut (q.v.) and began writing for *An-Nahār*. He became editor of the popular cultural supplement of the newspaper, which contained a melange of politics and literature. His poetry did not follow the established norms of classical Arabic (q.v.) literature; his first book of poetry (*Lan*) appeared in 1960. He translated several plays from French into Arabic and his newspaper columns were collected in book form. He was not politically partisan, although he was sympathetic to the Palestine Liberation Organization in the 1960s and early 1970s. He was, however, partisan in his praise for the singer Fayrūz (q.v.). His poetry did not have a lasting impact; it was original in style but vague in substance. He now serves as editor-in-chief of *An-Nahār*.

ḤAKĪM, 'ADNĀN al- (1914–1990). This Sunni (q.v.) party leader was born in Beirut (q.v.) and educated at Al-Maqāṣid (q.v.) secondary schools. He was associated with Sunni sectarian politics at an early age and, in 1936, along with Beiruti notables, founded the Helpers (Najjādah) Party (q.v.) to counter the organized movement of the Maronites (q.v.). He was an enthusiastic champion of Jamāl 'Abdul-Nasser (q.v.), and his political party never developed an ideology beyond this allegiance. He was critical of moderate Sunni politicians and accused Ṣā'ib Salām (q.v.) and others of abandoning Sunni political interests in return for political power. He was supportive of Fu'ād Shihāb (q.v.) and considered him fair on sectarian questions. He served in parliament and in cabinets but failed to win a seat in 1972. His role during the 1975 civil war (q.v.) was minimal, although he tried to form a militia to revive the role he had played in 1958. His last years were spent in political obscurity.

ḤAMĀDAH, FARĪD. *SEE* YAZBAKI LIBERATION FRONT.

ḤAMĀDĪ, MARWĀN (1939–). This follower of Walīd Jumblāṭ (q.v.) was born in Beirut (q.v.). Son of a diplomat (and later brother-in-law of

Ghassān Tuwaynī, q.v.), he was educated at St. Joseph University (q.v.). He worked in the press as a columnist for *L'Orient–Le Jour* (q.v.) before assuming various responsible positions within the *An-Nahār* (q.v.) media empire. Although he was never active in party politics, he was chosen by Walīd Jumblāṭ to be his Druze (q.v.) representative in a 1980 cabinet during the administration of Ilyās Sarkīs (q.v.). Ḥamādī was known for his moderation and his access to most political leaders in Lebanon, especially Progressive Socialist Party (q.v.) president Jumblāṭ. He won a seat in the 1992 and 1996 parliamentary elections. He has never deviated from Jumblāṭ's political line.

ḤAMĀDĪ, ṢABRĪ (1905–1976). This former speaker was born in Hirmil to the wealthiest and most powerful Shi'ite (q.v.) family in the region, which had dominated even parts of Kisrawān centuries ago. He received little if any formal education; his identity card had to be forged to permit him to run for election the first time (he was under the official minimum age). Ḥamādī was first elected in 1925 and held parliamentary and ministerial positions up until his death. He was speaker of parliament for most of the 1960s; he was also a key supporter of Fu'ād Shihāb (q.v.). He was reluctant to declare the victory of Sulaymān Franjiyyah (q.v.) in 1970, because he supported his rival, Ilyās Sarkīs (q.v.) for the presidency. He was a marginal figure during the 1975 civil war (q.v.). Ḥamādī was known for his bitter political rivalry with his brother-in-law, former speaker Kāmil al-As'ad (q.v.), with whom he fought for the speakership position during much of the 1960s.

ḤARAKAH AL-ISLĀMIYYAH FĪ LUBNĀN, AL. *SEE* ISLAMIC MOVEMENT IN LEBANON.

ḤARAKAH AL-WAṬANIYYAH AL-LUBNĀNIYYAH, AL. *SEE* LEBANESE NATIONAL MOVEMENT.

ḤARAKAT AL-MAḤRŪMĪN. *SEE* AMAL MOVEMENT.

ḤARAKAT AL-QAWMIYYĪN AL-'ARAB. *SEE* MOVEMENT OF ARAB NATIONALISTS.

ḤARAKAT AL-WIḤDAWIYYĪN AL-NĀṢIRIYYĪN. *SEE* MOVEMENT OF UNIONIST NASSERISTS.

ḤARAKAT AMAL. *SEE* AMAL MOVEMENT.

ḤARAKAT AMAL AL-ISLĀMIYYAH. *SEE* ISLAMIC AMAL MOVEMENT.

ḤARAKAT AN-NĀṢIRIYYĪN AL-MUSTAQILLĪN. *SEE* MOVEMENT OF THE INDEPENDENT NASSERISTS—AL-MURĀBITŪN.

ḤARAKAT AT-TAGHYĪR. *SEE* MOVEMENT OF CHANGE.

ḤARAKAT AT-TAWḤĪD AL-ISLĀMĪ. *SEE* ISLAMIC UNIFICATION MOVEMENT.

ḤARAKAT RUWWĀD AL-IṢLĀḤ. *SEE* MOVEMENT OF THE PIONEERS OF REFORM.

ḤARAKAT 24 TISHRĪN. *SEE* OCTOBER 24 MOVEMENT.

ḤARB AL-JABAL. *SEE* WAR OF THE MOUNTAIN.

ḤARB, BUṬRUS (1944–). He has emerged as one of the most effective and independent Maronite (q.v.) politicians in Lebanon (q.v.). He was born in Tannūrīn in 1944 and was educated at St. Joseph University (q.v.), where he received a law degree. He belonged to a "political family" and ran the campaign of his uncle, Jan, in 1960. He first won a parliamentary seat in 1972, in which he maintained an independent course. In 1979, Ḥarb helped found of the Bloc of Independent Maronite Deputies (q.v.), which was established to distance the deputies from the Lebanese Forces (q.v.) and their political hegemony over Maronite political life. He served in ministerial positions in the administration of Ilyās Sarkīs (q.v.) and was widely respected during his government service. As minister of education in 1979, he initiated Flag Day, a day when students expressed devotion to the Lebanese flag. He was clearly interested in underlining his patriotic credentials. He has harbored presidential aspirations and has maintained good relations with almost all Lebanese groups. Ḥarb was also a minister in the government of Ilyās Hrāwī (q.v.) and was known for his mild reforms of the educational system. He boycotted the elections of 1992 but without burning his bridges with Syria (q.v.) and its supporters in Lebanon. He surprised political observers in 1996 when he won a parliamentary seat with a large margin, despite negative signals from the Syrian regime.

ḤARĪRĪ, RAFĪQ (1944–). Although he became a billionaire, he was born to a low-income Sunni (q.v.) family in Sidon (q.v.). He obtained a degree in accounting from the Beirut Arab University (q.v.). He left at the age of 22 for Saudi Arabia (q.v.), at a time when so many Lebanese dreamed of making a fortune in the oil-rich states. He taught math before opening a construction company in the 1970s. Ḥarīrī developed a deep friendship with Crown Prince Fahd, was awarded Saudi citizenship in 1978, and founded the Oger International Company the following year. His business interests extend all around the world. He founded the Ḥarīrī Foundation in the 1980s to assist needy Lebanese students in their education. This foundation has granted some 20,000 scholarships to date. He serves on the board of trustees of the American University of Beirut (q.v.).

Ḥarīrī has been prime minister since 1992. He has accumulated power, not because the constitutional changes in aṭ-Ṭā'if Accords (q.v.) shifted the center of political gravity away from the president but because his regional and international reputation overshadows the president. He conducts international negotiations and is on a first name basis with many heads of state. Ḥarīrī has been criticized for reconstructing Lebanon into a service economy and for not taking into consideration the interests of small landowners in downtown Beirut (q.v.). Unlike previous prime ministers, he has never tried to enrich himself in office. Ḥarīrī entered the Lebanese parliament for the first time in the 1996 election.

HĀSHIM, JOSEPH al- (1937–). A former official of the Lebanese Phalanges Party (q.v.), he is closely linked with the Phalangist-run Voice of Lebanon (q.v.), the most listened-to radio station in the country during the 1975 civil war (q.v.). He was born in the village of Burjayn and educated at St. Joseph University (q.v.), where he received a degree in Arabic (q.v.) literature. He taught Arabic in a number of public and private schools. He joined the Phalanges Party and wrote a column for its daily newspaper *Al-'Amal*. He is known for his oratorical skills and for his command of the written and spoken Arabic language. His name became famous during the war, when he founded and managed the Voice of Lebanon, broadcasting a daily commentary, which was partisan but eloquent. He was very close to the Gemayyel family and was appointed minister in 1984 by Amīn Gemayyel (q.v.). Within the Phalanges Party, he represented the "Arabist" line, which espoused ending the isolation of the party within the Arab world, and ending its alliance with Israel (q.v.). Al-Hāshim is still active in politics and may run in the next parliamentary election. He published a book containing a collection of his radio commentaries.

HĀSHIM, JOSEPH AL-. *SEE* ZAGHLŪL AD-DĀMŪR.

***ḤAWĀDITH, al-*.** This newsmagazine became, in the 1960s and 1970s, the most widely read Arabic publication in the entire Middle East. Its gifted editor, Salīm al-Lawzī, bought the publication in 1955 from its owner in Tripoli (q.v.) and transformed it into a political voice in the Arab world that openly supported Jamāl ‘Abdul-Nasser (q.v.). It reached the height of its popularity only after 1967, when it led an attack against Nasser and other Arab regimes, recruiting gifted writers from around the Arab world. It published investigative reports about aspects of Lebanese life and was one of the first Arab publications to dispatch correspondents around the world. Its prominence gave it unprecedented access to Arab and world leaders, who often used its pages to send political signals. It became a subservient voice of Arab oil regimes, especially Saudi Arabia (q.v.), in the 1970s. After the outbreak of civil war (q.v.) in 1975, al-Lawzī moved his magazine to London, where he maintained his residence. Al-Lawzī's criticisms of the Syrian regime reportedly led to his assassination in 1980, when he returned to Beirut (q.v.) to attend his mother's funeral.

ḤĀWĪ, KHALĪL (1925–1982). One of the most gifted and original poets in the Arab world, he was born to a poor family in Shuwayr. He first worked as a construction worker. He graduated from secondary school in Shuwayfāt in 1947 and received various scholarships and fellowships to complete his education, first at the American University of Beirut (AUB) (q.v.) and then at Cambridge University, where he wrote a dissertation on Khalil Gibran (q.v.) under the noted Orientalist A. J. Arberry. He returned to Lebanon in 1959 to teach Arabic (q.v.) literature at AUB and to lecture at the Lebanese University (q.v.). He joined the Syrian Social National Party (q.v.) in his youth but did not last long as a card-carrying member, although he remained loyal to the party's ideals throughout his life. His first book of Arabic poetry appeared in 1957; others appeared in the 1960s. He rarely made important poetic contributions in the 1970s and was unhappy about the popularity of less-talented poets, like Nizār Qabbānī. He suffered from a psychological illness and shot himself in 1982, days after Israel (q.v.) invaded Lebanon.

HELPERS PARTY (*Ḥizb al-Najjādah*). Founded in 1936, this was a major political vehicle for Beirut Sunnis (qq.v). It participated in the civil war of 1958 (q.v.), and adopted Nasserism after that. Some of its members have held parliamentary and ministerial seats over the years. In 1974, the military cadres of the party split off to form the Corrective Movement led by Jamīl Da‘būl. The party lost its political significance as early as the 1970s. Its veteran and autocratic leader. ‘Adnān al-Ḥakīm (q.v.), passed away in 1990.

HILĀL AL-KHAṢĪB, AL. *SEE* FERTILE CRESCENT.

ḤILŪ, CHARLES (1912–). Born in Beirut (q.v.), he earned a law degree from St. Joseph University (q.v.) and edited French-language newspapers in Aleppo and Beirut. His work for *Le Jour* (q.v.) introduced him to Lebanese political life and to the Lebanese political class. He was one of the five founders of the Lebanese Phalanges Party (q.v.) but later left because he knew his membership would harm his political aspirations. Ḥilū was an extraordinary envoy to the Vatican, which he viewed with special regard. He was closely associated, both culturally and politically, with France (q.v.) and the Vatican. He believed that Lebanon had a special Christian mission. He served in various cabinets and was serving as minister of education in 1964 when he became the surprise choice for president by the Lebanese parliament. Although he was a protege of Fu'ād Shihāb (q.v.), Shihāb later regarded him with disdain. Ḥilū embarked on a moderate foreign policy, trying to maintain excellent relations with the West without alienating Jamāl 'Abdul-Nasser (q.v.) and other Arab leaders. He was regarded as a well-educated and intelligent president; he worked hard to master the Arabic (q.v.) language, which was largely unfamiliar to him upon his election.

Ḥilū allowed the Deuxième Bureau (q.v.) to retain the power it had under Shihāb, when it blackmailed and harassed politicians. The bureau, however, could not stem the tide of public opposition and resentment. The Israeli bombing of South Lebanon and the issue of the Palestinian struggle split the Lebanese population; some urged that the Lebanese Army (q.v.) be used in support of the Palestine Liberation Organization; others wanted to avoid antagonizing Israel (q.v.). Ḥilū coined the slogan, "Lebanon's strength lies in its weakness," arguing for insulating Lebanon from the Arab-Israeli conflict. He almost resigned in 1969 when his Sunni (q.v.) prime minister Rashīd Karāmī (q.v.) boycotted him to protest the army's treatment of the Palestinians in Lebanon (q.v.). The crisis produced the Cairo Agreement (q.v.), which recognized Palestinian political and military rights in Lebanon. Ḥilū delivered a very precarious country to his successor and was not heard from in the 1970s until the 1975 civil war (q.v.), when he emerged to give his support to the Lebanese Front (q.v.). His influence, however, was minimal; he was needed only to lend legitimacy to the Christian coalition.

He remained active in his old age and has written his memoirs in Arabic and French. Ḥilū has been mostly active in the Association of French-Speaking Countries and has served as its chairperson. The Lebanese disagree on his legacy; some blame him for the civil war; others think that if he had been president during the war he could have ended it.

ḤIWĀR. This literary journal was published bi-monthly between 1962 and 1966. It was founded and edited by Tawfīq Ṣā'igh, who suffered for years from accusations, printed in an American publication, that he had received funding from the United States (q.v.) government. A nation-wide boycott of the journal drove Ṣā'igh to close it down. He never recovered from this experience, and it isolated him from Arab literary circles.

ḤIZB AD-DĪMŪQRĀṬĪ, AL. *SEE* DEMOCRATIC PARTY.

ḤIZB AD-DĪMŪQRĀṬĪ AL-MASĪḤĪ AL-ISHTIRĀKĪ-ḤIZB AL-'AMAL, AL. *SEE* SOCIALIST CHRISTIAN DEMOCRATIC PARTY.

ḤIZB AL-'AMAL AL-ISHTIRĀKĪ AL-'ARABĪ-LUBNĀN. *SEE* SOCIALIST ARAB ACTION PARTY—LEBANON.

ḤIZB AL-'ARABĪ AD-DĪMUQRĀṬĪ, AL. *SEE* ARAB DEMOCRATIC PARTY.

ḤIZB AL-BA'TH AL-'ARABĪ AL-ISHTIRĀKĪ. *SEE* ARAB SOCIALIST BA'TH PARTY.

ḤIZB AL-DĪMŪQRĀṬĪ AL-ISHTIRĀKĪ, AL. *SEE* DEMOCRATIC SOCIALIST PARTY.

ḤIZB AL-KATĀ'IB AL-LUBNĀNIYYAH. *SEE* LEBANESE PHALANGES PARTY.

ḤIZB AL-KUTLAH AL-WAṬANIYYAH. *SEE* NATIONAL BLOC PARTY.

ḤIZB AL-WA'D. *SEE* PROMISE PARTY.

ḤIZB AL-WAṬANIYYĪN AL-AḤRĀR. *SEE* NATIONAL LIBERAL PARTY.

ḤIZB AN-NAJJĀDHAH. *SEE* HELPERS PARTY.

ḤIZB ASH-SHUYŪ'Ī AL-LUBNĀNĪ, AL. *SEE* LEBANESE COMMUNIST PARTY.

ḤIZB AS-SŪRĪ AL-QAWMĪ AL-IJTIMĀ'Ī, AL. *SEE* SYRIAN SOCIAL NATIONAL PARTY.

ḤIZB AT-TAḤARRUR AL-'ARABĪ. *SEE* PARTY OF ARAB LIBERATION.

ḤIZB AT-TAQADDUMĪ AL-ISHTIRĀKĪ, AL. *SEE* PROGRESSIVE SOCIALIST PARTY.

ḤIZB ḤURRĀS AL-ARZ. *SEE* GUARDIANS OF THE CEDARS.

ḤIZBULLĀH. *SEE* PARTY OF GOD.

HOLY SPIRIT UNIVERSITY AT AL-KASLĪK. This university was founded in 1962 by the Maronite Monastic Order. The languages of instruction are French and Arabic (q.v.). It has faculties in theology, philosophy and human sciences, letters, law, management, fine arts, agronomy, and music. It was considered the intellectual nerve center of the Maronite (q.v.) establishment during the 1975–90 civil war (q.v.), when theologians at the university produced a number of pamphlets in which the Christian identity of Lebanon (q.v.) was affirmed. Other professors advanced ideas of federalism and confederalism, which—in the eyes of its critics—pose a threat to the territorial integrity of Lebanon. Its program in theology is highly regarded. In 1991–92, it had 2,186 students.

HOMOSEXUALITY. As in other Arab countries, homosexual sex is specifically prohibited by law in Lebanon. The state rarely prosecutes offenders, although a few unfortunates (always from poor families) are sometimes arrested. Homosexuality is less condemned by Islam than in Christianity. The Qur'an only briefly mentions homosexuality, but Islamic law prohibits homosexual acts. Lesbianism is less covered by the law. In recent times, homosexual groups have become more active, although society is opposed to homosexual advocacy organizations. Christianity is more intolerant of homosexuality, and this is partly reflected in the Lebanese culture. Yet, many prominent Lebanese politicians were known homosexuals, and a bill proposed in the 1960s by then deputy Munīr Abū Fāḍil to ban homosexuals from holding public office never passed.

HRĀWĪ, ILYĀS (1930–). He was born into a large landowning family that regularly represented Zaḥlah (q.v.) in parliament. His two deceased brothers served in parliament before him, and his uncle became deputy in 1943. He did not have a university education and was mostly an agrarian businessman before winning a parliamentary seat in the 1972 election on the list of Joseph Skāf. He was supportive of Sulaymān Franjiyyah (q.v.) and was considered a moderate Maronite (q.v.) politician who maintained good ties with most sides and with the Syrian (q.v.) government, which has a lot of influence in his region. He tried to establish a militia of his own during the 1975 civil war (q.v.) but could not compete with the more powerful forces of the Lebanese Phalanges Party (q.v.) and the National Liberal Party (q.v.).

He remained close to the Lebanese Forces and the Lebanese Front (qq.v.) during the war, without severing his ties with the Syrian regime. In fact, he often served as a mediator between the two sides especially when Bashīr Gemayyel (q.v.) provoked the Syrian troops in Lebanon. He served as a minister in the administration of Ilyās Sarkīs (q.v.) His election to the presidency was surprising; the assassination of president Rene Mu'awwaḍ (q.v.) in 1989 brought Hrāwī forward as a compromise candidate, and he was elected within days of Mu'awwaḍ's assassination. His administration has been closely and consistently aligned with Syrian interests in Lebanon. He succeeded in implementing many of the terms of the aṭ-Ṭā'if Accords (q.v.), including the dissolution of the militias with the exception of armed groups in South Lebanon, which comprise the bulk of the National Resistance (q.v.) movement against Israeli (q.v.) occupation of Lebanon.

Hrāwī appointed his son-in-law, Fāris Buwayz (q.v.), as foreign minister, and he has been his closest advisor. His son, however, was defeated in the 1992 elections. Hrāwī is well-liked among Muslims but lacks popular support in his own Maronite community. He is criticized for being too subservient to Syrian wishes and dictates. His loyalty to Syria, however, has paid off: the Lebanese parliament amended the constitution (q.v.) in 1995 to permit him to serve three years beyond his six-year term. His association with Rafīq Ḥarīrī (q.v.) helped his administration, given Ḥarīrī's influence and international connections. Ḥarīrī, however, managed to take on much of Ḥrāwī's presidential power due to his regional and international standing.

ḤUBAYQAH, ELIE. *SEE* PROMISE PARTY.

ḤUBAYQAH, NAJĪB (1869–1906). This educator was born in Shuwayr and received his college education in Beirut at St. Joseph University (qq.v.). He excelled in Arabic (q.v.) literature and taught Arabic at St. Joseph University. He later taught Arabic at Al-Ḥikmah school. In 1903, he assumed the editorship of *Al-Miṣbāḥ*. His articles also appeared in *Al-Mashriq* (q.v.) and *Al-Maḥabbah*. He was interested in theater and wrote and translated several plays. Ḥubayqah is best known for school textbooks on Arabic (*Darajāt Al-Inshā'*).

HUNCHAK PARTY. This originally Marxist-oriented party, which was founded in 1887 in Geneva, moderated its doctrine to fit the environment in Lebanon (q.v.). The party has avoided taking extreme and controversial positions in Lebanese politics for fear of jeopardizing the status of the Armenians (q.v.) in Lebanon. It has maintained good ties with the Dashnak Party (q.v.), the major Armenian party in Lebanon, although the two parties engaged in bloody clashes in the 1950s. This party has recruited working-class Armenians, although it has intellectuals and professionals in its leadership and membership. One party leader was elected to parliament in 1992.

ḤURRIYYAH, al-. This magazine was published between 1964 and 1969 as the weekly mouthpiece of the Movement of Arab Nationalists (q.v.). It was edited by Muḥsin Ibrāhīm, who turned it into an effective leftist polemical publication. After the dissolution of the Movement of Arab Nationalists, the magazine was turned over to the Democratic Front for the Liberation of Palestine, which published it as its weekly mouthpiece.

ḤUSAYNĪ, ḤUSAYN al- (1937–). He was born to a prominent family in Shmisṭār near Ba'albak (q.v.). He first ran for public office in 1964, entering the parliament in 1972, through his close friendship with Imām Mūsā aṣ-Ṣadr (q.v.). His political role in Lebanese political life was small before 1978, when he became an active parliamentarian. He was once beaten up by thugs working for rival Shi'ite (q.v.) leader Kāmil al-As'ad (q.v.), who detested aṣ-Ṣadr for his threat to al-As'ad's leadership. In 1978, after years of working behind the scenes in the Amal Movement (q.v.) , al-Ḥusaynī assumed the leadership of the movement after the mysterious "disappearance" of aṣ-Ṣadr during an official trip to Libya (q.v.). His tenure at the helm of Amal was not smooth; he often clashed with more militant members. In 1980, Nabīh Birrī (q.v.), his arch rival, assumed the leadership role.

In 1984, al-Ḥusaynī assumed the most powerful position a Shi'ite can hold; with strong backing from Syria (q.v.), he was elected speaker of parliament. He held the position until 1992, when his arch rival, Birrī, again unseated him. Al-Ḥusaynī's showing in the 1992 election was poor; candidates of the Party of God (q.v.) achieved great success at his expense. A member of his list who was elected with him, Yaḥyā Shamaṣ (q.v.), was tried and convicted of drug trafficking in 1996. Al-Ḥusaynī has been a vocal critic of Rafīq Ḥarīrī (q.v.), and he seems to blame his showing in the 1992 election on Ḥarīrī. In the 1900s he has been marginalized in the Shi'ite community, although he was reelected to parliament in the 1996 elections.

ḤUṢṢ, SALĪM al- (1929–). This former prime minister is now one of the most important Sunni (q.v.) politicians in Lebanon (q.v.). His entry into Lebanese political life was relatively late. He was an orphan but excelled in school first at the International College and then at the American University of Beirut (AUB) (q.v.), where he studied economics. He then earned a Ph.D. in economics from Indiana University. He taught at AUB for years and did consulting work for the Kuwaiti government in the 1960s. While he did not take an overt political role in Lebanon, he was appointed in 1967 as chair of the state council that monitors banking activities in Lebanon. He became a close friend of Ilyās Sarkīs (q.v.), who was then the governor of the central bank. Al-Ḥuṣṣ was married to a Christian woman (she died in 1990), which is not common among people with political ambitions in Lebanon.

When Sarkīs was elected president in 1976, he appointed al-Ḥuṣṣ prime minister, a post he filled in the following two administrations (under Amīn Gemayyel, and under Ilyās Hrāwī, qq.v.). While he was considered a political moderate, he was criticized bitterly by some Maronite (q.v.) leaders for standing up to Sarkīs, with whom he had frequent disagreements over both internal appointments (and their sectarian repercussions) and foreign policy. In general, however, al-Ḥuṣṣ remains one of the most widely respected figures in contemporary Lebanon; his name has not been tainted by any scandal or rumors of corruption. He is seen as a principled politician among a group in which principles are often traded like money. His views tend to conform to the moderate views of the Sunni political establishment, although he appoints on the basis of merit and qualifications and does not engage in sectarian agitation. He ran his campaign for parliament in the 1992 election on a platform of "salvation and reform." He is strongly critical of the Israeli occupation of South Lebanon and has maintained close ties with the Syrian (q.v.) regime. He is seen as less subservient to Damascus, however, than most political leaders in Lebanon.

Al-Ḥuṣṣ has published three books on his experience in government and remains active in Lebanese political life. His power base is Beirut (q.v.), but his popularity extends to most parts of Lebanon. He is committed to the free enterprise system but believes that the government has a role in reducing the gap between the rich and the poor. He is highly critical of Western governmental support of Israel (q.v.) in the region. Al-Ḥuṣṣ served as de facto president in most of Lebanon in 1988 when Amīn Gemayyel (q.v.) appointed the commander-in-chief of the army as president. He assumed acting presidential powers until the election of Rene Mu'awwaḍ (q.v.) in 1989. He won a seat in the 1996 election, contrary to the wishes of Prime Minister Rafīq Ḥarīrī (q.v.).

ḤŪT, SHAFĪQ al-. This independent member of the Palestine Liberation Organization (PLO) who consistently refused to join any PLO organization has been immersed in Lebanese political life since the 1950s. A journalist, he wrote and edited several publications, including *Al-Ḥawādith* and *Al-Muḥarrir* (qq.v.). He is praised for his honesty and moderation. He broke with Yāsir 'Arafāt (q.v.) after the latter signed the Oslo Agreement in 1993. The administration of president Ilyās Hrāwī (q.v.) has forbidden al-Ḥūt from re-opening the PLO's office in Beirut (q.v.).

-I-

IBRĀHĪM, EMILY FĀRIS (1914–). This pioneer feminist was born in New York City and left shortly thereafter for Lebanon (q.v.). She was educated in Beirut (q.v.) and worked as a translator. She was one of the first feminists in Lebanon, calling attention to the lack of female representation in parliament. In 1953, she was the first woman to run for parliament. She subsequently ran in several elections but did not win.

IBRĀHĪM, MUḤSIN. *SEE* COMMUNIST ACTION ORGANIZATION.

'ĪD, 'ALĪ (1942–). This former deputy was born to an 'Alawite (q.v.) family in Tripoli (q.v.). He received his education at the American University of Beirut (q.v.), where he was known as a pro-Syrian (q.v.) activist. During the 1975 civil war (q.v.) he was an ally of Syrian Vice-president Rif'at Al-Asad and was a founder of several pro-Syrian organizations. His groups were notorious for their corruption and thuggery. His latest party is called the Democratic Arab Party. He was elected to the 1992 parliament but failed to win a seat in the 1996 election.

IDDĪ, EMILE (1886–1949). He was president of Lebanon (q.v.) during the French Mandate (q.v.) and is associated in the minds of the Lebanese with resistance to Lebanese independence. A Maronite (q.v.) Christian lawyer, he was more French than Lebanese, at least in cultural affinity and political orientation. He never wanted a Lebanon that contained a large Muslim population: Muslims were too Arab and too non-Western for his tastes. The Muslims were as unfriendly toward him, especially when the statement: "Let the Muslims go back to Mecca" was attributed to him. He served in the administration of the mandate and was elected president in 1936. He held several meetings with Zionist leaders and expressed sympathy for Zionist goals, which he found similar to his objective of establishing a Christian home in Lebanon free of Muslim-Arab influence. He founded the National Bloc Party (q.v.) in the 1930s to support the French presence and influence in Lebanon against the Constitutional Bloc (q.v.), which stood for Muslim-Christian understanding. Iddī was unwilling to grant the Muslims the necessary political concessions that made Lebanese sectarian coexistence possible. His loyalty to France (q.v.) was exemplified in 1939, when he accepted the presidency even when the French authority suspended the constitution (q.v.) and when most Lebanese politicians were critical of France. After independence, Iddī was discredited, and he was expelled from parliament. *See also* Iddī, Raymond.

IDDĪ, PIERRE (1921–1997). This Lebanese politician and son of Emile Iddī (q.v.) was never able to match the power and charisma of his brother Raymond (q.v.). He became known to the Lebanese in the 1940s as his father's timid secretary. He served in various parliaments and cabinets, especially in the area of finance. He was mainly involved in business in Brazil and abandoned political life in 1975, although his name was sometimes mentioned as a candidate for high office.

IDDĪ, RAYMOND (1913–). He is one of the most dynamic legislators in the contemporary history of Lebanon. A son of Emile (q.v.), he was born in Alexandria and moved to Beirut (q.v.) to earn a degree in law from St. Joseph University (q.v.). He succeeded his father in the leadership of the National Bloc Party (q.v.), but charted an independent political course. With the exception of the 1964 election, when he refused to run in the controversial election, he was a member of parliament from 1953 until 1992. In the 1968 election, Iddī aligned himself with Kamīl Sham'ūn (q.v.) and Pierre Gemayyel (q.v.) to form the Tripartite Alliance and won in a landslide victory.

Iddī distinguished himself in ministerial posts and was known for his honesty and integrity, which has won him support even among Muslim voters. He was an opposition voice in all administrations, but was an especially bitter enemy of Fu'ād Shihāb (q.v.) because he opposed military intervention in politics. Iddī considered Shihabism, communism, and Zionism as the three most dangerous threats to Lebanese security and prosperity. The list of his legislative accomplishments includes the creation of special security troops (Force 16); the elimination of progressive taxes on agricultural land; the joint accounts' law; banking secrecy laws; and criminal laws regarding the execution of murderers. Iddī was an early critic of governmental neglect of South Lebanon; he urged the government to invite U.N. troops to protect the border areas from Israeli raids and incursions. He ran for the office of president several times and was still considered a serious presidential contender in the 1990s.

Iddī's political path shifted in 1975 when he broke with the Maronite (q.v.) establishment and accused the Lebanese Phalanges Party (q.v.) of working for the destruction of Lebanon (q.v.). He resided in West Beirut (q.v.), away from right-wing influence, and struck a new alliance with Kamāl Jumblāṭ (q.v.) and the Palestine Liberation Organization. Iddī was a vocal critic of Syrian (and Israeli) intervention in Lebanese affairs. He accused Syria (q.v.) of plotting his assassination and left Lebanon for Paris in 1976, in the wake of an assassination attempt. He continued his political activities from exile, often making statements and issuing directives to the party in Lebanon. His analysis of the 1975 civil war (q.v.) is conspiratorial; he accuses Henry Kissinger (q.v.) of planning and guiding the destruction of Lebanon as a service to Israel (q.v.). In 1996, he called for the boycott of the parliamentary election.

IDRĪS, SUHAYL. This writer was born in Beirut (q.v.) and educated in Paris, where he earned a Ph.D. in Arabic (q.v.) literature. He wrote well-received novels and coauthored one of the best French-Arabic dictionaries. He devoted his career, however, to the publishing house he founded, *Al-Ādāb,* which has published since 1953 a monthly literary magazine by the same name and, in addition, he published works by writers from different Arab countries. He espoused an Arab nationalist, pro-Palestinian line. His son, Samāḥ, has assumed the editorial responsibilities of the magazine in recent years.

IHDIN. A town 38 kilometers from Zghartā in the north, it is the seat of the Franjiyyah family. It underwent tremendous development and construction during the presidential term of Sulaymān Franjiyyah (q.v.), who linked it to other towns through major highways. Franjiyyah also built himself a palace there.

IMĀM. This Arabic (q.v.) word originally meant a person who leads the Muslim community in prayer and stems from a root that means "in the forefront of." In the Shi'ite (q.v.) twelvers tradition, it refers to one of the twelve *imāms*, beginning with 'Alī and ending with the missing *imām,* the Awaited, Rightly-Guided One. It is also used in some Shi'ite circles to refer to somebody high in the religious hierarchy. It was used by Imām Mūsā aṣ-Ṣadr (q.v.), and was adopted by his successor, Muḥammad Mahdī Shams ad-Dīn.

INQILĀB. This Arabic (q.v.) word means coup d'état and in Lebanon refers to the only two coups d'état in modern Lebanese history. The first *inqilāb* was the December 1961 attempt by the Syrian Social National Party (q.v.) to seize power through control of the military. The attempt failed, the party was crushed, and its members were subjected to years of harassment, which changed and radicalized the party. This *inqilāb* represented the most successful infiltration of the Lebanese Army (q.v.) by any political party.

The second *inqilāb,* in March 1976, was led by 'Azīz Al-Aḥdab, a Sunni (q.v.) general of the Lebanese Army, who, with the support of the Palestine Liberation Organization proclaimed a movement to end the 1975 civil war (q.v.). The *inqilāb* lasted only a few weeks, because al-Aḥdab's force was easily outgunned.

INSTITUT DE RECHERCHE ET DE FORMATION EN VUE DU DÉVELOPPEMENT (IRFID). IRFID was a French mission invited by President Fu'ād Shihāb (q.v.) to assess social and economic conditions in the country. The commission published its report in Arabic (q.v.) and French in May 1961, noting the "enormous disparities in living standards" between Beirut (q.v.) and Mount Lebanon on the one hand, and other regions of the country. The report intensified calls for social and economic reforms to avert political destabilization.

INTRA BANK CRASH. The Intra Bank, owned by naturalized Palestinian businessman Yūsuf Baydas, was once the largest bank in Lebanon (q.v.), with financial powers equal to, if not exceeding, those of the Lebanese government. Its crash in October 1966 left a lasting impact on the Lebanese economy. Baydas had holdings in Europe and the United States (q.v.), but his Palestinian identity was not forgotten by his many enemies in Lebanon. There is no consensus on the reasons for the crash, but it is clear that it was deliberately planned while Baydas was away. Sunni (q.v.) politician Ṣā'ib Salām (q.v.) and others in the predominantly Catholic financial elite were perhaps responsible for circulating a leaflet warning bank clients about a severe liquidity problem at the bank. When clients began withdrawing funds, the bank was suddenly in a cash crisis. The central bank, however, going against its own mission, rejected Baydas's repeated appeals for cash aid (prompting the *New York Times* to observe: "The credit squeeze against Intra was spearheaded by the Central Bank.") The collapse of Intra coincided with the financial collapse of Baydas, who died in exile in 1969. As a result of the crash, the number of Lebanese banks dropped and foreign banks increased their hold over the Lebanese economy. Arab oil money was also moved to banks in Europe and the United States.

***IQṬĀ'*.** Literally, it means "feudalism," but it refers to the semi-feudal system in Lebanon and elsewhere, where inheritance of estates was not the norm and so is distinguished from the feudalism of Europe.

***'IRFĀN, al-*.** This journal was one of the first of its kind in Lebanon. It was founded as a monthly publication in 1909 in Sidon (q.v.) by Shaykh Aḥmad 'Ārif az-Zayn (1881–1960). It carried articles on history, literature, ethics, society, and science. It was a rare voice for Shi'ites (q.v.) in the Middle East at a time when their very existence was controversial and their beliefs were ridiculed by the Sunni (q.v.) majority. It is now studied by historians who look for indications of Shi'ite public opinion in the first half of this century. It still publishes, notwithstanding several interruptions over the years.

ISḤĀQ, ADĪB (1856–1885). He was born in Damascus and grew up in Beirut (q.v.). He edited the newspaper *At-Taqaddum* in Beirut before leaving for Egypt, which used to attract many Syrian intellectuals. He founded the newspaper *Miṣr,* which he subsequently turned into a daily newspaper and renamed *At-Tijārah.* He then left for Paris, where he published an Arabic journal. He was later appointed head of the translation section in the Ministry of Culture in Egypt. He met and was highly influenced by famed Islamic revolutionary Jamāl ad-Dīn al-Afghānī. He returned to Beirut after the British occupation. He is famous for political commentary, which was then new in Arabic literature. He was opposed to foreign domination of Arab affairs and urged the people to seek progress.

ISLAMIC AMAL MOVEMENT (*Ḥarakat Amal al-Islāmiyyah*). This movement, headed by Ḥusayn al-Mūsawī, split from the Amal Movement (q.v.) in June 1982 when Nabīh Birrī (q.v.) joined the Salvation Committee, which president Ilyās Sarkīs (q.v.) formed after the Israeli invasion of 1982 (q.v.), and which included, among other members, Bashīr Gemayyel (q.v.). Al-Mūsawī considered Birrī's participation tantamount to treason, given Bashīr's relations with the Israelis and his anti-Muslim attitude. Furthermore, Islamic Amal rejected what it considered the "secular" orientations of Amal. Al-Mūsawī has shaped and molded the party according to his own beliefs and has resisted Iranian pressure to merge the party with the Party of God (q.v.). For a brief period, he sat on the leadership council of the Party of God, but he withdrew in order to retain organizational independence. The movement seems to be confined to areas near Ba'albak (q.v.), from which al-Mūsawī hailed. Al-Mūsawī has been linked in press reports to various anti-U.S. actions in Lebanon during the 1980s, although he has denied responsibility.

ISLAMIC COMMUNITY (*Al-Jamā'ah al-Islāmiyyah*). This Sunni (q.v.) militant fundamentalist movement was founded in 1964 in Tripoli (q.v.) and was led by influential Sunni fundamentalist thinker Fatḥī Yakan (q.v.) and Sunni writer Muḥammad 'Alī aḍ-Ḍinnāwī. It advocated the establishment of an Islamic society in Lebanon based solely on Islamic law. The organization believed in political violence and established its own military arm, *al-Mujahidūn* (Religious Strugglers) in 1976. The militia participated in the 1975 civil war (q.v.) on the side of the leftist-Islamic coalition in Tripoli. Fatḥī Yakan, who is a widely known author among Islamic fundamentalists throughout the Arab world, brought prestige and publicity to the movement. He and two colleagues were elected to parliament in 1992. The party was engaged in a bitter feud with the al-Ḥabashī Group (q.v.) in the 1990s.

ISLAMIC JIHAD ORGANIZATION (***Munaḍhḍhamat Al-Jihād Al-Islāmī***). It is not known that there is a real organization with this name. It is certain, however, that some political group used that name to claim responsibility for several violent acts against the U.S., French, and Israeli presence in Lebanon (qq.v.) in the 1980s. Bombings of American diplomatic and military sites, in addition to hostage taking, were perpetrated in the name of this organization. Press reports linked it to a variety of Shi'ite (q.v.) fundamentalist organizations, but those reports relied on rumors and speculation. The Party of God (q.v.), for one, denies any links to this organization.

ISLAMIC MEETING (***Al-Liqā' al-Islāmī***). This grouping had its origins in meetings held by Muftī (q.v.) Ḥasan Khālid (q.v.) in his house in 'Aramūn in 1975 to coordinate Muslim affairs among key politicians and officials. It was later formalized and called *at-tajammu' al-Islāmī* (Islamic Grouping). It embraced the "club" of traditional Sunni (q.v.) politicians, mostly prime ministerial aspirants. It includes former prime ministers, former ministers, current and former deputies, and individual traditional Sunni politicians. The Islamic Meeting takes a relatively moderate stance, usually in support of the incumbent prime minister, particularly in the face of Christian attacks. Meetings of the group decreased after the death of Khālid.

ISLAMIC MOVEMENT IN LEBANON (***Al-Ḥarakah al-Islāmiyyah fī Lubnān***). This highly secretive organization announced its existence in a leaflet in 1983, but its leader, Shaykh Ṣādiq al-Mūsawī, had been active in militant Shi'ite (q.v.) politics since the 1970s. This obscure organization was probably the first Shi'ite group, long before the creation of the Party of God (q.v.), to call for the immediate establishment of an Islamic republic in Lebanon (q.v.). It considered the Party of God too moderate and not sufficiently dedicated to the Iranian line in Lebanon. The movement called for the election of a Shi'ite cleric as president in 1988. Al-Mūsawī had close ties to the Iranian government and was frequently featured in the Iranian press, where he sometimes wrote commentaries on Lebanese affairs.

ISLAMIC RESISTANCE. *SEE* NATIONAL RESISTANCE.

ISLAMIC UNIFICATION MOVEMENT (***Ḥarakat at-Tawḥīd al-Islāmī***). This Tripoli-based movement is one of the most famous Sunni (q.v.) fundamentalist groups in Lebanon (q.v.). Its leader (or "prince," according to the movement's terminology), Shaykh Sa'īd Sha'bān, was able to assert his authority over the whole city in 1983 in defiance of Syria (q.v.) by attracting the city's numerous and highly active lumpenproletariat. Sha'bān was a member of the conservative, pro-Saudi movement of Muslim Brotherhood before founding the movement in 1982. The movement was the result of a merger of three Tripoli-based Islamic fundamentalist groups: Jundullāh, al-Muqawāmah ash-Sha'biyyah, and the Movement of Arab Lebanon. The first two groups had split from the Islamic Unification Movement by the summer of 1984, denying Sha'bān important power bases in the neighborhoods of Tibbānah and Abū Samrā in Tripoli (q.v.). Sha'bān saw no way out of the 1975–90 civil war (q.v.) except through an application of Islamic laws. Strongly hostile to communism, the movement engaged in bloody massacres against local communists in 1983. The Syrian army later intervened and ended Sha'bān's rule in the city. In recent years, Sha'bān has become an enthusiastic ally of Iran and has improved his relations with the Syrian government.

ISMA'ILI SECT. There are only a few hundred Isma'ilis in Lebanon (q.v.). They are also known as "Seveners," because they believe Isma'īl was the seventh *imām*. The sect is divided into two branches: the Mustalian branch is found primarily in Yemen, and the Nizari branch is found in the Iranian district of Salamiya, Afghanistan, Central Asian states, India, the Chitral and Gilgit areas of Pakistan, and East Africa. The split was over a succession dispute. The current Nizari *imām* is revealed and known as the Agha Khan.

ISOLATION OF THE PHALANGISTS. This slogan was raised by Kamāl Jumblāṭ (q.v.) and his supporters in the wake of the massacre of Palestinians (q.v.) in 'Ayn Ar-Rummānah (q.v.) in 1975. He called for a national isolation of the Lebanese Phalanges Party (q.v.) in national political life. The Palestine Liberation Organization supported Jumblāṭ and his leftist allies in their efforts to undermine the credibility of the party in Lebanese popular opinion and to force the party to assume responsibility for the massacre, which triggered the 1975 civil war (q.v.). The policy failed miserably, as the Phalanges gained sympathy and support from many Christians.

ISRAEL. Israeli interest in Lebanon (q.v.) preceded the establishment of the Jewish state. Many Zionist leaders found common ground between them and Maronite (q.v.) leaders. Recent studies have disclosed the extent of Maronite-Zionist contacts before and after the establishment of the state of Israel. Indeed, it has been revealed that the Lebanese Phalanges Party (q.v.) received aid and support from Israel as early as the 1950s, even though most Lebanese assumed that Israeli-Phalangist contacts were triggered by the Lebanese civil war in 1975 (q.v.). Official Lebanon, of course, had to abide by the Arab consensus, paying lip service to the Palestinian cause. In 1948, contrary to official Lebanese textbooks, Lebanon avoided combat with the Jewish state, and when fighting loomed, Lebanese armed forces were withdrawn from the southern border area, allowing Israel to occupy a strip of land.

The Arab-Israeli conflict affected Lebanese politics in several ways. Lebanon received an influx of Palestinian (q.v.) refugees who had lost their homes, and many Lebanese became hostile to Israel because of their sympathy with the uprooted Palestinians. In addition, the requirements of Arab solidarity affected the implementation of the National Pact (q.v.). Some Lebanese were eager for their country's participation in a collective Arab action to restore Arab rights in Palestine, while others wished to insulate Lebanon from the Arab-Israeli confrontation. The conflict created hostility toward the West in general, and the United States (q.v.) in particular, and there were constant demands in Lebanon for political confrontation with the United States. Many called on the government to sever its ties with the U.S. to punish it for its unequivocal support of the Jewish state.

The Lebanese dream of living on a political island separated from the region's problem was dashed in the 1960s when armed Palestinian groups emerged in Lebanon, many of them engaging in infiltration attacks against targets in Israel. Israeli responses were swift and massive, often punishing Lebanese civilians and government installations to put pressure on the political elite to end its toleration of Palestinian revolutionary activity. The Lebanese government, or a segment of it, was sympathetic to the Israeli position, because Maronite leaders knew that the political and military weight of Palestinian resistance would strengthen the bargaining position of Lebanese Muslims. They also knew that the prestige of the Lebanese Army (q.v.) would suffer if the state tolerated the "revolution within," or—in the language of Phalangist leaders—the "state-within-a-state" (q.v.).

The escalation of the Palestinian-Israeli war on Lebanese soil made the "Jordan solution," that is, the military elimination of the Palestine Liberation Organization (PLO) forces in Lebanon, all the more desirable. The relocation of PLO headquarters from Jordan to Lebanon in the wake of Black September (when King Ḥusayn's forces expelled PLO forces from Jordan) increased the pressure on the Lebanese ruling elite to act. Right-wing militias made it clear that if the state did not act they were themselves willing to act, clearly overestimating their own military strength or hoping for large-scale Israeli military intervention. Sulaymān Franjiyyah (q.v.) was the perfect man for the job, in the eyes of Lebanese nationalists. His anti-Palestinian credentials are impeccable and his own militia was formed under the pretext of safeguarding Lebanon's sovereignty, a euphemism for preparing for the ultimate showdown with the Palestinians in Lebanon. The Lebanese attempt in 1973 to crush the PLO was a failure. The Lebanese Army was weak and poorly trained, and at least half of the population was more sympathetic to the PLO than to the state. Moreover, Arab official reactions were strong, and Syria (q.v.) closed its borders with Lebanon, which cost the economy millions of dollars worth of trade.

The outbreak of the civil war, the collapse of the state, and the gradual demise of the Lebanese armed forces allowed Israel to enter South Lebanon and occupy a border area under the pretext that Lebanon was no longer able to protect its border. It established contacts with Lebanese Christians and promised them humanitarian assistance. It also began training and salarying young armed Lebanese men to form the nucleus of what would later emerge as the South Lebanon Army (q.v.). But the entrance of Israel into Lebanon increased, rather than decreased, the intensity of the Palestinian-Israeli conflict and allowed Israel to establish itself as one of the key external powers in Lebanese internal affairs, and Israel and Syria emerged as the most important regional players in the Lebanese civil war.

By 1978, after Israel's invasion of 1978 (q.v.), the southern border region came under direct Israeli rule when the South Lebanon Army was formed and Sa'd Ḥaddād (q.v.) was installed as its head. He was treated almost as a head of state by Israel, and Israeli prime ministers paid official visits to Ḥaddād, hailing him as a hero and a friend of the "free world." The presence of the United Nations Interim Force in Lebanon (q.v.) did not affect the hostility between the PLO and Israel and the Israeli-Palestinian war intensified until 1981, when an American-mediated cease-fire was arranged. The agreement was beneficial to both sides: the PLO enjoyed full control of its mini-state in Lebanon, while Israeli occupation of the southern strip was recognized. They both wanted to be spared attacks by the other.

The 1982 Israeli invasion (q.v.) constituted a watershed in Israel's role in Lebanon. During the first few months, the invasion was a success from the Israeli perspective. Militarily, the Israeli army was victorious, despite stiff resistance; the PLO was cornered and squeezed within West Beirut (q.v.), and Israel's allies in Lebanon were about to seize power. Israeli success, however, did not continue. Lebanese popular passivity to Israeli occupation of the South, after years of the PLO's rule of corruption and misconduct, eventually changed to hostility. Israeli occupation practices, and the disruption of daily lives, produced mass resentment. A resistance movement was formed, and Israeli casualties mounted. More important, Israel's choice for the presidency, Bashīr Gemayyel (q.v.) was assassinated days after his election, and his, successor Amīn Gemayyel (q.v.), was too intimately aware of the delicate internal balance of the country to serve Israel as obediently as his brother had.

By 1985, Israel gave up on its plan to control Lebanon or to force Syria out of Lebanon. Instead, it withdrew back to the border area it had been occupying since at least 1976. While the PLO was evicted from Lebanon, a new anti-Israeli force emerged: the Shi'ite (q.v.) fundamentalist movement was born within the womb of the Israeli invasion, which had left 20,000 Lebanese and Palestinian dead. The Islamic-oriented resistance movement, which Israel labeled "terrorist," continued its attacks against the Israeli presence in South Lebanon. The hope of a peace treaty was completely dashed in 1984 when the 1983 May 17 Agreement (q.v.) was officially abrogated (the parliament followed suit in 1987). Lebanon participated in the Madrid Conference and the ensuing Arab-Israeli talks, but no progress was made. Lebanon was calling for an immediate and complete Israeli withdrawal from Lebanon according to the terms of U.N. Security Council Resolution 425 (q.v.), while Israel insisted on the disarming of "terrorist groups" in Lebanon. Israeli bombing raids continued almost on a weekly basis, and in April 1996 the Israeli army invaded Lebanon, driving 500,000 Lebanese from their houses. As had been the case before, the fighting stopped only when the United States intervened diplomatically. The Lebanese antipathy toward Israel is now more prevalent than ever.

ISRAELI INVASION OF 1978. Following a raid in Israel by the Fatḥ (q.v.) movement, the government of Menachem Begin in Israel (q.v.) launched an invasion of Lebanon (q.v.) in March 1978, eventually occupying all of South Lebanon. The international community put pressure on Israel to withdraw, and the United Nations Security Council issued Resolution 425 (q.v.), which called on Israel to withdraw to the international borders between the two countries. U.N. peacekeeping force (United Nations Interim Force in Lebanon, q.v.) was deployed to separate the combatants. Israel withdrew but retained a strip of land in South Lebanon, from which it has not withdrawn. Fighting continued, and the U.N. troops were ignored.

ISRAELI INVASION OF 1982. This was the largest and most massive invasion of Lebanon by Israel (q.v.). When Israeli ambassador Shlomo Argov was shot by gunmen belonging to the Abū Niḍāl organization—which is not a member of the Palestine Liberation Organization— Israel responded by moving its army and occupying South Lebanon and parts of Beirut (q.v.). Some 20,000 Palestinians and Lebanese died as a result of the invasion and the massive and indiscriminate bombing that accompanied it. Israel insisted that PLO forces, which were concentrated in West Beirut (q.v.), be forced to leave Lebanon. A siege was imposed on West Beirut, where food, water, and electricity were denied to the city and its inhabitants. The deadlock, and the bombing, continued until American mediation brought about an agreement by which the PLO agreed to withdraw its forces from Lebanon. The evacuation of PLO forces was followed by a massacre of Palestinian refugees in the Ṣabrā and Shātīlā (q.v.) refugee camps, which prompted President Ronald Reagan to send American troops to Lebanon.

Some southern Lebanese were initially pleased that the PLO forces were expelled from their villages, but Israeli practices in South Lebanon changed public opinion against the Israeli occupation. An armed resistance movement was formed to force Israel out of Lebanon. Israel did withdraw but retained, as was the case in 1978, a strip of Lebanese territory that it called its "security zone," which was ruled by Israeli troops and their surrogate militia, known as the South Lebanon Army (q.v.). Israel also tried to influence domestic Lebanese politics by helping install right-wing militia leader Bashīr Gemayyel (q.v.) as president of Lebanon. He was elected president in the summer of 1982 but was killed before assuming the office. His brother, Amīn (q.v.), became president in his stead and signed the May 17, 1983, Agreement (q.v.) between the two countries (it was later abrogated).

ITTIḤĀD AL-ISHTIRĀKĪ AL-'ARABĪ, AL. *SEE* ARAB SOCIALIST UNION.

ITTIḤĀD AL-ISHTIRĀKĪ AL-'ARABĪ—AT-TANḌHĪM AN-NĀṢIRĪ, AL. *SEE* ARAB SOCIALIST UNION-THE NASSERIST ORGANIZATION.

ITTIḤĀD AL-'ULAMĀ' AL-MUSLIMĪN. *SEE* UNION OF ISLAMIC 'ULAMĀ'.

ITTIḤĀD QIWĀ ASH-SHA'B AL-'ĀMIL—AT-TANḌHĪM AN-NĀṢIRĪ. *SEE* UNION OF THE FORCES OF THE WORKING PEOPLE—THE NASSERIST ORGANIZATION.

-J-

JABHAH AL-LUBNĀNYYAH, AL. *SEE* LEBANESE FRONT.

JABHAT AT-TAḤRĪR AL-YAZBAKIYYAH. *SEE* YAZBAKI LIBERATION FRONT.

JACOBITE CHRISTIANS. The Jacobites, or Syrian Monophysites, often referred to as Syrian Orthodox, take their name from Jacob Baradeus, who spread the teachings of the church throughout Syria in the sixth century. The doctrinal position of the Jacobites is that, after the incarnation, Christ had only one divine nature. This is contrary to the Orthodox Christian position, which states that Christ had both a human and a divine nature. The church follows the Syriac liturgy of St. James and has an independent hierarchy under the patriarch of Antioch, whose seat was formerly at Mardin, in Turkish Kurdistan (q.v.) and is now at Hums, Syria (q.v.). There are only a few thousand Jacobites in Lebanon.

JA'JA', SAMĪR (1952–). The family background of this militia leader is modest although his extended family is one of the historical feudal families in the Bshirrī area; his father was a soldier in the Lebanese Army (q.v.). Ja'ja' was intensely religious and often volunteered in local churches. He had been active in Phalanges circles in his teens and continued these activities while a medical student at the American University of Beirut (q.v.). He was known for his extremism; mutual coexistence was repugnant to him. He did not complete his medical studies (although he was nicknamed *al-ḥakīm,* the physician), leaving them for military duties with the Phalangist militia in the 1975 civil war (q.v.). He had his own following within the Lebanese Forces (q.v.) and was noted for his courage.

Ja'ja''s name first became public in 1978, when Bashīr Gemayyel (q.v.) selected him to lead Lebanese Forces commandos in the massacre of the family of Toni Franjiyyah (q.v.). But Ja'ja' was critical of Bashīr, thinking he had made too many compromises to win the presidency in 1982. He argued, on religious grounds, for an alliance with Israel (q.v.) to keep Lebanon from falling under Arab-Islamic influence. When Elie Ḥubayqah, as commander of the Lebanese Forces, signed the Damascus-sponsored Tripartite Agreement (q.v.), Ja'ja' launched his uprising against his former comrade in January 1986, expelling Ḥubayqah from East Beirut (q.v.). Ja'ja' was the undisputed warlord of East Beirut until 1988, when Michel 'Awn (q.v.) was designated by Amīn Gemayyel (q.v.) as his interim successor to the presidency. 'Awn launched a war against Ja'ja' in 1989; the defeat of 'Awn in 1990 brought a respite for Ja'ja'. He reluctantly supported the aṭ-Ṭā'if Accords (q.v.), perhaps because Israel (q.v.) was no longer deeply involved in Lebanese affairs and Syria (q.v.) was. When the militias were disbanded in 1991, Ja'ja' retained his apparatus in secret, which put him at odds with the government and the Lebanese Army. He was appointed minister in the administration of Ilyās Hrāwī (q.v.) He was arrested in 1994, accused of the 1990 murder of his rival, Dānī Sham'ūn. He remains in jail, pleading his innocence. *See also* Lebanese Phalanges Party.

JALLŪD, 'ABDUL-SALĀM. This once influential leader of Libya (q.v.) and close aide to Colonel Mu'ammar Qadhdhāfī was dispatched to Lebanon several times during the 1975–76 civil war (q.v.) to mediate first between the warring factions and later between Syria and the coalition formed by the Palestine Liberation Organization and the Lebanese National Movement (q.v.). He has been out of public office for years.

JAMA'AH AL-ISLĀMIYYAH, AL. *SEE* ISLAMIC COMMUNITY.

JAM'IYYAH, AS-SŪRIYYAH al- (Syrian Society). This scholarly association was founded in Beirut (q.v.) in 1847. It comprised the most famous writers, teachers, scientists, and Orientalists of the East. It published its own journal in 1852, which was edited by Buṭrus al-Bustānī (q.v.).

JAM'IYYAT AL-MASHARĪ' AL-KHAYRIYYAH AL-ISLĀMIYYAH. *SEE* ḤABASHĪ GROUP.

JARĀJIMAH. These ancient Christian warriors, who hailed from Jarjūmah, near Antioch, served in the armed forces of the Byzantines, although their origins remain obscure. Their deeds are glorified in some Maronite (q.v.) popular legends, because of their raids on Arab conquerors. Many of them settled in the area of Lebanon in the seventh and eighth centuries and, it is speculated, were known as the Maradites, or al-Maradah (q.v.).

JEWS. Lebanese Jews historically have been an integral part of the diverse Lebanese population. In 1947, they were estimated to number 5,950. After the creation of the state of Israel (q.v.) in 1948, Lebanese

Jews did not emigrate to the Jewish homeland because they enjoyed a prosperous status in Lebanese society and had been granted equal legal rights by law. Moreover, they suffered no harm during the anti-Zionist demonstrations of 1947 and 1948. Nevertheless, the intensification of Arab-Israeli hostilities over the years has politicized attitudes toward local Jews, who were often associated with the policies of Israel. In the early 1950s, their synagogue in Beirut (q.v.) was bombed, and the Lebanese parliament legislated the legal exclusion of Jews from the Lebanese Army (q.v.).

During the 1967 Arab-Israeli war, when anti-Jewish sentiments were manifested around Lebanon, Lebanese authorities stationed guards in Jewish districts. Several hundred Jews chose to leave the country. During the 1975–76 phase of the 1975–90 civil war (q.v.), the Palestine Liberation Organization (q.v.) posted troops in the Jewish quarter in Wādī Abū Jamīl, which housed what remained of the dwindling Jewish community, now estimated at less than 3,000. The rise of Islamic fundamentalism in the 1980s, especially in the wake of the Israeli invasion of 1982 (q.v.), posed a direct threat to Lebanese Jewry. Organizations such as the Khaybar Brigades (q.v.) and the Organization of the Oppressed of the Earth (q.v.) claimed responsibility for the kidnapping and murder of several Lebanese Jews between 1984 and 1987. It is estimated that a few dozen Jews remain in Lebanon today.

***JINĀN, al-*.** This journal was founded by Buṭrus al-Bustānī (q.v.) in 1870. Its motto was "Loving one's homeland is part of the faith." The reputation of Buṭrus helped widen its circulation in the region, although his son, Salīm, wrote most of its articles. It ceased publication in 1886. It published articles by the most famous scientists of the region. The role of this journal can only be understood in the context of the literary and information revival that Buṭrus himself helped pioneer.

JOINT FORCES (*Al-Quwwāt Al-Mushtarakah*). In May 1976, the Lebanese National Movement (q.v.), the Palestine Liberation Organization, and the Army of Arab Lebanon (q.v.) unified their military forces into one joint force. It was supposed to come under the leadership of Kamāl Jumblāṭ (q.v.), although Yāsir 'Arafāt (q.v.) was in charge and frequently clashed with Jumblāṭ about policies and tactics.

***JOUR, Le*.** This official publication of the Constitutional Bloc of Bishārah al-Khūrī (qq.v.) was founded in 1934. Several of the country's leaders were associated with it, including Michel Chīhā and Charles Ḥilū (qq.v.), who served as editors. It merged with *L'Orient* (q.v.) in 1972 and was published under the name *L'Orient-Le Jour* (q.v.).

JUBAYL. *SEE* BYBLOS.

JUBRĀN KHALĪL JUBRĀN. *SEE* GIBRĀN, KHALĪL.

JUMBLĀṬ FAMILY. This is perhaps the most important Druze (q.v.) family in Lebanon (q.v.); it forms one of the two rival Druze family confederations (the other being the Yazbaki). The family is traced by historians to a Kurdish (q.v.) family, the Janbulad of Syria (q.v.), which came to Lebanon some time in the 17th century after a failed rebellion against the Ottomans. With the support of Prince Fakhr ad-Dīn II (q.v.), the family was invited to settle in the Shūf region. Its members converted to Druzism, and they subsequently benefited from the demise of the Ma'nid dynasty. Their emergence as the *shaykhs* (q.v.) of the Shūf region allowed them to extend their feudal domain south of the Shūf, posing a threat to the power of the Shihabi dynasty. In the 19th century, the family became one of the most important political families in Lebanon and its leaders were automatic *zu'amā'* (s. *za'īm,* q.v.). In the 20th century, the history of the family is indistinguishable from the history of Druzes in Lebanon. In the 1920s, the political leadership of the family was assumed by Naḍhīrah Jumblāṭ, who succeeded her husband, Fu'ād, in the leadership after his assassination. She was sympathetic to the French and prevented anti-French movements from sprouting among the Druzes.

The prominence of the family was undoubtedly boosted by the emergence of Kamāl Jumblāṭ (q.v.), Naḍhīrah's son, who, until his death in 1977, dominated not only Druze political leadership but all Lebanese political life. His espousal of progressive and socialist policies extended his leadership beyond his confessional community. His great personal achievement was in marginalizing the role of the Yazbaki Arsalān family (q.v.), thanks in large measure to the ineptitude of the head of the Arsalān family, Majīd (q.v.). The latter's association with the Maronite (q.v.) political establishment discredited him in Druze eyes, although he was successful in parliamentary elections because of Christian votes. In the 1975–76 civil war (q.v.), Jumblāṭ was the major spokesperson of the leftist-Muslim coalition. He was also a famous champion of the Palestinian cause in the Arab world and the Socialist world despite his frequent disagreements with Yāsir 'Arafāt (q.v.).

JUMBLĀṬ, KAMĀL (1917–1977). This Druze (q.v.) and ostensibly progressive leader was one of the few true intellectuals among the *za'īm* (q.v.) class in Lebanon (q.v.). He was born to a leading Druze family. His interests in his youth, and in later years, were mostly academic. He studied at St. Joseph University (q.v.), which produced most of the members of the political elite in pre- and post-independence Lebanon, and attended courses at the Sorbonne in Paris. He was equally interested in science and philosophy. Although he was known in his later years as a radical, Jumblāṭ was initially sympathetic to the French Mandate (q.v.) but later became a supporter of Bishārah Al-Khūrī (q.v.) in his pro-Arab orientation. He was forced to assume political responsibilities after the death of his mother, Naḍhīrah, who was also an able political leader. He was a leader of the opposition, which forced the resignation of President Bishārah al-Khūrī in 1952. Jumblāṭ founded the Progressive Socialist Party (q.v.) in the 1940s but failed to break the sectarian framework of the leadership. While his appeal went beyond his Druze community, and indeed beyond Lebanon, his party never materialized into a modern political party; it merely served as a tool for his Druze leadership.

Jumblāṭ lacked consistency in dealing with the sectarian issue; he championed secularization in Lebanon, while cultivating sectarian support among his Druze followers, who kissed his hand as a sign of respect and allegiance. He advocated socialist reforms while remaining a large landowner. He was successful, however, in establishing his Arab nationalist credentials when he led the uprising against Kamīl Sham'ūn (q.v.) in 1958. He also was an ardent supporter of Jamāl 'Abdul-Nasser (q.v.). In his political career, Jumblāṭ was at once the insider and the outsider. Although he held several ministerial posts from the 1940s on, he often spoke as the voice of the anti-establishment. In the 1960s, he formed a loose coalition of leftist and Muslim organizations to solidify popular support for the Palestine Liberation Organization and to call for major internal reforms in the Lebanese political system.

By 1975, he was one of the most visible leaders in the country and was also well-known in international socialist circles. He was awarded the Lenin Medal in Moscow. He led the Lebanese National Movement (q.v.) until his death. His conflict with Syria (q.v.) in 1976 over the course of the Lebanese civil war of 1975 (q.v.) and over internal reforms brought about his death at the hands of assassins, believed to be working for the Syrian regime.

While Jumblāṭ's critics often question his motives during the civil war (he was accused of venting his anger against a system that deprived him of the presidency), he assumed a role that far exceeded the historic role of the Jumblāṭ family (q.v.). Some say that he cemented the ties between the Druzes and Arabism. Others, especially within the Druze community, wanted him to focus more on the affairs of the sect.

JUMBLĀṬ, WALĪD (1949–). This Druze (q.v.) party leader was born in Beirut (q.v.) and received his education at the American University of Beirut (q.v.). Like his father (Kamāl Jumblāṭ, q.v.), Walīd did not seek a political career, nor did he seek the leadership of the Jumblāṭ family (q.v.). In his first years as leader, Walīd tried to follow in his father's footsteps. He, however, avoided antagonizing Syria (q.v.) and, in fact, mended fences with the Syrian regime as soon as he assumed his political responsibilities. Upon his father's death in 1977, he assumed the leadership of the Lebanese National Movement (q.v.) and the Progressive Socialist Party (q.v.). His early political years were characterized by hesitancy and weakness, but he soon asserted himself within the Druze community and the leftist coalition. Walīd continued his father's alliance with the Palestine Liberation Organization, although, like his father, he often clashed with Yāsir 'Arafāt (q.v.) over the latter's desire to impose his will on his Lebanese allies. The Progressive Socialist Party became more sectarian under Walīd, and he made no effort to expand his party's political base.

Walīd played no important political role during the 1982 Israeli invasion (q.v.), and he retired to his palace in al-Mukhtārah (q.v.), where he received Israeli military and political leaders despite his strong support of the Palestinian cause. His relations with Syria were strengthened during the administration of Amīn Gemayyel (q.v.), especially when the latter ignored domestic opposition and embarked on a pro-American course aimed at achieving peace with Israel (q.v.) at the expense of Lebanon's ties to the Arab world. He survived an assassination attempt against him in 1982, and emerged as a critic of Amīn Gemayyel and the Lebanese-Israeli May 17 Agreement (q.v.). He co-founded the National Salvation Front with Rashīd Karāmī and Sulaymān Franjiyyah (q.v.). He participated in the Lausanne and Geneva (qq.v.) Conferences for national reconciliation. He led and won the 1983–85 War of the Mountain (q.v.), and was hailed as the undisputed leader of the Druze community.

Jumblāṭ was appointed minister in 1984 and has been a minister ever since, with responsibilities dealing with displaced Lebanese. The disbanding of the militias in 1991 cost Jumblāṭ in terms of political popularity among the Druzes and allowed the rival Arsalān family (q.v.), which heads the Yazbaki family confederation of the Druzes, to reassert itself. Ṭalāl Arsalān (q.v.) is the most serious rival to Walīd's leadership. Jumblāṭ's relations with his former ally Nabīh Birrī (q.v.) have deteriorated, while his relations with Prime Minister Rafīq Ḥarīrī (q.v.) have improved. His parliamentary list achieved great success in the 1996 parliamentary election.

JUNAYNAH, al-. This was a commercial-political newspaper that appeared in Beirut (q.v.) in 1871. It was edited by Salīm al-Bustānī, son of Buṭrus al-Bustānī (q.v.). He published it four times a week in an attempt to turn it into a daily newspaper. It ceased publication in 1875.

JUNDULLĀH. *SEE* SOLDIERS OF GOD.

JUNŪB. This means "south" in Arabic; it refers to the predominantly Shi'ite (q.v.) region of South Lebanon. In the 1980s, the name Jabal 'Āmil became more fashionable.

-K-

KAFAR SHŪBĀ. This refers to a battle in December 1974 between Israeli troops and Palestinian forces (and their Lebanese supporters) in the village of Kafar Shūbā in South Lebanon. The inaction of the Lebanese Army (q.v.) during the events triggered massive demonstrations. Imām Mūsā Aṣ-Ṣadr (q.v.) declared his intention to form a "Lebanese resistance" to support the Palestinian revolution and to pressure the Lebanese government to protect its citizens in the South.

KAN'ĀN, GHĀZĪ. He is the Syrian ('Alawite) officer in charge of Syrian intelligence operations in Lebanon and one of the most influential men in the country. He succeeded Muḥammad Ghānim.

KANAFĀNĪ, GHASSĀN (1936–1972). This writer and radical activist was born in Acre, Palestine, and left his home in 1948 after the establishment of Israel (q.v.). He settled in Lebanon (q.v.) and later attended Damascus University (without obtaining a degree). He taught in Syria (q.v.) and emigrated to Kuwait in the 1950s. He returned to Lebanon in 1960, where he stayed for the rest of his life. He was attracted to Palestinian political activism early and in 1954 joined the Movement of Arab Nationalists (q.v.). He was one of the founders of the Popular Front for the Liberation of Palestine (PFLP) in 1967, when the Movement of Arab Nationalists was dissolved. He became a close political advisor to George Ḥabash. In the 1960s, writing under assumed names, and sometimes his own name, he wrote for *Al-Ḥawādith, Al-Muḥarrir* (qq.v.), and *Al-Anwār*. He was known for his novels and short stories, which made him famous in the Arab world. His novel *Men in the Sun* was translated into several languages, including English. He founded the PFLP's weekly, *al-Hadaf*, in 1969, and it quickly became the standard leftist publication for Arab radicals. He was a politburo member of the PFLP, in charge of the Information Department. He designed logos and posters for the PFLP in addition to serving as the front's press relations person. A bomb (set up by Israeli agents) was planted in his car, which killed him, along with his young niece.

KARAKALLĀ, 'ABDUL-ḤALĪM (1938–). He was born in Ba'albak (q.v.) and received a secondary education before studying dance. He is known as the energetic founder and director of a dance company named after him. The Karakallā Dance Company was established in 1970 and quickly became the unofficial folkloric dance troupe of Lebanon. It has performed in Lebanon (q.v.) and abroad, receiving numerous awards. It collaborated with the Raḥbānī brothers (q.v.) and participated in the Ba'albak International Festival. It continued to perform during the war.

KARAM, MILḤIM. He is the dean of the Syndicate of Journalists and is head of a media and publishing empire. His father, Karam Milḥim Karam, was a novelist, known for his command of the Arabic (q.v.) language. Milḥim published and edited *Al-Bayraq,* which he used to disseminate the statements and activities of his friends in political life. He is known for his moderation and his relations with Arab officials, especially in the Gulf. He often uses his eloquence to praise Arab kings and princes. He owns the publishing house Alf Layla wa Layla and the pro-Saudi magazine *Al-Ḥawādith* (q.v.), serving as its editor.

KARAM, YŪSUF BAYK. This Maronite (q.v.) rebel led an armed revolt against the government in 1864, during the rule of Dāwūd Pasha (q.v.), protesting the raising of taxes in the mountains. He was later persuaded to lay down his arms and leave for Paris in 1866. A statue of him stands in Ihdin (q.v.).

KARĀMĪ, RASHĪD (1921–1987). This former prime minister was the son of Tripoli-based leader 'Abdul-Ḥamīd Karāmī. Rashīd became the inheritor of the family's political tradition at a relatively early age. He studied law in Cairo and returned to Lebanon (q.v.) to pursue political activities. He strayed little from his father's pro-Arab, Islamic-oriented views. Karāmī first served in parliament in 1951 and became a permanent representative from Tripoli (q.v.). His first ministerial appointment was also in 1951. He was known for his honesty, integrity, and extreme seriousness. He became prime minister in 1955 and thereafter frequently held that post. He was one of the most visible and popular of all Sunni (q.v.) leaders, perhaps because he was the least compromising on "Muslim" political rights.

During the 1958 civil war (q.v.), Karāmī supported the opposition to Kamīl Sham'ūn's (q.v.) policies and advocated closer ties with the Arab world. He apparently agreed with the policies and orientations of Egyptian leader Jamāl 'Abdul-Nasser (q.v.) and opposed a Western orientation for Lebanon's foreign policies. Karāmī was close to Fu'ād Shihāb (q.v.) and was considered his favorite prime minister. His relations with his successor, Charles Ḥilū (q.v.), were not as good, especially when Ḥilū expressed displeasure with the role of the Palestine

Liberation Organization (PLO) in Lebanon. In 1969, in the wake of clashes between the army and the PLO, Karāmī boycotted Ḥilū, causing a governmental crisis. Egyptian mediation and the Cairo Agreement (q.v.) resolved the dispute. Karāmī became the most pro-Palestinian prime minister in Lebanon and enthusiastically recognized the PLO's right to conduct an "armed struggle" from Lebanon. His relations with Syria (q.v.) were consistently supportive: he was never in disagreement with the Syrian regime throughout the 1975 civil war (q.v.).

In deference to Christian public opinion, Sulaymān Franjiyyah (q.v.) did not appoint Karāmī to the prime ministership, but Muslim public opinion forced Franjiyyah to appoint Karāmī head of the cabinet in an effort to end the civil war. While he was prime minister, Karāmī clashed with Kamīl Sham‘ūn (q.v.) over the role of the Lebanese Army (q.v.), Karāmī opposing the deployment of its troops for fear of them attacking PLO forces. In the administration of Amīn Gemayyel (q.v.), Karāmī withdrew to his Tripoli (q.v.) base and coordinated his moves with the Syrian regime. He was a co-founder of the National Salvation Front, along with Sulaymān Franjiyyah and Walīd Jumblāṭ (q.v.). He participated in the reconciliation conferences at Geneva and Lausanne (qq.v.). In 1984, at the behest of the Syrian regime, he formed a government of national unity. The civil war, however, intensified. He blamed Amīn Gemayyel and refused to see him. He was assassinated in 1987, probably by agents loyal to the Lebanese Forces (q.v.). *See also* Karāmī, ‘Umar.

KARĀMĪ, ‘UMAR (1934–). This brother of Rashīd Karāmī (q.v.) was forced to assume the political leadership of the Karāmī family in the wake of Rashīd's assassination. ‘Umar had managed the family's fortune for years, and he trusted the political instincts and experience of Rashīd. He was appointed prime minister by Ilyās Hrāwī (q.v.) in 1990 but was forced to resign in May 1992, when riots spread through the nation protesting economic conditions. Karāmī established himself as a respected politician and continued on the path of his deceased brother. His relations with Syria (q.v.) and with Sulaymān Franjiyyah Jr. (q.v.) were preserved. He blamed unnamed enemies for the downfall of his cabinet, often implying that Rafīq Ḥarīrī (q.v.) was behind Lebanon's economic troubles. He has been a critic of Ḥarīrī's government. He won a seat in the 1992 and 1996 elections.

KHADDĀM, ‘ABDUL-ḤALĪM (1926–). This Syrian Sunni (qq.v.) politician, after studying law, joined the Arab Socialist Ba‘th Party (q.v.) in the 1950s. He became active in politics following the 1963 coup, which brought his party to power. He was appointed governor of Damascus in 1967 and minister in 1969. When Ḥāfiḍh al-Asad assumed power in

November 1970, Khaddām assumed the foreign ministry and was elected to the top command of the Ba'th Party. In 1984, he was appointed one of three vice-presidents with powers in the foreign policy area. He has traveled to Lebanon numerous times and has been the most influential policy maker on Lebanese affairs since the outbreak of the 1975 civil war (q.v.); no Lebanese can expect to receive Syrian support without his approval. Lebanese officials often refer their conflicts and feuds to him personally. He is close to Lebanese president Ilyās Hrāwī (q.v.).

KHĀL, YŪSUF al- (1917–1987). This writer was born in Tripoli (q.v.) and graduated from the American University of Beirut (AUB) (q.v.) in 1944. He came under the influence of right-wing ideologue Charles Mālik, who hired him as an instructor at AUB. He then was editor at the magazine *Ṣawt al-Mar'ah* (Voice of the Woman). In 1948, he moved to the United States (q.v.), working for the United Nations and editing the New York-based *Al-Hudā.* He subsequently returned to Lebanon and taught at AUB until 1958, when he devoted his time to the famous journal, *Shi'r* (q.v.). In 1967, he was appointed managing editor of the newly founded Dār An-Nahār publishing house. He wrote several books of poetry, the most famous of which are *Al-Bi'r Al-Mahjūrah* (1958) and *Qaṣā'id fī-l-Arba'īn* (1960). In the 1970s, al-Khāl surprised his friends by advocating that Lebanese Arabic (q.v.) dialect (the spoken language in Lebanon) be the written language. He wrote in this form but did not achieve literary acclaim for his style. He was closely associated with Christian nationalism in his last years. *See also Shi'r* and Adonis.

KHĀLID, MUFTĪ ḤASAN (1921–1989). He was born to a Sunni (q.v.) family in Beirut (q.v.) and was educated in al-Maqāṣid (q.v.) schools. He earned a degree from the school of Islamic jurisprudence (later renamed Azhar Lubnān) in Beirut in 1940. He was sent by the *muftī* (q.v.) of Lebanon to Egypt for an advanced religious degree from Al-Azhar University in Cairo. He was appointed upon his return to an administrative position in the Sharī'ah court in Beirut (q.v.). He later served as a religious judge in several places outside Beirut. He taught Islamic theology in the Azhar Lubnan school and delivered Friday sermons in Beirut mosques. He was appointed *muftī* in 1967 upon the death of his predecessor, Muḥammad 'Alāyā. His educational specialties were personal status laws and inheritance issues. He traveled in the Muslim world and was close to the Saudi government. He advocated a firm position against Maronite (q.v.) militias during the 1975 civil war (q.v.). He was killed by a car bomb in Beirut.

KHAṬĪB, SĀMĪ al- (1933–). This retired army officer and deputy is an example of the rewards of subservience to Syrian (q.v.) political interests in Lebanon (q.v.). He was born to a Sunni (q.v.) family in Jib Jannīn. He graduated from the military academy in 1955 and became part of Fu'ād Shihāb's military apparatus. He played a role in thwarting the 1961 coup d'état by the Syrian Social National Party (q.v.) and wielded tremendous political influence during the Shihāb and Ḥilū (q.v.) eras. He was one of the Shihabi military elite summoned for a trial early in the Sulaymān Franjiyyah (q.v.) administration. He fled to Damascus, where his relations with Syria (q.v.) became even closer. In 1977, he was recalled from retirement and chosen by Ilyās Sarkīs (q.v.), at Syria's behest, to head the Arab Deterrent Force (q.v.), which was predominantly Syrian in composition. He served in that capacity until 1983, when the force was dissolved. He was promoted to the rank of general in 1979 and given the rank of *liwā'* (distinguished general) before his final retirement. He was appointed minister of interior in 1990 and elected to the parliament in 1992. He is considered one of the most loyal friends of Syria in Lebanon.

KHATĪB, ZĀHIR al- (1944–). This leftist deputy was born to a Sunni (q.v.) family from the Shūf. He was a lawyer before he ran for a seat, following his father's death in 1970. He won as a member of Kamāl Jumblāṭ's (q.v.) list; he was reelected in 1972. He established a reputation as one of the most radical members of parliament. When his brother Ḍhāfir died in battle in 1976, he took over as the secretary-general of the Toilers' League (q.v.) and became a Marxist-Leninist who ardently supported the Palestinian left. His views underwent a radical transformation after 1982, when he distanced himself from radical politics. He was appointed minister in 1990 and became a close ally of Nabīh Birrī (q.v.). He won a seat in the 1992 elections.

KHAYBAR BRIGADES. The name is derived from the name of a battle between Muḥammad and Jewish tribes in the seventh century A.D. Little is known on this small organization. It claimed responsibility for the kidnapping of Jews in Lebanon in the 1980s.

KHAYYĀṬ BOOKSHOP. This is one of the oldest and most academic-oriented bookshops in Beirut (q.v.). It is located on Bliss Street, where the American University of Beirut (q.v.) is located. It was a gathering place for intellectuals before the war. It carried foreign and Arabic (q.v.) books, magazines, and newspapers and served as a publishing house of French and English scholarly books.

KHURAYSH, ANTOINE (1907–1986). This Maronite (q.v.) patriarch was born in 'Ayn Ibil in South Lebanon and was sent to Rome at the age of 13 to study Christian theology. He was ordained as a priest in Tyre (q.v.) in 1930 and rose quickly in the Maronite clerical hierarchy.

He taught philosophy and theology in a number of schools in Lebanon and Palestine and in 1950 was appointed by the pope to be titular bishop of Tarse. In 1957, he was appointed archbishop of Sidon (q.v.); in 1975 he was elected Maronite patriarch of Antioch and the East; and in 1983 he was made cardinal by Pope John Paul II. He resigned from this post in 1985. Khuraysh was probably a more popular political figure among Muslims than in his own Christian community. He was praised for his moderation and refused to bless the actions of the Maronite-oriented Lebanese Front or the Lebanese Forces (qq.v.). He was known for his support of the Palestinian cause and for his opposition to Israel (q.v.). His political preferences marginalized his role and restricted his activities to spiritual affairs. He urged moderation, peace, and reconciliation, rejecting war as a solution. It is believed that his resignation came as a result of political dissatisfaction.

KHŪRĪ, BISHĀRAH 'ABDULLĀH al (AL-AKHṬAL AṢ-ṢAGHĪR) (1885–1968). This poet and journalist was born and educated in Beirut (q.v.). He founded the newspaper *Al-Barq* in 1908; its publication was interrupted during World War I. He was elected dean of the Press Syndicate in 1925. His nickname al-Akhṭal aṣ-Ṣaghīr, meaning the Smaller Akhṭal, was that of a great Arab poet from the classical period. He was "crowned" the Prince of Poets in a major poetic event in Beirut in 1961. He left a book of poetry that is still read today. His style was traditionalist, following the classical form of Arabic (q.v.) poetry. Politically, he was an Arab nationalist who called attention to the dangers of Zionism in Palestine. He is considered obsolete by the standards of modern Arabic poetry.

KHŪRĪ, BISHĀRAH al- (1895–1964). He was the first president in independent Lebanon (q.v.). He studied law in Beirut (q.v.) and Paris and, unlike many of his French-educated contemporaries, achieved a mastery of the Arabic (q.v.) language. He was appointed a judge in the early 1920s and later became minister of the interior. When the French suspended the constitution (q.v.) and blocked his presidential election, he formed the Constitutional Bloc (q.v.), which led Lebanese parliamentary activity for years. He disagreed with the orientations of Emile Iddī (q.v.), and while the ideological differences between the two men are often emphasized, there was also an element of personal rivalry. Both wanted to be president. In the summer of 1943, al-Khūrī held a series of discussions with Sunni (q.v.) politician Riyāḍ aṣ-Ṣulḥ (q.v.), and produced a political understanding that became known as the National Pact (q.v.). It was intended to achieve Muslim-Christian coexistence, but other sects were not consulted. It basically formalized juridically the sectarian distribution of political power in Lebanon.

For a brief period in 1943, al-Khūrī and aṣ-Ṣulḥ , along with other politicians, were arrested by the French; as a result Lebanese history has elevated them to the level of national heroes. This brief conflict with the French was recorded in history books as a War of Independence. Al-Khūrī's first years in the presidency were successful, but his alliance with aṣ-Ṣulḥ did not last. Furthermore, although the constitution prohibits a president from serving two consecutive terms, he rigged the 1947 election to ensure the parliamentary majority needed to amend the constitution in his favor. In 1951, aṣ-Ṣulḥ was assassinated, and public opposition to the regime, which was notoriously corrupt, mounted (Al-Khūrī's brother was nicknamed Sultan Salīm, in reference to the great powers he had amassed). There were also accusations of senility. Al-Khūrī was forced to resign in 1952, and he spent the rest of his life in disgrace. He wrote a highly literary, three-volume memoir, but he was unable to resurrect his sagging reputation. A major city square in Beirut was named after him. *See also* France; French Mandate.

KHŪRĪ, KHALĪL al- (1923–). The son of Bishārah (q.v.), he was born in Beirut and educated in law at St. Joseph University (qq.v.). He made a fortune early in his life, thanks to his family connections, helping Western companies in their business transactions in Lebanon and the Middle East. He was elected deputy in 1960 and reelected twice in 1964 and 1968. He headed the Constitutional Bloc (q.v.) after the death of his father. He was a cabinet member and a known figure in the era of Fu'ād Shihāb (q.v.). Khalīl was known for his lavish parties and frequent travels; many political conflicts were resolved at his dinner parties. He moved to France (q.v.) after the 1975 civil war (q.v.) began, perhaps because his famously luxurious Beirut apartment was looted and burnt. He has not taken political positions in years.

KHŪRĪ, KHALĪL al- (1836–1907). A pioneering journalist, he was born in Shuwayfāt, in Mount Lebanon. He studied Arabic in Beirut (qq.v.), and later learned Turkish and French. He founded in 1858 what is considered the first Arabic newspaper, *Ḥadīqat Al-Akhbār* (q.v.). He also wrote Arabic poetry but is known only for his journalistic work. He claimed that he was a friend of the French poet Lamartine, but no evidence exists to support this claim. After the 1860 civil war (q.v.), he held several official appointments. He founded the Greek Orthodox Philanthropic Society.

KHŪRĪ, MAHĀ (1936–). She was born in Qarṭabā to a Maronite (q.v.) family and is widely known for winning her parliamentary seat in the controversial 1992 election with only 41 votes: Christians boycotted the election in her district, so she ran unopposed. She is often used as an example of the unrepresentativeness of the Lebanese election of 1992. She lost her seat in 1996.

KHŪRĪ, MICHEL al- (1926–). A politician, he is the son of Bishārah al-Khūrī (q.v.). He was born in Beirut (q.v.) and educated at Jesuit schools, earning a law degree from St. Joseph University (q.v.). In his early career, he worked with his uncle Michel Chīḥā (q.v.) to establish relations between the Vatican and Lebanon (q.v.) and as a journalist for the French-language newspaper *Le Jour,* which was owned by Chīḥā. He was sent on several diplomatic missions, joined the Lebanese Bar Association in 1948, and practiced law until 1953. Al-Khūrī stunned the political elite in 1950 with his fierce attack on the political establishment in a famous lecture titled, "Horizons of Lebanon" at *Nadwah Al-Lubnāniyyah* (q.v.). He had also been critical of his father's decision to seek reelection. In 1957, he became editor of *Le Jour;* in the 1960s, he timidly supported his brother Khalīl's political campaigns; and in 1964 he founded the National Council for the Development of Tourism, serving as its chairperson until 1971. In 1967, he was appointed minister of information. He was known for his close ties to the Shihabi elite. Over the years, he became more involved in business and co-founded the Banque Libano-Francaise. He was not heard from during the 1975–76 civil war (q.v.) but reappeared on the public scene in 1978, when Ilyās Sarkīs (q.v.) appointed him governor of the Central Bank. He resigned in 1983 and moved to Paris. His name appears often as a presidential candidate.

KHŪRĪ, RA'ĪF (1913–1967). This journalist was born in Nabyah in the al-Matn region and was educated in literature at the American University of Beirut (q.v.). He taught literature in Jerusalem, Damascus, and Beirut. He also wrote articles for several newspapers and magazines. His views were independently leftist. His most famous book, which was translated into English, is *Modern Arabic Thought: The Impact of the French Revolution on Its Social and Political Orientation.*

KIBBĪ. This famous Lebanese dish is a mixture of minced meat and bulgur. Sometimes it is fried in oil. It is most associated with the cuisine of North Lebanon, where it is often served uncooked.

KISSINGER, HENRY. Many Lebanese are convinced that this U.S. secretary of state personally plotted the destruction of Lebanon and continued to manipulate the 1975 civil war (q.v.) in Lebanon long after his departure from public office in the United States (q.v.). Believers in the

Kissinger conspiracy theory include prominent Maronite (q.v.) politicians Raymond Iddī and Sulymān Franjiyyah (qq.v.).

KŪRĀNĪ, HANĀ KASBĀNĪ (1870–1898). This feminist was born in Kafar Shīmā and received her education at schools run by American missionaries. She taught in Tripoli (q.v.) and married the writer Amīn Kūrānī. She represented Syrian women in 1892 at a women's conference in Chicago; her espousal of a moderate feminist position started a literary debate between her and Zaynab Fawwāz (q.v.). She later toured and lectured in several American cities. She left her husband and lived for three years in the United States (q.v.), supporting herself with income from speaking engagements and writing. She wrote novels and essays. She contracted tuberculosis and returned to Lebanon, where she died.

KURDISH DEMOCRATIC PARTY (*Al-Parti*). This party was founded by Jamīl Miḥḥū in 1960 and operated without a license until 1970. First and foremost, it espouses the cause of Kurdish nationalism and views as one of its primary activities instilling ethnic consciousness among the Kurds (q.v.) in Lebanon (q.v.). The party rose in Lebanon at a time when some Kurds obtained Lebanese citizenship, which had been denied them because of Maronite (q.v.) fears of increasing the demographic weight of the Muslims in Lebanon. According to one estimate, only 10,000 Kurds were naturalized out of over 75,000 living in Lebanon. Miḥḥū, ran for parliament in 1968 but lost. The party later suffered because of its support for the Iraqi regime, which is not a known friend of the Kurdish cause. The Syrian army also punished the party for its pro-Iraqi stance. The party was a member of the Lebanese National Movement (q.v.) during the 1975 civil war (q.v.) but was later replaced by a left-wing offshoot. *See also* Kurdish Democratic Party-Provisional Leadership.

KURDISH DEMOCRATIC PARTY-PROVISIONAL LEADERSHIP. In 1977, Muḥammad Miḥḥū, the son of Jamīl Miḥḥū, head of the Kurdish Democratic Party (q.v.), split off from his father's party and formed his own. He called for closer ties with the Lebanese National Movement (q.v.) and the Palestine Liberation Organization.

KURDISTAN. This is the historic national homeland of the Kurds (q.v.), who have been oppressed by Arab and Turkish governments, while the West has exploited their grievances. The Kurds of Lebanon, like Kurds elsewhere, hope for the political fulfillment of Kurdish national aspirations in Kurdistan, which is now under foreign, non-Kurdish rule.

KURDS. There are tens of thousands of Kurds in Lebanon, mainly in Beirut (q.v.), in the Wādī Abū Jamīl district. The Kurds originate in the Taurus and Zagros mountains of Iraq, Iran, Turkey, and Syria (q.v.), in what is known as Kurdistan (q.v.). The Kurds of Lebanon are Sunni Muslims (q.v.), but speak their own language. Not all of them have Lebanese citizenship; many Christian leaders have resisted demands for their naturalization for fear of increasing the demographic weight of Muslims. Kurds face discrimination and humiliation in Lebanon; the word "Kurd" in Lebanese popular use is equated with "lowly" and "dirty." The Kurds of Lebanon have their own political parties and their own publications.

KUTLAH AL-WAṬANIYYAH, AL. *SEE* CONSTITUTIONAL BLOC.

-L-

LAḤḤŪD, GĀBĪ. (1931–). This military and political leader was at one time the most influential man in the country, perhaps more powerful than president Charles Ḥilū (q.v.) himself during his administration. He was born in Bayt ad-Dīn (q.v.) and studied in Beirut (q.v.), graduating from the Military Academy in 1952. He attended several military courses in France and the United States (qq.v.) returning to Lebanon to teach at the academy. Fu'ād Shihāb (q.v.) appointed him to a senior post in the Deuxième Bureau (q.v.), which he headed in the last weeks of the Shihāb administration; his main missions were to track Palestinian and leftist political activities in the country and to sabotage the political careers of Shihāb's enemies. He exposed and aborted in 1969 a Soviet operation to hijack a French-made Mirage plane from Lebanon. He failed in 1970 to secure the election of Shihabi candidate Ilyās Sarkīs (q.v.) to the presidency. The election of Sulaymān Franjiyyah (q.v.) brought to an abrupt end the dramatic rise of the bureau, which ruled Lebanon for years. He left Lebanon in 1973 and was sentenced in absentia to seven years of hard labor. He founded an export-import company in Madrid and was able to secure an amnesty the next year. He has been inactive politically in recent years and avoids the press.

LAḤḤŪD, NASĪB (1944–). This parliamentarian was born to a traditional wealthy Maronite (q.v.) family in Ba'abdāt and educated in Jumhūr and at Loughborough University of Technology, England, where he received a degree in engineering. He founded and served as a chairperson of Lahhud Engineering Company. He was not known in political circles until 1990, when he was appointed by Ilyās Hrāwī (q.v.) as ambassador to the United States (q.v.), in which position he served—with distinction according to the Lebanese government—until 1991. He returned to Lebanon (q.v.) to begin his political life. He was elected in 1992 and has been active in the parliamentary committee on foreign affairs. He is a respected parliamentarian and his statements are given great weight in the Lebanese press. His staff is highly educated and professional. He is often mentioned as a presidential candidate and has not denied harboring presidential aspirations. Laḥḥūd maintains good ties with the Syrian (q.v.) regime and also has credibility among Christians. He was reelected to parliament in 1996.

LAḤḤŪD, ROMEO (1929–). One of the most famous and original artists in Lebanon, he was born to the famed Laḥḥūd family in Beirut (q.v.) and educated in ʻAyn Ṭūrah and the Fine Arts Academy in Paris. His specialty was interior design and decoration, but his career was dedicated to musical productions. He traveled with his performing folklore troupes to various parts of Europe. He created, produced, and directed a variety of musical shows at the Baʻalbak (q.v.) International Festivals in the 1960s. In 1972, he created the Martinez Theater in Beirut and the Cedars Festival. His collaboration with Lebanese star Ṣabāḥ (q.v.) brought him Arab-wide fame. His style marries Western and Eastern traditions of music, with an emphasis on Lebanese folkloric heritage. In the late 1970s and 1980s he worked closely with his sister-in-law, Salwā al-Quṭrīb.

LAUSANNE CONFERENCE. This conference of national reconciliation was held in Lausanne, Switzerland, in March 1984 as a follow-up to the Geneva Conference (q.v.). It came as a result of the diminution of the power of president Amīn Gemayyel (q.v.) and the success of the opposition in West Beirut (q.v.).

LAWZĪ, SALĪM AL-. *SEE* AL-ḤAWĀDITH.

LEBANESE AMERICAN UNIVERSITY. The origins of this university go back to a nineteenth-century school for girls. By the 1970s it had grown and had become the Beirut University College, a women's college; later expanding into a co-educational university. In 1992, it changed its name to the Lebanese American University. It has faculties of literature, science, arts, and applied sciences. The language of instruction is English; it follows the example of the American University of Beirut (q.v.). In 1991–92, it had 2,270 students.

LEBANESE ARMY. The origins of the Lebanese Army can be traced to the French Mandate (q.v.), when France (q.v.) formed the Troupes

Spéciales du Levant. These were intended as supportive forces and comprised both Lebanese and Syrian soldiers (they were commanded by French officers). The percentage of Arab officers increased with time, and the force attained a strength of more than 10,000 men in the early 1940s. Some members of this force fought with the French in World War II, but Lebanon (q.v.) was spared the horrors of that war. Lebanese units of the Troupes Spéciales, which were released after 1945, formed the embryo of the Lebanese Army. The organization of the new army was structured by Fu'ād Shihāb (q.v.), who was a consistent admirer of France and its ways. The Lebanese political elite deliberately kept the army weak: it was not designed to defend Lebanon's borders but only to keep the state apparatus in control in a country where most males are armed. The guiding principle of the army was Charles Ḥilū's (q.v.) slogan: "Lebanon's strength lies in its weakness." A strong army could force Lebanon into unwanted confrontations with Israel (q.v.).

Lebanon was adamant that it wanted no part of Arab-Israeli wars. Lebanese history textbooks created the myth of Lebanese Army heroism during the 1948 war, although Lebanese participation was token at best. In fact, when combat began, Lebanon withdrew its symbolic forces from the border, thereby allowing Israel to occupy a strip of land, which it held until Lebanon signed the armistice agreement with Israel in 1949.

The post-independence reconstruction of the army was shaped by the personality and preferences of Fu'ād Shihāb. This cautious man avoided the experiences of neighboring Arab countries, whose armies were deeply involved in internal political matters and were used to bring about political change. Shihāb was also keenly aware of the fragility of Lebanese society and wanted to avoid sectarian tensions and conflicts within. In 1958, he rejected Kamīl Sham'ūn's (q.v.) orders to deploy the army against opposition rebels in the country. Shihāb knew that the army would disintegrate along sectarian lines, which was exactly what happened during the 1975–76 civil war (q.v.). Shihāb performed independently in 1958, and he was rewarded by the office of the presidency.

Shihāb, however, did not oppose the intervention of the army in politics as such; he only wanted to prevent Lebanese sectarian leaders from using the army for petty sectarian interests and electoral benefits. He himself introduced the army into Lebanese political and social life, but he made sure that the apparatus of intervention, the Deuxième Bureau (q.v.), was multisectarian in composition. It included Druzes, Sunnis, and Maronites (qq.v.) (rarely Shi'ites, q.v.) working side-by-side to further Shihabism. That gave army officers great political power, and it was used frequently even in election times to reward the friends of Shihāb.

The army's role changed somewhat in the 1960s, when Arab-Israeli tensions forced parliament to increase the defense budget (to the financial profit of generals and politicians alike) and to treat the Palestinians in Lebanon (q.v.) as a national security threat. The army was concerned that the rise of the Palestinian resistance would tip the delicate sectarian balance in the country in favor of the Muslims. The commander-in-chief of the army is by tradition a Maronite and is appointed at the discretion of the president. The commanders of the army have been anti-Palestinian by political instinct and sectarian when it comes to the preservation of Maronite political privileges.

Historically, the Lebanese Army recruited from the ranks of "prominent" families among the Christians. Later the army was seen as a last resort choice for those who failed to get into good schools. The army continued to recruit, however, among poor Maronites in 'Akkār, although the percentage of Muslim officers continued to be disproportionately small. The ideology of the army was Lebanese nationalist, as defined by the various right-wing parties in the country. Emphasis was on the uniqueness and superiority of Lebanon. The Palestinians were portrayed as posing the most serious threat to Lebanese sovereignty. Long before the 1975–76 civil war (q.v.), the army's role became a key issue in political debates. In the 1960s, Israeli raids against Lebanon were increasing as the Palestine Liberation Organization (PLO) was restructured and re-organized under Yāsir 'Arafāt (q.v.). The army, however, did not respond to Israeli raids and was passive in the face of increasing tensions and destruction in South Lebanon. The leftists and Muslims wanted the army to take a stand against Israel, while Maronite-oriented rightists insisted on insulating Lebanon from the Arab-Israeli conflict.

The conflict between the army and the PLO reached the brink in 1970–71 in the wake of Black September in Jordan, when King Husayn's forces expelled PLO forces from Jordan. Sulaymān Franjiyyah (q.v.) wanted to follow Jordan's example when he assumed the presidency in 1970. What he discovered, however, was that the Lebanese situation was strikingly different from that of Jordan. He did try to smash the PLO's military power in Lebanon in 1973, but he was utterly unsuccessful. First, the PLO in Lebanon had a strong popular base among the Lebanese; many of its members were Lebanese Muslims (and some were Christians). National harmony would not last if the president went ahead with his plans against the Palestinian resistance. Second, the Lebanese Army was weak and unprepared for combat. It was poorly trained. Sectarian factors would have ensured fragmentation in its ranks.

The civil war brought fundamental changes to the army. Initially, the right-wing coalition wanted to deploy the army to end the war by defeating the coalition of the PLO and the Lebanese National Movement (q.v.). Muslim leaders and leftists warned against "extermination of the Palestinians." But the army intervened anyway. Not only were right-wing militias trained and armed, but officers fought alongside these militias. On the other side, Aḥmad Al-Khaṭīb and his comrades in 1975–76 defected and subsequently formed the Army of Arab Lebanon (q.v.). On the Christian front, Antoine Barakāt (q.v.) (a protege of Franjiyyah) openly joined the right-wing militias and coordinated the army and the militias. In al-Biqāʿ (q.v.), the army troops formed a pro-Syrian Vanguard of the Army of Arab Lebanon. In the South, Israel created its own army, named in 1978 the South Lebanon Army (q.v.). The army command in Yarzah outside of Beirut (q.v.), however, maintained that there was still a central and unified army. The longer the war continued, the more fragmented the army became. By the 1980s, the brigades of the army were sectarian in composition and loyal to the prevailing militias in the various provinces of the country. When Michel ʿAwn (q.v.) took over the presidential palace in 1988, he was left with only Christian troops sympathetic to right-wing militias. This is not to say that there were no tensions between the Lebanese Forces (q.v.) and Christian army troops in East Beirut (q.v.). There were; and this can be understood as classic political and military rivalries in a time of war competing for influence and tax collection.

ʿAwn's defeat in 1990 allowed the Lebanese government to begin rebuilding the army. Emile Laḥḥūd, a highly respected Maronite moderate, was appointed commander-in-chief by Ilyās Hrāwī (q.v.), and he integrated the militias into the army's ranks. This, of course, is a recipe for certain disaster in the event of a sudden breakdown in law and order. But the army is receiving new indoctrination with emphasis on the Arabness of Lebanon and its sectarian balance is respected more than before. The top command posts, however, remain reserved for Maronites. The ability of the army to emerge as an effective and credible apparatus will depend on the Lebanese government's performance in the years to come. The Syrian (q.v.) influence in Lebanon, and over the Lebanese Army itself, hurts the army's image among some Lebanese.

LEBANESE CIVIL WAR. *SEE* CIVIL WAR OF 1975–90.

LEBANESE COMMUNIST PARTY (*Al-Ḥizb ash-Shuyūʿī al-Lubnānī*). The LCP is one of the oldest parties in Lebanon (q.v.) and, indeed, in the entire Arab world. The roots of this organization go back to the 1920s, when romantic writers with socialist leanings used a local literary newspaper in Zaḥlah (q.v.) to call for class brotherhood.

With the death of V. I. Lenin in 1924 a middle-level employee at the Beirut port, Yūsuf Ibrāhīm Yazbak, wrote extensively about "the contributions of Lenin" and the meaning of socialism. Yazbak, along with Fu'ād ash-Shimālī (a Lebanese activist worker who was expelled from Egypt for his revolutionary activities) and a Bolshevik envoy, founded the Communist Party in October 1924.

The party comprised both workers and intellectuals. It deliberately camouflaged its ideology by adopting the name Lebanese People's Party, and ash-Shimālī was chosen as its first secretary-general. The party came out publicly in a big rally in a May 1 celebration in 1925 in Beirut (q.v.), where demands for the improvement of workers' conditions were presented. Party leaders and members were victims of French harassment during the French mandate (q.v.). Many of the party members were members of minority sects and ethnicities, but in 1930 Khālid Bakdāsh (a Syrian Kurd, qq.v.) began a movement to Arabize the party. In 1932, Bakdāsh put the party under his command and allowed the USSR to have almost complete control over its affairs. It sponsored a translation into Arabic (q.v.) of the works of Marx, Engels, and Lenin.

The credibility of the party was compromised in the 1930s when it softened its attacks against France (q.v.) as a result of the ascension of Leon Blum's socialist government in France. The party, presumably in return, gained official recognition, and its leaders were allowed to operate publicly. In the first national party congress in 1943, the party split into two parties: a Lebanese and a Syrian communist party. Lebanese communists had been striving to end the tyrannical rule of Khālid Bakdāsh.

The Palestinian problem, Soviet support for the partition of Palestine in 1947, and the Soviet recognition of Israel (q.v.) in 1948 made Arab ties to the USSR a political liability. The party tried to recover by throwing itself into the anti-Western, nationalist struggle of the 1950s, although its opposition to Jamāl 'Abdul-Nasser (q.v.), and to his United Arab Republic, further harmed its credibility. By the 1960s, members were questioning the pro-Soviet orientation of the leadership. In 1964, a group of party militants identified with the Maoist line of communism and later formed the pro-Chinese Socialist Revolution Party. Another faction, which included some veteran party leaders, split in 1964–65 and formed the *Ilā al-Amām* (Marching Forward) group, which condemned the personality cult in the party and other bureaucratic ills. This group later merged with the Union of Lebanese Communists (headed by journalist Nasīb Nimr), an organization that never gained popular support. Another split occurred in 1966, when two leading members, Hasan Quraytim and Ṣawāyā Ṣawāyā, disagreed with the party's analysis of the Intra Bank crash (q.v.).

The party held its second national congress in 1968 and it promoted a youthful leadership, which would take over at the outset of the Lebanese civil war (q.v.) in 1975. The new leadership supported the Palestine Liberation Organization (q.v.) wholeheartedly, after years of opposing "armed struggle." The party called for modest reforms in the Lebanese political system and advocated an expansion of political participation and a consolidation of democracy. The party participated in the 1975 civil war as a founding member of the Lebanese National Movement (q.v.), which was the Lebanese ally of the PLO. The great success of the party was in creating cells throughout the country, not a small achievement in a land of narrow loyalties. Right-wing militias banned any communist activities in areas under their control, and many Christian communists were forced underground. Secretary-general George Ḥāwī, a friend of Kamāl Jumblāṭ (q.v.), emerged as the most powerful communist in Lebanon and a key opposition figure. In recent years, the party has declined in size and significance. Ḥāwī resigned, withdrawing from public life amid charges of corruption. Shi'ite (q.v.) members seem to be more influential than before within the command structure. A Sunni Muslim (q.v.), Farūq Daḥrūj, became secretary-general after Ḥāwī's retirement, but failed to win a seat in the 1996 parliamentary elections.

LEBANESE FORCES (*Al-Quwwāt al-Lubnāniyyah*). The 1975 civil war (q.v.) led to the bizarre transformation of political parties into militias, and vice versa. The origins of the LF go back to the battle of Tal az-Za'tar and the 1975–76 military campaigns conducted by the rightist (predominantly Christian) militias and their allies in the Lebanese Army (q.v.) against the Palestinian and Lebanese Shi'ite (qq.v.) presence in the suburbs of predominantly Christian East Beirut (q.v.). The suspicious death of William Ḥāwī, head of the war council, the military organ of the Lebanese Phalanges Party (q.v.), paved the way for Bashīr Gemayyel (q.v.) to assume full control of the party's military arm and, eventually, of all Christian militias operating in East Beirut.

The LF was established in August 1976 upon the creation of its Joint Command Council. Its first chairperson, Bashīr Gemayyel, was dissatisfied with the policies of his father, Pierre (q.v.), and his comrades in the leadership of the Lebanese Phalanges Party. Bashīr gradually expanded his power base as part of a calculated plan to take over Christian political and military leadership. The Command Council initially comprised "the command" of the Lebanese Phalanges Party, the National Liberal Party (q.v.), The Organization (q.v.) (at-Tanḍhīm), Guardians of the Cedars (q.v.), and other non-affiliated armed groups in East Beirut.

Bashīr's formula for ending the war was simple: Lebanon would regain its sovereignty and peace would prevail only if the *aghrāb* ("aliens," i.e., the Palestinians and, after 1978, the Syrians) were expelled from Lebanese territory. Bashīr's first attempt to eliminate Maronite (q.v.) rivals began in earnest in June 1978 when Toni Franjiyyah (q.v.), the leader of the al-Maradah (q.v.) Forces, and his family were killed and his military force was defeated in the Ihdin (q.v.) massacre. By 1979, he had made it clear that he would not allow any rival military force to exist in East Beirut. He formed a new unified military force that, theoretically, was not affiliated with any political party but was, in truth, under his control. In July 1980, in one of the bloodiest episodes against his Maronite enemies, he ruthlessly exterminated the Tigers, the militia of the National Liberal Party.

Bashīr's leadership of the integrated force was characterized by an alliance with Israel (q.v.) and a vocal, and violent, campaign against the Syrian military presence in Lebanon. The Israeli invasion of 1982 (q.v.) sped Bashīr's rise in Lebanese political life, allowing for Bashīr's election as president. (He was, however, assassinated in September of the same year). The LF was never to recover from this loss. He was succeeded by Fādī Frem (q.v.), who was linked to the Ṣabrā and Shātīlā massacres (q.v.) in 1982. The former head of LF intelligence, Elie Ḥubayqah, became commander in 1985 after the brief tenure of Fu'ād Abū Nāḍir (q.v.), a relative and protege of Amīn Gemayyel (q.v.). Ḥubayqah, whose ties to Israeli intelligence were exposed in the investigations that followed the Ṣabrā and Shātīlā massacres, embarked on a rapprochement with Syria (q.v.) and signed in December 1985 a reform package—which was detested by the Christian establishment.

Ḥubayqah was deposed in January 1986, and Samīr Ja'ja' (q.v.), who had executed the massacres in Ihdin, became the new commander; he remained in that position until the government of Ilyās Hrāwī (q.v.) disbanded all militias on Lebanese territory. Ja'ja' was appointed minister, but boycotted the 1992 parliamentary elections. His political career was at a standstill in 1996 because of his 1994 arrest for plotting the assassination of a rival and the bombing of a church. He was cleared of the second offense. Although the LF no longer exists in theory, its followers are still organized in Lebanon and abroad. After the disbanding of militias in Lebanon, the Lebanese Forces under Ja'ja' obtained a license to operate as a political party. The party of the Lebanese Forces in the diaspora is headed by Robert Faraḥ.

LEBANESE FRONT (*Al-Jabhah al-Lubnāniyyah*). This is not a political party but rather a body comprising all the important Maronite- (q.v.) oriented parties, organizations, and personalities in East Beirut (q.v.). It defines itself as a general leadership council for all Christians in Lebanon. The front has its roots in Jabhat al-Ḥurriyyah wa-l-Insān fī Lubnān (Front of Freedom and Man in Lebanon), which declared its existence in January 1976 in a brief statement affirming the priority of "restoring sovereignty" to Lebanon. The statement was signed by Abbot Sharbil al-Qassīs (head of the Maronite Order of Monks); Kamīl Sham'ūn (q.v.), head of the National Liberal Party (q.v.); Pierre Gemayyel (q.v.), head of the Lebanese Phalanges Party (q.v.); Fu'ād al-Shimālī, head of The Organization (q.v.) (At-Tanḍhīm) militia; Shākir Abū Sulaymān, secretary-general of the Maronite League (q.v.); Charles Mālik, a well-known right-wing thinker; and Sa'īd 'Aql (q.v.), a famous poet and guide of the Guardians of the Cedars (q.v.). Charles Mālik was instrumental in drafting "the vow" of the front in February 1976, which included—among other things—affirmation of the unity of Lebanon (q.v.), a demand for the expulsion of the non-Lebanese "aggressors" from Lebanon (a reference to the Palestinians in Lebanon, q.v.), and praise for the free enterprise system.

This front was formed to unify political action in the Christian camp. Later, it developed into an ideological movement, gradually breaking with Lebanon's Arab solidarity and sanctioning Bashīr Gemayyel's (q.v.) alliance with Israel (q.v.). By 1977, the front's name became the Lebanese Front, and it included Kamīl Sham'ūn, as president; Sulaymān Franjiyyah (q.v.); Pierre Gemayyel; Edward Ḥunayn (a deputy who deserted the moderate National Bloc Party, q.v.), on which list he won the election in 1972), who served as its secretary-general and author of its eloquent statements; Abbot Sharbil al-Qassīs, head of the Permanent Congress of the Lebanese Monastic Order (q.v.) (he was succeeded by Abbot Būlus Na'mān); Charles Mālik; and Fu'ād Afrām al-Bustānī (q.v.), a former president of the Lebanese University (q.v.) and a distinguished Orientalist. The new front declared its "charter" at a special meeting at the monastery of Sayyidat al-Bīr in January 1977. This document emphasizes "the eternal existence of the Lebanese entity" and affirmed its commitment to the preservation of Lebanon's "distinctive characteristics," which—in Muslim and leftist eyes—were code words for Maronite political supremacy.

While the front was established as the political directorate of the Christian community living under right-wing militia control, the influence of Bashīr Gemayyel began to increase as soon as it was established. By 1980, when Bashīr eliminated the military presence of all rival Christian groups, including the Tigers militia of Sham'ūn, and in the wake of the withdrawal of Sulaymān Franjiyyah following the murder of his son Toni (q.v.), the Lebanese Forces (q.v.) became the dominant element in the leadership of the Lebanese Front. Bashīr was a regular participant in its meetings, although military commanders were ostensibly excluded from leadership positions. The death of Bashīr in 1982 and the death of Pierre Gemayyel in August 1984 weakened the front. The uprising of Elie Ḥubayqah in 1985 against Amīn Gemayyel's (q.v.) influence in the Lebanese Forces marginalized the front, and its headquarters was bombed in November.

The victory of Samīr Ja'ja' (q.v.) against Ḥubayqah in 1986 revived the front. Its leadership was expanded to include non-Maronite figures and organizations, like deputy Rāshid al-Khūrī; deputy Michel Sāsīn and Habīb Muṭrān from the National Liberal Party; Karīm Paqradūnī (q.v.) of the Lebanese Forces; Albert Milkī representing the League of Christian Minorities; Dimitrī Biṭār of the Lebanese League of the Greek Orthodox; and publisher Jubrān Tuwaynī (q.v.). The credit for the expansion of the front's leadership beyond the traditional confines should go to Samīr Ja'ja', who consistently expanded the movement to encompass all Christian sects and organizations. However, he insisted on blind obedience to his autocratic leadership.

The status of the front's leadership changed again in the summer of 1987, when its president, Kamīl Sham'ūn, died, and his place in the party leadership was taken by his son Dānī Sham'ūn. The leadership of the front went to George Sa'ādah, head of the Lebanese Phalanges Party. The signing of the aṭ-Ṭā'if Accords (q.v.) and the rise of Michel 'Awn (q.v.) split East Beirut, and the front had its last meeting in the fall of 1989, during the aṭ-Ṭā'if meetings. The front itself was split asunder: George Sa'ādah insisted that he was the legitimate president of the front, while Dānī Sham'ūn, who opposed the aṭ-Ṭā'if Accords and who had become 'Awn's staunch ally, claimed that the front had not been transferred to new hands.

The revived front (which began to meet in April 1990) became known as the "new" Lebanese Front. This latter front was no more than a tool in 'Awn's hands. Until his defeat in October 1990, the new front included Dānī Sham'ūn; Jubrān Tuwaynī; a representative of the Guardians of the Cedars; Walīd Fāris of the Socialist Christian Democratic Party (q.v.); the head of the Lebanese League of the Greek Orthodox; the head of the Northern Liberation Groupings (a pro-'Awn instrument); a representative of the General Greek Orthodox Organization; a representative of the Christian minorities; a representative of the Greek Catholic League; and other activists. With 'Awn's defeat, the front's role was ended, although Jubrān Tuwaynī continued to make statements on its behalf in Europe and Lebanon.

LEBANESE KURDISH PARTY (*Riz Kari*) I. This party was founded in 1975 by Fayṣal Fakhrū and was aligned with the Syrian (q.v.)

regime in Lebanon. It criticized the Miḥḥū family's party (the Kurdish Democratic Party, q.v.) for failing to appeal to a broad section of Kurds (q.v.) in the country. It also accused the Miḥḥū family of monopolizing Kurdish political representation in Lebanon. It supported Barazani's revolt in northern Iraq. In December 1976, the Kurdish Democratic Party (q.v.) and the Lebanese Kurdish Party put aside their differences and formed the Broad Kurdish National Front to unify Kurdish political ranks in Lebanon. When the party criticized its own past pro-Syrian policies, a dissident faction announced the exclusion of Fayṣal Fakhrū and continued the previous political line. Fakhrū, however, continued to claim that he represented the party. *See also* Kurdish Democratic Party.

LEBANESE KURDISH PARTY (*Riz Kari*) II. Following the creation of the coalition of the Kurdish Democratic Party (q.v.) and the Lebanese Kurdish Party I, a faction within the party split off and accused Fayṣal Fakhrū of catering to Jamil Miḥḥū and returning to Kurdish tribalism. It also protested the coalition's domination by Miḥḥū. This faction consistently supported Syrian (q.v.) policy in Lebanon and was a member of a pro-Syrian coalition of organizations.

LEBANESE MONASTIC ORDER (*al-Ruhbaniyyāt al-Lubnāniyyah*). The full title of this group is the Permanent Congress of the Lebanese Maronite Monastic Order. Originally nonpolitical, this changed in 1966 when the order condemned foreign ownership of land in Lebanon. The Permanent Congress was formed to follow up on this issue, to "defend Lebanese territory" from, presumably, Arabs. The order is organizationally independent of the local Maronite (q.v.) patriarchate and has representation worldwide. It enjoys rich financial resources, owning—according to one credible account—27 percent of the land in the Mount Lebanon region. The Maronite Order is the largest monastic order in Lebanon, with almost 500 monks in 1976.

The order's role was expanded in 1966 when the Holy Spirit (Kaslīk) University (q.v.) was founded in Jūnyah. The university hosted conferences and lectures dealing with "Lebanese nationalism" and Maronite history. The Lebanese Research Committee at the university played an important role in theorizing for the Lebanese Front and the Lebanese Forces (qq.v.). The order assumed a prominent political role in the 1975–76 phase of the civil war (q.v.). Its leader, Sharbil al-Qassīs, was a detested figure among Muslims for what was perceived to be his strong anti-Muslim bias. The most controversial stand of the order was its rejection of Muslim-Christian coexistence in Lebanon and its preference for a "pure" Christian political entity. Al-Qassīs was succeeded by Abbot Būlus Na'mān, a close advisor to

Bashīr Gemayyel (q.v.). Na'mān encouraged alliance with Israel (q.v.). In recent years, after the defeat of Michel 'Awn (q.v.) and the rise of Syrian (q.v.) influence after the Gulf War, the order has kept a low profile. The new president of the order, Abbot Hāshim, has not taken controversial political stands.

LEBANESE NATIONAL MOVEMENT (*Al-Ḥarakah al-Waṭaniyyah al-Lubnāniyyah*). This first operated in 1964 under the name of the Front of National and Progressive Parties, Bodies, and Personalities. It was reorganized in 1969 and was renamed the Grouping of National and Progressive Parties. Kamāl Jumblāṭ (q.v.) was the leader and founder of both of these earlier fronts, which were intended to support Palestinian revolution and a program of progressive reforms in Lebanon. The front championed the right of the Palestine Liberation Organization to operate militarily outside of—and inside—Lebanon (q.v.). In 1975, the front was renamed the Lebanese National Movement, which formally reorganized in July 1976, when the Central Political Council was formed to guide members of the movement. The council comprised representatives of the Progressive Socialist Party (q.v.), the Lebanese Communist Party (q.v.), the Communist Action Organization (q.v.), the Syrian Social National Party (q.v.), the Movement of Independent Nasserists (*Al-Murābiṭūn*) (q.v.), the Arab Socialist Ba'th Party (q.v.), the Lebanese Movement in Support of the Revolution, the Organization of the Arab Socialist Ba'th Party (q.v.), the Popular Nasserist Organization (q.v.), the Arab Socialist Union (the Nasserist Organization) (q.v.), *Al-Afwāj al-'Arabiyyah*, the Forces of Nasser, the Leftist Kurdish Party, the Socialist Arab Action Party-Lebanon (q.v.), the Democratic Christians, and such pro-Jumblāṭ figures as Albert Manṣūr (q.v.), Usāmah al-Fākhūrī, Muḥammad Qabbānī, 'Iṣām Nu'mān, 'Izzat Ḥarb, and Fu'ād Shbaqlū. The movement ceased to exist after the Israeli invasion of 1982 (q.v.).

LEBANESE PHALANGES PARTY (*Ḥizb al-Katā'ib al-Lubnāniyyah*). The Phalanges Party was founded in November 1936 by Pierre Gemayyel (q.v.) and four other Christians in the wake of a visit to Germany, when Gemayyel was a member of the Lebanese delegation to the infamous 1936 Olympic Games in Berlin. Gemayyel never denied his desire to replicate the youth organizations of Nazi Germany. In his own words: "In Germany, I witnessed the perfect conduct of a whole, unified nation." The party was founded as a response to the rise of "unionist" calls among Muslims and some Christian groups in Lebanon, who sought the unity of Lebanon with either Syria (q.v.) or another Arab country as part of a larger Arab nation. Al-Katā'ib means "battalions," to underline the military purpose of the organization. In 1943, Phalanges leaders broke with Emile Iddī (q.v.), who wanted to preserve French rule in the country, supporting instead the rising tide of popular opinion that called for immediate independence. This gave the party national legitimacy.

The party first fielded candidates in the by-election of 1945, but failed to win parliamentary seats until 1958, when the 1958 civil war (q.v.) boosted the popularity of the party in Christian eyes. As sectarian polarization tore the country apart, the Phalanges emerged as a well-organized party with a militia. Its recruitment and propaganda techniques became more sophisticated and the party won six parliamentary seats in the 1960 election. It emphasized the uniqueness of Lebanon (q.v.) and resisted the Arabization of Lebanese culture and foreign policy. A party ideologue published a manual in 1966 pledging strict dedication to traditional values: God, homeland, family. The party also is dedicated—according to the party manual—to democracy, private property, and the free enterprise system and is opposed to individualism, leftism, and communism. Membership in the party was predominantly Christian, specifically Maronite (q.v.), and the leadership was tightly in the hands of its founder, Pierre Gemayyel.

The Lebanese Phalanges Party founded the most powerful militia in Lebanon as early as the 1950s and attracted followers in the 1960s and 1970s by provoking clashes with the Palestine Liberation Organization forces. The party was the major fighting force of the right-wing coalition during the 1975 civil war (q.v.) and received aid and weapons from Israel (q.v.) while its enemies were receiving aid of the PLO and other Arab countries. The rise of Bashīr Gemayyel (q.v.) marginalized the party, although Bashīr (the son of Pierre) was also a leading member of the party.

The year 1982 was a watershed in the history of the party. First, Bashīr was elected president of Lebanon. After his assassination, his brother, Amīn (q.v.), became the first Phalangist to assume the presidency of the republic. In 1984, Pierre Gemayyel died, and Amīn insisted that Pierre's deputy, Elie Karāmah, a Greek Catholic (q.v.), become the permanent leader of the party. Karāmah's tenure marked the ultimate marginalization of the party in Lebanese politics. In 1986, George Sa'ādah, a Maronite, was elected to the presidency of the party and he remained president into the 1990s, despite efforts to unseat him by his opponents and by a splinter faction headed by Karāmah and supported by Amīn Gemayyel. The party boycotted the 1992 parliamentary election and did not win seats in the 1996 election. *See also* Lebanese Forces.

LEBANESE POPULAR CONGRESS (*Al-Mu'tamar Ash-Sha'bī Al-Lubnānī*). This broad organization was founded by Kamāl Shātīlā in

1981 to replace his old Union of the Forces of the Working People-the Nasserist Organization (q.v.), which was dissolved. Its creation coincided with Shātīlā's departure from Lebanon (q.v.) in the wake of a deep conflict with Syria (q.v.), his former patron. He has remained in exile in Paris but continues to head this organization. It is known for its skillful manipulation of the media and for its grassroots organization. It is restricted to the Sunni (q.v.) community and is strongest in the Burj Abī Ḥaydar neighborhood, the former residence of Shātīlā. Shātīlā accused the government in 1996 of preventing his return to Lebanon to participate in the parliamentary elections.

LEBANESE UNIVERSITY. This first public university in the country was founded in 1951, when the need arose for an affordable university (the two main universities in Lebanon at the time, the American University of Beirut (AUB) (q.v.) and St. Joseph University (q.v.), catered to the privileged class). It was originally a school for teachers. The idea of the university was first raised in a speech by deputy Ḥamīd Franjiyyah (q.v.) in 1948 and backed by student protests. In 1953, the university opened; Fu'ād Afrām Al-Bustānī (q.v.) was its first president. In 1959, the government decreed the establishment of the various colleges within its domain: the College of Letters and Humanities (1959); the College of Law and Political-Administrative Sciences (1959); the College of Science (1959); the Institute of Social Sciences (1959); the Institute of Fine Arts (1966); the College of Education (1967); the College of Communication and Documentation (1967); the College of Economic Sciences and Business Administration (1967, 1981 respectively); the College of Engineering (1980); the College of Agriculture (1981); and the College of Public Health (1981). There are plans for a medical school.

By 1975, all the colleges were concentrated in Beirut (q.v.) and its suburbs, but the eruption of the 1975 civil war (q.v.), and the inability of many Lebanese to move freely within their country, compelled the government to open branches of the university. Although the university was ostensibly tied together by one curriculum and headed by a central administration in Beirut, it was in effect partitioned according to sectarian and regional lines. Teachers were appointed and promoted on the basis of sectarian and political patronage. Professors with "wrong" views could be harassed, dismissed, or murdered. Many university buildings were confiscated by militias during the war, forcing the administration to rent temporary facilities.

Students pay only nominal fees. The language of instruction is Arabic (q.v.) except in cases when courses are given in the departments of foreign languages and literature. Degree programs are four years long. The university also grants master's and doctoral degrees. Graduates of the university are sometimes discriminated against in employment; it is assumed that they possess an inferior education compared to that attained by graduates of St. Joseph University and the AUB. Attendance is not always high; many students are not full-time and must work to support themselves or their families. Furthermore, many of them have to work because they may have left their homes in remote villages and cannot afford to live in the city, where housing is expensive. Two jobs may be necessary to support a person living alone in Beirut.

The post-war reconstruction of the university is proving difficult. The unregulated proliferation of branches of the university during the war produced 47 branches occupying 74 buildings, many of which were not designed for university purposes. Unification of the branches would violate the norms of sectarian and regional separateness that many Lebanese sectarian leaders prefer. Furthermore, the new Lebanese state is concentrating most of its efforts and resources on defense expenditure, not on education. This has left the university behind the other private universities. For every student at the Lebanese University there are some 13.2 books, while for a student at the AUB the figure is 243.7. There is one personal computer for every 155 students, while there is one for every 20 students at AUB. Finally, the university offers no incentives or funding for its professors to conduct research.

LEBANESE YOUTHS (*Al-Shabībah al-Lubnāniyyah*). This organization was founded within the National Bloc Party (q.v.) and was headed by Mārūn Khūrī, known as Bāsh Mārūn. Mārūn opposed Raymond Iddī's (q.v.) rejection of a separate militia for the party. Mārūn was supported by the Lebanese Phalanges Party (q.v.). After the end of the first phase of the Lebanese civil war (q.v.) (1975–76), the organization seems to have ceased to exist, and its members were incorporated into other militias in East Beirut (q.v.).

LEBANESE-ISRAELI ARMISTICE AGREEMENT. This was signed in March 1949. In 1948, Lebanon had refrained from fighting Israel (qq.v.) despite declarations to the contrary from Lebanese political leaders. When Lebanon withdrew its token troops from the border area, Israel occupied a strip of land that it did not evacuate until the signing of this agreement. The agreement contains mutual commitments to respect border demarcations and not to launch attacks against the other. The Lebanese government holds Israel to the letter of this agreement, to compel it to withdraw from territories it occupies in South Lebanon.

LEBANON. The word "Lebanon" (Arabic *Lubnān*) comes from a Semitic word meaning "whiteness," in reference to the snow-covered peaks of Mount Lebanon. The word has been used since Roman times to refer to the western range of the mountain, while Anti-Lebanon refers to the eastern range. The country did not exist in its current borders before this century, although Lebanese ultra-nationalists have claimed that the Lebanese "nation" has been in existence for thousands of years. Greater Liban (q.v.), which refers to the geographic entity that is today Lebanon, was declared by the French in 1920. Lebanon is a republic and is recognized as an independent and sovereign state. It is a member of the United Nations and the League of Arab States. *See also* France; French Mandate.

LEVANT. This French word originally referred to the East but was later modified to refer specifically to the Fertile Crescent (q.v.).

LIBYA. It did not take long for Libyan leader Mu'ammar Qadhdhāfī to realize the significance of the Lebanese political and information arena for his pan-Arab struggle. Lebanese newspapers provided a region-wide readership. Furthermore, Lebanese public opinion was vocal on issues dealing with Arab unity and the Palestinian question, both issues central to Libyan propaganda. Foreign preference for Lebanese newspapers is not new; president Charles Ḥilū (q.v.) used to greet Lebanese journalists with the remark, "Welcome to your second homeland, Lebanon."

Lebanon was also important for Libya because it contained among the Sunni (q.v.) population followers of Jamāl 'Abdul-Nasser (q.v.), whose mantle was claimed by Qadhdhāfī. He cultivated ties with most Lebanese Nasserist groups and donated generously to their causes. He also was instrumental in the establishment of the pro-Libyan newspaper *As-Safīr* (q.v.) in 1974 and the weekly *Al-Kifāḥ Al-'Arabī.* Libya also gave money and weapons to several Palestine Liberation Organization organizations. The 1975 civil war (q.v.) provided Libya with an opportunity for political intervention; in the conflict between Syria (q.v.) and the PLO Libya presented itself as a neutral player, on good terms with all sides. To that end, Libya even cultivated relations with right-wing forces; the missions of Libyan Prime Minister 'Abdul-Salām Jallūd (q.v.) during the 1975–76 phase of the civil war were universally praised, although the Lebanese National Movement (q.v.) urged Libya to observe "the isolation of the Phalangists" (q.v.). Libya, however, lost any claim to neutrality as years went by and as news of Israeli sponsorship of right-wing forces emerged. Libya became the main sponsor of the Lebanese National Movement after 1976.

Not that there were no disagreements between Libya and its Lebanese clients and allies. Qadhdhāfī wanted the Lebanese left to bring about a decisive defeat of the Lebanese Forces (q.v.) and was uncomfortable during the periods of the war where there was no fighting. In 1978, Imām Mūsā aṣ-Ṣadr (q.v.) "disappeared" while on a state visit to Libya, and several Libyan businesses were bombed, presumably by angry Lebanese Shi'ites (q.v.). By 1982, Qadhdhāfī lost any faith or hope in the ability of the PLO and its Lebanese allies to achieve military and political victory. He even urged PLO leaders to commit suicide during the siege of Beirut (q.v.) instead of implementing Israeli conditions. By the 1980s, the Libyan role had diminished, and its influence in Lebanon was minimal. The diplomatic isolation of Libya in the 1980s and 1990s ended its generous donations to Lebanese groups and publications, and the Libyan leader was too intimidated by the United States (q.v.) in the wake of the Gulf War to project Libyan power in the region.

LIḤFID COMMUNE. In this 'Āmmiyyah (q.v.), which took place in 1821, peasant masses from Jubayl, Batrūn, and Kisrawān protested increased taxation. The commune also attracted Shi'ites (q.v.) from the Jubayl region. The gathering of the masses took place in Liḥfid. The armies of Bashīr II the Shihabi (q.v.) and Bashīr Jumblāṭ united to brutally crush the rebellion. One account estimates that some 80 people were killed. One woman called Umm Khaz'a participated heroically in this communal uprising and urged her three sons to join the ranks of the rebels.

LIQA' AL-ISLĀMĪ, AL. *SEE* ISLAMIC MEETING.

LĪRAH. *SEE* CURRENCY.

LIWĀ' TANNŪRĪN. *SEE* TANNŪRĪN BRIGADE.

LUBNĀN. *SEE* LEBANON.

-M-

MA'LŪF, NAṢRĪ (1911–). A parliamentarian and one of the most eloquent deputies in Lebanon, he was born to a Greek Catholic (q.v.), historically literate family in Beirut (q.v.) and received a law degree from St. Joseph University (q.v.). He became one of the most famous lawyers in Lebanon; his court presentations were reported in detail in the press and eagerly anticipated by readers. He used his command of the Arabic (q.v.) language to write columns in the newspaper *Al-Jarīdah.* He served briefly as minister of finance in 1956–57. Ma'lūf espoused political moderation and believed in Muslim-Christian coexistence. He was first elected to parliament from Beirut in 1968 and was reelected in 1972. He avoided taking extremist positions during the 1975–90 civil war (q.v.), although he admired Kamīl Sham'ūn (q.v.) as a political leader. He won a parliamentary seat in a by-election in Beirut in the 1990s, when deputy Joseph Mughayzil died.

MAḤĀḌIR MAJLIS AN-NUWWĀB. These are the published minutes of the Lebanese parliament. Since 1924 the Lebanese parliament has been publishing and selling the full minutes of its sessions, with the exception of its secret sessions, which are closed to the public and the press. These minutes also print the full statements of cabinets and the results of voting on issues before the parliament.

MAḤMAṢĀNĪ, ṢUBḤĪ (1911–1986). This jurist was born in Beirut (q.v.) to a Sunni (q.v.) family and was educated at the American University of Beirut (q.v.). He later received a doctorate in law from the University of Lyons and a degree in law from the University of London. He was one of the first scholars in jurisprudence in Lebanon, combining a thorough knowledge of Western canon law and traditional Islamic law. He was one of the reformers of Islam, believing that Islam is compatible with Western political institutions and with human rights. Maḥmaṣānī was also one of the first writers on human rights in Arabic (q.v.), long before it became the subject of abundant literature in the 1980s and 1990s. Most of his works are descriptions of legal systems in Arab countries. In 1945, he served as legal advisor to Lebanese delegations at the League of Arab States and the founding conference of the United Nations. He represented Beirut in the 1964 election and was appointed minister of economy in 1966.

MAJLIS AL-JUNŪB (Council of the South). This body was founded in 1970 to meet the needs and demands of South Lebanon. The council was created as a result of the political campaigns of Imām Mūsā aṣ-Ṣadr (q.v.), who drew attention to the neglect and impoverishment of South Lebanon. He was also critical of Lebanese state indifference to the Israeli bombing of villages in the South. The council was marred by corruption as soon as it was created. During the administration of Sulaymān Franjiyyah (q.v.), it was called by people in the South *majlis al-juyūb* (council of pockets). The political machine of Shi'ite (q.v.) leader Kāmil al-As'ad (q.v.) turned the council into a tool for rewarding cronies and loyalists and punishing political rivals. There was very little evidence of its work and impact years after its creation. It is now considered the state's tool to appease Shi'ite public opinion.

MAJLIS AN-NUWWĀB. Literally, this means chamber of deputies. It is the official name of the Lebanese parliament.

MAJMŪ' FAWĀ'ID. This journal, founded by American missionaries in 1851, dealt with a variety of religious and scientific issues. It was printed at the famous American Printing House. It is considered the oldest Arabic (q.v.) journal. It ceased publication in 1855.

MANDATE. *SEE* FRENCH MANDATE.

MA'NID. *SEE* FAKHR AD-DĪN II.

MANṢŪR, ALBERT (1937–). This parliamentarian was born in Ra's Ba'albak (q.v.) to a Greek Catholic (q.v.) family and was educated in Jūnyah, at St. Joseph University (q.v.), and at the University of Paris, where he earned a Ph.D. in law in 1963. He was attracted to leftist ideas, but refrained from joining a political party, because his employment with the government prohibited him from affiliating with any party. Manṣūr taught at the Holy Spirit University at al-Kaslīk (q.v.) and the Lebanese University (q.v.). He was employed at the Social Security Agency, which is part of the Lebanese governmental machinery.

He won his first parliamentary seat in 1972 and became close to Druze leader Kamāl Jumblāṭ (qq.v.). His views underwent a transformation during the 1975–90 civil war (q.v.), and he abandoned his early radical views. He established relations with right-wing figures, including Michel 'Awn (q.v.), whom he backed for president in the 1980s. Manṣūr broke with 'Awn when the latter declared his "war of liberation" in 1989. Manṣūr was appointed minister of defense in 1989–90 and minister of information in 1990. His relations with President Ilyās Hrāwī (q.v.) soured over the years, especially after he published a book in which he claimed that Hrāwī's administration had deviated from the aṭ-Ṭā'if Accords (q.v.).

MAQĀṢID, al-. This is the foundation that supports various charitable and educational Muslim institutions. It was founded in 1878 by Sunni (q.v.) notables concerned about the growth of Christian educational missions and who wanted to offer an education that would not dilute the Muslim faith. The foundation became one of the main, and best-funded, of its kind. In this century, al-Maqāṣid was put under the control of the Salām family, and Sā'ib Salām (q.v.) specifically. It recruits supporters and establishes patronage networks. In 1996 it received a multi-million-dollar donation from King Fahd of Saudi Arabia (q.v.).

MAQDISĪ, SAMĪR (1932–). This scholar and educator received his education in Lebanon and the United States (qq.v.), where he received a

Ph.D. in economics from Columbia University. He has taught economics at the American University of Beirut (AUB) (q.v.) since his return and has chaired its Economics Department. In 1990, he founded the Institute of Financial and Banking Affairs at AUB. Maqdisī briefly held the acting president post at AUB. In 1992, he was appointed minister of finance. He is the second Protestant to hold a ministerial post in the independent era.

MARADAH, al-. The origins of this group are still disputed. Popular Maronite (q.v.) myth refers to tough mountain fighters opposing the Arab conquest of Lebanon. It is speculated that they were known as Jarājimah (q.v.), after their settlement in the area of Lebanon.

MARONITE COLLEGE IN ROME. It was founded in 1584 to cement Maronite (q.v.) ties to the Vatican and to train Maronite clergy in matters of theology. It served as a school for some of the Orientalists who helped translate the Qur'ān into Latin.

MARONITE LEAGUE. This sectarian association of Maronite (q.v.) professionals was founded in the 1950s but emerged on the political scene during the 1975–76 civil war (q.v.). It took less extremist positions than other Maronite-oriented militias and organizations, and its leader during the civil war, the lawyer Shākir Abū Sulaymān (q.v.), often urged moderation and compromise. It played an important role in settling disputes, and wars, in the Christian camp. The league elected former deputy Pierre Ḥilū as its president in 1997.

MARONITE SECT. The origins of this sect are disputed. It is certain, however, that Maronite communion in the Roman Catholic Church was established in 1182, broken thereafter, and formally reestablished in the 16th century. Lebanese Maronites retain their own rites and canon law and use Arabic (q.v.) and Aramaic in their liturgy as well as the Karshuni script with old Syriac letters. The word *maron,* or *mārūn,* in Syriac means "small lord."

The Maronite sect has been directed and administered by the patriarch of Antioch and the East. Bishops are generally nominated by a church synod from among the graduates of the Maronite College in Rome (q.v.). In 1996 Cardinal Nuṣrallāh Buṭrus Ṣufayr (q.v.) was the Maronite patriarch. Besides the Beirut archdiocese, eight other archdioceses and dioceses are located in the Middle East: Aleppo, Ba'albak (q.v.), Cairo, Cyprus, Jubayl al-Batrūn, Sidon (q.v.), Tripoli (q.v.), and Tyre (q.v.). Parishes and independent dioceses are also found in Argentina, Brazil, Venezuela, the United States (q.v.), Canada, Mexico, Cote d'Ivoire, and Senegal. There are four minor seminaries in Lebanon and a faculty of theology at Holy Spirit University in al-Kaslīk (q.v.). The patriarch is elected by a synod of bishops and confirmed by the pope in Rome. It is estimated that some 16 percent of the Lebanese population are Maronites. They are scattered throughout the country, with a heavy concentration in Mount Lebanon.

MARQŪQ. This is the name of flat, thin bread also known as *ṣāj* bread. It is consumed mostly in the mountain areas of Lebanon and is a staple in Assyrian and Armenian (q.v.) cuisine.

MARTYR'S SQUARE (***Sāḥat Ash-Shuhadā'***). This square in downtown Beirut (q.v.) is named in memory of the Christians and Muslims executed by the Turkish occupation army in 1916. A memorial in the center of the square is dedicated to the men whose deaths are mourned in the annual Day of the Martyrs. The square was heavily damaged during the 1975 civil war (q.v.).

MĀRŪN (Saint Maron). The Maronites (q.v.) are named after this monk, who lived in the fourth century and died in 410 in the area between Antioch and Cyrrhus. His followers moved after his death, so the legend goes, to Syria (q.v.), and later to the mountains of Lebanon (q.v.). *See also* Maronite Sect.

MAS'AD, BŪLUS (1806–1890). This Maronite patriarch was born in 'Ashqut and educated by a priest in Bshirrī. He entered 'Ayn Waraqah (q.v.) school and learned Syriac, Arabic (q.v.), Italian, and Latin. He went to Rome for advanced religious study at the Maronite College (q.v.), returning to Lebanon in 1830 to work as the secretary of Patriarch Yūsuf Ḥubaysh. In 1854, he was elected to the Maronite patriarchate. He left several works on Christian theology.

MASHAQQAH, MIKHĀ'ĪL (1800–1888). A writer and historian, he was born to a family of Greek origin in Dayr al-Qamar. He was taught the principles of secondary education by his father, Jirjis, and then traveled to Egypt, where he studied music. He returned to Mount Lebanon and worked for the Shihabi family. He later relocated to Damascus, where he established ties with the British and American delegations. In 1845 in Cairo, he studied medicine on his own, passed a state exam, and earned a medical degree. He returned to Damascus and worked as a deputy to the American Council while practicing medicine. He wrote a detailed chronicle of the 1860 events in Syria; the book was translated into English.

***MASHRIQ, al-*.** This journal was first published 1898 by the Catholic Press (q.v.). It edited by noted scholar Louis Cheikho (q.v.) and was and was closely associated with St. Joseph University (q.v.). It was perhaps the first scholarly journal published in Arabic (q.v.), thanks in large measure to Cheikho. The publication of the journal has been interrupted, but it remains in existence.

***MASHRIQ, al-*.** This term in Arabic refers to the East, specifically the eastern part of the Arab world, in contrast to *al-maghrib,* the western part of the Arab world. *Al-mashriq* includes Lebanon.

MATNĪ, NASĪB al- (?–1958). An anti-Sham'ūn Maronite (qq.v.) journalist whose murder on May 8, 1958, triggered the 1958 civil war (q.v.). He was the owner and publisher of *At-Telegraph.*

***MAWĀQIF*.** This monthly journal was founded by the famous poet Adonis (q.v.) in 1968 and published articles critical of social, political, economic, and cultural conditions in the Arab world. It represented Adonis' beliefs that only through a thorough social and cultural revolution will a desirable political outcome emerge.

MAY 17 AGREEMENT. Nothing damaged the image of president Amīn Gemayyel (q.v.) more than his 1983 signing of the May 17 Agreement with Israel (q.v.). Under pressure from the administration of U.S. president Ronald Reagan, Gemayyel began the first direct negotiations with the Jewish state in Lebanese history. The Lebanese delegation was headed by legal scholar Anṭoine Fattāl. The Lebanese wanted a peace treaty with Israel that would end Israeli occupation of South Lebanon. The Israeli government, however, wanted Lebanon to put its relations with Israel ahead of its Arab ties. The agreement would have allowed Israel to suppress Lebanese views hostile toward Israel and to force normalization between Lebanon and Israel. The Lebanese government pledged to curtail violent groups in Lebanon and to protect the border area. Israel, however, wanted to retain rights over Lebanese air space and territory. What the agreement left out was an agreement by Syria (q.v.) to withdraw its forces from Lebanon. Syria objected strongly to the agreement, calling it "the capitulation agreement." Many groups in Lebanon agreed with Syria, and public opinion forced the government to abrogate it in 1984; and the parliament finally abrogated it in 1987.

MELKART AGREEMENT. This was a follow-up agreement to the Cairo Agreement (q.v.) of 1969, which regulated relations between the Lebanese government and the Palestine Liberation Organization

(PLO). It was signed by representatives of the Lebanese government and the PLO, in the wake of the clashes between the Lebanese Army (q.v.) and PLO forces in the spring of 1973. It affirmed commitment to the Cairo Agreement, while imposing restrictions on Palestinian military activities. The outbreak of violence in Lebanon made this agreement obsolete.

MIḤḤŪ, JAMĪL. *SEE* KURDISH DEMOCRATIC PARTY.

MIḤḤŪ, MUḤAMMAD. *SEE* KURDISH DEMOCRATIC PARTY—PROVISIONAL LEADERSHIP.

MISSILE CRISIS. This refers to a critical episode during the 1975–90 civil war (q.v.). Bashīr Gemayyel (q.v.), encouraged by Israel's (q.v.) militant government, which expressed its desire to lend more military support to the Lebanese Forces (LF) (q.v.), infiltrated 100 LF militiamen into the city of Zaḥlah (q.v.) (which is close to the Syrian border and free of a Phalangist presence) and ordered them to attack Syrian military positions in Shtūrah. In response, the Syrian army imposed a siege on Zaḥlah, demanding the surrender of the LF gunmen. Gemayyel then claimed that Syria was executing a plan to exterminate the Christians of Lebanon and pleaded for Israeli help. Israel attacked, downing two Syrian helicopters outside of Zaḥlah. Syria's Ḥāfiḍh al-Asad immediately stationed SAM-6 surface-to-air missiles in the region, while Israel promised to attack the missile site. Fearing an escalation that might lead to a Syrian-Israeli war, U.S. President Ronald Reagan dispatched his special envoy, Philip Habib, to calm both sides. An agreement was reached, and Syria was allowed to keep the missiles in Lebanon.

MITHĀQ AL-WAṬANĪ, AL. *SEE* NATIONAL PACT.

MI'ŪSHĪ, BŪLUS. He was the Maronite (q.v.) patriarch during the 1958 civil war (q.v.). He surprised president Kamīl Sham'ūn (q.v.) by refusing to support him. His stance diminished the sectarian flavor of the conflict. He was praised for his stance by many Muslims.

MONOPHYSITES. *SEE* JACOBITE CHRISTIANS.

MOVEMENT OF ARAB NATIONALISTS (*Ḥarakat al-Qawmiyyīn al-'Arab*). The movement was founded at the American University of Beirut (AUB) (q.v.) by students George Ḥabash and Hānī al-Hindī, who were inspired by the famous professor of history at AUB, Constantine Zurayq (q.v.), who preached Arab nationalism, secularism, and scientific advancement. The movement called for a strategy for the liberation of Palestine; revenge was an element of its ideology. It also preached Arab unity and was closely identified with the regime of Jamāl 'Abdul-Nasser (q.v.) during much of the 1960s. The movement was active in Lebanese affairs as early as the late 1950s, when it led rebels in Tyre (q.v.) against the al-Khalīl family rule of the city. In the 1960s the movement became increasingly splintered; Muḥsin Ibrāhīm led a leftist faction with Marxist-Leninist ideas. Ḥabash was identified with the rightist faction, which resisted calls for class analysis of Arab society. The movement was dissolved in the wake of the 1967 defeat, and the Popular Front for the Liberation of Palestine was born.

MOVEMENT OF CHANGE (***Ḥarakat at-Taghyīr***). This pro-'Awn movement was founded in 1991 when Michel 'Awn (q.v.) was no longer on Lebanese territory. It is headed by Elie Maḥfūḍh and is perhaps the most consistently anti-Syrian movement in Lebanon. The movement calls for the boycott of elections as long as the Syrian (q.v.) army remains in Lebanon.

MOVEMENT OF NON-VIOLENCE. *SEE* NONVIOLENCE.

MOVEMENT OF THE DISINHERITED (***Ḥarakat al-Maḥrūmīn***) *SEE* AMAL MOVEMENT.

MOVEMENT OF THE INDEPENDENT NASSERISTS-AL-MURĀBIṬŪN (***Ḥarakat an-Naṣiriyyīn al-Mustaqillīn***). This movement is closely associated with its founder and leader, Ibrāhīm Qulaylāt (q.v.). It was founded in 1958 when young Ibrāhīm was a participant on the side of pro-Nasser forces in Beirut (q.v.). His movement was originally confined to the Sunni (q.v.) quarter of Abū Shākir, where his father had been a local leader. Ibrāhīm was considered a fanatic Nasserist, willing to do anything to support Nasserist principles in Lebanon and to punish Jamāl 'Abdul-Nasser's (q.v.) enemies. In 1961 he was accused of bombing the house of the minister of finance, who was regarded as anti-Nasser. Qulaylāt spent a month and a half in jail.

Qulaylāt became a prominent—albeit controversial—figure in 1966, when the Lebanese government alleged that he instigated the assassination of Kāmil Muruwwah (q.v.), the publisher and editor-in-chief of the Beirut daily, *Al-Ḥayāt*. Muruwwah was virulently anti-Nasser and supported pro-Western Arab regimes. Qulaylāt, who professed his innocence, was jailed for a year and a half and was then released without trial. The case made him a hero in some circles, particularly among Nasser's many Muslim admirers. After 1967, Qulaylāt informally used the name of Independent Nasserists to underline his independence from the numerous Nasserist organizations in Sunni Muslim areas of Lebanon. His armed men clashed with the authorities as early as 1969, and his quarter of Abū Shākir was immune from state police interference. The movement came to public attention when government troops tried to close its headquarters, which led to sympathy for the movement on the part of Muslims and leftists.

Qulaylāt often asserted that his organization was not a political party but rather a broad-based movement aimed at mobilizing Nasserists in Lebanon. The movement lacked an ideology as such, claiming the writings and speeches of Nasser as its source of ideological inspiration. It supported the Palestine Liberation Organization (PLO) in Lebanon and advocated "armed struggle" against right-wing forces in the country. Yāsir Arafāt's Fatḥ (qq.v.) supported the movement with generous financial and military aid, but the Libyan (q.v.) regime was believed to be the main benefactor of the movement. The movement emerged as a major militia in the 1975–76 phase of the civil war (q.v.), not so much because of its fighting but because Qulaylāt knew how to promote his movement in the press, sometimes pressuring local newspapers and magazines to run favorable stories. The promotion of the militia led to the association of the movement with the name of its militia, *al-Murābiṭūn,* which is the common name of the movement.

Qulaylāt ran the movement autocratically, although he created the facade of a collective leadership. Many Sunni professionals flocked to the movement after 1977, because they thought it provided opportunities for employment and upward mobility. The leadership was predominantly Sunni, although the token presence of one Shi'ite (q.v.) in the leadership was often advertised. The militia had in fact a significant Shi'ite component, but the sectarian orientation of the movement was of Sunni urban professionals. Between 1977 and 1982, Qulaylāt held sway in the streets of West Beirut (q.v.) and often received foreign dignitaries and ambassadors. His militia, like other militias in the city, engaged in plunder, blackmail, and thuggery. The Israeli invasion of 1982 (q.v.) dealt a setback to all elements of the Lebanese National Movement (q.v.), including *al-Murābiṭūn*. But Qulaylāt continued to operate in the city until 1984, when the Amal Movement and the Progressive Socialist Party (qq.v.) imposed their rule over the city and gradually eliminated rival Sunni militias in West Beirut. In 1985, Al-Murābiṭūn fighters were defeated in bloody battles, and Qulaylāt fled the country. In recent years, he has resided in Europe, dividing his time between Switzerland and France. He has continued to issue political declarations from exile.

MOVEMENT OF THE PIONEERS OF REFORM (***Ḥarakat Ruwwād al-Iṣlāḥ***). This movement, founded in 1973 by Tammām Salām, the son of traditional Sunni (q.v.) leader Ṣā'ib Salām (q.v.), was intended to compete with armed leftist groups popular among the Muslim masses. In 1975, the militia of the movement did not participate in armed combat, although it had abundant military resources thanks to Saudi support for Ṣā'ib Salām. Tammām Salām won a seat in the 1996 parliamentary election.

MOVEMENT OF UNIONIST NASSERISTS (***Ḥarakat al-Wiḥdawiyyīn an-Nāṣiriyyīn***). This small organization was founded by Ibrāhīm Qulaylāt's (q.v.) deputy in the Movement of Independent Nasserists-Al-Murābiṭūn (q.v.). In 1982, French-educated Samīr Ṣabbāgh rebelled against Qulaylāt's autocratic tendencies and formed a small organization called the National Grouping, which he later renamed the Movement of Unionist Nasserists. It is a small organization based in Beirut (q.v.) that claims to speak on behalf of Sunnis (q.v.) in West Beirut (q.v.). It is aligned with Syria (q.v.) and the Progressive Socialist Party (q.v.).

MU'AWWAḌ, NĀ'ILAH (1940–). A deputy, she is the widow of President Rene Mu'awwaḍ (q.v.). She was born to a Maronite (q.v.) family in Beirut (q.v.), and was educated in Lebanon (q.v.) and the United Kingdom. She received a degree from St. Joseph University (q.v.). Both her father and uncle served in parliament. She worked as a journalist at *L'Orient* (q.v.), the French-language newspaper, before marrying Rene. She ran for her husband's seat in the 1992 election and won. Nā'ilah has kept a high profile since the death of her husband, establishing charitable foundations in his honor. She became the second woman ever to serve in parliament in 1991 when she was appointed to a seat. She has been active on the Education Committee in parliament and in calling for an increase in female representation in political institutions. She was reelected in the 1996 parliamentary elections.

MU'AWWAḌ, RENE (1925–1989). He was born to one of the key Maronite (q.v.) families of the North and received his education in Tripoli and later in Beirut at St. Joseph University (qq.v.), where he received a degree in law. He opened his own law office in 1951 and ran for a parliamentary seat in the same year on the list of Ḥamīd Franjiyyah (q.v.) but lost. He first entered parliament in 1957 and was reelected in subsequent elections. He was a minister in the administrations of Fu'ād Shihāb (q.v.) and Charles Ḥilū (q.v.), who was his friend. His loyalty to Shihabism was stronger than his regional ties; he surprised his constituency in 1970 when he voted for Ilyās Sarkīs (q.v.), who lost the presidency to Sulaymān Franjiyyah (q.v.). He returned to the cabinet in the administration of his friend Sarkīs. He remained neutral during the 1975 civil war (q.v.) distancing himself from the policies of the Lebanese Forces (q.v.). He was consistently close to Syrian (q.v.) officials, like most politicians from the North. He was elected president in 1989 but was assassinated a few weeks later. He was succeeded in public office by his wife, Nā'ilah (q.v.).

MUDAWWAR, MIKHĀ'ĪL (1822–1889). A publisher, he was born in Beirut (q.v.) and studied Arabic (q.v.) and Italian in 'Ayn Ṭūrā. He worked first in commerce with his brothers but later devoted his time to his work as an official translator of the French consulate. He was a member of the Asiatic Society in Paris and the Syrian Scientific Society in Beirut. He funded the publication efforts of his friend Naṣīf al-Yāzijī (q.v.). Mikhā'īl also funded Khalīl al-Khūrī's newspaper, *Hadīqat Al-Akhbār* (qq.v.). He traveled in Europe after the 1860 civil war (q.v.) and purchased large estates in al-Biqā' (q.v.) after his return. His business ventures took more of his time in later years, and he lost interest in literary activities.

MUḌHAFFAR PAHSA (1837–1907). A Roman Catholic *mutaṣarrif* (q.v.), his birthplace is not known. He attended the French military school of St. Cyr, enlisted in the Ottoman army, and was appointed in 1867 a military aide to Sultan Abdulaziz. He then served Sultan Abdulhamid II and contributed to military reforms in the empire. He was later appointed commander of the Imperial Stable. In 1902, he was appointed *mutaṣarrif* for a term of five years. He died before the expiration of his term. Muḍhaffar was unpopular due to widespread corruption during his term.

MUFTĪ. Literally, it means "jurisconsult," or somebody who can issue religiously binding edicts. It is the highest religious post in Lebanon, and is funded by the government. The current muftī is Muḥammad Rashīd Qabbānī (q.v.), who held for years the title of acting muftī due to lack of consensus among Lebanon's Sunni (q.v.) leaders on a candidate for the post. He became a full muftī in 1996.

MUḤĀFAḌHAH. An administrative unit that means a "governorate." Lebanon is divided into six governorates: Beirut (q.v.), Mount Lebanon, Jabal 'Āmil, Nabaṭiyyah (q.v.), North, and al-Biqā' (q.v.).

MUḤĀFIḌH. The term means "governor," the official in charge of the larger administrative unit of *muḥāfaḍhah* (q.v.).

MUHAJJARŪN, AL. *SEE* DISPLACED PEOPLE.

MUḤARRIR, al-. This now defunct newspaper, founded in 1963 by Hishām Abū Ḍhahr, was pro-Palestinian and expressed a pro-Iraqi Ba'th party (q.v.) political line. It was widely read in the 1960s and 1970s and was often used by the Palestine Liberation Organization and the Lebanese National Movement (q.v.) to spread their messages. It was edited by Hishām Abū Ḍhahr and, later, by his brother Walīd Abū Ḍhahr. The newspaper remained critical of Syrian policy during the war, and as a result, pro-Syrian troops stormed the newspaper headquarters in 1976. The paper was forced to close down. Its mission was continued by its sister publication *Al-Waṭan Al-'Arabī,* which was published in Paris, although it too received threats and a massive car bomb.

MUJADDARAH. This famous Lebanese dish contains lentils, rice, and onions. It is favored by the poor—due to its affordable ingredients—but is served in most homes.

MUJAHIDŪN, AL. *SEE* ISLAMIC COMMUNITY.

MUKARZIL, NA'ŪM (1863–1932). A journalist, he was born in Furaykah and studied in Beirut (q.v.). He received a degree from St. Joseph University (q.v.), and moved to Egypt to teach at a Jesuit school. He returned to Lebanon (q.v.) to found a private school and later emigrated to the United States (q.v.), where he published the weekly *Al-'Aṣr* in Philadelphia. In 1898, he founded the weekly *Al-Hudā,* which later became a daily newspaper and the leading Arabic (q.v.) publication in the United States. He recruited some of the best writers as contributors, and his efforts energized Arabic publishing in the United States.

MUKHAYBIR, ALBERT (1914–). This Greek Orthodox (q.v.) physician-turned-politician was born in 1914 in Bayt Mirī. He was educated in Lebanon and Lausanne, Switzerland, where he received his medical degree. He practiced medicine and served a very loyal constituency, which encouraged him to seek public office. He was elected deputy in 1957 and served as a minister in 1958. He was reelected in 1960, 1964, and 1972. He served briefly as acting minister of education in 1972 and later served as deputy prime minister. Mukhaybir maintained an independent stance during the 1975–90 civil war (q.v.), and was the only deputy living in East Beirut (q.v.) who refused to vote for Bashīr Gemayyel (q.v.) in 1982. He is highly critical of Syrian (q.v.) involvement in Lebanon and has called for Lebanese-Israeli peace. He founded the Rally for the Republic (q.v.) in the 1990s and emerged as the leading Christian opposition voice. He lost the election in 1996, although he continues his opposition activities.

MUKHTĀR. Literally, it means "the selected one," and refers to the village headman.

MUKHTĀRAH, al-. This is the seat of the Jumblāṭ family (q.v.). It houses a grand palace, where Kamāl Jumblāṭ (q.v.) resided and where his son Walīd (q.v.) now resides. It contains a valuable art and book collection.

MULTINATIONAL FORCE. This force was formed in 1982 and was deployed in August of that year to protect Palestinian civilians while Palestine Liberation Organization forces were being evacuated from Beirut (q.v.) and all of Lebanon (q.v.) according to an agreement that Israel (q.v.) imposed after its 1982 invasion (q.v.) of Lebanon. The massacre of Palestinians (q.v.) in the Ṣabrā and Shātīlā (q.v.) camps occurred after the withdrawal of the force. It was redeployed and was later embroiled in the 1975–90 civil war (q.v.) on the side of the right-wing camp.

MUNAḌHḌHAMAT AL-'AMAL AL-ISHTIRĀKĪ ATH-THAWRĪ. *SEE* ORGANIZATION OF REVOLUTIONARY SOCIALIST ACTION.

MUNAḌHḌHAMAT AL-'AMAL ASH-SHUYŪ'Ī. *SEE* COMMUNIST ACTION ORGANIZATION.

MUNAḌHḌHAMAT AL-JIHĀD AL-ISLĀMĪ. *SEE* ISLAMIC JIHAD ORGANIZATION.

MUNAḌHḌHAMAT AL-MUSTAḌ'AFĪN FI AL-ARḌ. *SEE* ORGANIZATION OF THE OPPRESSED ON THE EARTH.

MUNICIPALITY. This smallest administrative unit is intended as a form of local government with mere procedural powers. It is found (and its members are elected) in any village, town, or city with a population that exceeds 300 people. No municipal elections were held during the 1975–90 civil war (q.v.). The Lebanese government has promised to arrange for comprehensive municipal elections in the country.

MUQTAṬAF, al-. This journal was founded in 1876 by Ya'qūb aṣ-Ṣarrūf (q.v.) and Fāris Nimr and carried articles on science and agriculture.

The founders credited their professor at the American University of Beirut (AUB) (q.v.), Cornelius Van Dyck (q.v.), with encouraging them and choosing its name. When press restrictions increased in Syria (q.v.), the founders moved the journal to Egypt in 1884. Also, the editors had been fired from AUB for supporting a professor who was dismissed for mentioning Darwin's name in a public lecture.

MURĀBIṬŪN, AL. *SEE* MOVEMENT OF THE INDEPENDENT NASSERISTS.

MURĀD, 'ABDUR-RAHĪM (1942–). This Sunni (q.v.) Nasserist was born in al-Biqā' (q.v.) and educated in Sidon (q.v.) and Brummānā. He obtained a degree from the Beirut Arab University (q.v.) in 1968. He joined the Arab Socialist Ba'th Party (q.v.) in his youth and was one of the founders of the Arab Socialist Union (q.v.) in the mid-1970s. He has advocated Libyan foreign policy in Lebanon, and his party received financial and military aid from Libya (q.v.) during the 1975–90 civil war (q.v.). His businesses in Brazil used to keep him out of Lebanon for months at a time. He founded, with Libyan help, charitable educational institutions in poverty-stricken al-Biqā' and named them after a famed Libyan independence war hero, 'Umar al-Mukhtār. He was elected to parliament in 1992 and served in the cabinet of Ilyās Hrāwī (q.v.). He was reelected in 1996.

MURR, MICHEL (1931–). This Greek Orthodox (q.v.) politician was born in Btighrīn and educated at St. Joseph University (q.v.), from which he received an engineering degree. He was elected to parliament in 1968 and was appointed minister in 1969. He reappeared on the public scene, after years of successful business ventures, in 1976, when he was appointed minister. He was appointed again in 1980. He supported Bashīr Gemayyel (q.v.) in 1982 and was responsible for paying off hesitant deputies. He established close ties with Syria (q.v.) after 1982 and was appointed minister of defense and deputy prime minister in 1990. He was elected to parliament in 1992 and reelected in 1996. His critics attacked his management of the Lebanese elections in 1996.

MURUWWAH, KĀMIL (1915–1966). A journalist, he was born to a Shi'ite (q.v.) family in a village near Sidon (q.v.) and received a degree in political science from the American University of Beirut (q.v.). He worked as a journalist at *An-Nidā'* and *An-Nahār* (qq.v.). In 1946, he founded the daily newspaper *Al-Ḥayāt*, which soon emerged as one of the leading newspapers in the Middle East. His journalistic career was based on his ability to stand up to Jamāl 'Abdul-Nasser's (q.v.)

influence in Lebanon and the Arab world. He openly supported Gulf regimes and turned his newspaper into a powerful anti-communist vehicle. Muruwwah ridiculed Nasser and the leftist movement in Lebanon. He was accused by his enemies of receiving funds from Western intelligence agencies, but no evidence for this exists. His newspaper was closely read because it carried news about Nasser's enemies (in Lebanon and abroad) that other newspapers would not carry. In 1952, he founded the English-language newspaper *Daily Star,* the first serious English-language daily in the Arab world. It ceased publication only during the 1975–90 civil war (q.v.).

On May 15, 1966, Muruwwah was assassinated by a fanatic Nasserist. It was alleged that Lebanese Nasserist leader, Ibrāhīm Qulaylāt (q.v.), was behind the assassination. *Al-Ḥayāt* was resurrected in London in the 1980s by the former editor of *Daily Star,* Jihād al-Khāzin, who managed it with Kamīl's son Karīm. In 1990, Saudi Prince Khālid Bin Sulṭān bought the newspaper and kept al-Khāzin as its editor. It quickly became the leading Arabic (q.v.) daily in the world.

MŪSAWĪ, ḤUSAYN, AL. *SEE* ISLAMIC AMAL MOVEMENT.

MUSHĀRAKAH. Literally, it means "participation." Ṣā'ib Salām (q.v.) and others use it refer to the desire of Sunnis (q.v.) to attain greater political power. Specifically, it characterizes Sunni demands for increasing the power of the prime minister and was a key political term in pre-1975 Lebanon.

MU'TAMAR ASH-SHA'BĪ AL-LUBNĀNĪ, AL. *SEE* LEBANESE POPULAR CONGRESS.

MUTAṢARRIF. This title of the governor of the semi-autonomous province of Mount Lebanon was devised in 1861 in the wake of 1860 civil war (q.v.). *See also Mutaṣarrifiyyah.*

MUTAṢARRIFIYYAH. This is the official name of the administrative province of Mount Lebanon, which was created in 1861 according to the Règlement Organique (q.v.).

MUṬRĀN, KHALĪL (1872–1949). A poet and journalist, he was born in Ba'albak and received his education in Beirut (q.v.). He was a student of Ibrāhīm al-Yāzijī (q.v.), who helped him master Arabic (q.v.) and French. He emigrated to Egypt and settled in Alexandria, where he worked as a journalist and met the famous Egyptian poet Aḥmad Shawqī. Mutran was a journalist at *Al-Ahrām,* which he later edited.

His articles were also published in *Al-Mu'ayyid* and *Al-Liwā'*. He founded a bi-weekly publication, *Al-Majallah Al-Miṣriyyah,* which closed down after three years. He also founded the daily *Al-Jawā'ib,* which lasted for five years. Mutran, however, was not known for his journalistic work. He is now known by students in Lebanon and other Arab countries for his poetic writings. He also translated many of Shakespeare's works into poetic Arabic. His poetry was similar to that of his friend Aḥmad Shawqī; it followed faithfully the traditional forms of poetic expression, with no innovative techniques or forms. He was at his best describing scenes in nature.

MUTWĀLĪ (pl., matāwilah). A word of disputed etymological origins, it probably refers to a person who believes in the right of 'Alī to the caliphate, or *tawliyat,* hence the name. It is used as a pejorative term to refer to Shi'ites (q.v.) in Lebanon. It is close to the old term of *rawāfiḍ* (rejectionists) used by Sunni (q.v.) Arabs to refer to Shi'ites.

-N-

NABAṬIYYAH. This city, in South Lebanon, has served since 1975 as a center of a new *muḥafaḍhah* (q.v.), called Jabal 'Āmil. It was formerly part of the *muḥafaḍhah* of South Lebanon.

NADWAH AL-LUBNĀNIYYAH, an-. This monthly journal was published by a forum known as An-Nadwah Al-Lubnāniyyah, founded by Mishel Asmar, who brought into his "club" politicians and scholars of various political views to present lectures on topics of their choice. The journal and the lectures were intended to encourage debate and consultation among members of the Lebanese educated elite. The journal was published between 1947 and 1968.

NAFĪR SŪRYĀ. This was a publication founded in 1860 by Buṭrus Al-Bustānī (q.v.) to call for unity and brotherhood/sisterhood between Muslims and Christians.

NAHĀR, an-. Founded in 1933 by Jubrān Tuwaynī (q.v.), it soon emerged as the leading newspaper in Lebanon and the entire Arab world. Its circulation witnessed a tremendous increase under the leadership of Jubrān's son, Ghassān (q.v.), who took over the editorship in 1948. He steered the paper along an independent political line, not affiliating with any political party or regime. While the paper was considered right-wing and conservative by leftist critics, Ghassān also hired journalists who did not share his centrist political views. The paper's influence reached its peak in the 1960s and the 1970s, when its editorials, frequently written by Ghassān Tuwaynī or Michel Abū Jawdah, were widely read and discussed, sometimes causing political crises. Even Jamāl 'Abdul-Nasser (q.v.) admitted to reading this paper, which did not share the region's admiration for his leadership.

The newspaper was considered pro-Western and pro-American in a region where hatred of United States (q.v.) policies is widespread. Abū Iyād of the Palestine Liberation Organization accused its columnists of taking their orders from the U.S. Central Intelligence Agency. Its offices were repeatedly bombed, and in 1974 its leading columnist, Michel Abū Jawdah was kidnapped and beaten. The newspaper survived the 1975–90 civil war (q.v.) with difficulty, and its circulation dropped drastically due to competition from militia publications. The paper was clearly sympathetic to the Christian establishment, even though it did not endorse militia activities. Its cultural pages were famous in the 1960s and 1970s, but their quality dropped during the war. The paper thrived when Lebanon had a modicum of press freedom and when it was possible to criticize Arab regimes. That climate no longer exists.

NAHJ, AN. *SEE* COURSE.

NAHR AL-KALB. *SEE* DOG RIVER.

NAJJĀDAH PARTY. *SEE* HELPERS PARTY.

NAKHLAH, RASHĪD (1873–1939). A poet, he was born in Bārūk and studied in 'Ayn Zḥaltā. He joined the civil service in the *Mutaṣarrifiyyah* (q.v.), and after the creation of Greater Lebanon (q.v.). He edited the newspaper *Al-Arz* and also wrote for other newspapers. He founded the newspaper *Ash-Sha'b* in 1912 in 'Ayn Zḥaltā. Nakhlah won a contest in 1926 for the best national anthem lyrics: his poem, *Kullunā Lil Waṭan* (We all are for the Homeland), remains the national anthem of Lebanon. He was named the prince of *zajal* (q.v.) in 1933. The government dedicated a statue in his honor in 1950.

NAQQĀSH, ALFRED (1888–1978). A former president of Lebanon, he was born in Ḥasrūn and received his education at St. Joseph University (q.v.) and the University of Paris. He lived in Egypt while writing for *La Bourse Egyptienne* and *Le Journal du Caire*. He returned to Lebanon after WWI and practiced law. He later served as an appeals judge and as a member of the supreme court. He was appointed president when Emile Iddī (q.v.) resigned from the presidency in 1941. He is remembered for insisting on sparing Beirut the horrors of World War II, or so he claimed in his retirement. He was dismissed from office because he wanted to be consulted about the designation of the time of the election. He was elected in 1943 and 1953 and served as a minister in the administration of Kamīl Sham'ūn (q.v.). He was a diplomatic envoy of President Fu'ād Shihāb (q.v.) on more than one occasion. He avoided taking any partisan positions during the 1975–90 civil war (q.v.).

NAQQĀSH, MĀRŪN (1817–1855). A theatrical performer, he was born in Sidon and grew up in Beirut (qq.v.). He traveled to Syria (q.v.) and Egypt before settling briefly in Italy, where he learned Italian, French, and Turkish. He brought from Italy a determination to produce theatricals in the Middle East and started the first theatrical group in the region, which performed Western plays that he translated. He is considered the founder of theater in the Arab world.

NAṢRALLĀH, EMILY (1931–). A writer, she was born in Al-Kafīr (near Ḥāsbayyā) and was educated in Shuwayfāt. She moved to Beirut in 1954, where she taught Arabic (q.v.). She continued her studies and earned a degree in literature from the American University of Beirut (q.v.). She joined the staff of *Aṣ-Ṣayyād* (q.v.) in 1955, writing on non-political affairs. Her most famous novel is *Ṭuyūr Aylūl* (1962).

NASSER. *SEE* 'ABDUL-NASSER, JAMĀL.

NASSER'S FORCES (*Quwwāt Nāṣir*). This is a splinter (and self-declared corrective movement) of the Union of the Forces of the Working People-the Nasserist Organization (q.v.). 'Iṣām al-'Arab split off from the union in 1974 to protest Kamāl Shātīlā's support of Anwar al-Sadāt's policy at the time. Al-'Arab was supportive, instead, of Libya (q.v.), which backed his movement financially and militarily during the 1975–90 civil war (q.v.). The movement was active in the civil war on the side of the anti-Phalangist coalition, but it always had a small membership and limited effectiveness. Al-'Arab was assassinated in the mid-1980s.

NATIONAL BLOC PARTY (*Ḥizb al-Kutlah al-Waṭaniyyah*). This party, a vehicle for a traditional *za'īm* (q.v.), began in pre-independence times as a gathering of supporters of Emile Iddī (q.v.). It emerged officially in 1936 when the Lebanese parliament split into two blocs: one was the Constitutional Bloc of Bishārah al-Khūrī (qq.v.), which wanted complete independence for Lebanon and called for close ties between Lebanon and the Arab world; the other was the National Bloc (q.v.), which supported Iddī's line of Lebanese ultranationalism and rejected identification with the Arab world, calling for a continued French presence in the country. It defined Lebanon's cultural identity as Phoenician (q.v.). Iddī was blatantly sectarian and was accused by Muslims of calling for their expulsion to Mecca. Iddī emphasized the Christian character of Lebanon and lobbied Lebanese emigrants to return so as to increase the Christian demographic weight.

Lebanese independence in 1943 dealt a severe blow to Iddī's agenda. He suffered political isolation and was expelled from parliament, and his supporters were purged from the civil service. In May 1946, Iddī revived his political movement by forming the National Bloc Party. Its platform stated that "the Lebanese people form one nation" and that "Lebanon is a sovereign, independent state." This latter affirmation was needed to distance Iddī from his controversial past. Iddī served as the first *'amid* (dean) of the party, and he attracted supporters in Mount Lebanon. Following the death of Iddī in 1949, his son Raymond (q.v.) became *'amīd,* and the party has since been inextricably linked to him. His brother Pierre (q.v.) also played an important role in the party; both brothers assumed several ministerial posts. Raymond's strong and charismatic personality was an asset to the party. This *za'īm,* who always harbored presidential ambitions, transformed the party from a pro-French movement into a modern organization that has had a significant impact on public debate.

The party supports the free enterprise system and the democratic system of Lebanon. It does not have a distinctive ideology; rather, it stands for general principles that many right-wing parties in Lebanon share. In the 1960s, Raymond Iddī stressed that the three dangers that faced Lebanon were communism, Shihabism, and Zionism. His stiff opposition to the government of President Fu'ād Shihāb (q.v.), and to that of his successor, earned him the wrath of the state apparatus, which fought his candidates in state and local elections.

Raymond Iddī was an active and respected parliamentarian who took his duties seriously. He was responsible for the banking secrecy laws of Lebanon, the creation of the special security forces (Troop 16), and for a sizable body of legislation. He was also a constant critic of government policy toward South Lebanon. Although his party was regarded in the 1960s as part of the traditional Maronite (q.v.) establishment, he took a distinctly independent political stance during the 1975–90 civil war (q.v.). He broke with the Maronite-oriented coalition and resided in West Beirut (q.v.). The outbreak of the war in 1975 led to the marginalization of his party, because Iddī refused to create a militia of his own. The political position that almost cost Iddī his life was his adamant opposition to Syrian (q.v.) intervention in Lebanon. Iddī considered the Syrian army an occupation force, and he consistently called for its withdrawal from Lebanon. He also took a principled position against Israeli (q.v.) occupation of parts of Lebanon and called for an end to Israeli intervention in Lebanese affairs. In 1976, in the aftermath of an assassination attempt, for which Iddī held Syria responsible, he chose to leave Lebanon and settle in Paris, where he remains. His party boycotted the 1992 and 1996 parliamentary elections to express displeasure at Syrian political and military dominance in the country.

NATIONAL GROUPING (*At-Tajammu' Al-Waṭanī*). This political association was founded in November 1996 by Amīn Gemayyel (q.v.), Michel 'Awn (q.v.), and leader of the National Liberal Party (q.v.), Dūrī Sham'ūn. The formation of this grouping was announced in Beirut (q.v.) although the three leaders reside in exile. The grouping also included other personalities formerly associated with the Lebanese Front (q.v.). It was intended to unify Maronite-oriented opposition figures who share an antipathy to Syrian (q.v.) military and political influence in Lebanon.

NATIONAL LIBERAL PARTY (*Ḥizb al-Waṭaniyyīn al-Aḥrār*). This party was founded in 1958 by Kamīl Sham'ūn (q.v.), a charismatic *za'īm* (q.v.) who saw the influence of party mobilization in the 1958 civil war (q.v.). He did not want to be outflanked by the well-organized Lebanese Phalanges Party (q.v.). The party was an informal group and it did not publish a program until the mid-1960s. Sham'ūn, who previously was active in the Constitutional Bloc (q.v.), was identified with a pro-Western policy that alienated many of his former Muslim and Christian supporters. The party, which included even some non-Maronite and non-Christian members in its leadership, is classified as Maronite-oriented because it was closely associated with Sham'ūn. In the lexicon of Lebanese politics, this party should be understood more as a *kutlah* (parliamentary bloc) than as a regular political party. The charisma of Sham'ūn, however, guaranteed that the party could muster enough supporters and members for public rallies and party festivals. The party joined an alliance with the Phalanges Party in the 1960s and agreed that the free enterprise system should be preserved in Lebanon. It accepted Lebanon's membership in the League of Arab States but rejected any role for Lebanon in Arab-Israeli confrontations. It also regarded communism as an international evil and wanted Lebanon to join the American-led crusade against Soviet interests during the cold war.

Like the Lebanese Phalanges Party, the National Liberal Party began organizing a militia (Tigers) long before the outbreak of the 1975–90 civil war (q.v.). Benefiting from financial and military aid from his friend King Ḥusayn of Jordan, Sham'ūn believed that the

Palestinians in Lebanon (q.v.) posed a threat that the Lebanese state was unwilling or unable to cope with. The party's militia was active in the early part of the civil war, but it was overshadowed by the more powerful and better organized militia of the Phalanges Party and, later, by the Lebanese Forces (q.v.). The party was no more than an instrument for the Sham'ūn family. Thus, Kamīl's son Dūrī was "elected" secretary-general and his other son Dānī was "elected" secretary of defense. Bashīr Gemayyel's (q.v.) fighters massacred the Tigers in July 1980 in Ṣafrā. This was the party's worst crisis. Nevertheless, Kamīl Sham'ūn did not boycott the Lebanese Front (q.v.), and he continued his political alliance with Bashīr Gemayyel until Gemayyel's death in 1982.

After the 1982 Israeli invasion, Dānī Sham'ūn tried to revive the party and its militia, but he was not able to compete with the Lebanese Forces (q.v.). The death of Kamīl Sham'ūn in 1987 caused an organizational crisis in the party. Young, educated activists apparently took advantage of Sham'ūn's death to press for democratization within the party and to end the Sham'ūn family's dominance. The issue was not resolved, and a small faction defected and formed an alternative party. The party as a whole remained marginal until 1989, when Dānī Sham'ūn headed the "new" Lebanese Front to promote the agenda of Michel 'Awn (q.v.). In 1990 Dānī Sham'ūn was assassinated by forces loyal to Maronite rival Samīr Ja'ja' (q.v.). He was replaced in the leadership of the party by his brother, Dūrī.

NATIONAL MUSIC INSTITUTE (Conservatoire). This was founded in 1959 and falls under the jurisdiction of the Ministry of Education. Its mission states that it is responsible for the teaching of music and the production of musical events. It is divided into two sections: an Eastern (specializing in music of the region) and a Western (specializing in European and American music).

NATIONAL PACT (*Al-Mithāq al-Waṭanī*). This 1943 unwritten agreement between Bishārah al-Khūrī and Riyāḍ aṣ-Ṣulḥ (qq.v.) stipulated that Christians would not seek Western protection and that Muslims would renounce their dreams of Arab or Syrian unity. It also devised a formula for the arithmetic distribution of political power on a sectarian basis. It stated that the president shall be a Maronite (q.v.), the speaker a Shi'ite (q.v.), and the prime minister a Sunni (q.v.). The spirit of the pact remains in effect in Lebanon although it came under attack from various sides during the 1975–90 civil war (q.v.).

NATIONAL PALESTINIAN LIBERATION MOVEMENT. *SEE* FATḤ MOVEMENT.

NATIONAL RESISTANCE. This refers to all those organizations which joined in "armed struggle" against Israeli troops in South Lebanon since the 1982 Israeli invasion (q.v.). In the early phase of the movement, the founding organizations were communist, including the Socialist Arab Action Party-Lebanon, the Lebanese Communist Party, and the Communist Action Organization (qq.v.). The official title of the movement was the National Resistance Front. Later, Islamic fundamentalist organizations, notably the Party of God and the Amal Movement (qq.v.) took over the movement and marginalized the communist organizations, which did not have as many members as the Islamic-oriented groups. In recent years, the Party of God has formed the backbone of the movement, and it prefers to call it the Islamic Resistance.

NA'ŪM PASHA (1846–1911). A *mutaṣarrif* (q.v.), he was born in Istanbul to a Roman Catholic (q.v.) family. He was recruited early in life for training in the Ottoman administration and joined the foreign ministry upon completing his studies, serving in the Ottoman Embassy in St. Petersburg. He later moved to Istanbul, where he worked on foreign correspondence. He was appointed *mutaṣarrif* in 1892 for a five-year term, which was later extended five more years. He returned to Istanbul in 1902 to resume his old job. In 1907–08, he was appointed ambassador to Paris, where he died.

NESTORIAN CHURCH. *SEE* ASSYRIAN CHURCH.

NIDĀ', an-. This daily newspaper, the mouthpiece of the Lebanese Communist Party (q.v.), was founded in 1970. It was considered a serious newspaper, despite its obvious political orientation. It was closed down in the 1980s, when the party concentrated its resources in its radio and television ventures.

NON-VIOLENCE. The movement for non-violence was founded by Lebanese intellectuals in late 1966. Its first declaration was published in 1967. The Movement of Non-violence was headed by Khuḍur Nubuwwah. The movement, limited to a small number of writers and professionals, was never taken seriously because political violence was popular among the Arab people, who considered the Palestinian revolution their only hope. During the 1975–90 civil war (q.v.), the non-violent movement staged a series of protests and demonstrations, but its activities were often met with bombing and sniping. The official end of the war has revived calls for non-violence in Lebanon.

NU'AYMAH, MIKHĀ'ĪL (1889–1988). A writer, he was born in his beloved Biskintā and received his education in a Russian missionary school, which later enrolled him in the teachers' institute in Nazareth. In 1906 he received an education scholarship to study in Boltava, Russia. He returned to Lebanon (q.v.) in 1911 after studying Russian literature. He emigrated to the United States (q.v.) in 1912, where he received a law degree from the University of Washington, Seattle, in 1916. Nu'aymah served in the American forces during World War I, although he was critical of superpower politics—and of war in general. He spent a year studying French literature in France (q.v.). In 1919, he settled in New York City, where he focused on his writing, which he had begun during his student days in Seattle. He also worked as a salesperson to support himself. He participated in the establishment of *Ar-Rābiṭah Al-Qalamiyyah* (Pen's League) with Khalīl Gibrān (q.v.) (Jubrān Khalīl Jubrān) and was elected as its first secretary. A book of his literary criticism appeared in 1923 under the title *Ghurbāl,* and it was praised in reviews throughout the Arab world.

He returned to Lebanon in 1932 following the death of his friend Jubrān. He surprised Jubrān's admirers in Lebanon, however, when he published a controversial biography of Jubrān in which he exposed Jubrān's weaknesses for alcohol and sex. Like Jubrān, whose shadow hung over his literary career, Nu'aymah wrote prose and poetry, although he is best known for his essays and short stories. He avoided involvement in Lebanese political affairs and lived in social isolation for much of his life. During his lifetime, he was praised and honored as the best living writer in Lebanon. He translated several of his books into English, hoping to achieve the success that Jubrān had with *The Prophet* but failed in that endeavor. He wrote a three-volume literary autobiography which was well received.

NŪR AL-HUDĀ. This artist-singer was born in Turkey. Her real name is Alexandra Badrān. She was a famous singer in the 1940s and 1950s, when she worked in Egypt and appeared in a number of feature films. She returned to Lebanon, but her fame was eclipsed by Ṣabāḥ and Fayrūz (qq.v.) in the 1960s.

NUSŪR AL-BIQĀ'. *SEE* EAGLES OF AL-BIQĀ'.

-O-

OCTOBER 24 MOVEMENT (***Ḥarakat 24 Tishrīn***). This small, Tripoli-based organization takes its name from the revolt by its leader, Fārūq al-Muqaddam, on October 24, 1969, when—with Fatḥ's (q.v.) help—he occupied the city's fortress to protest government policies against the Palestinians in Lebanon (q.v.). This charismatic leader was a student in France in the 1960s; he returned to

Lebanon to further the Palestinian cause and to press for progressive reforms. He stayed outside the framework of the Lebanese National Movement (q.v.), which he considered too moderate. Yet, the 1972 election tempted him to run for the parliamentary seat of Tripoli (q.v.), which he lost. This organization, like others, lacks a coherent ideology. The literature of the movement combines Nasserist rhetoric with romantic socialist ideas. The movement idolized "armed struggle" and participated in the 1975–76 phase of the civil war (q.v.) in the Tripoli region. The movement underwent some mysterious changes in the late 1970s, when Muqaddam improved ties with the Lebanese state. He was often accused of ties to the Lebanese intelligence services. In the early 1980s, he aligned himself with the Lebanese Phalanges Party (q.v.), and, later, with the regime of Amīn Gemayyel (q.v.). He relocated to East Beirut (q.v.) and was said to have resided in France (q.v.) in the 1980s and 1990s.

OHANNIS PASHA (1852–?). A *mutaṣarrif* (q.v.), he was born in Istanbul to an Armenian Roman Catholic family. He joined the foreign ministry and married a Maronite (q.v.) woman. He was appointed *mutaṣarrif* in 1912 for a term of five years. He resigned in 1915 over disagreements with Cemal Pasha. He died in Rome.

ORGANIZATION, THE (***At-Tanḏhīm***). This small party was founded in 1969 in the wake of major clashes between the Palestinian forces in Lebanon and the Lebanese Army (q.v.). The latter was aided by right-wing militias. Its founders split off from the Lebanese Phalanges Party (q.v.) in protest against its reluctance to engage in the nationwide military training and arming of the Lebanese people to launch an all-out war against the Palestinians (q.v.). The existence of this ostensibly secret organization was made public in 1973, when the organization participated in clashes between Palestinian forces, on the one hand, and the coalition of Lebanese army troops and right-wing militias, on the other. The organization developed into a political party in 1975 and became an active (albeit insignificant) member of the Lebanese Forces (q.v.). Its role in the 1980s and 1990s was minimal.

ORGANIZATION OF LEFTIST KURDISH PARTY. This faction of the Kurdish-oriented *Parti* (Kurdish Democratic Party, q.v.) opposed the 1976 formation of a joint front by the Kurdish Democratic Party and the Lebanese Kurdish Party (q.v.), and cautioned against the insulation of Kurdish forces from the Lebanese conflict. The new faction asserted that Jamīl Miḥḥū (leader of the *Parti*) was an anti-leftist traditionalist. The Lebanese National Movement (q.v.) welcomed the party within its structures.

ORGANIZATION OF REVOLUTIONARY SOCIALIST ACTION (***Munaḍhḍhamat al-'Amal al-Ishtirākī al-Thawrī***). This is the Lebanese sister party of the Popular Front for the Liberation of Palestine-General Command (PFLP-GC) that participated briefly in the 1975–90 civil war (q.v.). Its claim to fame was is its proclamation of responsibility for the kidnapping of U.S. Colonel Morgan, who was released in 1975 after the United States (q.v.) Embassy delivered shipments of food to refugee camps.

ORGANIZATION OF THE OPPRESSED ON THE EARTH (***Munaḍhḍhamat al-Mustaḍ'afīn fī al-Arḍ***). Little is known about this ultra-secret organization. It claimed responsibility for the hijacking of a Trans World Airlines plane in 1985 and for the kidnapping of Jews in Lebanon in the 1980s. It is believed to be close to the Party of God (q.v.). The group has not been heard from in the 1990s.

L'ORIENT. This daily French newspaper was founded in 1923–24 and reflected the views of Emile Iddī (q.v.) and his French friends and sponsors. It was edited for a while by noted journalist George Naqqāsh, who raised questions about the feasibility of the National Pact (q.v.). The paper merged with *Le Jour* (q.v.) in 1971 and was published as *L'Orient-Le Jour* (q.v.). It was only read by members of the French educated elite.

L'ORIENT-LE JOUR. This leading French daily in Lebanon came about in 1971 when *Le Jour* (q.v.) and *L'Orient* (q.v.) merged. It espouses a moderate political line and is against radicalism on both sides of the political spectrum. It is only read by members of the French educated elite and does not have a mass readership.

-P-

PALESTINE LIBERATION ORGANIZATION. *SEE* PALESTINIANS IN LEBANON.

PALESTINIANS IN LEBANON. Between 100,000 and 170,000 Palestinians entered Lebanon when Israel was established in 1948 (qq.v.). Some had been evicted from their homes, others had fled the war out of fear and panic. They were mostly Muslim Arabs, but there was a minority of Armenians (q.v.), Greeks, and Circassians. Palestinian Christians were awarded citizenship, because successive Maronite (q.v.) presidents, especially Kamīl Sham'ūn (q.v.), were alarmed at the high Muslim birth rate in the country. They were also concerned about the potential added demographic weight of Palestinian Muslims, as far as the delicate sectarian (im)balance is concerned. The Palestinians were immediately treated as a security threat to the state, and their affairs were managed by a special office within the Ministry of Interior. Most Palestinians lived in the 16 official refugee camps administered by the United Nations Relief and Works Agency (UNRWA) (q.v.). Only 13 camps survived the 1975–90 civil war (q.v.). Right-wing militias destroyed the Palestinian refugee camps in East Beirut (q.v.). Bashīr Gemayyel (q.v.) suggested turning them into playgrounds and zoos. Middle-class and wealthy Palestinians, however, lived among the Lebanese, not in camps.

The Lebanese state's attitude to the Palestinians changed in the 1960s, when armed Palestinian groups and the Palestine Liberation Organization (PLO) emerged on the scene. Lebanese officials feared that the precarious Lebanese order would collapse under pressure from the Palestinian resistance. Muslims and leftists, on the other hand, used the Palestinian armed presence in Lebanon as leverage in dealing with the state. The Lebanese Army (q.v.) immediately lost some of its credibility and intimidating power because the PLO was seen as a stronger and better trained force. The Muslims wanted to use the presence of the Palestinians as a bargaining chip for demands for a better share of political power. The state tried to eliminate the Palestinian resistance movement on more than one occasion but failed; a segment of the population was in favor of Palestinian military activity inside and outside of Lebanon.

Support for the Palestinians, however, has diminished among most, if not all, Lebanese groups. The arrogant and corrupt rule of the PLO during the years of the civil war alienated most former supporters and sympathizers. Only those on the PLO payroll continued to chant pro-Palestinian slogans. The evacuation of PLO forces from Lebanon in 1982 was welcomed by most Lebanese, who were eager for the end of PLO rule in their cities and villages. Hostility against the Palestinians often assumed a racist cast, with the Lebanese swearing that the Palestinians were biologically and genetically inclined to nastiness and cruelty. The post-1982 period witnessed added hardships for the Palestinians, who experienced hostility from all directions. Shi'ite (q.v.) and other militias, often at the behest of Syria (q.v.), bombed refugee camps, and Israel continued its decades-old practice of constant bombing. Although the Palestinian presence has dwindled, some 400,000 Palestinians remain in Lebanon, living precarious lives. They await the results of the multilateral talks (between Israel and its Arab neighbors), which will ostensibly deal with their status and destiny.

PAQRADŪNĪ, KARĪM (1944–). This Phalangist leader and Christian lawyer was born in Beirut (q.v.) to an Armenian (q.v.) family. He was educated at St. Joseph University (q.v.) and emerged as a student leader of the Lebanese Phalangist Party (q.v.). He led a reformist campaign within the party, emphasizing the need for the incorporation of youthful leadership, attention to social issues, and openness toward the Arab world. He practiced law in the late 1960s but was soon more involved in party activism. He represented his party in years of negotiations with the Palestine Liberation Organization. He was also responsible for the temporary alliance between right-wing forces and Syria (q.v.) in 1976. He then emerged as a key advisor to Bashīr Gemayyel (q.v.), a surprising move, given the latter's ties to Israel (q.v.). After 1986, he became an advisor to Samīr Ja'ja' (q.v.). He later distanced himself from Ja'ja' and cooperated with the civilian leadership of the Phalangist Party after the defeat of Michel 'Awn (q.v.) in 1990. He now serves as advisor to Phalanges Party president George Sa'ādah. His book, *The Missing Peace* (published in Arabic and French), was widely read for its insights into Lebanese-Syrian relations and the administration of Ilyās Sarkīs (q.v.), for whom he worked as a behind-the-scenes advisor.

PARLIAMENT. *SEE* MAJLIS AN-NUWWĀB.

PARTI, AL. *SEE* KURDSH DEMOCRATIC PARTY.

PARTITION (*Taqsīm*). Leftist and Muslim forces accused the right-wing coalition of plotting to partition Lebanon into small, sectarian states in order to create a Maronite (q.v.) homeland under Israeli (q.v.) protection. Some Maronite leaders denied the accusation and expressed their support for the territorial integrity of Lebanon; others openly promoted such federal and confederal solutions.

PARTY OF ARAB LIBERATION (*Ḥizb at-Taḥarrur al-'Arabī*). This small organization was formed by the late Sunni prime minister Rashīd Karāmī (qq.v.). It was a renamed version of a parliamentary bloc formed by his father, 'Abdul-Ḥamīd Karāmī, in the 1940s.

PARTY OF GOD (*Ḥizbullāh*). *Ḥizbullāh* was officially established in the wake of the Israeli invasion of 1982 (q.v.); however, its formation can be traced to the 1960s, to Shi'ite (q.v.) militants displeased with the agenda of Imām Mūsā aṣ-Ṣadr (q.v.). The party, however, came into existence only after Nabīh Birrī (q.v.), of the Amal Movement (q.v.), joined the Salvation Committee, which was formed by president Ilyās Sarkīs (q.v.) and which included Bashīr Gemayyel (q.v.). Amal's representative in Iran, Shaykh Ibrāhīm al-Amīn (now known as Ibrāhīm al-Amīn as-Sayyid, q.v.), held a press conference in the offices of an Iranian newspaper during which he attacked the committee and its members. It was then that the party was formed, under the sponsorship of the Iranian Revolutionary Guards stationed in al-Biqā' (q.v.) at the time, although the organization declared its existence officially in 1984, when a statement commemorating the massacres of Ṣabrā and Shātīlā (q.v.) was issued over the party's signature.

The role of Shaykh Muḥammad Ḥusayn Faḍlallāh (q.v.) in the establishment of the party remains unclear. He denies any official capacity, although he is believed to enjoy influence with leaders and members of the party. Ḥizbullah's ideology emphasizes the Qur'anic origins of its terminology. The word *ḥizbullah* itself comes from the Qur'ān, but it was not used to advocate party activity in the modern sense. The party has close ties to Iran, and it has never wavered in its support for Iranian policies in the region. The dramatic rise in the fortunes of the party occurred after 1984, when it undertook various acts against the U.S. Marine presence in Lebanon. The association of Ḥizbullāh with the bombing of the U.S. Marine barracks in Beirut and the hostage takings boosted the radical credentials of the party. The Trans World Airlines hijacking in 1985 focused more attention on the party (although the party never admitted responsibility for hostage taking or hijacking acts). The party published its manifesto in 1985, three years after its birth. It is primarily known for its strategic objective: the creation of an Islamic republic in Lebanon.

The party lured members away from the Amal Movement, and a war between the two organizations erupted between 1988 and 1990. The party intensified its activities in South Lebanon against Israeli occupation forces and their allies. Israel (q.v.) assassinated the party's secretary-general, 'Abbās al-Mūsawī, who was succeeded by Ḥasan Naṣrallāh. The party surprised the public in 1992 when it participated in the parliamentary election and won eight seats.

PHALANGES PARTY. *SEE* LEBANESE PHALANGES PARTY.

PHOENICIANS. This ancient people are at the core of Lebanese national myths. Lebanese popular culture, under the influence of the state and of Jesuit Orientalist education, elevated the Phoenicians to the status of a universal civilization. Lebanese poet Sa'īd 'Aql (q.v.) and scholar Fu'ād Afrām Al-Bustānī (q.v.) popularized in school curricula and political discourse notions of Phoenician greatness and achievements that attributed most of the accomplishments of the Greek and Roman empires to those "ancient Lebanese people." The name *phoenix* was invented by the Greeks to refer to people residing in the coastal areas of what is today Lebanon. The Phoenicians were also known as Canaanites (q.v.). Contrary to Lebanese national legend, the Phoenicians did not constitute a single nation, but lived in separate, often feuding, city-communities. The Phoenicians spoke a language belonging to the Semitic family, which also includes Hebrew, Aramaic, and Arabic. In the second millennium B.C., the Phoenicians devised an alphabet that influenced the alphabets of other languages.

POPULAR FRONT FOR THE LIBERATION OF PALESTINE. *See* KANAFĀNĪ, GHASSĀN.

POPULAR NASSERIST ORGANIZATION (*At-Tanḍhīm ash-Sha'bī an-Nāṣirī*). This organization, based in Sidon (q.v.), is closely associated with local activist Ma'rūf Sa'd (q.v.), whose assassination in 1975 marked for some the beginning of the Lebanese 1975–90 civil war (q.v.). Ma'rūf founded the party in 1970, after years of pro-Nasser political activity in his home city. He was succeeded in the leadership of the movement by his son Muṣṭafā Sa'd (q.v.), formerly an engineering student in Moscow. Muṣṭafā modernized the organization's militia, which was later named the Popular Liberation Army. It benefited from the Palestine Liberation Organization and Libyan (q.v.) help. Sa'd survived a car bomb near his house in 1985, which killed his daughter and cost him his eyesight. The entry of the Lebanese Army (q.v.) into Sidon in 1991 did not undermine the power of Sa'd, who—to the surprise of his rival, Prime Minister Rafīq Ḥarīrī (q.v.)—won a parliamentary seat in the 1992 election. The movement lacks an ideology, notwithstanding its belief in Nasserist goals, and should be considered merely a local gang. Sa'd was reelected to parliament in the 1996 election.

POVERTY BELTS. The term, probably coined by Imām Mūsā aṣ-Ṣadr (q.v.), refers to the impoverished southern suburbs of Beirut (q.v.), where hundreds of thousands of Shi'ites (q.v.) from South Lebanon migrated beginning in the 1960s to escape the Israeli bombardment of their villages. The belts generated social and political stress in the Lebanese political system, and many of their residents were recruited by leftist and Palestinian organizations and, later, by Shi'ite fundamentalist organizations.

PRINTING. The cultural-literary awakening in Lebanon, indeed in the whole Middle East, is closely associated with the printing and publishing efforts of missionaries and monasteries in Lebanon. The first press to produce a book in Arabic (q.v.) was at the monastery of Dayr Mār Qazḥayyā in 1610, when the Psalms were published in Syriac characters. The first printing in Arabic script was in Aleppo in 1702.

Another press was founded at Dayr Mār Yuḥannā as-Sabigh in 1735 and produced several books in Arabic script. In 1751, a Greek Orthodox (q.v.) opened a press in Beirut (q.v.) to produce religious books for his community.

High-quality printing, however, was first introduced by the American Mission when it moved its printing press, known as the American Press, or *Al-Maṭba'ah Al-Amīrkiyyah,* from Malta to Beirut (q.v.) in 1834. It was intended to produce the first accessible translation of the Bible. The founding of St. Joseph University (q.v.) by French Catholic Jesuits led to the establishment of the Catholic Press (q.v.) in 1853, which—under Jesuit scholar Louis Cheikho (q.v.)—was partly responsible for the circulation of Arabic works of literature on a mass scale and in elegant form. The Syrian Press was established in 1857 and the Eastern Press in 1858. The founding of many other presses quickly turned Lebanon into a center for publishing and printing in Arabic, serving the entire Arab world. It is estimated that Lebanon today has more printing and publishing houses than the entire Arab world combined.

PROGRESSIVE SOCIALIST PARTY (PSP) (*Al-Ḥizb at-Taqaddumī al-Ishtirākī*). This party is closely associated with its founder, Kamāl Jumblāṭ (q.v.), who hails from one of the leading Druze (q.v.) families in Lebanon (q.v.). This highly educated politician founded the party in 1949, along with an impressive group of intellectuals from various sects. It presented a program of moderate socialist reforms. Jumblāṭ quickly became a key parliamentary leader and was instrumental in the formation of a front in 1952 that led to the downfall of the administration of Bishārah al-Khūrī (q.v.). The party's militia took part in the 1958 civil war (q.v.) against the troops of pro-American president Kamīl Sham'ūn (q.v.). The secular and progressive rhetoric of the party helped Jumblāṭ extend his leadership and appeal well beyond his community, but it failed to make the party a nonsectarian organization, at least as far as membership composition is concerned.

By 1975, Jumblāṭ had become a major Arab figure, admired for his staunch support of the Palestine Liberation Organization. He also became closely aligned with the communist movement in Lebanon. Jumblāṭ was the main spokesperson for the leftist-Muslim coalition, although his party did very little fighting because he wanted to spare the Druze regions the horrors of the 1975–90 civil war (q.v.). He was instrumental in organizing and shaping the Lebanese National Movement (q.v.) and in formulating its reformist program in August 1975, which called for the diminution of sectarian representation in the political system. The major political crisis in Jumblāṭ's life was his conflict with Syria (q.v.) in 1976, when Syrian troops opposed the defeat of right-wing forces. He was assassinated in 1977 and was succeeded by his son Walīd (q.v.) in the leadership of the Druze community and the party.

Walīd ended the feud with the Syrian regime and reorganized the party's militia in preparation for a major showdown with the Lebanese Forces (q.v.). The Israeli invasion of 1982 (q.v.) led the Lebanese Forces to deploy troops in the Druze heartland, which triggered the 1983–85 War of the Mountains (q.v.). It was one of the bloodiest chapters in the civil war and resulted in the eventual victory of Druze fighters. Walīd's standing with the community rose. The party won five seats in the 1992 parliamentary election.

PROGRESSIVE VANGUARDS ***(Aṭ-Ṭalā'i' at-Taqaddumiyyah).*** This small, Beirut-based organization was founded in 1973 by Muḥammad Zakariyyā al-'Ītānī, and was never more than a pro-Syrian gang. It was not active after 1978.

PROMISE PARTY (*Ḥizb Al-Wa'd*). It would be misleading to call this group a political party; in reality, it is the clique, or gang, of the former head of the Lebanese Forces (q.v.), Elie Ḥubayqah, who was linked to the massacre of Palestinians at Ṣabrā and Shātīlā (q.v.) in 1982. Ḥubayqah was the commander of the Lebanese Forces until January 1986, when Samīr Ja'ja' (q.v.) staged a coup within the leadership and ousted Ḥubayqah for his acceptance of the Tripartite Agreement (q.v.) of December 1985, which was signed in Damascus by Ḥubayqah, representing the Lebanese Forces; Nabīh Birrī, representing the Amal Movement (qq.v.); and Walīd Jumblāṭ, representing the Progressive Socialist Party (qq.v.). The agreement was opposed by some Christian factions because it gave more power to Muslims and because it guaranteed Syrian (q.v.) political supremacy in Lebanon.

After his defeat, Ḥubayqah, a trainee of Israeli (q.v.) intelligence, moved to Zaḥlah (q.v.), claiming to represent the "authentic" Lebanese Forces (q.v.). He subsequently became a loyal ally of the Syrian regime and set up an office in Damascus. With millions of dollars from the Lebanese Forces' budget, Ḥubayqah was able to maintain a militia of his own, although he always wanted to return to East Beirut (q.v.). He entered East Beirut victoriously in October 1990 in the wake of the defeat of Michel 'Awn (q.v.). He served in various ministerial positions, and his party won two seats in the 1992 parliamentary election.

PROSTITUTION. The law of *baghā'* (prostitution), issued in February 1931, allowed women over voting age to practice prostitution provided it took place in legally designated houses (*buyūt da'ārah*) and the women were examined regularly by a state physician. Prostitutes in Lebanon, unlike in Western societies, do not work for a pimp but keep their own income, although they pay fees to the state. Illegal prostitution constitutes a very small segment of prostitution. The law is strict, though it is often not implemented: prostitutes, for example, are not supposed to (but do) leave their houses on religious holidays and weekends, presumably so as not to corrupt holy festivities. The state on occasion closes down illegal brothels. In the 1950s a major ring was closed down, and a house was found serving famous politicians. There was a similar case in 1996, and rumors circulated about the involvement of famous names from politics and the arts.

PROTEIN COMPANY. Kamīl Sham'ūn (q.v.) served as the board chairperson and general manager of this company, which planned to monopolize the fishing industry in Lebanon. Government licensing of the company triggered massive demonstrations by leftist groups, and a national strike day was proclaimed in February 1975. Demonstrators in Tripoli (q.v.) were met by Lebanese Army (q.v.) troops, who shot Ma'rūf Sa'd (q.v.). His death is considered by some the spark of the civil war of 1975 (q.v.).

PROTESTANT CHURCHES. The Protestants in Lebanon were all converted by missionaries, primarily British and American, during the 19th and 20th centuries. They are divided into a number of denominations, the most important being Presbyterian, Congregational, and Anglican. Typically, Lebanese Protestants are well educated and belong to the professional middle class. Many of them have retained close ties to the Protestant-affiliated American University of Beirut (q.v.). They constitute no more than 1 percent of the Lebanese population and live primarily in Beirut (q.v.).

PROTESTANT SYRIAN COLLEGE. *SEE* AMERICAN UNIVERSITY OF BEIRUT.

PUBLIC SECURITY DEPARTMENT. This government department was founded in 1959 with a mission to collect political, economic, and social information. It was also charged with protecting borders and issuing of visas and work permits to foreigners. It falls under the jurisdiction of the Ministry of the Interior. It is also the key agency for uncovering espionage and for monitoring suspected spies. It has been used in the past to collect information on leftist and Palestinian groups. This department also monitors and censors all foreign publications and books before they enter Lebanon. It served the political interests of the presidency, not those of the minister in charge. Presidents commonly appoint a trusted person to this position.

-Q-

***QABAḌĀYY*.** The word, of Turkish origin, means a "strong man" or "tough guy." It has been used in Lebanon to refer to thugs employed by political leaders to render services, sabotage rival political campaigns, and on rare occasions, assassinate enemies.

QABBĀNĪ, MUḤAMMAD RASHĪD (1942–). *Muftī* (q.v.) of the republic, he is the son of a *shaykh* (q.v.), and was guided toward religious education at an early age. In 1962, he graduated from the Sunni (q.v.) religious school in Lebanon, known today as Azhar Lubnān, and received an advanced degree from Al-Azhar University in Cairo in 1966. He completed his Ph.D. in Islamic jurisprudence at Al-Azhar in 1976, when he became director-general of Islamic Waqf (religious endowment) in Beirut (q.v.). He also taught courses at Beirut Arab University (q.v.) and Al-Maqāṣid (q.v.) schools. He was appointed acting *muftī* in 1989, when *Muftī* Ḥasan Khālid (q.v.) was assassinated. In 1996, after years of delay and intra-communal conflict, Qabbānī was confirmed as *muftī* of the republic.

***QAḌĀ'*.** It is a smaller administrative unit than the *muḥāfaḍhah* (q.v.). Each *muḥāfaḍhah* is subdivided into several *qaḍā'*s.

***QĀ'IMMAQĀM*.** This is the official in charge of the small administrative unit, *qaḍā'* (q.v.), within the governorate (*muḥāfaḍhah,* q.v.).

QĀNĀ MASSACRE. This refers to the Israeli bombardment of the Fijian battalion of the United Nations Interim Force in Lebanon (UNIFIL) (q.v.) in the village of Qānā in South Lebanon on April 18, 1996. It is estimated that more than 100 persons were killed and a larger number injured. The events galvanized Lebanese public and official opinion and resulted in Arab condemnation of Israel (q.v.). Israel denied that it knew that civilians were seeking refuge in the compound, but an official U.N. report disputed Israeli claims of ignorance.

QAṢṢĀR, 'ADNĀN (1930–). President of the Chamber of Commerce and one of the wealthiest businessmen in Lebanon, he was born to a Sunni (q.v.) family. He received a law degree from St. Joseph University (q.v.) but did not practice law. He is the owner and founder of many businesses in Beirut (q.v.) and abroad. He is the co-owner (with his brother) of Adnān and Adel Kassar. He is also chairman and general manager of Fransabank SAL. He has been president of the Lebanese Chamber of Commerce and Industry since 1972. He serves on the boards of many banks and companies and is frequently mentioned as a ministerial candidate.

QĀWARMĀ. This is a traditional mountain dish of preserved meat dipped in fat.

QAYSI-YEMENI CONFLICT. This is perhaps one of the oldest political-tribal conflicts in Lebanon. The Druzes (q.v.) of Lebanon were for centuries divided into Qaysi and Yemeni confederations. This split is sometimes traced to an old division in Arabia between northern Arabs and southern Arabs. The Yemeni power was eliminated in the Battle of 'Ayn Dārah in 1711, when the Qaysi forces emerged victorious.

QULAYLĀT, IBRĀHĪM (1934–). A Nasserist leader, he was born in Beirut (q.v.) to a middle class family. He attended several schools, finishing his secondary education at Al-Maqāṣid (q.v.). He held a clerical job at the electric company in Beirut. The 1958 civil war (q.v.) elevated him to the status of street leader as he was one of the most enthusiastic supporters of Jamāl 'Abdul-Nasser (q.v.) in Lebanon. He joined the armed rebels working for the downfall of the regime of Kamīl Sham'ūn (q.v.). He later attended the law school at Beirut Arab University (q.v.) but did not complete his studies. His name was linked in 1966 to the assassination of editor Kāmil Muruwwah (q.v.), but he denied responsibility. He was the founder and leader of the Movement of the Independent Nasserists—Al-Murābiṭūn (q.v.). He was one of the key warlords in West Beirut (q.v.) during the 1975–90 civil war (q.v.). When his militia was defeated in 1987, he fled to Europe, where he remains, living in Geneva and Paris.

QURM, CHARLES (1894–1963). A poet, he was born in Beirut (q.v.), the son of the Christian-oriented artist Dāwūd Qurm. He studied at Jesuit schools before beginning a career in commerce. His interests, however, were Lebanese nationalist. He celebrated the "uniqueness" of the Lebanese historical experience and founded in 1920 *La Revue Phoenicienne,* which promoted ultra-Lebanese nationalism. He also founded a publishing house by the same name. He founded a Lebanese club in 1935 as a gathering place for members of the Lebanese nationalist elite.

QUWWĀT AL-LUBNĀNIYYAH, AL. *SEE* LEBANSE FORCES.

QUWWĀT AL-MARADAH. *SEE* FORCES OF MARADAH.

QUWWĀT AL-MUSHTARAKAH, AL. *SEE* JOINT FORCES.

QUWWĀT ḤUSAYN AL-INTIḤĀRIYYAH. *SEE* SUICIDAL FORCES OF HUSAYN.

QUWWĀT NĀṢIR. *SEE* NASSER'S FORCES.

-R-

RĀBIṬAT ASH-SHAGHGHĪLAH. *SEE* TOILERS' LEAGUE.

RĀFI'Ī, 'ABDUL-MAJĪD ar- (1928–). This pro-Iraqi Ba'thist leader was born to a Sunni (q.v.) family from Tripoli (q.v.). He was educated in Tripoli and Lausanne, Switzerland, where he received his medical degree. He worked for years as a physician, treating many poor patients free of charge. He recruited vigorously in Tripoli for the pro-Iraqi Arab Socialist Ba'th Party (q.v.). He was a member of the National Command and befriended top Iraqi leaders, including Saddām Ḥusayn. He was elected by a large margin in 1972, shaking the traditional political establishment of Tripoli. He was a respected parliamentarian who spent as much time in Iraq as in Lebanon, especially when Syrian (q.v.) influence increased in the country. After the late 1970s, Rāfi'ī avoided visiting West Beirut (q.v.) and other areas under Syrian control, especially after many of his colleagues in the party leadership were assassinated. He resided temporarily in East Beirut (q.v.) in the 1980s, when the Iraqi regime improved its ties with the right-wing establishment. He has lived outside of Lebanon for several years.

RAḤBĀNĪ, ILYĀS (1938–). A musician, he is one of the three famous Raḥbānī brothers who have produced scores of musicals and songs in Lebanon. He studied music in Beirut (q.v.) and became a music composer and producer at the Lebanese radio station. He composed music for numerous singers and for feature films in Lebanon and Egypt. He was one of the first Arab musicians to incorporate synthesizers and keyboards into musical production. His music is strongly influenced by French music. In the 1970s, he composed for Fayrūz (q.v.), but critics did not find their collaboration successful. He made a fortune writing jingles for advertisers.

RAḤBĀNĪ BROTHERS (Manṣūr [1925–], and 'Āṣī [1923–1986]). This refers to 'Āṣī Ar-Raḥbānī and his brother Manṣūr Ar-Raḥbānī. They worked as policemen before they devoted their life to music and the musical theater. 'Āṣī's marriage to Fayrūz (q.v.) began his life of devotion to Fayrūz's voice. These two brothers wrote well over 300 songs for Fayrūz and established a name for themselves in the Arab world. ʻĀṣī's stroke in 1972 ended the two brothers' collaboration and proved—to nobody's surprise—that ʻĀṣī was the real genius behind their success. After ʻĀṣī's death, Manṣūr continued to write music and poetry but has not collaborated with Fayrūz.

RALLY FOR THE REPUBLIC ***(At-Tajammuʻ min Ajl al-Jumhūriyyah).*** This small but vocal opposition movement is headed by former deputy Albert Mukhaybir (q.v.) and comprises former deputies generally sympathetic to the politics of Michel ʻAwn (q.v.). It criticizes Syrian (q.v.) influence in Lebanon and calls for an end to the state of war between Lebanon and Israel (qq.v.). Mukhaybir is widely respected in Lebanon although he did not win a seat in the 1996 elections. He has accused the government of electoral fraud.

RAMGAVAR PARTY. This party, founded in 1921 when two liberal and democratic Armenian (q.v.) parties merged, is considered the party of Armenian intellectuals. It has benefited from the conflict between the Dashnak Party and Hunchak Party (qq.v.). It has emphasized the preservation of Armenian culture and heritage in the diaspora. In the 1960s the party joined with others in opposing the political dominance of the Dashnak Party.

RAYYIS, RIYĀḌ NAJĪB ar- (1937–). A publisher, he was born to a Syrian-Lebanese family and educated at Cambridge University in the United Kingdom. He worked in the 1960s as a journalist specializing in Arab affairs at *Al-Ḥayāt* and became the chief foreign correspondent at *An-Nahār* (q.v.). He wrote several novels and political books. In the 1980s, he founded the publishing house Riyad Ar-Rayyis Books, in London, and produced a large number of books, some of which had never been printed before in Arabic (q.v.) because of their sensitive political or social contents. He also edited the literary monthly *An-Nāqid,* which published articles dealing with political, sexual, social, and religious subjects that Arab censors would not have permitted. It suspended publication in the 1990s due to a lack of circulation (many Arab capitals banned it).

RED LINE UNDERSTANDING. When Syria (q.v.) intervened militarily in Lebanon in 1976, the Israeli (q.v.) government was not necessarily opposed because the targets of Syrian bombing at the time were Palestine Liberation Organization forces and their Lebanese allies. Israel tolerates the Syrian military presence in Lebanon as long as Syria does not advance its troops south of the Liṭānī River.

RÈGLEMENT ORGANIQUE. This is the French, and official, name of the legal-political order established in Mount Lebanon in the wake of the 1860 civil war (q.v.), which led to international intervention. It was officially agreed upon by representatives of Britain, Austria, Russia, France (q.v.), Prussia, and the Ottoman government in June 1861. It constituted Lebanon (q.v.) as a semi-autonomous province of the Ottoman Empire under the supervision of the signatories. In 1867, Italy was added to the list of signatories. The country, defined as Mount Lebanon, was to be governed by a Catholic, Christian, non-Lebanese, Ottoman citizen. His appointment had to be approved by the European powers. The governor, called *mutaṣarrif* (q.v.), was to be assisted in his task by an administrative council of 12 elected members representing the Maronites (q.v.) (four seats), the Druzes (q.v.) (three seats), the Greek Orthodox (q.v.) (two seats), the Greek Catholics (q.v.) (one seat), the Sunnis (q.v.) (one seat), and the Shi'ites (q.v.) (one seat). Tax collection was to support the new region; any surplus would go to Istanbul. This order came to an end in 1918, when the French occupied Lebanon.

LE REVEIL. This French newspaper was founded by Alexander Khūrī in 1908. It was out of business for decades before it was purchased by Amīn Gemayyel (q.v.) in 1977, who relaunched it to disseminate his political opinions. It has not been published regularly due to war conditions and to the struggles within the Lebanese Phalanges Party (q.v.).

REVOLUTION FROM ABOVE (*Thawrah min Fawq*). This slogan was coined by Prime Minister Ṣā'ib Salam (q.v.) as an alternative to the radical and reformist programs of Lebanese leftist groups.

REVOLUTIONARY COMMUNIST BLOC (*At-Tajammu' ash-Shuyū'ī ath-Thawrī*). One of the smallest of the numerous, clandestine communist organizations in Lebanon, it adheres to Marxist Trotskyism and calls for violent revolutionary change in Lebanon. It is one of the few organizations of the left that has taken a consistently anti-Syrian line. Its membership is small and multisectarian.

REVOLUTIONARY NASSERIST ORGANIZATION (*At-Tanḍhīm ath-Thawrī an-Nāṣirī*). This is an offshoot of Nasser's Forces (q.v.). In 1977, 'Iṣām al-'Arab's deputy, Ḥasan Qubaysī, split off from the forces to form this small Nasserist organization. The movement had some Shi'ite (q.v.) members.

RIḌĀ, RASHĪD (1865–1935). This Islamic thinker was born to a religious Sunni (q.v.) family in Qalamūn, near Tripoli (q.v.), where he received a religious education. He emigrated to Egypt, where he met Muḥammad 'Abduh, who left a lasting impression on him. He founded the journal *Al-Manār* in 1898, which remained in publication for 40 years. It was dedicated to the interpretation of the Qur'ān, explanations of Ḥadīth, religious opinions, and the challenges of modernity. Riḍā is considered one of the key Islamic reformers of this century; he visited Islamic countries, preaching pan-Islam. In 1920, he headed the Damascus council that drafted the constitution of Prince Fayṣal's government. He was also elected vice-president of the Jerusalem-based Syrian-Palestinian Congress. He wrote dozens of books dealing with Islamic law and also a biography of his mentor, Muḥammad 'Abduh.

RIFĀ'Ī, NUR AD-DĪN ar- (?–1979). In May 1976, Sulaymān Franjiyyah (q.v.) recalled this retired commander of the internal security forces and asked him to head a cabinet of military officers (and one civilian). The protest against this unprecedented move was enormous in a country opposed to military cabinets, forcing ar-Rifā'ī and his cabinet to resign after two days.

RIFQAH, FU'ĀD (1930–). A poet, he was born in Kara'ūn in Syria (q.v.) and received his education at the American University of Beirut (q.v.) and later at Göttingen University, Germany, where he earned a Ph.D. in philosophy. He received Lebanese citizenship and taught at Beirut University College (later renamed Lebanese American University, q.v.). He produced very little in his field of philosophy and was known through his surrealistic poetry, which published in *An-Nahār* (q.v.). He has published several books of poetry but has never had a mass appeal.

RIḤĀNĪ, AMĪN (1876–1940). This writer was born in Furaykah, where he received an elementary education. In his teens, he moved to the United States (q.v.) and studied drama, returning to Lebanon to teach English and to study Arabic (q.v.). He later moved back to the United States, where he was active in the Arab immigrant community. He was a prolific writer, with passionate Arab nationalist ideas, attacking sectarianism and calling for Arab unity. He traveled a great deal in the Arab world and wrote a book about his impressions of the Arab kings and princes he had met. His best writings deal with detailed descriptions of his travels in Lebanon and abroad. Riḥānī also authored a book of poetry (published after his death), which is considered one of the first examples of free verse in Arabic. His brother Albert founded a publishing house dedicated to the distribution of his works.

RIYĀḌ CONFERENCE. This conference, held in Riyāḍ, Saudi Arabia, in October 1976, brought together representatives of Lebanon (q.v.), Syria (q.v.), the Palestine Liberation Organization (PLO), Kuwait, Saudi Arabia (q.v.), and Egypt. They had been invited to Riyāḍ by Prince Fahd to end the 1975–90 civil war (q.v.) in Lebanon. The conference recognized Syrian supremacy in Lebanon and agreed to form the Arab Deterrent Force (q.v.) to end the fighting. The outcome was a defeat for Syria's rivals in Lebanon: the PLO and the Lebanese National Movement (q.v.). *See also* Cairo Conference.

RIZ KARI. *SEE* LEBANESE KURDISH PARTY.

ROMAN CATHOLIC CHRISTIANS. Catholics who accept the full primacy of the Holy See and follow the Latin rite comprise less than 1 percent of the population of Lebanon. The Lebanese refer to these Catholics as Latins, to distinguish them from Uniate groups. Many of their laity and clergy are Europeans. As Roman Catholics, they acknowledge the supreme authority of the pope in Rome.

RUHBANIYYĀT AL-LUBNĀNIYYAH, AR. *SEE* LEBANESE MONASTIC ORDER.

RUSSIA. There is very little diplomatic communication between Lebanon (q.v.) and Russia, or between Lebanon and the republics of the former USSR. The USSR took an interest in Lebanon and exploited Lebanese freedoms of the press to publicize Soviet achievements in space and science. The Lebanese communist movement, which has never wavered in its dedication to orthodox Marxist-Leninist Stalinism, vigorously defended the communist cause and received money and weapons from Russia. The Lebanese government, on the other hand, maintained uneasy, though cordial, ties with the communist regime. Lebanon took its democratic claims very seriously and identified strongly with the "free world." The philosophical foundations of Lebanese nationalism, as formulated by right-wing groups, were deeply rooted in anti-communism.

Censorship in pre-war Lebanon often targeted "communist propaganda." Many political parties, including the relatively moderate National Bloc Party (q.v.) of Raymond Iddī (q.v.), expressed open enmity to the communist ideology. The state also showed its preference for the West in its arms purchases, always buying arms from Europe and the United States. Despite these signs, Soviet diplomacy was active in Lebanon, and many Lebanese parliamentarians visited the Soviet Union on official visits, including members of right-wing parties. The Soviet Union also tried to win the sympathy of the Lebanese people by awarding college scholarships in Soviet bloc countries to poor Lebanese, who were sponsored by Lebanese communist and socialist parties and sympathetic parliamentarians.

Soviet involvement in Lebanon, of course, increased during the 1975–90 civil war (q.v.). The joint forces of the Palestine Liberation Organization and the Lebanese National Movement (q.v.) received weapons and aid from Soviet bloc countries. The Soviet Union saw in the Lebanese civil war an opportunity for the advancement of its cause in a strategically located country. Its dilemma was in balancing its support for the PLO with its relations with Syria (q.v.). The 1976 Syrian military intervention posed an embarrassing challenge for Soviet policy makers because it forced the USSR to tolerate the crackdown against the left in Lebanon. In return, Syria continued to improve its ties with the communist government in Moscow without having to further the cause of leftism in Lebanon. The collapse of the USSR almost ended Russian influence in Lebanon. Protocol and routine visits by Russian officials still take place, but they generate little excitement and scant press coverage. *See also* Lebanese Communist Party.

RUSTUM, ASAD (1897–1965). This historian was born in Shuwayr and studied in Zaḥlah (q.v.). He received undergraduate and graduate degrees in history from the American University of Beirut (AUB) (q.v.). He began his Ph.D. program at the University of Chicago in 1922 and was hired to teach at AUB upon his graduation. He was invited to Egypt in 1930 by King Fu'ād I to classify the Royal Archives and published a multi-volume work based on the archives. In 1943, he resigned from AUB and joined the American Embassy in Beirut (q.v.) as a Near East expert. He resigned from his post in 1949 to teach at the Lebanese University (q.v.). He was also a consultant with the command of the Lebanese Army (q.v.).

RUSTUM PASHA (1810–1885). A *mutaṣarrif* (q.v.), he was born in Italy to a Latin family. He received his education in his homeland, but financial needs forced him seek a career in the Ottoman foreign service. He moved to Istanbul, acquired Ottoman citizenship, and was promoted rapidly in the bureaucratic ranks. He worked primarily as a translator and advisor. He was appointed ambassador to St. Petersburg before becoming *mutaṣarrif* in 1873. His rule was considered honest, although the clerics opposed his raising of government fees. He completed a 10-year term and died in London.

-S-

SA'ĀDAH, ANṬŪN (1902–1949). An ideologue, he was born to a Greek Orthodox (q.v.) family in Brazil. He returned to Lebanon in 1930 and taught German at the American University of Beirut (q.v.). He used his university platform to advocate the union of the countries that formed, in his opinion, Greater Syria (q.v.). In his politics, Sa'ādah was equidistant from the advocates of Arab nationalism and the advocates of Lebanese nationalism. Inspired by German and Italian fascism, he founded the Syrian Social National Party (q.v.) in 1932 as a centrally structured organization under his complete control. Party members pledged allegiance to him, as the *za'īm* (q.v.) of the party. Intellectuals of various sects flocked to the party and carried his message to others. Eventually, the party was banned, and Sa'ādah fled Lebanon—without, however, losing control of the party. He returned to Lebanon in 1947, eager to push the party toward the ultimate seizure of power. Palestinian, Syrian, Lebanese, and Jordanian members made the party a major political force. Many of the top intellectuals of the Eastern Arab world were at one point or another members of this party. Sa'ādah declared a revolt against the state and was arrested and executed in 1949. To this day, party members are required to pledge allegiance to him. He left a number of works, the most famous of which is *Nushū' Al-Umam* (The Evolution of Nations).

ṢA'B, HASAN (1929–1990). A scholar and political advocate, he was born to a Sunni (q.v.) family in Beirut (q.v.), and educated at Cairo University and Georgetown University, United States, where he earned a Ph.D. in government. He worked for years in the diplomatic service of Lebanon, returning to Beirut in the late 1940s to work in the press section of the Foreign Ministry. He lectured at the American University of Beirut (q.v.) in the late 1950s and later taught at St. Joseph University (q.v.) and the Lebanese University (q.v.). Ṣa'b published a number of books and articles in Arabic (q.v.) and a few in English. He believed that modernization was compatible with Islam. He served as an unofficial advisor to the Sunni *muftī* (q.v.) of the republic. He ran for a parliamentary seat in the 1972 election and lost.

SĀBĀ, AS'AD. This famous *zajal* (q.v.) poet, and president of the League of Lebanese *Zajal,* was born in Ghusta where he was educated. He worked in the government-owned radio station for 17 years. He also edited magazines specializing in *zajal*. His poetry is published in book form.

ṢABĀḤ (FGHĀLĪ, JEANNETTE). Lebanese still debate the age of this seemingly ageless singer-entertainer. She was born some time in this century in Wādī Shaḥrūr and began her singing career early in her life. She later moved to Egypt, where she appeared in more than 40 feature films. She settled in Lebanon in 1964 and was frequently the star of the Ba'albak (q.v.) International Festival. Known for her six failed marriages, she has now been married for years to singer-dancer

Fādī Lubnān. She was a visible presence in the social life in Lebanon before the 1975–90 civil war. In the 1970s, her career was boosted by collaboration with Romeo Laḥḥūd (q.v.), who produced and directed several plays for her. She has collaborated with the best musicians of the Arab world. She maintains residences in Cairo and Beirut.

SABBĀḤ, ḤASAN KĀMIL as- (1894–1935). An inventor, he was born to a poor Shi'ite (q.v.) family in Nabaṭiyyah (q.v.) where he received his elementary education. He excelled in arithmetic and foreign languages at an early age. He studied engineering for one year at the American University of Beirut (q.v.) before he was summoned for military service. He taught arithmetic in Damascus after World War I. He later emigrated to the United States (q.v.) where he studied first at the Massachusetts Institute of Technology and then at the University of Illinois. He joined General Electric as a designer. The Lebanese tend to exaggerate his genius, claiming that he invented much of modern technology and was not given credit because of his Arab-Muslim origins. He died in a car accident in the United States. Conspiracy theorists in Lebanon claim, without evidence, that he was assassinated by Zionist forces to prevent him from benefiting the Arab world and uplifting it from its scientific backwardness.

ṢABRĀ AND SHĀTĪLĀ MASSACRES. On September 16, 1982, president-elect Bashīr Gemayyel (q.v.) was assassinated. On the same evening, right-wing militiamen of the Lebanese Forces and South Lebanon Army (qq.v.) entered the refugee camps at Ṣabrā and Shātīlā and massacred more than 700 Palestinians (q.v.). It was revealed later that Israeli troops had been in the area and that some officers watched the events from rooftops. The massacres are commemorated by Palestinians around the world.

SA'D, ḤABĪB BĀSHĀ as- (1886–1966). This former president was born to a Maronite (q.v.) family in 'Ayn Trīz and educated in Jesuit schools. He held several administrative positions before and after the French Mandate (q.v.). He was a local administrator and served as president of the Administrative Council. He was elected to parliament in 1922 and 1929. In 1925, he was appointed secretary-general of the highest French official in Lebanon. He was appointed to the Senate in 1926 and 1927. During the era of Charles Dabbās (q.v.), he served as prime minister. In 1934, the high commissioner appointed him to a one-year term as president, following the resignation of his predecessor. He was, according to some accounts, the first Christian to be awarded the title *pasha* (or *bāshā* in Arabic, which is incorporated into his name).

SA'D, MA'RŪF (1910–1975). the name of this Nasserist leader is synonymous with the 1975–90 civil war (q.v.). He was born in Sidon (q.v.) to a Christian mother and a Sunni Muslim (q.v.) father. He excelled in athletics and was a teacher of physical education in Lebanon, Saudi Arabia, Syria (qq.v.), and in Palestine. Sa'd was involved in anti-Zionist activities in 1936 during the Great Rebellion, when Palestinians revolted against British and Zionist domination of their homeland, and joined the Syrian Social National Party (q.v.) shortly thereafter. His militant activities landed him in jail in Lebanon on numerous occasions. In the later 1940s, he was a school principal in Sidon; in 1949 he joined the local police force. He won his first parliamentary seat in 1957. In the 1958 civil war (q.v.), he was a local rebel leader. He served in parliament in the 1960s and was close to the Shihabi political-military apparatus. Sa'd founded the Popular Nasserist Organization (q.v.) in 1970, heading it until his death. He lost the 1972 election to his rival, Nazīh Bizrī, and accused the government of Sulaymān Franjiyyah (q.v.), which never forgave him for his pro-Shihabi activities, of electoral fraud. On February 26, 1975, he was shot by, it is widely believed, a Lebanese Army (q.v.) sniper and died the following month. His death is considered by some the spark that set off the civil war. He was succeeded in the leadership of the party by his son, Muṣṭafā (q.v.).

SA'D, MUṢṬAFĀ (1950–). This Nasserist leader was born in Sidon (q.v.) and received his college education in agricultural engineering in Russia (q.v.). He interrupted his studies in 1975 to return to Lebanon upon the assassination of his father, Ma'rūf Sa'd (q.v.). He immediately assumed political responsibility and modernized the Nasserist political organization he inherited from his father, the Popular Nasserist Organization (q.v.). Sa'd took extremist positions during the war and his fighters engaged in ferocious fighting with Syrian (q.v.) troops in 1976, when the Syrians intervened militarily on the side of the right-wing militias. Even Kamāl Jumblāṭ (q.v.) thought he went too far in the fighting against Christian villages and nicknamed him "Admiral Nelson Sa'd" because of his fighters' attacks from the sea. Sa'd later mended fences with the Syrian regime, without, however, becoming a Syrian client, unlike most other leftist and nationalist leaders in the country. He led the mobilization efforts in his region against the Israeli (q.v.) occupation of the South. He was blinded in 1985 (and his daughter killed) when a car bomb exploded outside of his house. He received medical treatment and reconstructive surgery in the United States (q.v.) and resumed his political activities upon his return. Sa'd, one of the leading personalities in Sidon, is on unfriendly terms with Prime Minister Rafīq Ḥarīrī (q.v.). He surprised observers in 1992 when he won a seat despite the well-funded campaigns of his rivals. He was reelected in 1996, despite efforts by Ḥarīrī to defeat him.

ṢĀDIQ, PIERRE. One of the most famous political cartoonists in Lebanon, he studied classical art in Lebanon but was attracted to political cartoons. He joined the satirical magazine *Ad-Dabbūr* (q.v.) and also contributed to the publications of *Dār Aṣ-Ṣayyād* Publishing House. In 1959, Ṣādiq joined *An-Nahār,* contributing a daily cartoon that was one of the most popular items in this leading newspaper. His satirical style often angered the authorities and led to the closing of the paper. In 1970, his cartoon on the death of Jamāl 'Abdul-Nasser (q.v.), which showed the Sphinx crying, was carried in international publications. Ṣādiq surprised his readers during the 1975–90 war (q.v.) by defecting to the daily *Al-'Amal,* the mouthpiece of the Lebanese Phalanges Party (q.v.). His cartoons during the war were intensely partisan, anti-Palestinian, and anti-Syrian. In 1986 he started drawing for the television station of the Lebanese Forces. Later, he returned to *An-Nahār*.

ṢADR, IMĀM MŪSĀ aṣ- (1918–1978[?]). This mysterious Shi'ite (q.v.) cleric was one of the leading men in the contemporary history of Lebanon. Born in Qum, Iran, the son of a Lebanese father, he descends from a family of *'ulamā'* (doctors of religion). He studied at Najaf and at Teheran University. As-Ṣadr returned to Lebanon in 1959 (where he settled in Tyre, q.v.) and began to have an impact on Lebanese political life. He struggled for the legal recognition of Lebanese Shi'ites, who were often represented by Sunni (q.v.) political leaders. In the late 1960s, with support from speaker Ṣabrī Ḥamādī (q.v.), he founded the Higher Islamic Shi'ite Council, which centralized the organization of the sect's affairs.

Aṣ-Ṣadr had great charismatic qualities, even with his Persian-accented Arabic. He supported social programs for the Shi'ites, criticized state neglect of South Lebanon, and advocated arming the Shi'ite masses to defend their territories from Israeli (q.v.) bombings. He posed a serious threat to the established Shi'ite traditional *zu'amā'* (s., *za'īm,* q.v.), especially to that of Kāmil al-As'ad (q.v.), who detested him. He helped found the Movement of the Disinherited (*Ḥarakat al-Maḥrūmīn*) and its military arm, the Amal Movement (q.v.). He rendered a great religio-political service to the Syrian (q.v.) regime in 1973 by recognizing the 'Alawite sect (q.v.) as a branch of Shi'ism. As-Ṣadr remained loyal to the Syrian regime and was marginalized during the 1975–90 civil war (q.v.). He disappeared while on a state visit to Libya (q.v.) in 1978, and a cult grew around his "disappearance." Shi'ite leaders still refuse to acknowledge his death.

ṢĀFĪ, WADĪ' aṣ- (1921–). This famous singer was born in Lebanon (q.v.) and received a secondary education. He started singing at an early age and was recognized for his powerful voice and his preference for the Lebanese folkloric style. He participated in several of the musicals of the Raḥbānī brothers (q.v.) but later worked with other musicians. He often sings accompanied only by his *'ūd* (a stringed instrument). He left Lebanon during the 1975–90 war and performed in a Lebanese restaurant in Paris. He returned to Lebanon after the end of the civil war, having avoided antagonizing any political party or militia.

SAFĪR, as-. This newspaper was founded in 1974 by Shi'ite (q.v.) journalist Ṭalāl Salmān (q.v.). It was clear that the Libyan (q.v.) government was behind the newspaper, because it often carried long essays exalting the virtues of Mu'ammar al-Qadhdhāfī and praising his regime, and also frequently carried long interviews with the Libyan leader. The paper benefited from the strong leftist tide in the country at the time, and its circulation increased sharply after the pro-Iraqi newspaper *Al-Muḥarrir* (q.v.) was closed by Syrian troops in Lebanon in 1976. *As-Safīr* publishes the reports of leftist journalists who previously wrote for mainstream publications. Salmān's editorials, which are characterized by poetic use of the Arabic (q.v.) language, are also widely read. The paper emphasizes the Arab cultural aspects of Lebanon and features many Palestinian artists and writers previously albeit unofficially banned from the Lebanese press. Its cultural editor, Ilyās al-Khūrī, emerged as one of the most original novelists in Arabic, and some of his books have been translated into English. (Khūrī later left the paper to join the rival *An-Nahār*.)

The paper served as the main mouthpiece for the establishment in West Beirut (q.v.) during the 1975–90 civil war (q.v.) while *Al-'Amal,* of the Lebanese Phalanges Party (q.v.), expressed the establishment viewpoints in East Beirut (q.v.). The paper supported the Palestinian resistance in Lebanon even when most Lebanese had become disillusioned with the Palestinian revolution. It has distanced itself from Libya in recent years and is now closely associated with the Syrian (q.v.) regime. It has also moderated its political stance; it is far less critical of conservative (oil-rich) Arab regimes than it used to be. It remains one of the two leading newspapers in the country.

ṢAḤĀFĪ AT-TĀ'IH, aṣ-. This magazine, published by Iskandar Riyāshī between 1922 and 1959, was first headquartered in Zaḥlah (q.v.) but later moved to Beirut (q.v.). It was the first magazine to carry socialist articles. Yūsuf Ibrāhīm Yazbak, one of the founders of the Lebanese Communist Party (q.v.), was one of its contributors. It represented unorganized, romantic visions of socialism. It also introduced readers to the names of key Marxists.

SĀḤAT ASH-SHUHADĀ'. *SEE* MARTYRS' SQUARE.

SA'ĪD, 'ALĪ AḤMAD. *SEE* ADONIS.

ṢĀ'IGH, SALMĀ (1889–1953). This writer was born in Beirut (q.v.), and studied under Shaykh Ibrāhīm al-Mundhir. She later studied dentistry, but World War I interrupted her studies. She moved to Brazil looking for a missing brother and joined the Arabic literary society of *Al-'Uṣbah Al-Andalusiyyah*. Ṣā'igh returned to Lebanon (q.v.), where she spent her life teaching Arabic (q.v.). She was also active in philanthropic work, founding many women's organizations. She served as editor-in-chief of the magazine *Ṣawt Al-Mar'ah* (Voice of the Woman). Ṣā'igh's most famous book is *An-Nasamāt,* published in Beirut in 1923.

ṢĀ'IGH, TAWFĪQ. *SEE ḤIWĀR.*

SAINT MARON. *SEE* MĀRŪN.

ṢĀ'IQAH. This pro-Syrian organization was active in Lebanon (q.v.) in the 1960s and 1970s. Its close ties with the Syrian (q.v.) regime allowed it to operate relatively freely in Lebanese territory. Its former leader, Zuhayr Muḥsin, was notorious for his involvement in petty Lebanese affairs. The organization is popularly associated with wartime corruption, theft, and thuggery, although almost all Lebanese militias engaged in similar activities.

ṢĀJ. *SEE* MARQŪQ.

SALĀM, ṢĀ'IB (1905–). A former prime minister and a doyen of the Sunni (q.v.) political establishment, he was born in Beirut (q.v.) to a leading political family. He was educated in Beirut at the American University of Beirut (q.v.) and later at the London School of Economics, although he did not earn a degree from either. He was a large landowner and in the 1930s was accused of selling land in Palestine to the Jews. He founded Middle East Airlines-Air Liban in 1943. He became a deputy from Beirut in 1943 and represented the city for years, with a few exceptions. He served as minister of the interior in 1946 and was known for his firmness and public theatrics. Salām held the prime ministership numerous times and has one of the most recognizable faces in Lebanese public life. He built an impressive political machine through the al-Maqāṣid (q.v.) charitable schools, which he headed and from which he recruited supporters.

Salām was detested by the Shihabi apparatus but returned to the prime ministership when his friend Sulaymān Franjiyyah (q.v.) was elected president in 1970. He won a seat in the 1972 election and served as prime minister in 1970–73. He clashed with Franjiyyah in 1973, when the latter refused to dismiss the commander-in-chief of the army in the wake of a successful Israeli commando attack in the heart of Beirut. Salām was one of the opposition figures who held Franjiyyah responsible for the outbreak of the 1975–90 civil war (q.v.). He has been known as Saudi Arabia's (q.v.) faithful voice in Lebanese politics and has not deviated from the political line of the Saudi royal family, from which he has been reported to receive huge sums of money. In the 1982 siege of Beirut, Salām mediated between the United States (q.v.) and the Palestine Liberation Organization (PLO). He is a close friend of many PLO leaders, although he has been critical of Palestinian military behavior in Lebanon. In 1982, he was chosen by Amīn Gemayyel (q.v.) as his special envoy but later parted company with him. Salām retired in the mid-1980s to Geneva, returning in the early 1990s at the end of the civil war.

ṢALĪBĪ, KAMĀL (1929–). A historian, he was born to a Protestant family in Bḥamdūn and was educated at the American University of Beirut (q.v.) and London University, where he completed a Ph.D. dissertation under the noted Orientalist Bernard Lewis. He returned to Lebanon in 1953 to teach Middle East history at AUB. Ṣalībī has written a number of books on Lebanese history, including the first scholarly treatment of the modern history of Lebanon, titled as *The Modern History of Lebanon.* His views have undergone changes over the years; from espousing extremist pro-Phalangist views, Ṣalībī has been associated since the 1975–90 civil war (q.v.) with progressive pro-Arab policies. He has been critical of right-wing forces and Israel (q.v.). He resided in West Beirut (q.v.) during the war; when his life was threatened in the 1980s, he relocated temporarily to Jordan, where he worked on a book on modern Jordanian history. In his later years, Ṣalībī published a number of controversial books in which he claimed that certain Biblical places were in Arabia and not in Palestine.

SĀLIM, ELIE (1930–). A foreign minister, he was born to a Greek Orthodox (q.v.) family in Btirrām, Kūrah (North Lebanon), and was educated at the American University of Beirut (AUB) (q.v.), the University of Cincinnati, and the School of Advanced International Studies (SAIS) in Washington, D.C., where he worked with Majid Khadduri. Sālim taught at SAIS for a few years before joining the faculty of the political science department at AUB. He chaired the department and later became dean of the School of Arts and Sciences.

Sālim did not serve in government until 1982, when Amīn

Gemayyel (q.v.) appointed him foreign minister and deputy prime minister. He served in that post until 1984, when he became special advisor to the president. His tenure in office was fraught with controversial decisions: he was seen as serving the interests of the United States (q.v.) in Lebanon and as the person who rationalized the Lebanese-Israeli treaty of the May 17 Agreement (q.v.). After leaving public office, he founded the Lebanese Center for Policy Studies, which has published a number of useful journals, magazines, and books. He recently served as president of the new Greek Orthodox-affiliated University of Dayr al-Balamand (q.v.). Sālim is the author of a number of books and articles in English and Arabic (q.v.), including a memoir of his brief political experience.

SALMĀN, ṬALĀL (1938–). A journalist and publisher, he was born to a Shi'ite (q.v.) family in Shmisṭār near Ba'albak (q.v.). He started his journalist career at *Ash-Sharq* (q.v.) before moving to *Al-Ḥawādith* (q.v.) (1957–59). He worked at *Aṣ-Ṣayyād* (q.v.) in the mid-1960s, where he was known as a staunch pro-Palestinian. Salmān worked at a number of other publications before he returned to *Aṣ-Ṣayyād* in 1970. His articles are critical of the Lebanese political system and of Arab official neglect of the Palestinian cause. His views gained him access to the top leaders of the Palestine Liberation Organization (PLO), and his reports on Palestinian organizations helped publicize Palestinian goals and objectives. He published his writings on the Palestinian revolution in a well-received book.

Salmān became famous, however, only when he founded *As-Safīr* (q.v.) in 1974 and served as its editor-in-chief. The newspaper espoused a leftist line and received its financial support from the Libyan regime, which was covered favorably in the paper. The newspaper benefited from the demise of another leftist paper, the pro-Iraqi *Al-Muḥarrir* (q.v.). *As-Safīr* was widely read during the 1975–90 civil war (q.v.) and was considered second only to *An-Nahār* (q.v.) in circulation. While *An-Nahār* took a conservative, pro-regime perspective during the war, *As-Safīr* was unabashedly supportive of the PLO and the Lebanese National Movement (q.v.). Salmān's relations with Libya (q.v.) have deteriorated in recent years, and the paper now expresses Syrian (q.v.) political views. Its cultural section is considered an important platform for Arab intellectuals.

SALMĀN, ZĀHYAH (1914–). A philanthropist and social reformer, she was born in Brummānā and received an education in sociology from the American College for Girls. She was active in charitable organizations dealing with issues of children and families and has been a voice for the improvement of the status of women in Lebanon.

Salman is founder and president of the Association for the Protection of Childhood in Lebanon and has served as an advisor to the National Council of Lebanese Women.

SAMMĀN, GHĀDAH. A writer, she was born in Damascus and received a degree in English literature from Damascus University. In 1966, she received a master's degree in English literature from the American University of Beirut (q.v.). Upon her graduation, she joined the University of London to work on a Ph.D. in English literature but was unable to complete her studies. Sammān has written articles for the Lebanese press and was known as a daring journalist, not afraid to challenge conventional views on social, religious, and political issues. She returned to Beirut in 1969 and became a full-time correspondent for *Al-Ḥawādith* (q.v.). She produced several novels known for their original style and feminist portrayal of women. Sammān recently published the love letters between herself and the famous Palestinian writer-activist Ghassān Kanafānī (q.v.), who was one-sidedly in love with her, as it was revealed in this book.

SARKĪS, ILYĀS (1924–1980s). This Lebanese president was born in Shbāniyyah to a family of modest means. He was educated in Beirut (q.v.) and received a law degree after he had begun working in the department of rail stations. He resigned to practice law, later becoming a judge. In 1953, he was appointed to the auditing office (*diwān al-muḥāsabah*), which is the accountability department of the Lebanese administration. His honesty and intelligence was admired by Fu'ād Shihāb (q.v.), who appointed him as his legal advisor in 1959. In 1962, his closeness to Shihāb was established when the latter appointed him to the highest civil service job in the country: director-general of the Presidency of the Republic. He was appointed governor of the central bank in 1967 and played a role in resolving the Intra Bank Crash (q.v.) in that same year.

Sarkīs was encouraged by Shihab to run for the presidency in 1970 (he lost by one vote). He was elected president in 1976 with strong Syrian support. Sarkīs charted a moderate political course but drew closer to the right-wing establishment during his presidency. He was regarded as a weak president because, unlike most previous presidents, he lacked an independent power base. Sarkīs relied on the Lebanese Front (q.v.) to bolster his popularity among Christians. His relations with Syria (q.v.) were fraught with tension and he contemplated resigning in 1978 when Syrian forces bombarded the Christian heartland and East Beirut (q.v.). He selected Salīm al-Ḥuṣṣ (q.v.) as his prime minister; the two later had their disagreements. In his last years in office, he championed the candidacy of Bashīr Gemayyel (q.v.) but urged him to moderate his stance.

Sarkīs was totally disempowered in the last years of his administration, when the country was ruled by militias and Syrian and Israeli (qq.v.) armies. He also relied on a weak and unpopular prime minister, Shafīq al-Wazzān (q.v.). After his term expired in 1982, Sarkīs withdrew completely from public life and retired to Paris where he died of cancer. He never married.

ṢARRŪF, YA'QŪB (1852–1927). A publisher, he was born in Ḥadath, near Beirut (q.v.) and was educated at the American University of Beirut (q.v.) and was a member of the first graduating class. He taught sciences and literature at his alma mater. In 1876, he co-founded, with Fāris Nimr, the journal *Al-Muqtaṭaf,* which, along with general news, carried news on new scientific discoveries. The journal later relocated to Egypt.

SAUDI ARABIA. For much of the country's history, Saudi Arabia was not involved in Lebanese affairs, although Saudi money began being funneled into conservative Sunni (q.v.) organizations, like elements of the Muslim Brotherhood, during the 1960s. The Arab cold war between Jamāl 'Abdul-Nasser (q.v.) and Saudi Arabia pushed the Saudi royal family toward more involvement in internal Arab affairs. Many Lebanese politicians were too intimidated by Nasser to accept Saudi patronage, but Nasser's death expedited Saudi entry into Lebanon. Ṣā'ib Salām (q.v.) was an early Saudi client in Lebanon, rarely expressing disagreement with Saudi foreign policy. His Al-Maqāṣid (q.v.) schools benefited from this political loyalty to the oil-rich state.

The Sunni religious establishment was also a recipient of Saudi money, and the Sunni *muftī* (q.v.) was always careful to celebrate Muslim holidays, which follow the lunar calendar and which are not celebrated on the exact day by all Muslims, because some still wait to visually see the moon. There were reports during the 1975 phase of the civil war (q.v.) that the Saudi government was supplying right-wing militias with weapons and money to defeat the communist-led coalition of leftist forces. No evidence, however, was ever provided to support this allegation, often made in *Al-Muḥarrir* (q.v.).

In the 1980s, Saudi Arabia participated, through its ambassador to the United States, Bandar Bin Sulṭān, in mediation efforts in Lebanon and supported the various diplomatic missions of Rafīq Ḥarīrī (q.v.), who held dual Lebanese-Saudi citizenship. Harīrī's interest in Lebanon increased Saudi interest, and the government of Saudi Arabia hosted the meeting in 1989 that produced the aṭ-Ṭā'if Accords (q.v.). Saudi financial support to Lebanon continued over the years, but it was always smaller than what Lebanon demanded or needed. The designation of Rafīq Ḥarīrī as prime minister in 1992 was considered a great diplomatic victory for Saudi influence in Lebanon.

Saudi interest in Lebanon was exemplified in 1997 when Crown Prince 'Abdullāh paid an official visit to the country.

SAWDĀ, YŪSUF as- (1889–19?). A diplomat and politician, he was born in Bakfayyā and studied in Beirut (q.v.), where he received a degree from St. Joseph University (q.v.). He earned a law degree in Paris and practiced law in Alexandria, Egypt. He was an enthusiastic champion of the formation of modern Lebanon and lobbied the French government to grant Lebanon special status. He founded the Lebanese Union, a Lebanese nationalist advocacy group. He returned to Lebanon in 1921, where he founded the daily *Ar-Rāyah.* In 1945, he became a diplomat and later served in parliament and government. His most famous book is *Fī Sabīl Lubnān* (1919).

SAWMĀ, EDWARD (1926–). An engineer and agronomist, he was born in Beirut and educated at St. Joseph University (qq.v.) and the University of Montpellier, France, where he received an advanced degree in agronomy. He was a director-general of the National Agriculture Research Institute in Beirut and has served as the director-general of the United Nations Food and Agriculture Organization (FAO). He has turned down opportunities to serve in Lebanese cabinets.

ṢAWT AL-AḤRĀR. *SEE AḤRĀR, AL-.*

ṢAWT AL-'URŪBAH. This newspaper was founded by 'Adnān al-Ḥakīm (q.v.), leader of the Helpers (Najjādah) Party (q.v.) as the mouthpiece of Sunni (q.v.) Nasserism in Lebanon. It was considered a publication of narrow partisan sectarianism, very much as *Al-'Amal* was for the Lebanese Phalanges Party (q.v.). It was commercially unsuccessful, although reports indicated that it received support from Arab countries.

ṢAYDĀ. *SEE* SIDON.

ṢAYYĀD, aṣ-. This political weekly, founded by Sa'īd Furayḥah (q.v.) in 1943, quickly became popular, for it combined serious political essays with satirical caricatures of public officials and the French Mandate (q.v.). In the 1960s, it was reliably pro-Nasser, although during the 1975–90 civil war (q.v.) its politics became closer to that of the Maronite (q.v.) establishment. In the 1980s and 1990s, the magazine became less political, emphasizing, instead, fashion, arts, and society.

SAYYID, IBRĀHĪM AMĪN As- (Ibrāhīm Al-Amīn) (1950–). This leader of the Party of God (q.v.) refuses to reveal any information about himself for fear of "filling American intelligence files," as he puts it. He was known in the early 1980s as the representative of the Amal Movement (q.v.) in Tehran. As-Sayyid broke with the movement in the summer of 1982, when Nabīh Birrī (q.v.) joined the Salvation Committee formed by Ilyās Sarkīs (q.v.) to seek a solution to Lebanon's immense problems in the wake of the Israeli invasion of 1982 (q.v.). As-Sayyid opposed the membership of Bashīr Gemayyel (q.v.) on the committee, denounced Birrī, and returned to Lebanon to help found the Party of God. He served for years as the official spokesperson of the party. He was elected to parliament in 1992 and again in 1996.

SECTARIANISM. It refers to narrow loyalty to one's sect at the expense of loyalty to the nation, and is a feature of Lebanese political identities where many Lebanese tend to define themselves first and foremost as members of their sectarian groups. The term also refers to the distribution of political power and governmental posts according to a sectarian formula. This was formalized in the National Pact (q.v.) and in Article 95 (q.v.) of the constitution (q.v.).

SERVICE TAXI. This kind of taxicab service picks up passengers along Beirut's (q.v.) major routes, charging a small fraction of what the usual taxicab ride costs. Passengers share rides.

SEVENERS. *SEE* ISMA'ILI SECT.

SHABAKAH, ash-. This magazine, which began publication in 1955, was founded by Sa'īd Furayḥah (q.v.), the founder and owner of Dār aṣ-Ṣayyād, the publishing house and media empire. Its first editor was Yāsir Hawwārī, but it was shaped by the efforts of its current editor, George Ibrāhīm al-Khūrī, who is close to the Arab world's best artists and performers. It devotes its pages to news about society and entertainment; celebrities from the Arab world—often in revealing pictures—are featured on its pages. It achieved the highest circulation figures of any magazine in the 1970s, when it passed the 100,000 mark. It has many imitators, but it remains one of the best-selling magazines in the region.

SHA'BĀN, SHAYKH SA'ĪD. *SEE* ISLAMIC UNIFICATION MOVEMENT.

SHABĪBAH AL-LUBNĀNIYYAH, AL. *SEE* LEBANESE YOUTHS.

SHAHHĀL, RUḌWĀN (1915–). An artist, he was born in Tripoli (q.v.), where he received his secondary education. He was a well-known cartoonist and writer, and his illustrations appeared in numerous newspapers, magazines, textbooks, and art galleries. He was interested in Arabic (q.v.) literature and wrote a book on al-Mutanabbī. Shahhāl was a communist sympathizer and wrote an "epic" glorifying Lenin.

SHĀHĪN, ṬĀNYUS (1815–1895). A peasant leader and Maronite (q.v.), he was born to a poor family in Rayfūn. He emerged in the 1850s as a popular hero and in the late 1850s led a rebellion against the Maronite feudal families, expelling the Khāzin family, a large landowning family, from their estates. The peasant movement later degenerated into blatant sectarian warfare.

SHAKĪB EFENDI'S REGLEMENT. This revision of the *double qa'immaqamate* (q.v.) system was proposed by Ottoman Foreign Minister Shakīb Efendi. In the wake of sectarian fighting in 1845, he helped disarm inhabitants of the region and proposed consultative councils to assist the *qā'immaqām* of each district. The council, which included representatives of the various sects, decided matters of tax collection and other cases brought to it by the *qā'immaqām*. This reduced the powers of the large landowning families.

SHAMAṢ, YAḤYĀ (1945–). A convicted drug trafficker and deputy, he was born in Ba'albak (q.v.) and received a degree in commerce. He is a member of the powerful Shamas clan in his region. He was a businessman, although rumors in Lebanon connected him to drug trafficking, which is widespread in his region. He was elected in 1992 on the list of Ḥusayn al-Ḥusaynī (q.v.), and was reported to have funded the latter's electoral campaign. In 1995, he was arrested and convicted of drug trafficking. A parliamentary committee that examined the evidence against him stripped him of his parliamentary immunity. He remains in jail, asserting his innocence.

SHAM'ŪN, KAMĪL (1900–1987). One of the most influential politicians in modern Lebanon, he was born in Dayr al-Qamar. After finishing his secondary education, he obtained a law degree. He was first elected deputy in 1934 and was involved in politics for the rest of his life. He was the country's first ambassador to Britain and later headed Lebanon's delegation to the United Nations. He was identified in his early life with a pro-Arab, pro-Palestinian policy, utilizing his linguistic skills to defend the Arab cause in world forums. Sham'ūn was a member of the Constitutional Bloc (q.v.) of Bishārah al-Khūrī (q.v.), and he disagreed with those who wanted to isolate Lebanon from the Arab world. In the last years of al-Khūrī's administration, Sham'ūn joined the opposition and was seen as the likely successor to al-Khūrī in the presidency.

Sham'ūn was elected president in 1952. His political career underwent a transformation during his presidency when he appointed the pro-Western Charles Mālik (q.v.) as his foreign minister. Sham'ūn then embarked on an anti-communist, anti-Nasser foreign policy, which alienated large segments of the population, including influential Christians. He also lost many of his former allies by repeating the mistake of his predecessor: rigging elections to guarantee an amendment to the constitution (q.v.) so that he could be reelected. The 1958 civil war (q.v.) followed, which caused Sham'ūn to ask for American military help under the pretext that his country was facing an external leftist conspiracy. Intercession from Egypt and the United States (q.v.), however, could not deliver a second term to Sham'ūn, who reluctantly stepped down.

Sham'ūn became a symbol of the violation of the National Pact (q.v.), which prevented Lebanon from seeking an alliance with the West. Sham'ūn was detested by Muslims and leftists, although he was quite popular in some Christian circles, which admired his defiance and courage in the face of Nasserist attacks. He went on to found his own political party, the National Liberal Party (q.v.), and to continue an active political life. He reemerged in the 1968 election as one of the most popular Maronite (q.v.) leaders, along with Pierre Gemayyel (q.v.). The two, along with Raymond Iddī (q.v.), were the members of the Tripartite Alliance that led the Maronite establishment in the 1960s. His party played a role in the 1975–90 civil war on the side of right-wing factions, and he was a key figure in the Lebanese Front (q.v.).

Sham'ūn returned to government service briefly during the civil war but clashed continuously with Prime Minister Rashīd Karāmī (q.v.), who opposed the deployment of the Lebanese Army (q.v.) because he feared a massacre of Palestinians in Lebanon (q.v.). Sham'ūn's role within the Lebanese Front was overshadowed by that of Bashīr Gemayyel (q.v.), who quickly monopolized decision making within the Christian right-wing camp. Sham'ūn died in 1987; his two sons, Dūrī and Dānī, succeeded him in the political leadership of the family.

***SHARQ, ash-*.** This daily newspaper was founded in 1926 by 'Abdul-Ghanī al-Ka'kī. The newspaper did not achieve success until the 1970s, when its loyalty to the Syrian regime attracted curious readers, who wanted to understand Syrian intentions toward Lebanon. To increase circulation, the newspaper prints pictures of nude women. It is known as Syria's (q.v.) daily mouthpiece in Lebanon.

SHARTŪNĪ, ḤABĪB. He planted the massive bomb at the headquarters the Lebanese Phalanges Party (q.v.) in Beirut (q.v.) in September 1982, which killed president-elect Bashīr Gemayyel (q.v.) and many other party leaders. Shartūnī was a member of the Syrian Social National Party (q.v.). He was captured but was released in the 1980s when the state collapsed. His whereabouts are unknown.

SHĀTĪLĀ, KAMĀL. *SEE* LEBANESE POPULAR CONGRESS.

SHAYKH. This Arabic (q.v.) word has several meanings. It originally meant "old person" but later referred to a tribal elder, or leader. In the context of Lebanon, it is used by wealthy families as a prestigious title. In the religious Sunni (q.v.) context, it refers to a religious man, or cleric.

SHAYKH SHABĀB. An Arabic (Lebanese dialect) term used in the 19th century to refer to the village peasant leader who led the populace against feudal oppression. It literally means "elder of the youths." The most famous *shaykh shabāb* was Ṭānyus Shāhīn (q.v.).

SHAYKHŪ, LUWĪS. *SEE* CHEIKHO, LOUIS.

SHIDYĀQ, AḤMAD FĀRIS ash- (1804–1887). A scholar and linguist, he was born in 'Ashqūt, Lebanon, to a Maronite (q.v.) family. He studied Arabic (q.v.) and Syriac at the famed 'Ayn Waraqah (q.v.) school. He moved to Egypt in 1825 and wrote for the Egyptian publication *Al-Waqā'i' Al-Miṣriyyah*. Also in 1825, his brother, As'ad (q.v.), was seized and later tortured to death by Maronite clerical authorities for converting to Protestantism (q.v.). Aḥmad Fāris realized then a hatred for the clerical establishment that remained with him for the rest of his life.

He achieved a rare mastery of the Arabic language and in 1834 was invited by American Protestant missionaries to Malta, to manage the American Printing House. Aḥmad Fāris stayed with them for 14 years, teaching in their school, improving their Arabic, and eventually converting to the Protestant faith. He wrote the first manual of Arabic intended for non-Arabic speaking people and a book on the social and cultural situation in Malta.

He traveled for 10 years in Europe, meeting Orientalists and visiting libraries. He made his living from translations of the Bible and tutoring students of Arabic. He wrote a book on European affairs, probably the second book of its kind (after a similar one by the Egyptian R. Ṭahṭāwī). In Paris, he wrote and published his major satirical work, *As-Sāq 'Ala-s-Sāq*. This unique book is part biography, part observations, and part commentary on the intricate linguistic details of the Arabic language. While in Paris, he met the Tunisian ruler, Ahmad Bey, whom he praised in a long poem. Aḥmad Faris accompanied him to Tunisia and, while in Tunisia, converted to Islam and added "Aḥmad" to his name. He was invited to Istanbul in 1857, and there enjoyed the respect of the political and cultural elite. He produced the journal *Al-Jawā'ib,* in which he published his observations and linguistic opinions, in addition to official statements. He wrote a long book in which he criticized a classical Arabic dictionary by Fayruzabādī. He also wrote, but did not publish, at least two books against Catholicism. In his old age, Aḥmad Fāris visited Egypt, where he was honored by its rulers. He returned to Istanbul, where he died.

He is considered a liberal thinker and reformer; he coined many of the modern technical and political terms used in Arabic and expressed enlightened—albeit inconsistent—views on women, not common among men of the age. His name is famous, although his main book, *As-Sāq,* has not been reprinted in full since 1920, when an Egyptian edition appeared. A Lebanese edition appeared in the 1960s, which remains in print, but it censored what it considered "technical."

SHIDYĀQ, AS'AD ash- (1798–1829). An educator and brother of the noted scholar Aḥmad Fāris Ash-Shidyāq (q.v.), he was educated in 'Ayn Waraqah (q.v.), where he excelled in Arabic (q.v.). In the 1820s, he assisted American missionaries in their translation and educational work. He converted to Protestantism (q.v.) in 1825 but was immediately handed over by his family to the Maronite (q.v.) Patriarch, imprisoned and tortured. He died in 1829. His brother, Aḥmad Fāris, who was pained and enraged by this, wrote a book about his ordeal, but no copies exist. Buṭrus Al-Bustānī (q.v.) also wrote a book about the case. It was reprinted in Beirut in 1994 by Dār Al-Ḥamrā'.

SHIHĀB, FU'ĀD (1902–1973). This influential figure is the only president in Lebanese history whose name was incorporated into an "ism." Fu'ād Shihāb was born into a princely family that gave Lebanon many of its leaders. He was recruited into the Lebanese armed forces (known as the Special Troops) during the French Mandate (q.v.). He was appointed commander-in-chief of the Lebanese Army (q.v.) when the French forces left Lebanon in 1946. He is credited with building the Lebanese Army according to French military tradition, transforming a disorganized collection of armed men into a relatively modern army. His biggest challenge was in transcending sectarian considerations.

Shihāb rose to prominence in 1952, when he became interim president during the transition following the resignation of Bishārah al-

Khūrī (q.v.). His prestige, both nationally and internationally, was enhanced in 1958 when he refused orders from President Kamīl Sham'ūn (q.v.) to use the army to suppress the opposition. He was against using the army in sectarian and political battles. Shihāb emerged as the consensus candidate for president after the expiration of Sham'ūn's term, and the United States (q.v.) and Egypt, which were crucial power brokers at the time, admired his leadership abilities. His term was unique in contemporary Lebanese history because he was unusually private and because he abhorred Lebanese political life and its sectarian rules and methods.

Although Shihāb previously opposed the army's intervention in politics, he ruled through his army and its intelligence apparatus because he distrusted the political class, which he nicknamed the *fromagiste*. He expressed his wishes early on to retire from politics, but Muslim and Christian political leaders agreed that he was needed to restore amity and concord among the Lebanese people.

Shihāb initiated a package of social and economic reforms but did not address the inequality in political representation among the various Lebanese sects. He managed to conduct a credible foreign policy; he did not alienate Jamāl 'Abdul-Nasser (q.v.), although he was primarily focused on internal Lebanese affairs and did not want to give the Palestine Liberation Organization a military role in Lebanon. His reforms were partially successful in the administrative realm, although he did not end the unbalanced sectarian distribution of posts and powers. Shihāb tolerated abuse of power by his security services and refused to curtail the role of the military. He could have easily achieved the necessary parliamentary majority to amend the constitution (q.v.) to enable him to run for a second term, but he was eager to retire from politics. He never gave press interviews and refused in 1970 to run for the presidency.

He handpicked his successor, Charles Ḥilū (q.v.), but quickly lost respect for him. Shihāb's supporters, from various sects, adhered to "Shihabism," in reference to his brand of moderate, non-sectarian Lebanese nationalism.

SHIHABISM. *SEE* SHIHĀB, FU'ĀD.

SHI'ITE MUSLIMS. Most Shi'ites of Lebanon are adherents of the Twelver Shi'ite branch of Shi'ism. They believe that succession to the prophet, not only in his political capacity, passed to 'Alī ibn Abī Ṭālib and to his male descendants after him until the disappearance of the 12th *Imām, al-Mahdī al-Muntaḍhar* ("the Awaited, Rightly-Guided One"). Twelver Shi'ites believe that the return of the 12th *Imām* will usher in an era of justice and prosperity. The Shi'ites generally occupy the lowest stratum of Lebanese society; they are peasants or workers except for a small Shi'ite bourgeoisie and a few large landowners. The Shi'ites are concentrated chiefly in the poor districts of South Lebanon and al- Biqā' valley (q.v.). From these poor rural areas, neglected by the central government, some Shi'ites emigrated to West Africa, and many Shi'ites migrated to the suburbs of Beirut. *See also* Poverty Belts.

The Shi'ites of Lebanon, who constitute at least half of the population, lacked historic, state-recognized, religious institutions, independent of Sunni Muslim (q.v.) institutions, until 1968, when Imām Mūsā aṣ-Ṣadr (q.v.) created the Higher Shi'ite Islamic Council in Lebanon, which was supposed to represent Lebanese Shi'ites at both the political and religious levels.

SHI'R. This important literary-cultural journal was first published in 1957 under the editorship of Yusuf al-Khāl (q.v.) and Adonis (q.v.). It played an important role in breaking the old established rules of Arabic expression and introduced the free verse movement to a wide audience of readers in the Arab world. The journal also published translations of modern poetry from Europe and the United States. It represented an enlightened trend in modern Arab political thought and was considered a voice of Arab intellectuals. It ceased publication in 1964 but was resumed briefly after 1967.

SHTŪRAH AGREEMENT. The agreement is named after the town in which it was signed on 25 July 1977. In it, the Syrian government forced the Palestine Liberation Organization to accept the Lebanese interpretation of the Cairo Agreement (q.v.), according to which all refugee camps would be surrounded by Syrian troops uniformed as the Arab Deterrent Force (q.v.). These troops were to collect all arms that violated the Cairo Agreement. The Shtūrah Agreement also called for the disarming of groups in South Lebanon and for the deployment of Lebanese troops in that region. The agreement was never implemented.

SHUḤRŪR AL-WĀDĪ (1894–1937). This is a nickname for As'ad al-Khūrī Fghālī, one of the most accomplished *zajal* (q.v.) poets in Lebanon. He was born in Bdādūn and received some secondary education before going to work in the local police force. He was credited with forming the first *zajal* troupe in the country, and he performed in various cities and villages. A book of his poetry was published in 1939.

SIDON (ṢAYDĀ). The seat of the Jabal 'Āmil province and a key city in the South, it was once a Phoenician (q.v.) city and is rich in antiquities. It is predominantly Sunni (q.v.), but other sects reside there as well. The murder of Ma'rūf Sa'd (q.v.), an act that sparked the

1975–90 civil war (q.v.), was perpetrated in Sidon. Prime Minister Rafīq Ḥarīrī (q.v.), who was born in Sidon, has devoted much of his enormous financial resources to the modernization of the city.

SKĀF, ILYĀS (ELIE) (1948–). A politician and large landowner, he was born in New Zealand to a famous Greek Catholic (q.v.) family. His father was a major *za'īm* (q.v.), who served in parliament until the 1972 election. He was also a minister in many cabinets. Ilyās returned to Lebanon to receive his education and earned a degree in agricultural engineering from the American University of Beirut (q.v.). He was elected to the 1992 parliament. He assumed the leadership of his family upon the death of his father in 1991. He has maintained close ties with the Syrian (q.v.) regime and is one of the most popular politician in al-Biqā' (q.v.) due, at least partly, to his enormous wealth and his ability to wield patronage and power. His work in parliament focuses on agricultural affairs that affect his region. He was reelected to parliament in 1996.

SNIFFING DOGS INCIDENT. This refers to a 1974 incident at the New York City airport when President Sulaymān Franjiyyah (q.v.) was searched and dogs sniffed for drugs in the luggage of the official delegation. Franjiyyah was in New York to address the United Nations on behalf of the League of Arab States and in reference to the Palestinian question. He never forgave the Americans for the humiliation. It reinforced his view that the United States (q.v.), U.S. government, and Henry Kissinger (q.v.) personally, planned the destruction of Lebanon.

SOCIALIST ARAB ACTION PARTY-LEBANON (***Ḥizb al-'Amal al-Ishtirākī al-'Arabī-Lubnān***). When the Movement of Arab Nationalists (q.v.) was dissolved, George Ḥabash's supporters in the Lebanon branch formed an organization of their own. The party, founded in 1969, presented itself as an alternative to the moderate and reformist Communist Action Organization (q.v.) and the Lebanese Communist Party (q.v.). The party declared itself a revolutionary communist party that admired the Bulgarian version of Marxism-Leninism; it was known as the Lebanese sister party of the Popular Front for the Liberation of Palestine (PFLP) (q.v.).

The party held its first congress in 1975 and elected an Iraqi-born union leader, Hāshim 'Alī Muḥsin (Abū 'Adnān), as its leader. The party, which has advocated armed struggle throughout its history, participated enthusiastically in the 1975–90 civil war (q.v.). It was linked by Abū Iyād to the assassination of the American ambassador to Lebanon in 1976 and has consistently advocated intensification of hostilities to achieve revolutionary change. Its links with the PFLP gained it representation in the Lebanese National Movement (q.v.). In 1981, the PFLP severed its ties with the party. The party has remained insignificant. After the death of 'Alī Muḥsin, Ḥusayn Ḥamdān was elected its leader.

SOCIALIST CHRISTIAN DEMOCRATIC PARTY-THE ACTION PARTY (***Al-Ḥizb ad-Dīmuqrāṭī al-Masīḥī al-Ishtirākī-Ḥizb al-'Amal***). This party is associated with Walīd Fāris, who was until 1989 the head of the "immigrants' apparatus" of the Lebanese Forces (q.v.). He sided with Michel 'Awn (q.v.) in his conflict with the Lebanese Forces and joined the ranks of the "new" Lebanese Front (q.v.) and was put in charge of immigrant affairs. The party combines the anti-Syrian stand of 'Awn with vague formulations about the necessity for Christian socialism in Lebanon.

SOCIETY FOR THE CARE OF THE MOTHER AND THE CHILD. This society was founded in 1944 to assist mothers and their children. It financially sponsors some 500 families, pays school tuition for needy students, offers free literacy classes, and runs a school to train seamstresses. In 1979, it opened a nursery for working mothers. The society offers classes to educate first-time expectant mothers about motherhood and health. This society is not a feminist organization; it only reinforces the traditional roles of women. It associates parenthood with motherhood and assumes that fathers will not be involved in parenting. It also encourages women to work in those occupations traditionally associated with women. The society is run and managed mostly by wealthy Sunni (q.v.) women from Beirut (q.v.). It provides opportunities for politicians' wives to prove their social involvement.

SOCIETY OF ISLAMIC PHILANTHROPIC PROJECTS. *SEE* ḤABASHĪ GROUP.

SOLDIERS OF GOD (***Jundullāh***). This is not a political party but a small armed group in the quarter of Abū Samrā in Tripoli (q.v.). This militia stood for the establishment of an Islamic order in Lebanon, and its fighters have acted on their own, refusing to cooperate with the Lebanese National Movement (q.v.).

SOUTH. *SEE* JUNŪB.

SOUTH LEBANON ARMY. Following the 1978 Israeli invasion (q.v.) of South Lebanon, Israel (q.v.) was forced to withdraw from territories it occupied in the country but insisted on retaining full control of a strip of land along the border. There, in an attempt to obfuscate, it installed a surrogate army, which it trained and financed. It is clear, however, that this South Lebanon Army was created by Israel for its own purposes. Army troops are often targets of attacks by members of the resistance movement.

ST. GEORGE HOTEL. According to legend, this hotel served as a center for international intrigue and espionage in the 1950s and 1960s. It is located on St. George's Bay, Beirut (q.v.), for decades a playground for the rich. The hotel was built in 1932 and quickly established itself as the most famous luxury hotel in the region, hosting international celebrities. It was severely damaged during the 1975–90 civil war (q.v.) and was closed. There are plans for its reopening.

ST. JOSEPH UNIVERSITY. Nothing helped the cause of education in Lebanon more than the competition between Protestant (q.v.) and Catholic missionaries in the region. This university was founded by the Society of Jesus and was affiliated with the University of Lyons in France. It has branches in Tripoli, Sidon, and Zaḥlah (qq.v.). This university was the primary educational institution for the Lebanese political elite; a law degree from St. Joseph University was almost the prerequisite for entry into Lebanese political life, at least for members of rich families. Furthermore, graduates of St. Joseph University and the American University of Beirut (AUB) (q.v.) were often favored in high-paying jobs.

The language of instruction is French, although some classes are offered in Arabic (q.v.) and English. The Oriental Institute at the university produced a significant body of scholarship early in the century but has been relatively inactive in recent decades. The university has faculties of law and political sciences, medical sciences, letters and human sciences, economic sciences, engineering, and management and has institutes for theology, Islamic-Christian studies, technology, pedagogy, languages and interpretation, theatrical and audiovisual studies, information and technology, and agricultural sciences. The university, like AUB, has been primarily an elite university, inaccessible to the majority of poor Lebanese. Its fees, however, are less exorbitant than those of AUB. It was affected, like all other aspects of life in Lebanon, by the 1975–90 civil war (q.v.), during which many foreign professors fled the country. In 1991–92, it had 5,398 students.

STATE-WITHIN-A-STATE. This phrase has been used in Lebanon since the 1960s to refer to the growing power of the Palestine Liberation Organization (PLO) in Lebanon. Right-wing factions and their supporters claim that the Palestinian political movement established a state within Lebanon, in violation of national sovereignty and independence. Palestinian leaders insisted, however, that their only national destination was Palestine. Yet, few disagree that the rising influence of the PLO and its military apparatus in Lebanon contributed to the decline of state power. *See also* Palestinians in Lebanon.

ṢUFAYR, NAṢRALLĀH BUṬRUS (1920–). A Maronite (q.v.) Patriarch, he was born in Rayfūn and educated at the Maronite seminary in Ghazīr and later studied theology at St. Joseph University (q.v.). He was ordained a priest in 1950. He served in the priesthood in Rayfūn, was secretary of the Maronite Archdiocese of Damascus, taught Arabic (q.v.) literature in a Maronite college in Jūnyah, and was ordained bishop in 1961. His name became a household word in 1986, when he was elected patriarch of Antioch and the East. He was later promoted to the rank of cardinal by Pope John II. Unlike his predecessor, Antoine Khuraysh (q.v.), Ṣufayr has been deeply involved in political matters and is generally sympathetic to the goals of the Maronite establishment. Michel ʻAwn (q.v.), in 1989, ordered his followers to break into Ṣufayr's house, attack him, and humiliate him. Ṣufayr was opposed to inter-Christian fighting at the time. While he was critical of the transgressions of right-wing militias during the 1975–90 war (q.v.), he has became sympathetic to their cause in recent years. In statements and interviews he strongly denounces Syrian (q.v.) influence in Lebanon and the heavy-handed manner in which Lebanese Forces (q.v.) officials were treated by the administration of Ilyās Hrāwī (q.v.). Ṣufayr is the most respected voice among Christians today.

SUICIDAL FORCES OF ḤUSAYN (***Quwwāt Ḥusayn al-Intiḥāriyyah***). This little-known Shiʻite (q.v.) organization has participated in the fighting in the heavily Shiʻite populated area of ash-Shiyyāḥ. The organization has not been heard from in several years.

ṢULḤ, ʻALYĀ aṣ-. A newspaper columnist and political advocate, this daughter of Lebanon's "founding father" Riyāḍ aṣ-Ṣulḥ (q.v.) was born in Beirut. She was an outspoken critic of the Lebanese political elite before the war. She wrote columns for *An-Nahār* (q.v.) in the 1960s supporting the Palestinian revolution. She was also a champion of Ḥāfidh Al-Asad. In 1969, she edited the entertainment magazine *Al-Ḥasnā'*. Her television appearances were widely watched because she was daring in her criticism of Lebanese politicians, whom she once compared to animals. She left Lebanon for Paris during the 1975–90 civil war (q.v.) and has not returned. Her views have changed over the years; she has been supportive of Bashīr Gemayyel (q.v.) and other right-wing forces in Lebanon. She is a bitter critic of Syrian (q.v.) influence in Lebanon.

ṢULḤ, RASHĪD aṣ- (1926–). A prime minister, he was born in Beirut to a Sunni (qq.v.) political family and educated at Al-Maqāṣid schools and at St. Joseph University (qq.v.), where he earned a law degree. He worked as a lawyer and a judge. He first won a parliamentary seat in 1964 and was elected again in 1972. His critics, like Raymond Iddī (q.v.), considered him bright but deceptive. Ṣulḥ was appointed prime minister and minister of the interior in 1974 by Sulaymān Franjiyyah (q.v.) and served until May 1975, when he delivered a resignation speech in parliament in which he blamed the Lebanese Phalanges Party (q.v.) for the ʻAyn ar-Rummānah massacre (q.v.) and for creating a climate of fear and conflict in Lebanon. Ṣulḥ was close to Kamāl Jumblāṭ (q.v.) and the leftist trend in the country. He moderated his views over the years and maintained good ties with parties in East Beirut (q.v.) during the 1975–90 civil war (q.v.). He was appointed prime minister again in 1992 in the administration of Ilyās Hrāwī (q.v.), but served only briefly. He won a seat in the 1992 elections.

ṢULḤ, RIYĀḌ aṣ- (1894–1951). A politician, he was born to a wealthy Sunni (q.v.) family and studied law in Beirut (q.v.) and Turkey. He joined the Arab nationalist movement in his youth and was part of the administration of King Fayṣal I in Damascus. Ṣulḥ was cofounder of *Al-Istiqlāl* party. After the demise of Fayṣal's government, he fled to Egypt and Europe, where he met Zionist leaders. Newly released documents from the Israeli archives indicate that he might have been on the payroll of Zionist leadership. He tried to moderate the views of the Palestinian leadership. Ṣulḥ returned to Lebanon in 1936. In the summer of 1943, when he was already the most prominent Muslim politician in Lebanon, with contacts throughout the Arab world, he collaborated with Bishārah al-Khūrī (q.v.) on the formulation of the National Pact (q.v.). He firmly believed in Muslim-Christian understanding. Ṣulḥ held the prime minister post for five years in the administration of al-Khūrī. He was assassinated in 1951 by a member of the Syrian Social National Party (q.v.), which held him responsible for the 1949 execution of its leader, Anṭūn Saʻādah (q.v.).

ṢULḤ, SĀMĪ aṣ- (1887–1968). A prime minister, he was born in Acre, Palestine, to a family of notables. He studied under private tutors and learned some Turkish, French, and Greek. He later moved to Istanbul, where he earned a law degree. He joined Arab nationalist secret societies and moved to Paris to complete a Ph.D. in jurisprudence. Ṣulḥ returned to Lebanon and ran, in 1914, for a parliamentary seat, but lost. He was hunted by Turkish forces, according to his own account, for his nationalist activities and was later exiled to Istanbul. In the French Mandate (q.v.) period, he was appointed judge, and he served on the bench for 22 years. He was first appointed prime minister in 1942 and held that position several times. Ṣulḥ was a favored prime minister of Kamīl Sham'ūn (q.v.) because of his loyalty and weak personality. His support for Sham'ūn made him an outcast among Muslims, and his house was burnt down. He fled to predominantly Christian areas, but he was later forgiven and won in the 1964 elections. He was nicknamed "the father of the poor" for his modesty and his concern for poor people. He lost his seat in his last parliamentary campaign in 1968.

ṢULḤ, TAQIYY-ID-DĪN aṣ- (1909–1988). A prime minister, he was born in Beirut and educated at the American University of Beirut (qq.v.) and its affiliated secondary school. He wrote for *An-Nidā'* (q.v.) and *Ad-Diyār,* while teaching literature at the French Lycee in Beirut. He held diplomatic positions and advised his relative, Riyāḍ aṣ-Ṣulḥ (q.v.). In the 1940s, he was elected president of the Press Syndicate. He also entered parliament in 1947 and was reelected in 1964. He served as a minister in the mid-1960s. Sulaymān Franjiyyah (q.v.) chose him to fill the prime minister's position after the resignation of Ṣā'ib Salām (q.v.) and of his successor, Amīn Al-Ḥāfiḍh (q.v.). Ṣulḥ was known as a moderate politician who advocated compromise and reconciliation. He had been close to the Iraqi faction of the Arab Socialist Ba'th Party (q.v.) in his youth but, after his experience in the prime ministership, he improved his relations with the Syrian (q.v.) regime.

SUNNI MUSLIMS. Orthodox Sunni Muslims (q.v.) regard the Qur'an, supplemented by the traditions of the prophet, as the sole embodiment of the Muslim faith. They do not generally recognize priests as mediators of the faith to the community of believers. Religious leadership of the Sunni community in Lebanon is based on principles and institutions deriving partly from traditional Islam and partly from French influence. Under the French Mandate (q.v.), the French established the Supreme Islamic Council at the national level, headed by a grand *muftī* (q.v.), and the national Directorate of Waqfs; these institutions remain in present-day Lebanon. *Shaykh* (q.v.) is an honorary title given to any Muslim religious man in Lebanon. As a result of the 1975–90 civil war (q.v.) and the intensification of sectarian consciousness, religious leaders of the Sunni community assumed a more political role, especially with the rise of Islamic fundamentalism. The highest religious title is held by the *muftī,* Shaykh Muḥammad Rashīd Qabbānī (q.v.).

The majority of Sunnis reside in urban centers; more than two-thirds of them live in Beirut, Sidon, and Ba'albak (qq.v.). The few rural Sunnis live in the 'Akkār region, in Western al-Biqā' valley (q.v.), around Ba'albak, and in the Shūf mountains. Large and wealthy Sunni families have enjoyed political power and social prestige; the most prominent among them are the Ṣulḥs, Bayhums, Dā'ūqs, Salāms, and Ghandūrs in Beirut; the Karāmīs, Muqaddams, and Jisrs in Tripoli (q.v.); and the Bizrīs in Sidon. Sunnis constitute perhaps a quarter of the Lebanese population. Non-Arab Sunnis in Lebanon include the Kurds (q.v.).

ṢŪR. *SEE* TYRE.

SURSUQ, YVONNE LADY COCHRANE. A socialite and art curator, she was born in Beirut (q.v.) to the wealthy Sursuq family. She was educated in Beirut and London and earned a degree in town planning. She was president of the Nicolas Sursuq Museum and president and founder of the Association for the Protection of Sites and Ancient Buildings. She was president of Les Jeunesses Musicales of Lebanon in the early 1970s. She was also an active member of the committee that founded and managed the Ba'albak (q.v.) International Festival. She was a well-known socialite before the war.

SYRIA. Relations between Syria and Lebanon (q.v.) have always been odd; the two neighboring countries have been close, but their ties were never clarified. Historically, the countries of the region did not exist as separate, independent political units. The boundaries between the various administrative units of the Ottoman Empire were either nonexistent or were purely cultural, not political. Syria and Lebanon have been particularly close, with Lebanon being part of the general area of Syria known as "natural Syria." The creation of Lebanon in 1920 was not a happy event for many Lebanese Muslims, nor was it welcome news for Syria. Syrian and Lebanese Muslims hoped that Lebanon would one day unite with Syria in a larger Arab entity. Many Lebanese Christians, however, viewed Lebanon as a distinct national entity and did not want an association between Arabness and Islam. Many Syrian leaders feared that the creation of Lebanon would increase Western influence in Lebanon and that Israel (q.v.) might find an ally in Lebanon.

The relations between the two countries were also based on mutual suspicion. Christians in Lebanon were concerned that Syria's Arab nationalists might encourage Arabs in Lebanon to destabilize the state. Christian fears increased when the Arab Socialist Ba'th Party (q.v.) rose in popularity and when support for "armed struggle against Israel" was widespread. Lebanese leaders did not want Arab pressure to drag their country into an unwanted confrontation with Israel, especially when the Palestinian question split the Lebanese people and intensified sectarian sensibilities.

In more recent times, the Ba'th Party emerged as the most important ideological factor in Syrian-Lebanese relations; the Lebanese state was accused of harming Arab interests by identifying with the West and of not supplying armed support for the Palestinians in Lebanon (q.v.). The Palestinian question and Lebanon's official antipathy to collective Arab action (despite its juridical commitment to a joint Arab defense as part of the obligations of membership in the Arab League) also created friction. Further, Beirut (q.v.) housed many Arab dissidents, and some critics of Syrian regimes, including former rulers in Damascus, sought asylum in Lebanon. The Lebanese press, representing a variety of Lebanese and Arab interests, carried articles by and interviews with Syrian dissidents.

The election of Sulaymān Franjiyyah (q.v.) to the presidency warmed Lebanese-Syrian relations. The Franjiyyah family had known the al-Asad family for a long time, and Tonī Franjiyyah (q.v.) was a close friend and business associate of Ḥāfiḍh al-Asad's brother, Rif'at al-Asad. Franjiyyah, however, was unable to convince Ḥāfiḍh al-Asad to visit Lebanon, something he still has not done. In 1973, the Syrian government closed its borders with Lebanon to protest the Lebanese Army's (q.v.) bombing of Palestinian camps during clashes with the Palestine Liberation Organization (PLO) forces. Negotiations and consultations were necessary before the Syrian government would reopen the borders.

Before the outbreak of the 1975–90 civil war (q.v.), the Syrian government had a presence in Lebanon through its intelligence apparatus and through the pro-Syrian Ṣā'iqah organization, which was active in Lebanese and Palestinian affairs. Ṣā'iqah also recruited among the Lebanese people. The civil war changed the nature of Syrian-Lebanese relations and increased Syria's role in Lebanon. In the early phase of the war, the Syrian government sent its Foreign Minister, 'Abdul-Ḥalīm Khaddām (q.v.) to Lebanon in an attempt to achieve a cease-fire agreement and to mediate between the warring factions. Syria urged President Franjiyyah to accept some of the opposition's reform demands. It, however, soon discovered that the PLO and the Lebanese National Movement (LNM) (q.v.) were hoping to bring about the overthrow of the regime, which Syria did not want. A radical government in Lebanon would provoke Israel and eventually drag Syria into a confrontation with Israel. The Syrian government thus formed an alliance with the right-wing establishment in 1976. When the PLO-LNM forces were about to take over the country, Syria—which had earlier infiltrated thousands of its troops into Lebanon—intervened militarily to save the Christian camp.

The entry of the Syrian army into Lebanon would guarantee Syrian political and military influence for years to come. The Syrian government became involved in the most minute issues of Lebanese politics, and Lebanese politicians made repeated "political pilgrimages" to Damascus. 'Abdul-Ḥalīm Khaddām quickly emerged as the main arbiter of Lebanese internal affairs. Neglect of Lebanon by the regional and world community also allowed Syria a foothold. Furthermore, Lebanese leaders have historically used external powers to achieve local political gains. In other words, the Lebanese themselves are not blameless in the steady diminution of Lebanese sovereignty. The Israeli intervention in Lebanon, which started long before the civil war, made Syrian intervention understandable from the standpoint of the Arab-Israeli problem.

Syria's honeymoon with the right-wing coalition did not last; in 1978, an all-out war erupted between the two sides. Israel emerged as the patron of the Lebanese Forces (q.v.) under Bashīr Gemayyel (q.v.). Syria later tolerated an anti-Syrian enclave in Lebanon (in East Beirut (q.v.) and the southern border area) but maintained its political and military hegemony over the rest of the country. The Israeli invasion of 1982 (q.v.) was intended to end Syria's presence in Lebanon, but Israel underestimated Lebanese popular antipathy to the Zionist state, and Amīn Gemayyel (q.v.) overestimated the degree of American interest in this small country. The fragmentation within the Christian camp, and the successful resistance to and violence against Israeli occupation of the South, helped the Syrian cause.

Israel gave up on its dream of shaping Lebanon, and the intra-Christian war exhausted the right-wing militias and shifted their political orientation. In October 1990, Syria defeated Michel 'Awn (q.v.), the last symbol of anti-Syrian defiance in Lebanon. Syria's choice for the presidency, Ilyās Hrāwī (q.v.), returned victorious to East Beirut, and in May 1991 the Treaty of Brotherhood, Cooperation, and Coordination (q.v.) was signed, giving Syria juridical influence in Lebanon and Lebanon recognition of its full independence and territorial integrity.

SYRIAN MONOPHYSITES. *SEE* JACOBITE CHRISTIANS.

SYRIAN PROTESTANT COLLEGE. *SEE* AMERICAN UNIVERSITY OF BEIRUT.

SYRIAN SCIENTIFIC SOCIETY. This society, founded in 1868 by scholars of various sects in Syria, served as a scholarly association for deliberation and intellectual discussion among the educated class. Its publication, managed and edited by Buṭrus al-Bustānī (q.v.), contained articles on a variety of scientific subjects.

SYRIAN SOCIAL NATIONAL PARTY (SSNP) ***(Al-Ḥizb as-Sūrī al-Qawmī al-Ijtimā'ī).*** This is one of the oldest political parties in the Arab East. It was founded by Anṭūn Sa'ādah (q.v.), in 1932, according to a rigid, hierarchical system. It preferred clandestine operations to visible political activity. In 1937, party members had their first serious clash with Lebanese authorities. By 1939, it had become one of the most influential parties in the entire Arab East and was particularly popular among intellectuals. Some of the most prominent names in contemporary Arabic (q.v.) literature and political thought were at one point members of the party.

The party advocated the unity of Greater Syria (q.v.), which includes the Fertile Crescent (q.v.) and Cyprus. Sa'ādah spelled out his vision with the slogan, "Syria is for the Syrians, and the Syrians form one nation." He also opposed sectarianism and called for Christian-Muslim brotherhood within the context of Syrian nationalism. Sa'ādah also attacked clerical authorities and called for secularization in Lebanon to solve the acute sectarian problems. His experience in South America (where he had lived) convinced him that a new ideology should be formulated to unify the Syrians split by sectarian and particularistic sentiments.

In the first constitution of the party in 1934, Sa'ādah was declared "the leader [*za'īm,* q.v.] of the party for life; . . . members absolutely support the leader in all his constitutional legislation and administration." The fascist inclinations of the party were evident in its ideology and organizational structure. While Sa'ādah called for the unification of Syria into one nation, he was adamant about the exclusion of Jews. In fact, the party's ideology is virulently anti-Semitic. Even the non-Jewish enemies of Sa'ādah were called *Yahūd ad-dāhkhil* (the Jews of the interior). He understood nationalities only in racial terms. In 1949, after declaring armed revolt against the Lebanese government, he was executed. His death expanded the party's appeal and gave it a principled, uncompromising image, but it suffered in the 1950s from schismatic tendencies, and from the ideological isolation caused by the rise of Jamāl 'Abdul-Nasser (q.v.) and the Arab Socialist Ba'th Party (q.v.). The SSNP became known as a right-wing party that supported Kamīl Sham'ūn's (q.v.) administration in Lebanon and was close to the Jordanian regime and its Western patrons. Ironically, the party fought in 1958 in support of Sham'ūn against the same organizations that were to become allies in 1975.

The most serious crisis in the party's history was its 1961 attempted coup d'état, the only *inqilāb* (q.v.) (coup d'etat) in Lebanon's history, if one excludes the comical coup of Azīz al-Aḥdab in 1976. The failed coup led the Shihabi regime to ruthlessly persecute suspected party members and sympathizers. This almost destroyed the party, but the prison experience of party leaders led to a revolutionary change in its ideology. Party leaders like In'ām Ra'd and Munīr Khūrī read Marxist works and introduced new interpretations of Sa'ādah's writings that—while continuing to idolize the *za'īm*—were intended to end the party's political isolation. The party espoused social justice and equitable income distribution; it also ended its ideological opposition to Arab nationalism and began preaching reconciliation between Arab nationalism and Syrian nationalism; and it championed the Palestinian revolution and identified with the Lebanese leftist coalition headed by Kamāl Jumblāṭ (q.v.). The release of party leaders from jail in 1969 and the convocation of the Melkart party congress led to the institutional legitimization of Arabization and the introduction of Marxist influences into the party's ideology. This led to a split, which came into the open in 1974. The main party was led by In'ām Ra'd; the smaller faction was led by Ilyās Qunayziḥ, who was closely aligned with the Syrian (q.v.) regime. The main party participated in the 1975–90 civil war (q.v.) and was a member of the Lebanese National Movement (q.v.).

The factions reunited in 1978 under veteran party leader, 'Abdallāh Sa'ādah, who improved ties with Syria, while continuing special relations with the Libyan regime. But the unity was artificial and did not affect the cells of the two factions. The 1982 Israeli invasion (q.v.) intensified the split. The party elected 'Iṣām al-Maḥāyrī, a close ally of the Syrian regime, as head of the party, but schismatic tendencies were still at play, and the two factions split again in 1987. Maḥāyrī's branch (the main party) added the title Majlis aṭ-Ṭawāri' (the Emergency Council); the other branch added the title Al-Majlis al-A'lā (the Higher Council). The main party is headed by 'Alī Qānṣū and the smaller faction (which follows Libya and Yāsir 'Arafāt, qq.v.) is headed by In'ām Ra'd. The main party won six seats in the 1992 parliamentary elections. In 1997, a third faction was also claiming to represent the authentic party.

SYRIAN SOCIETY. *SEE* JAM'IYYAH AS-SŪRIYYAH, AL-.

-T-

TABBŪLAH. A famous Lebanese dish, it is a salad mixture of onions, parsley, tomatoes, and bulgur wheat. It is eaten as an appetizer and is served in homes all over the country.

ṬĀHĀ, RIYĀḌ (1927–1980). A journalist, he was born in Hirmil and studied in Beirut (q.v.) and Ḥumṣ, Syria (q.v.). He started his journalistic career during his student days, when he co-founded the magazine *As-Sirāj,* and in Beirut he founded *Al-Awtār.* He edited the magazine *Aṭ-Ṭalā'i'* before assuming editorial responsibilities at *An-Niḍāl.* Ṭāhā purchased the magazine *Akhbār Al-'Ālam* and became its editor-in-chief in 1947. In 1949, he established the first local news agency in the Middle East (News Agency of the Middle East). In the same year he published the new magazine *Al-Aḥad.* In 1958, he published *Al-Kifāḥ,* which was associated with his name. In his youth, Ṭāhā was a radical revolutionary who took a stance against the political and economic domination of the feudal landlords and their *za'īm* (q.v.) clientalism. This pitted him against the influential Ḥamādī family in his Ba'albak region. He ran for office against them but did not win. He was elected dean of the Press Syndicate in 1967 and remained in this post until his assassination in 1980. Speculation continues on the identity of his assailants, but it is highly likely that his pro-Iraqi Arab Socialist Ba'thist (q.v.) sympathies won him many enemies in Syria. Ṭāhā was unreserved in his Arab nationalist leanings but was not known for any sectarian biases.

ṬĀ'IF ACCORDS aṭ-. These accords were formulated in the city of aṭ-Ṭā'if, Saudi Arabia (q.v.). In September 1989, the Lebanese parliament met in this city to discuss formulas and plans for constitutional and political reforms. It was attended by 31 Christian and 31 Muslim deputies out of the 73 surviving members of the 1972 parliament. They met again in October of the same year and officially approved the accords, which shifted some powers from the presidency to the Council of Ministers and called for equal sectarian representation between Christians and Muslims. The accords also promised an eventual end to "political sectarianism," although no timetable was specified. They included a comprehensive settlement of the 1975–90 civil war (q.v.), entailing the dissolution of all militias in Lebanon. Lebanon was declared to be Arab, and Lebanon's relations with Syria (q.v.) were officially characterized as "distinctive." The agreement included a promise of Syrian evacuation of troops from Lebanon. In 1990, the Lebanese constitution (q.v.) was amended to incorporate the reforms of these accords.

TAJAMMU' AL-WAṬANĪ, AT. *SEE* NATIONAL GROUPING.

TAJAMMU' AN-NUWWĀB AL-MAWĀRINAH AL-MUSTAQILLĪN. *SEE* BLOC OF INDEPENDENT MARONITE DEPUTIES.

TAJAMMU' ASH-SHUYŪ'Ī ATH-THAWRĪ, AT. *SEE* REVOLUTIONARY COMMUNIST BLOC.

TAJAMMU' MIN AJL AL-JUMHŪRIYYAH, AT. *SEE* RALLY FOR THE REPUBLIC.

TAJĀWUZĀT. This is Arabic for "excesses" or "transgressions" and has been used by the Lebanese to refer to the acts of thuggery and illegality committed by Palestinian armed groups in Lebanon. Curiously, it is not used to refer to similar acts by Lebanese militia groups.

ṬALĀ'I' AT-TAQADDUMIYYAH, AṬ. *SEE* PROGRESSIVE VANGUARDS.

TAL AZ-ZA'TAR. This was the site of the largest of the Palestinian refugee camps in Lebanon. It was put under siege by the coalition of right-wing forces in 1976, and—after months of resistance—was eventually razed. Hundreds of its inhabitants were killed in the bombing, and all of the surviving residents were evacuated from East Beirut (q.v.). Its fall is still commemorated by Palestinians around the world.

TAMAMMU' AL-LIJĀN WA-L-RAWĀBIṬ ASH-SHA'BIYYAH. *SEE* GROUPING OF THE POPULAR COMMITTEES AND LEAGUES.

TANḌHĪM, AT. *SEE* THE ORGANIZATION.

TANḌHĪM ASH-SHA'BĪ AN-NĀṢIRĪ, AT. *SEE* POPULAR NASSERIST ORGANIZATION.

TANḌHĪM ATH-THAWRĪ AN-NĀṢIRĪ, AT. *SEE* REVOLUTIONARY NASSERIST ORGANIZATION.

TANNŪRĪN BRIGADE (*Liwā' Tannūrīn*). The brigade was formed by deputy Buṭrus Ḥarb (q.v.) in the Batrūn region to serve as his own militia. It fought alongside right-wing factions but was later dissolved, as Ḥarb could not compete with the more powerful militias in East Beirut (q.v.) and other Christian areas.

TAQIYYAH. This means "dissimulation" in Arabic. It refers to the practice by which Druzes or Shi'ites (qq.v.) are permitted, under circumstances that endanger their lives, to falsely proclaim their allegiance to the dominant faith while privately maintaining their genuine religious beliefs. It was practiced in the past to protect the survival of persecuted minorities.

TAQIYYIDĪN, DIANĀ. A musician, she was born to a Druze (q.v.) family in Davo in the Philippines. After receiving a secondary education, she studied music in a number of countries. She also received a degree from the American University of Beirut (AUB) (q.v.). She was a famous concert pianist and taught music at AUB. She immigrated to the United States (q.v.) during the 1975–90 civil war (q.v.).

TAQLĀ, PHILIP (1915–). A diplomat and parliamentarian, he was born to a Greek Orthodox (q.v.) family in Zūq and was educated in law in France (q.v.). He was elected to the parliament in 1945 and appointed minister in 1959. He distinguished himself, however, as a foreign minister in the 1960s in the administration of Fu'ād Shihāb (q.v.). Taqlā sought a moderate foreign policy that maintained Lebanon's special ties to France and the West without alienating Arab countries and the Muslim population in Lebanon. He served in 1964 as governor of the central bank. In 1967, he represented Lebanon at the General Assembly of the United Nations. Between 1968 and 1971, he was ambassador in France. In 1974, Sulaymān Franjiyyah (q.v.) appointed him minister of foreign affairs. Taqlā avoided any involvement in the 1975–90 civil war (q.v.) and is one of the few post-independence politicians who has not taken a position on any political party's side.

TAQSĪM. *SEE* PARTITION.

ṬARĀBULSĪ, MUḤAMMAD KHAYR (1952–). This weight-lifter was born to a poor Sunni (q.v.) family in Beirut (q.v.). He also worked as a firefighter. He participated in many international weight-lifting contests in Lebanon and abroad. In 1972, he received a hero's welcome in Lebanon when he came back from the Munich Olympic Games with a gold medal. He resumed his work in the fire department in Beirut.

ṬARĪQ, Aṭ-. This bi-weekly journal was founded in 1941 under the sponsorship of the communist-oriented Anti-Fascist, Anti-Nazi League. It carried analytical articles on literature, society, and politics. It emerged in the 1970s as a serious theoretical journal specializing in Marxist analysis.

TAṬHĪR. Literally, it means "purging," and refers to the drastic administrative measures taken during the administration of Charles Ḥilū (q.v.) to eliminate corrupt bureaucrats from the government. It resulted in the expulsion of a number of officials and the trial of others. It is suggested that the measures did not go far enough and that political considerations influenced the selection of the cases.

THĀBIT, AYYŪB (1884–1951). This former president was born in Bḥamdūn aḍ-Ḍay'ah to the Protestant (q.v.) faith. He was active in the decentralization movement during the Ottoman Empire, which sought more freedom for the Arab provinces than the government was willing to grant. He received a medical degree and left for New York City long before WWI. Thābit was active among Lebanese Christian immigrants in New York and seemed to play on Western fears of and antipathy toward Islam and Muslims. He presented an independent Lebanon as the only guarantee for Christian survival in the East. He returned to Lebanon after World War I and was active in Christian associations. He was elected to parliament in 1922, 1924, 1937, and 1943; he was appointed minister in 1936 and in 1943 was appointed president by the French following the dismissal of Alfred Naqqāsh (q.v.). Although he was one of the few Lebanese politicians who lived, studied, and worked in the United States (q.v.), he remained loyal to France (q.v.) and its culture throughout his life.

THAWRAH MIN FAWQ. *SEE* REVOLUTION FROM ABOVE.

TIGERS. *SEE* NATIONAL LIBERAL PARTY.

TISHBĪḤ. This colloquial Arabic word is used by Lebanese to refer to acts of showing-off or thuggery by individuals during the 1975–90 war (q.v.). Some of these individuals carried in the streets heavy weapons in order to attract attention.

TOILERS' LEAGUE (*Rābiṭat ash-Shaghghīlah*). This very small, Marxist-Leninist organization is headed by deputy Zāhir al-Khaṭīb (q.v.), who replaced his brother Ḍhāfir, who died in combat early in the 1975–90 civil war (q.v.). Founded in 1974, it was a self-styled revolutionary organization that called for the violent overthrow of the government. The league is an insignificant player but has benefited from Zāhir's close ties to Syria (q.v.).

ṬRĀD, PETRO (1886–1947). A former president, he was born in Beirut (q.v.) and educated in Paris, where he earned a degree in law. He started his political activities as an admirer of France (q.v.) and joined other Christians in 1913 in asking for French protection of Lebanon and Syria (qq.v.). This led to a Turkish death sentence against him, and some of his friends were executed. He established his name as a successful lawyer and was elected to parliament in 1922, 1924, 1927, 1929, 1934, and 1937. He served as speaker of parliament in 1934 and 1938. He was selected in 1943 to serve as president and to supervise the parliamentary elections.

TREATY OF BROTHERHOOD, COOPERATION, AND COORDINATION. This treaty was signed by the representatives of the Lebanese and Syrian governments in May 1991. For a long time, Syria (q.v.), which does not maintain an embassy in Lebanon (q.v.) because some Syrians consider Lebanon a part of Syria, has urged the Lebanese government to recognize the special and *mumayyazah* (distinctive) relations between the two countries. This treaty juridically formalizes Syrian military, political, and security roles in Lebanon and covers all aspects of relations between the two countries, including cultural and economic. Critics of the treaty were mistaken when they warned of the economic consequences of the treaty: there has been no change in the Lebanese economic system as a result of the signing of the treaty. Its significance, however, lies in Lebanon's official recognition of Syria's role in Lebanon; Lebanon allows Syria, for example, to control the Lebanese "file" vis-a-vis Arab-Israeli negotiations. Not that the Lebanese would otherwise make peace with Israel (q.v.). On the contrary, Lebanese public opinion is probably more critical of Israel and of Arab-Israeli talks than is the Syrian government. But the treaty diminishes Lebanese diplomatic power and guarantees for Syria a sympathetic Lebanese armed force. Implementation of the treaty is supervised by a Supreme Council, comprising the presidents of the two states. A secretary-general for the council was appointed in 1993.

TRIPARTITE AGREEMENT. This is a Syrian-sponsored agreement between Nabīh Birrī (q.v.), representing the Amal Movement (q.v.); Walīd Jumblāṭ (q.v.), representing the Progressive Socialist Party (q.v.); and Elie Ḥubayqah, representing the Lebanese Forces (q.v.). It was signed on December 28, 1985, and included a series of reforms, among which was an increase in the Muslim share in the power structure. It also aimed at recognizing and increasing Syria's (q.v.) influence in Lebanon.

TRIPOLI. This coastal city, the regional capital of North Lebanon, has served as an outlet to the sea for that part of Lebanon and for northern and western Syria as well. It is noted for its attachment to traditions and religious piety. The population is predominantly Sunni (q.v.), and the Karāmī family has monopolized the political leadership of the city for much of the contemporary history of the country. The government has promised to invest in the development of the city's infrastructure and its facilities. *See also* Karāmī, Rashīd; Karāmī, 'Umar.

TURK, NIQULA (1763–1828). He was born in Dayr al-Qamar to a family of Greek origin. He spent four years in Egypt, receiving advanced education in Arabic (q.v.) literature and Islamic jurisprudence.

He wrote one of the first local accounts of the impact of the French Revolution on the region in a chronicle of the Napoleonic invasion of Egypt. He returned to Lebanon to work for Bashīr II (q.v.), who later made him his personal poet and tutor to his sons. Turk wrote poetry emulating the classical tradition of the Arabic heritage.

TUWAYNĪ, GHASSĀN (1926–). This publisher, diplomat, and journalist was born to a Greek Orthodox family in Beirut (qq.v). His father was a politician and the publisher of *An-Nahār* (q.v.). He was educated at the American University of Beirut (q.v.), and at Harvard University, where he earned a master's degree in political science in 1947. Tuwaynī joined the Syrian Social National Party (SSNP) (q.v.) in his youth and was favored by SSNP leader Anṭūn Sa'ādah (q.v.). When Tuwaynī left the party in the late 1940s, Sa'ādah felt the loss and tried in vain to win him back. Tuwaynī remained, however, sympathetic to the party, and his newspaper printed sympathetic articles about Sa'ādah after his death. He assumed the editorship of *An-Nahār* in 1948. Tuwaynī first served in parliament in 1951 and was one of the leading opposition figures in the last years of the administration of Bishārah al-Khūrī (q.v.). He joined the Lebanese delegation to the United Nations in 1957 and later served as a special envoy to President Charles Ḥilū (q.v.). He served as minister of education and information in 1970–71, but his relations with president Sulaymān Franjiyyah (q.v.) deteriorated, and he was detained in jail for several weeks. The Lebanese intelligence apparatus was instructed by Franjiyyah to urge advertisers to boycott his newspapers.

An-Nahār, however, partly because of the negative attention, remained the most widely read newspaper in the country and in fact grew into a media empire, producing magazines, books, comic books, and cassette tapes. Tuwaynī later was chosen by Prime Minister Rashīd Karāmī (q.v.) to serve in his cabinet in 1975. While he avoided taking sides during the 1975–90 civil war (q.v.) and abhorred the use of violence, he was assumed to be sympathetic to the right-wing coalition. President Ilyās Sarkīs (q.v.) appointed him permanent representative of Lebanon at the United Nations (1977–82), where he played an important role in persuading the international community to take action against the Israeli invasions (q.v.) of Lebanon. He was instrumental in the passage of U.N. Security Council Resolution 425 (q.v.). In the administration of Amīn Gemayyel (q.v.), he served as an unpaid special advisor to the president and as the coordinator of the Lebanese team during the negotiations with Israel (q.v.) that led to the May 17 Agreement (q.v.). Tuwaynī remains active as a columnist in *An-Nahār*.

TUWAYNĪ, JUBRĀN (1957–). A journalist and political advocate, this son of Ghassān Tuwaynī (q.v.) was born in Beirut (q.v.) and educated in journalism at the Ecole Superieure de Journalisme in Paris. In 1979, with his father's financial and moral support, he served as the first general manager and editor-in-chief of the weekly magazine *An-Nahār Al-'Arabī wa-d-Duwalī,* the sister publication of *An-Nahār* (q.v.). Tuwaynī championed the cause of the right-wing militias and opposed Syrian (q.v.) influence in Lebanon. In 1988, he emerged as a major spokesperson for Michel 'Awn (q.v.). He was a leading figure in the "new" Lebanese Front (q.v.). He lived in Paris for a while, before returning to Beirut, where he still practices journalism.

TUWAYNĪ, JUBRĀN, Sr. (1890–1947). This journalist and parliamentarian was the father of Ghassān Tuwaynī (q.v.). He was born in Beirut (q.v.) and received a secondary education. He traveled to Paris in 1908 and wrote in Arabic (q.v.) publications. He later lived in Egypt for 10 years, where he wrote for most Egyptian newspapers of the time. Tuwaynī returned to Beirut in 1923 to work as a journalist. In 1924, he co-founded the daily newspaper *Al-Aḥrār* (q.v.), which was the mouthpiece of the Freemasons. He founded the leading Arabic daily *An-Nahār* (q.v.) in 1933. In 1931, he was appointed minister of education. He was later appointed ambassador to Latin American countries. He died in Chile.

TYRE (Ṣūr). A key city in the South and a famous Phoenician (q.v.) port city, it was until the time of Alexander the Great an island. Today it is a peninsula. It is predominantly Shi'ite (q.v.) but had always has a substantial number of Greek Catholics (q.v.). It is one of the few Lebanese cities that was not a site of heavy fighting during the 1975–90 civil war. However, it was severely hit in Israeli bombing.

-U-

UNION OF THE FORCES OF THE WORKING PEOPLE-THE NASSERIST ORGANIZATION (***Ittiḥād Qiwā ash-Sha'b al-'Āmil [at-Tanḍhīm an-Nāṣirī]***). This organization was born in the midst of the revolutionary upheavals of April 1969, when the Lebanese Army (q.v.) clashed with Palestine Liberation Organization (PLO) forces in Lebanon and with their Lebanese supporters. It was founded by a Sunni (q.v.) student leader, Kamāl Shātīlā, who remains the head of the organization. The organization used the legacy of Jāmal 'Abdul-Nasser (q.v.) to recruit students from public schools and the state-run Lebanese University (q.v.). The movement achieved national fame in 1972 when its Greek Orthodox candidate, Najāḥ Wākīm (q.v.), won the Greek Orthodox (q.v.) seat in West Beirut (q.v.). His landslide victory, made possible by Muslim votes, displeased the Greek Orthodox establishment. The movement was also known for its total devotion to the Syrian regime.

In the spring of 1976, the movement suffered a tremendous setback when its offices and bases in Beirut (q.v.) were occupied by troops of the Lebanese National Movement (LNM) (q.v.) and the PLO. Leaders of the movement were arrested and forced to criticize Syria (q.v.). They were later allowed to relocate to Damascus. When Syria gained the upper hand in Lebanon, the movement was allowed to return, with Syria ensuring that it played a prominent political role. In 1976, Kamāl Shātīlā (by this time, deputy Najāḥ Wākīm had left the movement permanently) announced the formation of *Al-Jabhah al-Qawmiyyah* (the [Pan-Arab]National Front) to counter the weight of the LNM. The front comprised all pro-Syrian organizations and gangs in Lebanon, but it failed to attract a mass following. The LNM continued to outflank the National Front, which experienced a slump in popular support.

The Union of Working People suffered a crisis in the early 1980s, when Syria forced Shātīlā and his organization out of Lebanon. It is still unclear just what ruined the special relations between Shātīlā and Damascus, but it was rumored that he leaked a copy of a top secret Syrian Ba'th document to an anti-Syrian magazine in Lebanon (*Al-Ḥawādith,* q.v.), embarrassing the Syrian government. Shātīlā lives in Paris, where he follows a pro-Saudi line. His followers in Lebanon have since 1981 operated under the name of *al-Mu'tamar ash-Sha'bī al-Lubnānī* (the Lebanese Popular Congress). Since 1981, this latter organization replaced the Union of the Forces of the Working People as Shātīlā's political vehicle.

UNION OF ISLAMIC 'ULAMĀ' (***Ittiḥād al-'Ulamā' al-Muslimīn***). The union emerged in 1982, when West Beirut (q.v.) was under siege by the Israeli Defense Forces. It was supported by Iran and included Sunni and Shi'ite (qq.v.) clerics who shared the view that the application of *sharī'ah* (Islamic Law) would end Lebanon's problems. It was unique in its Sunni-Shi'ite sectarian composition. The union collapsed in the 1990s.

UNITED NATIONS INTERIM FORCE IN LEBANON (UNIFIL). After Israel's invasion (q.v.) of Lebanon in 1978, which was intended to expand the Israeli zone of influence in the country, the United Nations dispatched a 6,000-man peacekeeping force to ensure the Israeli withdrawal to pre-1978 lines and to maintain peace and order in the border area. The presence of the troops, however, did not stop the combatants from engaging in attacks and shelling. The force, which became largely confined to social and humanitarian services for the people of the region, has been largely ignored by the armed groups operating in the South. Furthermore, the Israeli government resists efforts to extend the mandate of the force into areas it calls "the security zone," the area in South Lebanon occupied by Israel. In June 1982, and several times thereafter, Israel ignored the presence of UNIFIL when it invaded Lebanon. Many UNIFIL members were killed while on duty in Lebanon.

UNITED NATIONS RELIEF AND WORKS AGENCY (UNRWA). The agency was founded in 1949 by the United Nations General Assembly to run the Palestinian refugee camps after the end of the first Arab-Israeli war, which preceded and followed the establishment of Israel. It primarily deals with health and education. It faced difficulties in its work in Lebanon after 1982 because the Lebanese government has not facilitated its activities. *See also* Israel.

UNITED NATIONS SECURITY COUNCIL RESOLUTION 425. This resolution, voted by the Security Council of the United Nations in 1978 following an invasion of South Lebanon by Israeli troops, calls on Israel (q.v.) to withdraw its troops from Lebanon and for the formation of a UN peacekeeping force. Israel refuses to relinquish control over a strip of land on the border. The Lebanese government still asks the international community to implement the terms of this resolution, especially in the wake of the Gulf War. *See also* Israeli invasion of 1978.

UNITED STATES. Lebanon has prided itself on its good relations with its neighbors (with the exception of Israel [q.v.]) and with the Western world. Lebanon's relations with the United States have been close over the years, and the American ambassador in Lebanon played a role that transcended the traditional role of foreign diplomats. American diplomats in Lebanon often expressed views on domestic issues, and presidential elections were closely watched by experts at the American Embassy, perhaps because Lebanon, from the standpoint of American foreign policy, contained too many destabilizing elements. During the cold war, the communist movement was a source of alarm to American policy makers and the rise of the Palestine Liberation Organization (PLO) worried those officials, who hoped that Lebanon would be the first Arab country to sign a peace treaty with Israel.

American concerns about developments in Lebanon were clearly illustrated in 1958, when President Dwight Eisenhower dispatched the U.S. Marines to the country, ostensibly to maintain law and order. The marines did not engage in battle and were quickly withdrawn. Their presence, however, enabled Washington to play a crucial role in the Lebanese election that brought Fu'ād Shihāb (q.v.) to the presidency. The 1975–76 civil war (q.v.) was of great concern to the United States. Initially, there were reports of American intelligence and military support for the right-wing militias, probably because the cold war was the prism through which the American government watched and analyzed events in Lebanon. It seems, however, that it did not take long for the American government to lose faith in the Lebanese Forces (q.v.) (and their predecessors). The U.S. State Department constantly called for internal reforms, recognizing the unfairness of the Lebanese political system, which did not reflect the actual demographic weights of the various sects. When Lebanon's security conditions deteriorated, American ships, in cooperation with PLO forces, evacuated American civilians from Lebanon. A few of those who stayed behind were later captured as hostages.

Washington lost interest in Lebanon until the advent of the Reagan administration and the intensification of the cold war during his term. Lebanese and Palestinian events were explained in conspiratorial terms: the PLO was understood, and treated, merely as a Soviet tool for the expansion of its interests in the region. In Bashīr Gemayyel (q.v.), the Reagan administration, probably with prodding from Israel, found an ally willing to make peace with Israel and to open his country to an American military presence. Gemayyel was also eager to put pressure on Syria (q.v.). Aware of these considerations, Gemayyel sprinkled his speeches with references to "the free world" and Lebanon's status in it.

The American position quickly changed when Amīn Gemayyel (q.v.) assumed the presidency. Early on, the American government, represented by Secretary of State George Schultz, took an interest in the country and saw a golden opportunity to achieve peace between Israel and a second Arab state. When the May 17 Agreement (q.v.) fell apart as a result of domestic and regional pressures, and when Gemayyel showed little consideration for his country's internal sectarian balance, the American government pushed for internal reforms and understood the need for an increase in Shi'ite (q.v.) political representation. The kidnapping of Americans in Lebanon and the rise of the bitterly anti-American Party of God (q.v.) shifted America's attention away from Lebanon. Assistant Secretary of State Richard Murphy tried in 1988 to avert a constitutional vacuum by trying to convince the Christian camp to accept the presidency of Mikhā'īl aḍ-Ḍāhir (q.v.). His efforts failed, and chaos followed. The American government would not recognize the representativeness of Michel 'Awn (q.v.) and urged the recognition of President Ilyās Hrāwī (q.v.).

The United States has returned to Lebanon in recent years; Secretary of State Warren Christopher visited Lebanon more than once during his shuttle trips in the region. Washington's interest in Lebanon, however, is motivated by the diplomacy of Arab-Israeli peace and by the progress, or lack thereof, in the American-sponsored peace process. As America's relations with Syria have improved, as has been the case since the 1990–91 Gulf War, American tolerance of the Syrian presence in Lebanon has increased. When tensions arise in Syrian-American relations, the U.S. government usually points to Syrian—but not Israeli—violations of Lebanese sovereignty. The last remaining issue in American-Lebanese relations deals with the constant—almost automatic—renewal of the ban on travel to Lebanon. The ban (which is symbolic; many Americans do travel to Lebanon, anyway, and rarely is anyone prosecuted) undermines Lebanese officials' efforts to change Lebanon's image around the world and to attract foreign investors and tourists.

UNIVERSITY OF AL-MANĀR. This university was founded in 1993 in Tripoli (q.v.) as an Islamic university. It offers degrees in Islamic theology and jurisprudence.

UNIVERSITY OF DAYR AL-BALAMAND. This university, founded in 1990 by the Greek Orthodox (q.v.) church, had served for decades as a high school. It has a faculty of letters and human sciences, and sciences and technology, and has incorporated the Lebanese Academy of Fine Arts. Its first president was Ghassān Tuwaynī (q.v.), who helped in fund-raising efforts. Its current president is former foreign minister Elie Sālim (q.v.). In 1991–92, it had 295 students.

***'URWAH, al-*.** It was published between 1936 and 1955 as the official mouthpiece of the al-'Urwah al-Wuthqah Club at the American University of Beirut (q.v.). The club was sponsored by the popular professor Constantine Zurayq (q.v.) and served as a gathering place for Arab nationalist students. Many later leaders of the Arab world, including George Ḥabash and Wadī' Ḥaddād of the Popular Front for the Liberation of Palestine, were members. It was also a center for students involved in the Palestinian refugee problem.

'USAYRĀN, 'ĀDIL (1905–). A Shi'ite (q.v.) and former speaker, he received degrees in political science from the American University of Beirut (q.v.) and was first elected to parliament in 1943. He was reelected regularly, with the exception of the 1960 and 1964 elections. He served in numerous ministerial positions and was speaker of parliament several times in the 1950s, when he was aligned with Kamīl

Sham'ūn (q.v.). He is considered an "independence" hero, having been arrested by the French in 1943 for pro-independence activities. He is known for his seriousness and intelligence, although he lost interest in politics before the 1975 civil war (q.v.), when his son 'Abdullāh was murdered. 'Usayrān was succeeded in parliament in 1992 by his son 'Alī.

'USAYRĀN, LAYLĀ (1934–). A writer, she was born in Baghdad to Lebanese Shi'ite (q.v.) parents. She studied in Cairo and received a degree in political science from the American University of Beirut (q.v.) in 1954. She was active in her student days in nationalist organizations and advocated "armed struggle" against Israel (q.v.). She wrote for Lebanese publications and became a correspondent for Egyptian weeklies. Her interest in the Palestinian question is evident in her novels, most of which were published in the 1960s. She was a close friend of Palestine Liberation Organization leader, Yāsir 'Arafāt (q.v.).

USSR. *SEE* RUSSIA.

-V-

VAN DYCK, CORNELIUS (1818–1896). An Orientalist and educator, he was born in the United States (q.v.) to a Dutch immigrant family. He studied Latin and Greek and helped his father in his pharmacy. He received a medical degree from the University of Pennsylvania and was sent to Syria—geographic Syria, here—by American missionaries. Van Dyck arrived in Beirut (q.v.) in 1840 but was recalled to Jerusalem to tend to the medical needs of his colleagues. He returned to Beirut and embarked on the study of the Arabic (q.v.) language, which put him in touch with Buṭrus al-Bustānī (q.v.), who became his closest friend. He also studied Arabic under Naṣīf al-Yāzijī and Yūsuf al-Asīr (qq.v.). Van Dyck achieved a command of the Arabic language rarely seen among Western Orientalists; he could speak, write, and read the language fluently. He was one of the few Orientalists able to write in Arabic, and he spoke Arabic like a native speaker. He cofounded, with his friend, al-Bustānī, the famous school in 'Abayy.

Van Dyck realized the need for school textbooks in Arabic and wrote textbooks in geography, algebra, geometry, and biology. He lived for a while in Sidon (q.v.). In 1857 he was asked by an American missionary group to translate the Bible. During this work he managed the American Printing House, improving its script and adding diacritical marks. Van Dyck completed his Bible translation in 1864. When the Protestant Syrian College (later known as the American

University of Beirut, q.v.) was founded 1866, he was invited to teach science. He designed the medical school curriculum, and when he realized that the school had not hired a chemistry teacher, offered to teach it himself, spending his own money on laboratory equipment. He later taught astronomy and wrote an Arabic textbook on it. Van Dyck resigned from the university in 1882; he had been associated with the liberal, enlightened group of the faculty and protested the dismissal of a professor for mentioning Darwin's name in an official address. His son, William, later taught at the university.

VOICE OF LEBANON. This is the first major independent—albeit unlicensed—radio station not operated by the Lebanese government. It began its operation as the civil war (q.v.) started in 1975 and it became an effective propaganda tool of the Lebanese Phalanges Party (q.v.), which owned and operated the station. The station played an important role in the civil war because its transmission was more powerful than the government-run station and its news flashes provided listeners with up-to-date information on developing stories and bombing sites. In 1994, the Lebanese government ordered all private radio and television stations to cease broadcasting news and assumed sole power over news broadcasting. Most stations, however, have ignored the order. The popularity of the Voice of Lebanon has diminished over the years, because many other radio and television stations are now operating competitively.

-W-

WĀKĪM, NAJĀḤ (1946–). A Nasserist parliamentarian, he was born to a Greek Orthodox (q.v.) family in Barbārah and was educated in ʻAlayy and at the Beirut Arab University (q.v.), where he earned a law degree. He was a Nasserist activist in his youth and joined the Union of the Forces of the Working People-the Nasserist Organization (q.v.) headed by Kamāl Shātīlā. Wākīm was a surprise winner of the 1972 elections, shocking the political establishment by winning the largest number of votes. The Greek Orthodox community protested his election, because he was seen as an unrepresentative member of the sect. He has been a consistent critic of the Lebanese political system and supported the Syrian military intervention in 1976, when he was kidnapped by Palestine Liberation Organization forces and beaten. He later resigned from the union and charted an independent political course. He was known as an honest politician who did not enrich himself from the public coffers. Wākīm was one of the handful of deputies who opposed the May 17 Agreement (q.v.) in 1983. He survived several assassination attempts, including one at his house in 1987. He is one of the few supporters of the Palestinian (q.v.) cause left in Lebanon. His relations with Syria (q.v.) deteriorated over the years, and he is a vocal critic of Rafīq Ḥarīrī (q.v.). Wākīm won a seat in the 1992 and 1996 elections.

WAR CONDITIONS. Civil war, like Lebanon's civil war of 1975–90 (q.v.), hits all inhabitants of a country, but not equally: the poor possess far fewer options than the rich. Most members of Lebanon's wealthy class either fled the country (to France, q.v., or some other country) or at least sent their families abroad. The majority of Lebanese, however, could only move in with relatives when armed combat and shelling made their lives impossible. The most immediate impact of the war is, of course, the routinization of death and injury and the effects of constant fear. Most Lebanese have either lost a loved one to death or have known somebody who has.

Citizens of Lebanon also had to adjust to shortages of: water, electricity, food, and fuel. It was only in the mid-1990s that electric power was restored, with French help, to the city of Beirut (q.v.). Electric power blackouts, however, remained common, especially outside of the capital. The water supply was severely reduced. Food was often out of reach of the poor since no government price control was in place. One of the most severe crises in living conditions occurred in 1982, when Israel (q.v.) imposed a siege on West Beirut (q.v.) to pressure the Palestine Liberation Organization to surrender. Israeli forces, aided by Lebanese Forces (q.v.), ensured that no food or fuel was allowed into the capital. Loaves of bread were destroyed at checkpoints.

The physical destruction of Lebanon is still visible. The war left scarcely a house or building intact. The situation in Palestinian (q.v.) refugee camps was particularly difficult; many camps in East Beirut (q.v.) were demolished and their inhabitants either killed or expelled en masse. Displaced people (q.v.) numbered in the hundreds of thousands.

WAR OF THE CAMPS. The war between the Amal Movement (q.v.) and fighters in the Palestinian (q.v.) refugee camps in Lebanon started in 1985 near the refugee camp of Burj al-Barājinah, outside Beirut (q.v.), and quickly spread to other refugee camps in Beirut and Tyre (q.v.). Syria's desire to eliminate pro-'Arafāt (q.v.) forces in Lebanon was the contributing factor. The Shi'ites (q.v.), however, or some of them, had scores to settle too: they wanted to punish the remaining Palestinians in Lebanon for the corrupt rule of the Palestine Liberation Organization in South Lebanon prior to the 1982 Israeli invasion (q.v.) of Lebanon. The clashes lasted, with varying intensity, until 1989.

WAR OF THE MOUNTAIN *(Ḥarb al-Jabal).* This refers to the 1983–85 war in Mount Lebanon between the Druze (q.v.) forces and the Lebanese Forces (LF) (q.v.). Following the Israeli invasion of 1982 (q.v.), LF troops were stationed in the mountain. The right-wing militias had not been able to achieve a foothold in the area since 1975 (when Druze forces prevailed) without a war. Some Christians were killed, however, in 1977, following the assassination of Kamāl Jumblāṭ (q.v.). The presence of the LF troops in the Druze region provoked the Druze militias and started a bloody and destructive war. Although the Lebanese Army (q.v.), under the control of Amīn Gemayyel (q.v.), aided the LF, the Druzes won the war. Dozens of Christians were massacred and most of the Christian population in Mount Lebanon was displaced.

WASA PASHA (1824–1892). A *mutaṣarrif* (q.v.), he was born in Albania to a Roman Catholic (q.v.) family. He studied in Rome, acquiring knowledge of several languages. His interests were primarily literary, and he traveled to Istanbul eager to participate in its cultural life. He joined the foreign ministry and was appointed counselor in the Ottoman Embassy in London. He was later hired by the Interior Ministry, where he dealt with more domestic issues. He once served in Aleppo, where he studied Arabic (q.v.). He was appointed *mutaṣarrif* in 1883 but died before the end of his 10-year term. His brother-in-law, who accompanied him to Lebanon (q.v.), was known for selling favors and posts; bribery and corruption were massive. A local poet commented upon his death that the ringing of coins would bring him back to life. Wasa Pasha was buried in the Hazmiyyah area outside of Beirut (q.v.).

WĀSIṬAH (WĀSṬAH). Literally, it signifies "means" but refers to the complex system of political communication and interaction between the *za'īm* (q.v.) and his constituency. It specifically refers to the value of access and connection in attaining a job or in conducting a simple transaction with the Lebanese government. The concentration of governmental services and jobs in Beirut (q.v.) has strengthened the power of *zu'amā'* in remote areas of Lebanon.

WĀSṬAH. *SEE* WĀSIṬAH.

WAṬAN, al-. Benefiting from generous Libyan (q.v.) aid, the Lebanese National Movement (q.v.) published a daily newspaper that was distributed free of charge around the country. It lasted for the few years that Libyan donations to the LNM were generous.

WAZZĀN, SHAFĪQ al- (1925–). He was perhaps the weakest prime minister in contemporary Lebanese history. This Sunni (q.v.) politician was born in Beirut (q.v.) and educated at St. Joseph University (q.v.), where he obtained his law degree. He was elected in 1968 to parliament and was briefly a minister in 1969. He lost the election in 1972 but continued to be active politically through his own Islamic Council, which was merely a vehicle to exaggerate his political influence. Wazzān became a prime minister in 1980, when Ilyās Sarkīs (q.v.) was looking for a weak prime minister to succeed the independent Salīm al-Ḥuṣṣ (q.v.). He was chosen by Amīn Gemayyel (q.v.) to be his first prime minister, also, because he was subservient to the president. Wazzān lost his Muslim credibility as a result of his services under Gemayyel and retired from public life in 1984, although he still issues political statements.

WEST BEIRUT. The name was used after 1975 to refer to the predominantly Muslim section of the city after the outbreak of hostilities. Many Christians continued to live in West Beirut, especially in the Rās Beirut area, near the American University of Beirut (q.v.). Many militias ruled over the city and terrorized its population during the 1975–90 civil war (q.v.). Beirut was united only after October 1990 when the government of Ilyās Hrāwī (q.v.) established control over both sections of the city.

WORSHIPPERS OF THE COMPASSIONATE. *SEE* YAKAN, FATḤĪ.

-Y-

YĀFĪ, ‘ABDULLĀH al- (1901–1986). A former prime minister, he was born in Beirut to a Sunni (qq.v.) family. He received his education in Beirut and in Paris, where he received a Ph.D. in law. He was first elected to parliament in 1932 and first served as prime minister in 1938–39. Yāfī was a noted authority on constitutional law and was respected for his honesty and integrity. He served as prime minister under Kamīl Sham‘ūn (q.v.) but resigned in protest in 1956, when Sham‘ūn refused to sever diplomatic ties with France and Britain after the Tripartite (involving France, Israel, and Britain) invasion of Egypt in the same year. He soon emerged as a staunch Nasserist who wanted to orient Lebanon toward the Arab world. Yāfī served as prime minister in the 1960s and was known for his enthusiastic support of the Palestinian resistance movement and for the rights of Palestinians in Lebanon (q.v.) to bear arms. He won a seat in the 1968 election but lost in the 1972 election. He was not heard from during the 1975–90 civil war (q.v.) and faded from public life long before his death.

YAKAN, FATḤĪ (1933–). This fundamentalist leader and deputy was born in Tripoli to a Sunni (qq.v.) Muslim family. He received his education in Tripoli and later received degrees in engineering and a Ph.D. in history. Yakan has been active since the 1950s in Islamic fundamentalist affairs. In 1955, he founded the conservative Islamic fundamentalist group 'Ubbād Ar-Raḥmān (Worshippers of the Compassionate). He wrote more than 10 books on Islamic affairs, and his writings are widely circulated throughout the Arab world. His influence is strong even among Palestinian fundamentalist groups. Yakan was active in the 1975–76 civil war (q.v.) (and thereafter) as the leader of the Islamic Community (q.v.). He was elected to the 1992 parliament.

YAZBAKI FAMILY CONFEDERATION. *SEE* ARSALĀN FAMILY.

YAZBAKI LIBERATION FRONT (***Jabhat at-Taḥrīr al-Yazbakiyyah***). This small organization was formed by Farīd Ḥamādah, who hails from a prominent Druze (q.v.) family. He intended to oppose the leadership of the Jumblāṭ family (q.v.) by reviving the historical Yazbaki-Jumblati feud within the Druze community. His alliance with the Lebanese Forces (q.v.) and his residence in East Beirut (q.v.), however, discredited him in Druze eyes. The front plays an insignificant role in Lebanese politics; it was merely a tool for the Lebanese Forces to undermine Walīd Jumblāṭ's (q.v.) leadership.

YĀZIJĪ, IBRĀHĪM al- (1847–1906). A writer and linguist and son of Naṣīf al-Yāzijī (q.v.), he was born in Beirut (q.v.) and was taught by his father. He wrote poetry in his youth but not in his later years. He also studied Islamic jurisprudence with a famous doctor of religion in Beirut. He was hired by Jesuit missionaries to translate Christian texts. He studied Hebrew and Syriac and later learned French and English. Yāzijī also wrote scientific articles for a medical journal. In 1882, he began work on his father's manuscript, an elaborate interpretation of al-Mutanabbī's poetry. He finished this great task and published it over his father's name. It remains one of the best editions of Al-Mutanabbī's poetry. Yāzijī also wrote books on rhetoric, grammar, and philology, and re-edited many of his father's books. He traveled to Europe in 1894; he later settled in Egypt, where he founded the journal *Al-Bayān*. When it ran into financial difficulties, he founded (in 1898) a new journal *Aḍ-Ḍiyā'*. In 1904, he began working on a dictionary of synonyms but did not finish it.

YĀZIJĪ, NAṢĪF al- (1800–1871). A scholar and educator, he was born in Kafar Shīmā and educated by a priest. His father, who was a physician, had an appreciation for Arabic (q.v.) poetry, which was inherited by his son. He read voraciously and composed Arabic poetry at the age of 10. As printed books were rare at the time, he memorized whole books, copying what he could not memorize. Yāzijī was a prolific writer on Arabic literature and grammar. One of his books, *Faṣl Al-Khiṭāb,* was probably one of the first useful summaries of Arabic grammar; it has been used in many Arab countries for teaching of Arabic. He worked with American missionaries and composed for them some religious hymns in Arabic. He wrote a famous book of *Maqamāt* (an old form of writing Arabic prose) titled *Majma' Al-Baḥrayn.* Yāzijī worked as a linguistic editor in printing houses and was one of the founders of the Syrian Scientific Society. He left three books of poetry. He was praised for his ability to write exactly like classic Arab poets; by modern poets, he is criticized for his non-original forms. His reputation extended throughout the region, and he was briefly hired as the personal writer of the patriarch of the Greek Catholics (q.v.). He later worked for Prince Bashīr II (q.v.). Yāzijī memorized the Qur'ān and began an extensive interpretation of al-Mutanabbī's *diwān,* which was completed by his son Ibrāhīm (q.v.).

YĀZIJĪ, WARDAH al- (1838–1924). A writer and the daughter of famous scholar Naṣīf al-Yāzijī (q.v.), she was born in Kafar Shīmā and educated by her father, who trained her in the rules of Arabic (q.v.) poetry. She first composed poetry at the age of 13. A series of deaths in her family led her to write poetic obituaries in their memories. In 1899, after the death of her husband, Yāzijī left for Egypt, where she received advanced education and learned French. Her articles appeared in various newspapers and magazines. Her poetry was collected in one volume, *Ḥadīqat Al-Ward* (1867). There is a melancholic streak in her poetry.

YOUTHS OF 'ALI (***Fityān 'Alī***). This organization was a splinter of the Amal Movement (q.v.). It was led by a militant street leader, 'Alī Ṣafwān, who participated in the 1975–76 civil war (q.v.) on the Shiyyāḥ front.

YŪSUF PASHA (1856–?). A *mutaṣarrif* (q.v.), he was born in Istanbul to a Greek Catholic (q.v.) family. He studied in Mount Lebanon with private tutors before joining the office for foreign correspondence. He was appointed *mutaṣarrif* in 1907 for a term of five years. He later served in the Senate.

-Z-

ZAGHLŪL AD-DĀMŪR (1925–). This is a nickname for folk poet Joseph al-Hāshim, who was born in Būshriyyah. He formed the most famous operating *zajal* (q.v.) troupe in Lebanon, known as *Jawqat*

Zaghlūl ad-Dāmūr, which included, in addition to Joseph Al-Hāshim, Zayn Shu'ayb, As'ad Sa'īd, and Jān Ra'd. It broke up during the war due to the relocation of its members.

ZAḤLAH. This major city in al-Biqā' valley (q.v.) is nicknamed "bride of Biqā'" for its beauty. It is predominantly Christian and is in an area politically loyal to the Skāf family. *See also* Skāf, Ilyās.

ZA'ĪM* (pl., *ZU'AMĀ'). Literally, it means "leader" but refers to the class of political bosses who have monopolized political leadership and representation within the sects. They typically come from traditional families with inherited wealth. They belong to all the sects of Lebanon and did not retire from political life after the 1975–90 civil war. The death of a *za'īm* automatically leads to the selection of a member of the deceased's family—preferably his eldest son—as his successor. Many of the leaders of Lebanon today fit this category.

ZAJAL. This popular form of poetry is expressed in the Lebanese dialect of Arabic (q.v.). It does not adhere to the rules of classical Arabic but instead is simple, folkloric, even at times vulgar. *Zajal* groups tour villages and towns to perform critical poetry, troupe members poetically "attacking" one another, to the delight of the audience. Cassette tapes of *zajal* festivals are popular.

ZAYDĀN, JURJĪ (1861–1914). A writer and scholar, he was born in Beirut (q.v.), where he attended elementary school. He discovered the love of reading at an early age but was forced to quit his education for financial reasons. He studied English in a night school and entered the medical school at the American University of Beirut (q.v.). He left after the student disturbances in 1882, following the dismissal of a popular professor. Zaydān worked briefly with his father in commerce but later left for Egypt, where he had an illustrious journalistic career, publishing the highly acclaimed journal *Al-Hilāl.* He was a prolific writer, who wrote books on Islamic history and Arabic (q.v.) literature. He is best known for his historical novels, in which he narrates Islamic history through the romantic plot line. These novels are widely read in the Arab world.

ZAYN, 'ABDUL-LAṬĪF az- (1930–). A landlord and politician, this Shi'ite (q.v.) member of a traditional *za'īm* (q.v.) family was born in Kafar Rummān and educated in Beirut (q.v.), where he received a law degree from St. Joseph University (q.v.). He began practicing law in 1953, was first elected deputy in 1960, and has been reelected ever since. Zayn was close to the Shihabi establishment and was appointed a minister in 1969. He charted an independent political course during the 1975–90 civil war (q.v.), adjusting to the changing moods of his constituency. He has been known for his frequent visits and extended stays in his home village. He won a seat in 1992.

ZI'INNĪ, 'UMAR (1898–1961). A popular poet, he was born to a Sunni (q.v.) family in Beirut (q.v.). He received a religious education at an early age and graduated from the now-defunct Uthmāniyyah school in 1914. He developed a love for poetry and reading at an early age but was distracted from his scholastic pursuits by Ottoman conscription in 1914. Zi'innī graduated from the military academy in Ḥumṣ and worked in the Ottoman military administration during World War I. He taught Arabic (q.v.) at various schools, wrote poetry and plays, and worked as a clerk in a Beirut court in the 1920s. He attended law classes at St. Joseph University (q.v.) but did not obtain a degree. He started writing and reciting his biting satirical poetry in Beirut in the 1920s. He mixed in his unique style the classical and colloquial forms of the Arabic language. His subjects were social and political, and in 1939 Zi'innī wrote a famous poem in which he expressed satisfaction at French military defeats and glorified Hitler (as "the enemy of my enemy"). During the administration of Bishārah al-Khūrī (q.v.), his poetry landed him in jail. He often used his poetic skills to expose corruption and hypocrisy. Zi'innī developed a cult following after his death, and a compilation of his poetry has been published in Beirut.

ZIYĀDAH, MAYY (1886–1941). A writer, she was born in Nazareth to a Lebanese father. She moved to Lebanon and then to Egypt, where she studied French, English, Spanish, German, Italian, Latin, and modern Greek, in addition to Arabic (q.v.), which she mastered at an early age. Ziyādah wrote many articles for Arab publications, which have been published in a book form. She was known among the prominent writers of the Arab world, and her house became a gathering place for the Egyptian intellectual elite. Her independent lifestyle (she was not married) earned her enemies and harmed her reputation. She is also known for her literary correspondence with Jubrān Khalīl Jubrān (Khalīl Gibrān, q.v.), and experts still debate whether the two were lovers. She spent her last years in a mental asylum in Lebanon. Her defenders claim that Ziyādah was committed by her family for reasons relating to family inheritance, but Salāmah Mūsā, an Egyptian writer and friend of Ziyādah, remembers her as mentally disturbed in her last years.

ZU'AMĀ'. SEE ZA'ĪM.

ZURAYQ, CONSTANTINE (1909–). A scholar, he was born in Damascus and educated at the American University of Beirut (AUB) (q.v.), the University of Chicago, and Princeton University, where he received a Ph.D. in Middle East history. He taught history at AUB and served as an advisor to the Syrian mission in Washington, D.C. (1945–47). In 1952, Zurayq was appointed acting president of AUB, the first Arab to ever head the university. He has written a number of scholarly articles, but his books in Arabic (q.v.) have been more in the manifesto genre. His book *Ma'nā An-Nakabah* (Meaning of Disaster) was the first serious attempt to understand and explain the non-military reasons for the Arab defeat in the first war with Israel (q.v.) in 1948. He has been a passionate believer in Arab nationalism and in secularism. Zurayq's impact has been profound on AUB students, who now occupy positions of prominence in Arab ruling and opposition circles. George Ḥabash and Hānī al-Hindī, who founded the Movement of Arab Nationalists (q.v.), were both inspired by him. Zurayq left Lebanon during the war and settled in Washington, D.C., where he works for the Institute of Palestine Studies.

Appendix 1
Ottoman Mutaṣarrifs

Dāwūd Pasha (1861–1868)
Naṣrī Franco Pasha (1868–1873)
Rustum Pasha (1873–1883)
Wāsā Pasha (1883–1892)
Na‘um Pasha (1892–1902)
Muḍhaffar Pasha (1902–1907)
Yūsuf Franco Pasha (1907–1912)
Uhānnis Pasha (1912–1915)

Appendix 2
Lebanese Presidents

Before independence:

Charles Dabbās (1926–1934)
Ḥabīb Pasha as-Sa'd (1934–1936)
Emile Iddī (1936–1941)
Alfred Naqqāsh (1941–1943)
Ayyūb Thābit (1943)
Petro Ṭrād (1943)

After independence:

Bishārah al-Khūrī (1943–1952)
Kamīl Sham'ūn (1952–1958)
Fu'ād Shihāb (1958–1964)
Charles Ḥilū (1964–1970)
Sulaymān Franjiyyah (1970–1976)
Ilyās Sarkīs (1976–1982)
Amīn Gemayyel (1982–1988)
Ilyās Hrāwī (1989–)

Appendix 3
Prime Ministers

Before independence:

Uguste Pasha Adīb (1926–1927)
Bishārah al-Khūrī (1927–1928)
Ḥabīb Pasha as-Sa'd (1928–1929)
Bishārah al-Khūrī (1929)
Emile Iddī (1929–1930)
Ugust Pasha Adīb (1930–1932)
Khayr ad-Dīn al-Aḥdab (1937–1938)
Khālid Shihāb (1938)
'Abdullāh al-Yāfī (1938–1939)
Aḥmad ad-Dā'ūq (1941–1942)
Sāmī aṣ-Ṣulḥ (1942–1943)
Ayyūb Thābit (1943)

After independence:

Riyāḍ aṣ-Ṣulḥ (1943–1945)
'Abdul-Ḥamīd Karāmī (1945)
Sāmī aṣ-Ṣulḥ (1945–1946)
Sa'dī al-Munlā (1946)
Riyāḍ aṣ-Ṣulḥ (1946–1951)
Ḥusayn al-'Uwaynī (1951)
'Abdullāh al-Yāfī (1951–1952)
Sāmī aṣ-Ṣulḥ (1952)
Nāḍhim 'Akkārī (1952)
Ṣā'ib Salām (1952)
Fu'ād Shihāb (1952)
Khālid Shihāb (1952–1953)
Ṣā'ib Salām (1953)
'Abdullāh al-Yāfī (1953–1954)

Sāmī aṣ-Ṣulḥ (1954–1955)
Rashīd Karāmī (1955–1956)
'Abdullāh al-Yāfī (1956)
Sāmī aṣ-Ṣulḥ (1956–1958)
Rashīd Karāmī (1958–1960)
Aḥmad ad-Dā'ūq (1960)
Ṣā'ib Salām (1960–1961)
Rashīd Karāmī (1961–1964)
Ḥusayn al-'Uwaynī (1964–1965)
Rashīd Karāmī (1965–1966)
'Abdullāh al-Yāfī (1966)
Rashīd Karāmī (1966–1968)
'Abdullāh al-Yāfī (1968–1969)
Rashīd Karāmī (1969–1970)
Ṣā'ib Salām (1970–1973)
Amīn al-Ḥāfiḍh (1973)
Taqiyy ad-Dīn aṣ-Ṣulḥ (1973–1974)
Rashīd aṣ-Ṣulḥ (1974–1975)
Nūr ad-Dīn ar-Rifā'ī (1975)
Rashīd Karāmī (1975–1976)
Salīm al-Ḥuṣṣ (1976–1980)
Shafīq al-Wazzān (1980–1983)
Rashīd Karāmī (1983–1987)
Salīm al-Ḥuṣṣ (1987–1990)
'Umar Karāmī (1990–1992)
Rashīd aṣ-Ṣulḥ (1992)
Rafīq Ḥarīrī (1992–).

Bibliography

The bibliography on Lebanon is quite extensive, especially if one does not confine oneself to English-language sources. American libraries generally carry English-language books on Lebanon. The presence of Lebanese emigrants in the United States and the association between Lebanon and Eastern Christians generated interest in that country long before the outbreak of the civil war.

Only specialized Middle East collections, however, carry important materials in French and Arabic: libraries at Harvard University, the University of Pennsylvania, Georgetown University, the University of California at Berkeley and Los Angeles, Stanford University (the Hoover collection), the University of Texas, Princeton University, Yale University, the University of Michigan, Indiana University, Columbia University, the University of Utah, Oxford University, Cambridge University, the University of London; and the Boston Public Library, the New York Public Library, the Bibliothèque Nationale, and of course the Library of Congress. The late Philip Hitti's presence at Princeton University strengthened that university's collection on the Middle East, and he acquired many important manuscripts.

The library at the American University of Beirut, however, remains the most important source of information on Lebanon, although it is far behind most American universities in computerized cataloguing. The Centre for Lebanese Studies in Oxford, England, is an important source of information on Lebanon, as is the Beirut-based Lebanese Center for Policy Studies.

For centuries, Lebanon has attracted visitors from the West. Books by travelers often contain useful information, although they are often full of stereotypical depictions of and prejudiced assumptions about Arabs and Muslims. In the twentieth century, classical Orientalists began their studies of the actual conditions of countries, utilizing impressive linguistic skills. Lebanon was the subject of more studies than any other Arab country, perhaps with the exception of Egypt, because it was considered, at least partly, a Christian nation in a region of Islamic influence. Furthermore, the relatively democratic system invited social scientists who were curious about the viability of Western democracy in a developing country.

Studies about Lebanon, however, had many shortcomings. Few questions were raised about the injustices of the distribution of power or about the viability of the new nation. Assessments of the political system were naively optimistic, and Muslim grievances were too easily dismissed. The civil war, however, changed all that. The world was shocked by the transformation of the image of Lebanon from "the Switzerland of the East"—as Lebanese postcards would boast—to the horrors of civil war. The protracted conflict highlighted the weaknesses in the pre-war political system and linked the destiny of Lebanon to the fate of the Arab-Israeli conflict.

There are some superb books on Lebanon in English, although an advanced study of the country requires knowledge of Arabic and French. The bibliography on the civil war, for example, is far richer in Arabic than in any other language. Studies on pre-war Lebanon are available in English and French. The violence in the country during the civil war and the kidnapping of foreigners scared away scholars and journalists, although some brave individuals, like Tabitha Petran, Augustus Richard Norton, Helena Cobban, and Robert Fisk, conducted research under the most dangerous conditions.

Those interested in Lebanese history should read Kamal Salibi's *The Modern History of Lebanon*. Philip Hitti's *Lebanon in History* covers eras skipped by Salibi, and his book remains a classic regardless of the passage of time. Meir Zamir's *The Formation of Modern Lebanon* enhanced our understanding of the role of Lebanese emigrants and the origins of the modern entity of Lebanon. Kamal Salibi later provided a revisionist history of Lebanon in his *A House of Many Mansions,* in which he refutes the notion of a distinctive Lebanese history apart from the region's history. Those with knowledge of French are strongly encouraged to read Dominique Chevallier's *La Societé du Mont-Liban*. Readers of Arabic should consult the works of Mas'ud Dahir and Wajih Kawtharani.

The 19th century is well covered in Leila Tarazi Fawaz's *Occasion to War* and Engin Akarli's *The Long Peace*. Samir Khalaf's *Persistence and Change in 19th century Lebanon* deals with social history.

For Lebanese social conditions, consult Samir Khalaf's *Lebanon's Predicament*. To understand sectarianism and its social dimensions, one may rely on Su'ad Joseph's *Muslim-Christian Conflicts*. Halim Barakat's *Lebanon in Strife* focuses on the role of students in politics. Joseph Chamie's *Religion and Fertility* is a rare study of this important subject. *Crucial Bonds: Marriage among the Druze,* by Nura Alamuddin and Paul Starr, is the only book in English on marriage in Lebanon. Those with command of Arabic should read Zuhayr Ḥatab's *Taṭawwur Bunā Al-Usrah Al-'Arabiyyah.*

For information on the various sects in the country, one has to study them separately. On the Christians of the East, Robert Betts' *Christians in the Arab East* remains a classic, while Robert Haddad's *Syrian Christians in Muslim Society* is more historical. Sami Makarem's *The Druze Faith* is an informative albeit uncritical treatment of the subject, while Robert Betts' *The Druze* is more scholarly. Augustus Richard Norton's *Amal and the Shi'a* is by far the best study of Lebanon's Shi'ite community, while Fouad Ajami's *The Vanished Imam* focuses on Imam Musa as-Sadr. Matti Moosa's *The Maronites in History* is a highly informative look at this important sect.

Studies of Lebanese culture and literature are rare in English, although translations of Lebanese literary works are now being made available. Miriam Cooke's *War's Other Voices* looks specifically at the war through the works of literature. Jamīl Jabr's *Lubnān fī Rawā'i' Aqlāmihi* contains a compilation of the best writings by Lebanese authors, with brief biographies of each. Emily Faris Ibrahim's early *Adibāt Lubnāniyyāt* studies the contribution of female writers.

The study of pre-war Lebanon occupies a relatively large number of books in French and English. Michael Hudson's *The Precarious Republic* remains the most influential study of Lebanese politics. Leonard Binder's *Politics in Lebanon* contains contributions by some of the most noted scholars of Lebanon. Michael Suleiman's *Political Parties in Lebanon* is still the only English language book on the subject. John Enterlis' *Pluralism and Party Transformation in Lebanon* is a study of the Lebanese Phalanges Party. Elie Salem's *Modernization without Revolution* is often cited as an example of pre-war glorification of the Lebanese political model.

The civil war has been extensively studied in English although most accounts are journalistic. Kamal Salibi's *Crossroads to Civil War* covers the first two year of war, and so does Walid Khalidi's *Conflict and Violence in Lebanon*. For analytical accounts, one should read *Essays on the Crisis in Lebanon* by Roger Owen, and *Lebanon in Crisis,* by Edward Haley and Lewis Snider. The later developments of the war are covered in Marius Deeb's *The Lebanese Civil War* and in Robert Fisk's *Pity the Nation*. Rashid Khalidi's *Under Siege* offers a scholarly study of the Israeli invasion of Lebanon. Augustus Richard Norton's *Amal and the Shi'a* studies the Shi'ite dimension of the war. Halim Barakat's *Towards a Viable Lebanon* and Deirdre Collings' *Peace for Lebanon?* both contain contributions by scholars on Lebanon. The most recent scholarly study of Lebanon is Theodor Hanf's *Coexistence in Wartime Lebanon,* which has been translated from the German.

General Works and Historical Sources

Abū An-Naṣr, 'Umar. *Tārīkh Sūryā wa Lubnān* (History of Syria and Lebanon). Beirut: n.p., n.d.

Christopher, John. *Lebanon: Yesterday and Today*. New York: Holt, Rinehart, 1966.
Cobban, Helena. *The Making of Modern Lebanon*. Boulder, CO: Westview, 1985.
Collelo, Thomas. ed. *Lebanon: A Country Study*. Washington, D.C.: Government Printing Office, 1989.
Dibs, Al-Muṭrān Yūsuf. *Tārīkh Sūryā* (History of Syria). Beirut: Al-Maṭba'ah Al-'Umūmiyyah, 1893–1902.
Hitti, Philip. *Lebanon in History*. New York: St. Martin's, 1957.
———. *A Short History of Lebanon*. New York: St. Martin's, 1965.
Hourani, Albert. *Syria and Lebanon*. London: Oxford University Press, 1946.
Ismail, Adel. *Le Liban: Histoire d'un Peuple*. Beirut: Dār Al-Makshūf, 1968.
Al-Khāzin, Philip, and Farīd Al-Khāzin. *Majmū'at Al-Muharrarāt As-Siyāsiyyah wa-l-Mufāwaḍāt Ad-Duwaliyyah 'An Sūryā wa Lubnān 1840–1910* (The Collection of Political Documents and International Negotiations on Syria and Lebanon, 1840–1910). Junya: Maṭba'at Aṣ-Ṣabr, 1910.
Lyautey, Pierre. *Le Liban Moderne*. Paris: Julliard, 1964.
As-Sawdā, Yūsuf. *Fī Sabīl Lubnān* (For the Sake of Lebanon). Beirut: Dār Laḥd Khāṭir, 1988.
———. *Tārīkh Lubnān Al-Ḥaḍārī* (The Civilizational History of Lebanon). Beirut: Dār An-Nahār, 1972.
Tibawi, Abdul Latif. *A Modern History of Syria, including Lebanon and Palestine*. Edinburgh: Macmillan, 1969.
Ziadeh, Nicola. *Syria and Lebanon*. New York: Praeger, 1957.

History, to 1800

Abu-Husayn, Abdul-Rahim. *Provincial Leaderships in Syria, 1575–1650*. Beirut: American University of Beirut, 1985.
Aubet, Maria Eugenia. *The Phoenicians and the West*. New York: Cambridge University Press, 1987.
Autran, C.. *Phéniciens: essai de contribution à l'histoire antique de la Méditerranée*. Paris: Geuthner, 1920.
Baramki, D. *Phoenicia and the Phoenicians*. Beirut: Catholic Press, 1961.
Būlus, Jawād. *Tārīkh Lubnān* (History of Lebanon). Beirut: Dār An-Nahār, 1972.
Chami, Joseph. *De la Phénicie*. Beirut: Librairie du Liban, 1967.
Chebli, Chebli. *Fakdreddine II Maan, Prince du Liban, 1572–1635*. Beirut: Imprimerie Catholique, 1946.

———. *Une Histoire du Liban à l'époque des émirs, 1635–1841*. Beirut: Catholic Press, 1955.

Chevallier, Dominique. *La société du Mont-Liban à l'époque de la Révolution Industrielle en Europe*. Paris: Librairie Orientale, 1971.

Culican, William. *The First Merchant Ventures: The Ancient Levant in History and Commerce*. London: Thames and Hudson, 1966.

Ḍaww, Buṭrus. *Tārīkh Al-Mawārinah* (History of the Maronites). Beirut: Dār An-Nahār, 1975–1980.

Dunand, Maurice. *Byblos: Its History, Ruins, and Legends*. Beirut: 1973.

Duwayhī, Isṭifān. *Tārīkh Al-Azminah* (History of Time). Beirut: Al-Maṭba'ah Al-Kāthūlīkiyyah, 1951.

Grainger, John D. *Hellenistic Phoenicia*. London: Clarendon, 1991.

Gray, John. *The Canaanites*. London: Thames and Hudson, 1964.

Haddad, Robert. *Syrian Christians in Muslim Society*. Princeton: Princeton University Press, 1970.

Harden, Donald. *The Phoenicians*. London: Thames and Hudson, 1962.

Al-Ḥūrānī, Yūsuf. *Naḍhariyyat At-Takwīn Al-Fīnīqī* (The Phoenician Theory of Formation). Beirut: Dār An-Nahār, 1970.

Ibn Yaḥyā, Ṣāliḥ. *Tārīkh Bayrūt* (History of Beirut). Beirut: Lebanese University, 1969.

Jidejian, Nina. *Byblos Through the Ages*. Beirut: Dar el-Mashreq, 1968.

Khāṭir, Laḥd. *Mukhtaṣar Tārīkh Lubnān* (A Concise History of Lebanon). Beirut: n.p., 1914.

Al-Khūrī, Salīm Yūsuf. *Lamḥah 'an Al-Fīnīqiyyīn* (A Glance at the Phoenicians). Sidon: n.p., 1924.

Lammens, Henri. *Tasrīḥ Al-Abṣār* (Surveying the Archeology that Lebanon Has). Beirut: Al-Maṭba'ah Al-Kāthūlīkiyyah, 1914.

———. *La Syrie, précis historique*. Beirut: Catholic Press, 1921.

Martan, Al-Ab Al-Yasū'ī. *Tārīkh Lubnān* (History of Lebanon). Beirut, 1889.

Mathews, Samuel. "The Phoenicians, Sea Lords of Antiquity." *National Geographic Magazine* 146, pt. 2 (August 1974): 149–189.

Mizhir, Yūsuf. *Tārīkh Lubnān Al-'Ām* (General History of Lebanon). n.p. and n.d.

Moosa, Matti. *The Maronites in History*. Syracuse: Syracuse University Press, 1986.

Moscati, Sabatino. *The World of the Phoenicians*. New York: Praeger, 1968.

———, ed. *The Phoenicians*. New York: Abbeville, 1988.

Qara'lī, Būlus. *Fakhr Ad-Dīn*. Harisa: Al-Majallah Al-Baṭriyarkiyyah, 1938.

Rawlinson, George. *History of Phoenicia*. London: Longman, Green, 1889.

Rīḥānī, Amīn. *An-Nakabāt* (The Disasters). Beirut: Dar Ar-Rīḥānī, 1948.

Aṣ-Ṣafadī, Aḥmad Al-Khālidī. *Lubnān Fī 'Ahd Al-Amīr Fakhr Ad-Dīn* (Lebanon in the era of Fakhr Ad-Din). Beirut: Lebanese University, 1969.

History, 1800–1861

Abkarius, Iskandar. *Lebanon in Turmoil*. Trans. J. F. Scheltema. New Haven: Yale University Press, 1920.
Abraham, Anthony. *Lebanon at Mid-Century*. Lanham, MD: University Press of America, 1981.
Abū Shaqrā, Ḥusayn. *Al-Ḥarakāt fī Lubnān* (Movements in Lebanon). Beirut: Maṭba'at Al-Ittiḥād, 1952.
Anonymous. *Ḥasr Al-Lithām 'an Nakabāt ash-Shām* (Unveiling the Disasters of Syria). Cairo, 1895.
Barbir, Karl. *Ottoman Rule in Damascus*. Princeton: Princeton University Press, 1980.
Baz, Salim. *Pièces diplomatiques relatives aux évenéments de 1860 au Liban*. Beirut: Librarie Antoine, 1974.
Churchill, Charles. *The Druzes and the Maronites under Turkish Rule from 1840 to 1860*. New York: Arno, 1973.
———. *Mount Lebanon: A Ten Years' Residence from 1842 to 1852*. London, 1853.
Fawaz, Leila Tarazi. *Merchants and Migrants in Nineteenth-Century Beirut*. Cambridge: Harvard University Press, 1983.
———. *An Occasion for War*. Berkeley: University of California Press, 1994.
Harik, Iliya. *Politics and Change in a Traditional Society: Lebanon, 1711–1845*. Princeton: Princeton University Press, 1968.
Ismail, Adel. *Reversement et déclin du feudalisme libanais 1840–1860*. Beirut: Bajjani, 1958.
Kerr, Malcolm, ed. and trans. *Lebanon in the Last Years of Feudalism, 1840–1868*. Beirut: American University of Beirut, 1959.
Khalaf, Samir. *Persistence and Change in 19th Century Lebanon: A Sociological Essay*. Beirut: American University of Beirut, 1979.
Polk, William. *The Opening of South Lebanon*. Cambridge: Harvard University Press, 1963.
Poujade, M. *Le Liban et la Syrie 1845–1860*. Paris, 1860.
Ash-Shidyāq, Ṭannūs. *Kitāb Akhbār Al-A'yān fī Jabal Lubnān* (The Book of the Tales of Notables in Mount Lebanon). Beirut: Al-Maṭba'ah Al-Kāthūlīkiyyah, 1970.
Al-Shihābī, Amīr Ḥaydar Aḥmad. *Lubnān fī 'Ahd Al-Umarā' Ash-Shihābiyyīn* (Lebanon in the Era of the Shihabi Princes). Beirut: Lebanese University, 1969.

Smilianskaya, I. M. *Al-Ḥarakāt Al-Fallāḥiyyah fī Lubnān* (Peasant Movement in Lebanon). Trans. 'Adnān Jāmūs. Beirut: Dār Al-Fārābī, 1972.

Van Leeuwen, Richard. *Notables and Clergy in Mount Lebanon: The Khazin Sheikhs and the Maronite Church (1736–1840)*. Leiden: Brill, 1994.

Historical Accounts of Travelers

Baptiste, Jean. *Memoires du Chevalier d'Arvieux, contenant ses voyages à Constantinople, dans l'Asie, la Syrie, la Palestine, l'Egypte, et la Barbarie*. Paris, 1735.

Beaufort, Emily. *Egyptian Sepulchres and Syrian Shrines, including Some Stay in the Lebanon, at Palmyra, and in Western Turkey*. 2 vols. London: Longman, Green, Longman and Roberts, 1861.

Bidulph, William. *The Travels of Certaine Englishmen into Africa, Asia, Troy, Bythinia, Chracia, and the Black Sea. And into Syria, Cilicia, Pisidia, Mesopotamia, Damascus, Canaan, Galile, Samaria, Judea, Palestina, Jerusalem, Jericho, and to the Red Sea and sundry other places Begunne in the Yeare 1608*. London, 1609.

de Binos, Abbe. *Voyage par l'Italie, en Egypte, au Mont Liban et en Palestine ou Terre Sainte*. 3 vols. Paris, 1787.

———. *Voyage au Mont Liban*. Paris, 1809.

Burckhardt, J. L. *La France au Liban*. Paris, 1879.

———. *Travels in Syria and the Holy Land*. London, 1822.

Carnarvon, Fourth Earl of. *Recollections of the Druses of the Lebanon, and Notes on Their Religion*. London: J. Murray, 1860.

Carn, John. *Syria, the Holy Land, Asia Minor*. London, 1837.

Castlereagh, Viscount. *A Journey to Damascus through Egypt, Nubia, Arabia, Petraea, Palestine, and Syria*. 2 vols. London, 1847.

Damas et le Liban: extraits du journal d'un voyage en Syrie au printemps de 1860. London, 1861.

Damoiseau, L. *Voyage en Syrie et dans le desert*. Paris, 1833.

De Damas. *Souvenirs du Mont Liban*. Paris, 1860.

De Paris, Comte. *Damas et le Liban*. London, 1861.

De Tott, F. *Memoirs*. London, 1786.

Guys, Henri. *Beyrouth et le Liban*. Paris, 1850.

Jessup, H. *Fifty Three Years in Syria*. New York: Fleming Revell, 1910.

Kent, S. H. *Gath to the Cedars: Travels in the Holy Land and Palmyra*. London, 1872.

Lamartine, A. *Voyage en Orient*. Paris, 1903.

Lortet, Dr. L. *La Syrie d'aujourd'hui*. Paris, 1884.

Louet, E. *Expédition de Syrie 1860–1861*. Paris, 1862.

Mariti, M. l'Abbe. *Voyages dans l'isle de Chypre, la Syrie et la Palestine*. Paris, 1791.
Neale, F. A. *Eight Years in Syria, Palestine, and Asia Minor, from 1842–1850*. London, 1852.
Riskallah, Habeeb. *The Thistle and the Cedar of Lebanon*. London, 1854.
Robinson, E., and E. Smith. *Biblical Researches in Palestine, and the Adjacent Regions*. London, 1860.
Stanhope, Lady Hester. *Memoirs of Lady Hester Stanhope*. 3 vols. London, 1845.
Taylor, Bayard. *The Lands of the Saracens, or Pictures of Palestine, Asia Minor, Sicily, and Spain*. New York, 1855.
Urquhart, D. *The Lebanon (Mount Souria) A History and A Diary*. London, 1860.
Volney, C. F. *Voyage en Syrie et en Egypte*. Paris, 1787.
Warburton, Eliot. *The Crescent and the Cross, or, Romance and Realities of Eastern Travel*. 2 vols. London, 1845.

History and Politics, 1861–1975

Abouchdid, Eugenie Elie. *30 Years of Lebanon and Syria*. Beirut: The Sader Rihani Printing Co., 1948.
Agwani, Mohammad Shafi. *The Lebanese Crisis 1958: A Documentary Study*. New York: Asia Publishing House, 1965.
Akarli, Engin Deniz. *The Long Peace: Ottoman Lebanon, 1861–1920*. Berkeley: University of California Press, 1993.
Akl, George, et al. *The Black Book of the Lebanese Elections of May 25 1947*. New York: Phoenicia Press, 1947.
Alem, Jean-Pierre. *Le Liban*. Paris: Presses Universitaires, 1963.
Ammoun, Blanche Loheac. *History of Lebanon*. Beirut: Syteco, 1972.
Amoun, Iskender. *Memoire sur la question libanaise*. Cairo: Imprimerie Maaref, 1913.
Anderson, R. *History of the Missions of the American Board of Missions to the Oriental Churches*. 2 vols., Boston, 1872.
Associated Business Consultants. *Lebanon: the New Future*. London: George Murray, 1974.
Al-Aswad, Ibrāhīm. *Dalīl Lubnān* (Lebanon's Guide). Ba'abdā: Al-Maṭba'ah Al-'Uthmāniyyah, 1906.
'Awaḍ, 'Abdul-'Azīz. *Al-Idarāt Al-'Uthmāniyyah fī Wilāyat Sūryā* (Ottoman Administration in the Wilayat of Syria). Cairo: Dar Al-Ma'arif, 1969.
'Awaḍ, Walīd. *Aṣḥāb Al-Fakhāmah Ru'asā' Lubnān* (Their Excellencies, the Presidents of Lebanon). Beirut: Al-Ahliyyah, 1977.

Baaklini, Abdo. *Legislative and Political Development: Lebanon, 1842–1972*. Durham: Duke University Press, 1976.

Bayhum, Muḥammad Jamīl. *Al-'Ahd Al-Mukhaḍram fī Sūryā wa Lubnān* (The Veteran Era in Syria and Lebanon). Beirut: Dār At-Talī'ah, 1968.

Betts, Robert C. *Christians in the Arab East*. Athens: Lycabettus Press, 1975.

Binder, Leonard. *Politics in Lebanon*. New York: Wiley and Sons, 1966.

Britt, George. "Lebanon's Popular Revolution." *Middle East Journal* 7 (1953): 1–17.

Bustani, Emile. *March Arabesque*. London: Hale, 1961.

Chehab, Maurice. *Rôle du Liban dans l'histoire de la soie*. Beirut: Université Libanaise, 1967.

Cheikho, Louis, ed. *Lubnān: Mabāḥith 'Ilmiyyah wa Ijtimā'iyyah* (Lebanon: Social and Scientific Research Studies). Beirut: Lebanese University, 1969.

Chiha, Michel. *Politique Intérieure*. Beirut: Trident, 1964.

Corbeiller, J. le. *La guerre de Syrie, juin-juillet 1941*. Paris: Éditions Dufuseau, 1967.

Dahdah, Najib. *Évolution historique du Liban*. Mexico City: Oasis Editions, 1967.

Ḍāhir, Mas'ūd. *Al-Judhūr At-Tārīkhiyyah li-l-Mas'alah Aṭ-Ṭā'ifiyya-l-Lubnāniyyah* (The Historical Roots of the Lebanese Sectarian Question). Beirut: Ma'had Al-Inmā' Al-'Arabī, 1981.

———. *Al-Istiqlāl, Aṣ-Ṣīghah wa-l-Mīthāq* (Lebanon: Independence, the Formula, and the Pact). Beirut: Dār Maṭbū'āt Ash-Sharqiyyah, 1984.

———. *Al-Intifāḍāt Al-Lubnāniyyah Ḍid-d-a-Niḍhām-i-l-Muqāṭa'jī* (The Lebanese Uprisings against the Feudal Order). Beirut: Dār Al-Fārābī, 1988.

Davet, Michel Christian. *La Double affaire de Syrie*. Paris: Fayard, 1967.

Dubar, Claude, and Salim Nasr. *Les classes sociales au Liban*. Paris: La Fondation Nationale des Sciences Politiques, 1976.

Entelis, John. *Pluralism and Party Transformation in Lebanon*. Leiden: Brill, 1974.

Fedden, R. *Syria and Lebanon*. London: John Murray, 1965.

Gaunson, A. B. *The Anglo-French Clash in Lebanon and Syria, 1940–1945*. London: Macmillan, 1987.

George, Lucien, and Toufic Mokdessi. *Les Partis Libanais en 1959*. Beirut: L'Orient-al-Jaridah, 1959.

Haddad, George. *Fifty Years of Modern Syria and Lebanon*. Beirut: Dar Al-Hayat, 1950.

Al-Ḥakīm, Yūsuf. *Bayrūt wa Lubnān fī 'Ahd Aāl 'Uthmān* (Beirut in the Era of the Ottomans). Beirut: Dār An-Nahār, 1980.

Hudson, Michael. "The Electoral Process and Political Development in Lebanon." *Middle East Journal* 20 (1966): 173–186.

———. "A Case of Political Underdevelopment." *Journal of Politics* 29 (1967): 821–837.

———. *The Precarious Republic*. New York: Random House, 1968.

Ismail, Adel. *Lebanon: history of a people*. Trans. Shereen Khairalah. Beirut: Dar Al-Makchouf, 1972.

Al-Jisr, Bāsim. *Mithāq 1943* (The 1943 Pact). Beirut: Dār An-Nahār, 1978.

Jouplain, M. *La question du Liban*. Paris: Librairie nouvelle de droit, 1908.

Kawtharānī, Wajīh. *Al-Ittijāhāt Al-Ijtimā'iyyah wa-s-Siyāsiyyah fī Jabal Lubnān, 1860–1920* (Social and Political Trends in Mount Lebanon, 1860–1920). Beirut: Ma'had Al-Inmā' Al-'Arabī, 1976.

Khair, Antoine. *Le Moutacarrifat du Mont-Liban*. Beirut: Lebanese University, 1973.

Khāṭir, Laḥd. *'Ahd Al-Mutaṣarrifiyyah fī Lubnān* (The Musarrifate Era in Lebanon). Beirut: Lebanese University, 1967.

Khuri, Fuad. *From Village to Suburb*. Chicago: University of Chicago Press, 1975.

Lerner, Daniel. *The Passing of a Traditional Society*. Glencoe, IL: Free Press, 1958.

Longrigg, Stephen. *Syria and Lebanon under French Mandate*. London: Oxford University Press, 1968.

Lubnān: Waṭan Qawmī li-n-Naṣārā (Lebanon: A National Homeland for Christians in the East) N.p., n.d.

Lyautey, Pierre. *Liban Moderne*. Paris: Julliard, 1964.

Mas'ad, Būlus. *Lubnān wa Sūryā: Qabla-l-Intidāb wa Ba'dahu* (Lebanon and Syria: Before the Mandate and After). Cairo: Al-Maṭba'ah As-Sūriyyah, 1939.

McLaurin, R. D., ed. *The Political Role of Minority Groups in the Middle East*. New York: Praeger, 1979.

Meo, Leila. *Lebanon, Improbable Nation*. Bloomington: Indiana University Press, 1967.

Mishaqa, Mikhayil. *Murder, Mayhem, Pillage, and Plunder*. Trans. Wheeler Thackston Jr. Albany: SUNY Press, 1988.

Nantet, Jacques. *Histoire du Liban*. Paris: Minuit, 1963.

Nawwār, 'Abdul-'Azīz. *Wathā'iq Asāsiyyah min Tārīkh Lubnān Al-Ḥadīth* (Basic Documents about the Modern History of Lebanon). Beirut: Beirut Arab University, 1974.

Nimeh, William. *History of the Lebanon*. Mexico City: Editora Nacional, 1954.

Qubain, Fahim. *Crisis in Lebanon*. Washington, D.C.: The Middle East Institute, 1961.

Rabbat, Edmond. *La Formation historique du Liban*. Beirut: Lebanese University, 1973.

Rizq, Charles. *Le Régime politique libanais*. Paris: R. Pichon, 1966.

Rondot, Pierre. *Les institutions politiques du Liban*. Paris: Institut d'Études de l'Orient, 1947.

Salem, Elie. *Modernization Without Revolution*. Bloomington: Indiana University Press, 1973.

Salibi, Kamal. *The Modern History of Lebanon*. Delmar, NY: Caravan, 1977.

Sayegh, Raymond. *Le Parlement libanais*. Beirut: Lebanese University, 1974.

Smock, David, and Audrey Smock. *The Politics of Pluralism: A Comparative Study of Lebanon and Ghana*. New York: Elsevier, 1975.

Spagnolo, John. *France and Ottoman Lebanon, 1861–1914*. London: Ithaca Press, 1977.

Suleiman, Michael. *Political Parties in Lebanon*. Ithaca: Cornell University Press, 1967.

———. "The Lebanese Communist Party." *Middle Eastern Studies* 3 (1967): 134–159.

———. "The Role of Political Parties in a Confessional Democracy: The Lebanese Case." *Western Political Quarterly* 20 (1967): 682–693.

Zamir, Meir. *The Formation of Modern Lebanon*. London: Croom Helm, 1985.

Zuwiyya, Jalal. *The Parliamentary Election of Lebanon, 1968*. Leiden: Brill, 1972.

The Lebanese Civil War, 1975–1990

Abdel Samad, Nadim. "La crise au Liban." *La Nouvelle Revue Internationale* 9 (1975): 114–125.

Abraham, Antoine. *Lebanon: A State of Siege (1975–1984)*. NewYork: Institute of Technology, Anthroscience Press, 1984.

AbuKhalil, As'ad. "Druze, Sunni and Shi'ite Political Leadership in Present-day Lebanon." *Arab Studies Quarterly* 7 (1985): 28–58.

———. "The Study of Political Parties in the Arab World: The Case of Lebanon." *Journal of Asian and African Affairs* 5 (1993).

———. "Lebanon and the New World Order." In Phyllis Bennis and Michel Moushabeck, eds. *The New World Order*. New York: Olive Branch, 1993.

———. "The Longevity of the Lebanese Civil War." In Karl Magyar and Constantine Danopoulos, eds. *Modern Prolonged Conflicts: Wars of the First Kind*. Maxwell Air Force Base: Air University Press, 1994.

———. "Arab Intervention in the Lebanese Civil War: Lebanese Perceptions and Realities." *The Beirut Review* 1 (1991).

———. "Ideology and Practice of Hizb-ul-Lah: The Islamization of Leninist Organizational Principles." *Middle Eastern Studies* 27 (July 1991).

———. Syria and the Shi'ites: Al-Asad's Policy in Lebanon." *Third World Quarterly* 12 (1990).

———. "The Presidential Crisis in Lebanon." *The World and I* (December 1988).

Accaoui, Selim. *Comprendre le Liban*. Paris: Savelli, 1976.

Ackermann, Fridolin. "Beirut: Life among the Ruins." *Swiss Review of World Affairs* 31 (1981): 8–12.

Adam, Heribert. "The Politics of Violence in Lebanon." *Middle East Focus* (Canada) 7 (1985).

Adams, William C. "The Beirut Hostages: ABC and CBS Seize an Opportunity." *Public Opinion* 8 (1985): 45–48.

Ahmad, Naveed. "The Lebanese Crisis." *Pakistan Horizon,* No. 1 (1976): 31–46.

Ajami, Fouad "The Shadows of Hell." *Foreign Policy* 48 (1982): 94–110.

———. "Lebanon and Its Inheritors." *Foreign Affairs,* 63 (1985): 778–799.

———. *The Vanished Imam*. Ithaca: Cornell University Press, 1986.

Alanov, V. "Origins of Lebanon's Tragedy." *International Affairs* 8 (1979): 38–45.

Alpher, Joseph. *Israel's Lebanon Policy: Where To?* Memorandum 12. Tel Aviv: Tel Aviv University's Jafee Center for Strategic Studies, 1984.

Aly, Hamdi, and Nabil Abdun-Nur. "An Appraisal of the Six-Year Plan of Lebanon." *The Middle East Journal* 29 (1975): 151–164.

Arbid, Marie Thérèse. *Ma guerre: pourquoi faire?* Beirut: Dar An-Nahar, 1980.

Aruri, Naseer. "The United States Intervention in Lebanon." *Arab Studies Quarterly* 7 (1985): 59–77.

Association France-Nouveau Liban. *Liban nouveau, uni, libre, souverain*. Lyon: Editions du Pylone, 1978.

Aucagne, J. "La crise libanaise et les prises de position religieuses." *Travaux et Jours,* Nos. 56–57 (1975): 69–73.

Aulas, M. "The Socio-Ideological Development of the Maronite Community: The Phalanges and the Lebanese Forces." *Arab Studies Quarterly* 7 (1985): 1–27.

Azar, Antoine. *Le Liban face à demain*. Beirut: Librairie Orientale, 1978.

Azar, Edward. *Lessons for Lebanon*. College Park: University of Maryland's Center for International Development and Conflict Management, 1984.

———. *United States Arab Cooperation*. College Park: University of Maryland's Center for International Development and Conflict Management, 1985.

———, ed. *The Emergence of a New Lebanon?* New York: Praeger, 1984.

Baaklini, Abdo. *Civilian Control of the Military in Lebanon: A Legislative Perspective*. Occasional Papers. Albany: State University of New York Graduate School of Public Affairs, 1977.

Bailey, John, et al. *About the Cause: Sketches of Lebanon's History*. Beirut: The Lebanese Resistance, 1982.

Bakst, Jerome. *Casualties in Lebanon: Origins of the Propaganda's Numbers Game*. Research Report. New York: 1982.

Balasone, G. "Le falange libanais." *Annali Ca' Foscari,* No. 3 (1975): 31–36.

Balta, Paul. "L'Algérie et la tragédie libanaise." *Revue Française d'Etudes Politiques Méditerranéennes,* Nos. 20–21 (1976): 28–33.

Al-Banna, Sami. "The Defense of Beirut." *Arab Studies Quarterly* 5 (1983): 105–115.

Barakat, Halim: *Lebanon in Strife*. Austin: University of Texas Press, 1977.

Bar-Zohar, Michael, and Eitan Hober. *The Quest for the Red Prince*. New York: William Morrow, 1983.

Bauberot, J. *Palestine et Liban: Promises et mensonges de l'occident*. Paris: Editions l'Harmatan, 1977.

Baudis, Mominique. *La passion des chrétiens du Liban*. Paris: Editions Franco-Empire, 1979.

Bawly, Dan, and Eliahu Salpeter. *Fire in Beirut: Israel's War in Lebanon with the PLO*. New York: Stein and Day, 1984.

Belmont, J. "Le drame du Liban." *Le Monde Moderne,* No. 11 (1975–76): 112–123.

Benassar. *Anatomie d'une guerre et d'une occupation*. Paris: Galilee, 1978.

Beydoun, Ahmed. *Identité confessionelle et temps social chez les historiens libanais contemporains*. Beirut: Lebanese University, 1984.

Boerma, Maureen. "The United Nations Interim Force in Lebanon." *Millennium* 8 (1979): 51–63.

Booth, Marilyn. "Seeds of Conflict Within Lebanon." *Harvard Political Review* 5 (1977): 11–14.

Born, Nicholas. *Die Falschung*. Hamburg: Rowohlt, 1979.

Bourgi, Albert, and Pierre Weiss. *Les Complots Libanais*. Paris: Berger-Lerrault, 1978.

Bowder, Geoffrey. "Lebanon in Turmoil." *The World Today,* No. 11 (1978): 426–434.

Bullock, John. *Death of a Country*. London: Weidenfeld and Nicolson, 1977.

———. "Civil War in Lebanon." In *Royal United Services Institution and Brassey's Defense Yearbook* (1976–77). London: Brassey's.

Burrel, M. "Lebanon: The Collapse of a State: Regional Dimension of the Struggle." *Conflict Studies,* No. 74 (1976): 19–30.

Cadir, Nada. "La guerre du Liban: dans la gouffre du confessionnalisme." *Khamsin,* No. 3 (1976): 101–123.

Caplan, Neil, and Jon Black. "Israel and Lebanon: Origins of a Relationship." *Jerusalem Quarterly,* No. 27 (1983): 48–58.

Carrol, W., and Samih Farsoun, "The Civil War in Lebanon: Sect and Class." *Monthly Review,* No. 28 (1976): 12–37.

———. "Die Libanesische Krise." *Dritte Welt Magazin,* Nos. 8–10 (1976): 11–17.

Centre Libanais D'Information *La guerre libano-palestinienne ou comment une poignée des jeunes firent échec aux jeux des nations*. N.p., 1978.

Chakhtoura, Marie. *La guerre des graffiti: Liban 1975–1978*. Beirut: Dār An-Nahār, 1978.

Chamie, Joseph. "The Lebanese Civil War: An Investigation into the Causes." *World Affairs,* No. 3 (1976–77): 171–178.

Chamussy, Rene. *Chronique d'une guerre*. Paris: Desclée, 1978.

Cobban, Helena. "Lebanon's Chinese Puzzle." *Foreign Policy,* No. 53 (1983–1984): 34–48.

———. *The Shia Community and the Future of Lebanon*. Washington, D.C.: American Institute for Islamic Affairs, 1985.

——— "Thinking about Lebanon." *American-Arab Affairs,* (1985): 59–71.

Cohen, A. "Roots of the Lebanese Crisis." *New Outlook,* No. 4 (1976): 21–29.

Colie, Stuart E. "A Perspective on the Shiites and the Lebanese Tragedy." *Middle East Review* 9 (1976): 16–23.

Collings, Deirdre, ed. *Peace for Lebanon?* Boulder, CO: Reinner, 1994.

Cooper, Mary H. "American Involvement in Lebanon." *Washington Congressional Quarterly* 1 (1984): 171–188.

Corm, George. *Géopolitique du conflit libanais*. Paris: la Découverte, 1986.

Costello, Mary. "Divided Lebanon." *Editorial Research Report* 1 (1980).

Creed, John. *United States Interests in Lebanon*. Washington, D.C.: Library of Congress, Congressional Research Service, 1985.

———. *Lebanon: Developments between February 1984 and July 1985*. Washington, D.C.: Library of Congress, Congressional Research Service, 1985.

Davidson, Larry. "Lebanon and the Jewish Conscience." *Journal of Palestine Studies* 12 (1983): 54–60.

Dawisha, Adeed."Syria's Intervention in Lebanon, 1975–76." *The Jerusalem Journal of International Relations,* Nos. 2–3 (1978): 245–263.

———. *Syria and the Lebanese Crisis*. New York: St. Martin's, 1980.

———. "Syria in Lebanon: Asad's Vietnam." *Foreign Policy,* No. 33 (1978–79): 135–150.

Deeb, Marius. *The Lebanese Civil War*. New York: Praeger, 1980.

Dekmejian, Richard Hrair. "Consociational Democracy in Crisis: The Case of Lebanon." *Comparative Politics,* No. 2 (1978): 251–265.

Dhibyān, Sāmī. *Al-Ḥarkah Al-Waṭaniyyah Al-Lubnāniyyah* (The Lebanese National Movement). Beirut: Dār Al-Masīrah, 1977.

Entelis, John. "Ethnic Conflict and the Reemergence of Radical Christian Nationalism in Lebanon." *Journal of South Asian and Middle Eastern Studies,* No. 3 (1979): 6–25.

———. "The Politics of Partition: Christian Perspectives on Lebanon's Nationalist Identity." *International Insight* 1 (1981): 11–15.

———. "Ethnic and Religious Diversity in Lebanon." *Society* 22 (1985): 48–51.

Eshel, David. *The Lebanon War: 1982*. Hod Hasharon, Israel: Eshel-Dramit, 1983.

Evron, Yair. *War and Intervention in Lebanon: The Israeli-Syrian Deterrence Dialogue*. London: Croom Helm, 1987.

Faksh, Mahmud. "Lebanon: the Road of Disintegration." *American-Arab Affairs,* No. 8 (1984): 20–30.

Faour, A. "Population Movements and Prospects for Development in South Lebanon." *Population Bulletin,* No. 25, UN Commission for Western Asia (1984): 49–88.

Farsoun, Samih. "Toward a Maronite Zion." *MERIP Reports* 44 (1976): 15–18.

Feldman, Shai, and Heda Rechnitz-Kijner. *Deception, Consensus and War: Israel in Lebanon.* Paper No. 27. Tel Aviv: Tel Aviv University's Jaffee Center for Strategic Studies, 1984.

Fisk, Robert. *Pity the Nation: The Abduction of Lebanon.* New York: Atheneum, 1990.

Franjie, Samir. "Liban: la rupture du Pacte National." *Le Monde Diplomatique* (July 1975).

Frankel, Ephraim. "The Maronite Patriarch: an Historical View of a Religious Za'im in the 1958 Crisis." *The Muslim World* 66 (1976).

Freedman, Robert O. "The Soviet Union and the Civil War in Lebanon." *The Jerusalem Journal of International Relations,* No. 4 (1978): 60–93.

———. "Moscow, Damascus, and the Lebanese Crisis of 1982–84." *Middle East Review* 17 (1984): 22–39.

Freiha, Adel. *L'Armée et l'état au Liban (1945–1980)*. Paris: Librairie Générale de Droit et de Jurisprudence, 1980.
Furlonge, Geoffrey. "The Tragedy of Lebanon." *Asian Affairs,* No. 2 (1978): 127–134.
Gabriel, Philip Louis. *In the Ashes: A Story of Lebanon*. Ardmore, PA: Whitmore, 1978.
Gabriel, Richard A. *Operation Peace for Galilee: The Israeli-PLO War in Lebanon*. New York: Hill and Wang, 1984.
Gale, Jack. *Zeitbombe Libanon*. Essen: Bund Sozialistischer Arbeiter, 1978.
Gates, C. L. "The Lebanese Lobby in the U.S." *MERIP Reports* 8 (1978): 17–19.
George, Lucien. "Liban: une nation éclatée." *Universalia* (1976): 307–313.
Gervasi, Frank. *The War in Lebanon: Media Coverage*. Washington, D.C.: The Center for International Security, n.d.
Ghali, Samir, and C. Hartwig. "France and the Lebanese Conflict." *Journal of South Asian and Middle Eastern Studies,* No. 1 (1979): 78–83.
Giannov, Chris. "The Battle for South Lebanon." *Journal of Palestine Studies* 11 (1982): 69–84.
Gillon, D. Z. "Arab World and South-West Asia: Lebanon's Savage War." *Annual of Power Conflict* (1976–77): 219–254.
Gilmour, David. *Lebanon: The Fractured Country*. New York: St. Martin's, 1983.
Gilsenan, Michael. "Economie, politique, et violence au Liban." *Revue Française d'Etudes Politiques Méditerranéennes,* Nos. 20–21 (1976): 78–94.
Godwin, P. "Linkage Politics and Coercive Diplomacy: A Comparative Analysis of the Two Lebanese Crises." *Air University Review,* No. 1 (1976): 80–89.
Goksel, Timur. "UNIFIL: Honour in Lebanon." *Army Quarterly and Defense Journal* 113 (1983): 391–411.
Golan, Galia. "The Soviet Union and the Israeli Action in Lebanon." *International Affairs* 59 (1982–83): 7–16.
Gordon, David. *Lebanon: The Fragmented Nation*. London: Croom Helm, 1980.
———. *The Republic of Lebanon*. Boulder, CO: Westview, 1983.
Goria, Wade. *Sovereignty and Leadership in Lebanon*. London: Ithaca Press, 1985.
Gubser, Peter. "The Politics of Economic Interest Groups in a Lebanese Town." *Middle Eastern Studies* 11 (1975): 262–283.
———. "Will Stability Return to Lebanon." *Middle East Journal,* No. 33 (1979): 365–368.

Haddad, Jean-Pierre. *Le combat du Liban, Pourqui? Pourqoui?* Meaux: H. Couchon, 1976.

Haddad, William. "Divided Lebanon." *Current History* 81 (1982): 30–35.

———. "Lebanon in Despair." *Current History* 82 (1983).

Hagopian, Elaina. "Redrawing the Map in the Middle East: Phalangist Lebanon and Zionist Israel." *Arab Studies Quarterly* 5 (1983): 321–336.

———. *Amal and the Palestinians: Understanding the Battle of the Camps*. Belmont, MA: Arab American University Graduates, 1985.

Haley, P. Edward, and Lewis Snider, eds. *Lebanon in Crisis*. Syracuse: Syracuse University Press, 1979.

Hammel, Eric. *The Root: the Marines in Beirut*. San Diego: Harcourt Brace Jovanovich, 1985.

Hanf, Theodor. *Der Libanonkrieg, von der Systemkrise einer Konkordanzdemokratie zum (Spanischen Burgerkrieg) der Araber*. Freiburg: Arnold Bergstraesser Institut, 1976.

———. *Coexistence in Wartime Lebanon*. Trans. John Richardson. London: I. B. Tauris, 1993.

Harik, Iliya. *Lebanon: Anatomy of Conflict*. Hanover, NH: American Universities Field Staff, 1981.

Haritz, Detlef. *Der Burgerkrieg im Libanon*. Offenbach: Verlag 2000, 1977.

Harris, William. "Syria in Lebanon." *MERIP Reports* 15 (July-August 1985): 9–14.

Hayani, Ibrahim. "Evaluating Syria's Objectives in its Lebanese Intervention." *International Perspectives* (May-June 1977): 39–43.

Heiberg, Marianne. "Lebanon and Premonitions of Battles to Come." *Journal of Peace Research* 20 (1983): 293–298.

———. *Observations on UN Peace Keeping in Lebanon: a Preliminary Report*. Oslo: Norwegian Institute of International Affairs, 1984.

Heller, Peter. "The Syrian Factor in the Lebanese Civil War." *Journal of South Asian and Middle Eastern Studies* 4 (1980): 56–76.

Hiro, Dilip. *Lebanon: Fire and Embers: A History of the Lebanese Civil War*. New York: St. Martin's, 1992.

Hof, Frederick. *Galilee Divided: The Israel-Lebanon Frontier 1916–1984*. Boulder, CO: Westview, 1985.

Hottinger, Arnold. "Der Burgerkrieg im Libanon: Das Ende eines Prekaren Gleichgewichts." *Europa Archiv,* No. 3 (1976): 75–84.

———. "Lebanon and Foreign Powers." *Swiss Review of World Affairs* 33 (1983): 12–13.

———. "Rebuilding Beirut." *Swiss Review of World Affairs* 32 (1983): 12–17.

Howard, Norman F. "Upheaval in Lebanon." *Current History,* No. 412 (1976).

———. "Tragedy in Lebanon." *Current History,* No. 423 (1977).

Hudson, Michael C. "The Lebanese Crisis and the Limits of Consociational Democracy." *Journal of Palestine Studies,* Nos. 3–4 (1976): 109–122.

———. *The Precarious Republic Revisited: Reflections on the Collapse of Pluralist Politics in Lebanon.* Washington, D.C.: Georgetown University's Center for Contemporary Arab Studies, 1977.

———. "The Palestinian Factor in the Lebanese Civil War." *The Middle East Journal,* No. 3 (1978): 261–278.

———. "Palestinians After Lebanon." *Current History* 84 (Jan. 1984).

———. "The Break-down of Democracy in Lebanon." *Journal of International Affairs* 38 (1985): 277–282.

Hussein, M. "Reflections on the Lebanese Impasse." *Monthly Review,* No. 6 (1976): 14–27.

Ignatius, David. "How to Rebuild Lebanon." *Foreign Affairs* 61 (1983): 57–64.

Inbar, Effraim. "Israel and Lebanon: 1975–1982. *Crossroads,* No. 10 (1983): 39–80.

Iverkovic, I. "Happenings in Lebanon." *Review of International Affairs,* No. 260 (1976): 31–34.

Jabbra, Joseph. "Sectarian Affiliation and Political Orientation of Lebanese Students." *The Muslim World* 66 (1976): 189–212.

Jansen, Michael E. *The Battle of Beirut: Why Israel Invaded Lebanon.* Boston: South End, 1983.

Johnson, Michael. *Class and Client in Beirut.* London: Ithaca, 1986.

Jullien, J. "Liban: les raisons d'une guerre civile." *Critique Socialiste,* No. 24 (1976): 75–84.

Jureidini, Paul, and R. D. McLauren. "Lebanon: A MOUT Case Study." *Military Review* 59 (1979): 2–12.

———. "Army and State in Lebanon." *Middle East Insight* 3 (1983): 28–34.

Kaisi, I. "Lebanon: Once Again, No Victor and No Vanquished." *The Middle East,* No. 26 (1976): 16–20.

Kamel, Michel. "Lebanon Explodes." *MERIP Reports,* No. 44 (1976).

Kapeliouk, Amnon. "Le rôle politique d'Israel dans la crise libanaise." *Le Monde Diplomatique* (Dec. 1977).

———. *Sabra and Shatila: Inquiry into a Massacre.* Belmont, MA: Arab American University Graduates, 1984.

Kass, Ilana. *The Lebanon Civil War 1975–1976: A Case of Crisis Mismanagement.* Jerusalem Papers. Jerusalem: Hebrew University, 1979.

———. "Moscow and the Lebanese Triangle." *Middle East Journal* 33 (1979): 164–187.

Kechichian, Joseph. "The Lebanese Army: Capabilities and Challenges in the 1980s." *Conflict Quarterly* 5 (1985): 15–39.

Kedouri, Elie. "Lebanon: The Perils of Independence." *Washington Review of Strategic and International Studies* 1 (1978): 84–89.

Kelly, John. "The CIA in the Middle East." *Counterspy* 3 (1978): 3–42.

Khalaf, Salah. *Palestinien sans patrie*. Paris: Fayolle, 1978.

Khalaf, Samir. "On the Demoralization of Public Life in Lebanon: Some Impassioned Reflections." *Studies in Comparative International Development* 17 (1982): 49–72.

———. *Lebanon's Predicament*. New York: Columbia University Press, 1987.

Khalidi, Rashid. "Problems of Foreign Intervention in Lebanon." *American-Arab Affairs,* No. 7 (1983–84): 24–30.

———. "The Palestinians in Lebanon: Social Repercussions of Israel's Invasion." *The Middle East Journal* 38 (1984): 255–266.

———. "Lebanon in the Context of Regional Politics: Palestinian and Syrian Involvement in the Lebanese Crisis." *Third World Quarterly* 7 (1985): 495–514.

———. *Under Siege: PLO Decisionmaking During the 1982 War*. New York: Columbia University Press, 1986.

Khalidi, Walid. *Conflict and Violence in Lebanon*. Cambridge: Harvard University Press, 1979.

Kimche, David. "Lebanon: The Horn of Truth." *Middle East Insight* 3 (1983): 4–7.

———. "Bloody Lebanon: Byzantine Collusion." *The New Republic* 174 (1976): 7–10.

———. "Blueprint for Conflict: Bleeding Lebanon." *The New Republic* 174 (1976): 12–15.

———. "Lebanon: the Prelude and the Postscript." *Midstream* 29 (1983): 3–6.

Kisirwani, Maroun. "Foreign Interference and Religious Animosity in Lebanon." *Journal of Contemporary History* 15 (1980): 685–700.

Koury, Enver. *The Crisis in the Lebanese System*. Washington, D.C.: American Enterprise Institute, 1976.

Laipson, Ellen, and Clyde Mark. *Conflict in Lebanon: from the Missile Crisis of April 1981 through the Israeli Invasion of August 1982*. Washington, D.C.: Library of Congress, Congressional Research Service, 1983.

Lambeth, Benjamin. *Moscow's Lessons from the 1982 Lebanon Air War*. Santa Monica, CA: Rand, 1984.

Lawson, Fred. "Syria's Intervention in the Lebanese Civil War 1976: A Domestic Conflict Explanation." *International Organization* 38 (1984): 451–480.

Lewis, Bernard. "Right and Left in Lebanon." *The New Republic* 177 (1977): 20–23.
Mahfoud, Peter. *Lebanon and the Turmoil of the Middle East*. New York: Vantage, 1980.
Mallison, Sally, and Thomas Mallison. *Armed Conflict in Lebanon, 1982: Humanitarian Law in a Real World Setting*. Washington, D.C.: American Educational Trust, 1985.
Mark, Clyde. *The Beirut Hostages: Background to the Crisis*. Washington, D.C.: Library of Congress, Congressional Research Service, 1985.
McCullin, Don. *Beirut: a City in Crisis*. Sevenoaks, Kent: New English Library, 1983.
Morgen, Geffrey A. "Lebanon: A Troubling Enigma." *Atlantic Community* 22 (1984): 77–85.
Moughrabi, Fouad, ed. *Lebanon: Crisis and Challenge in the Arab World*. Detroit, MI: Arab American University Graduates, 1977.
Muir, Jim. "Lebanon: Arena of Conflict, Crucible of Peace." *The Middle East Journal* 38 (1984): 204–219.
Muravchik, Joshua. "Misreporting Lebanon." *Policy Review,* No. 23 (1983): 11–66.
Nasr, Nafhat, and Monte Palmer. "Alienation and Political Participation in Lebanon." *International Journal of Middle East Studies* 8 (1977): 493–516.
Norton, Augustus Richard. "Israel and South Lebanon." *American-Arab Affairs,* No. 4 (Spring 1983): 23–31.
———. "Making Enemies in South Lebanon: Harakat Amal, the IDF, and South Lebanon." *Middle East Insight* 3 (1984): 13–20.
———. "Instability and Change in Lebanon." *American-Arab Affairs,* No. 10 (1984): 79–88.
———. "Occupation Risks and Planned Retirement: The Israeli Withdrawal from South Lebanon." *Middle East Insight* 4 (1985): 14–18.
———. *Amal and the Shi'a*. Austin: University of Texas Press, 1987.
O'Brien, William V. "Israel in Lebanon." *Middle East Review* 15 (1982–83): 5–14.
Odeh, B. J. *Lebanon: The Dynamics of Conflict*. London: Zed, 1984.
Owen, Roger. *Essays on the Crisis in Lebanon*. London: Ithaca, 1976.
———. "The Lebanese Crisis: Fragmentation or Reconciliation?" *Third World Quarterly* 6 (1984): 934–949.
Pelcovitz, Nathan. *Peacekeeping on Arab-Israeli Fronts: Lessons from Sinai and Lebanon*. Boulder, CO: Westview, 1984.
Perlmutter, Amos. "Lebanon: Can it Be Pieced together Again?" *Strategic Review* 11 (1983): 44–49.
Petran, Tabitha. *The Struggle over Lebanon*. NewYork: Monthly Review Press, 1987.

Philips, James A. *Standing Firm in Lebanon*. Background Paper 302. Washington, D.C.: The Heritage Foundation, 1983.

Picard, Elizabeth. *Liban: état de discorde*. Paris: Flammarion, 1988.

Quandt, William. "Reagan's Lebanon's Policy: Trial and Error." *The Middle East Journal* 38 (1984): 237–254.

Rabinovich, Itamar. *The War for Lebanon, 1970–1983*. Ithaca: Cornell University Press, 1984.

Raburn, Terry. *Under the Guns in Beirut*. Springfield, MA: Gospel, 1980.

Rasler, K. "Internationalized Civil War: A Dynamic Analysis of the Syrian Intervention in Lebanon." *Journal of Conflict Resolution* 27 (1983): 421–456.

Rees, John. "Perspective on the War in Lebanon." *Review of the News* 18 (1982).

Richards, Martin. "The Israeli-Lebanese War of 1982." *Army Quarterly and Defense Journal* 113 (1983): 9–19.

Rubin, Robin. "US Lebanese Right." *Counterspy* 3 (1979): 37–44.

Rubinstein, C. L. "The Lebanon War: Objectives and Outcomes." *Australian Outlook* 37 (1983): 10–17.

Ryan, Sheila. "Israel's Invasion of Lebanon: Background to the Crisis." *Journal of Palestine Studies* 11 (1982): 23–37.

Sahliyeh, Emile. *The PLO after the Lebanon War*. Boulder, CO: Westview, 1985.

Salem, Elie Adib. "Lebanon's Political Maze: The Search for Peace in a Turbulent Land." *Middle East Journal* 33 (1979): 444–463.

———. *Prospects for a New Lebanon*. Special Analyses 81–84. Washington, D.C.: American Enterprise Institute, 1982.

Salibi, Kamal S. "The Christians of Lebanon: the Lebanese Identity." *Middle East Review* 9 (1976): 7–13.

———. *Crossroads to Civil War: Lebanon 1958–1976*. Delmar, NY: Caravan, 1976.

Salman, Magida. "The Lebanese Community and their Little Wars." *Khamsin*, No. 10 (1983): 13–20.

Schahgaldian, Nikola B. "Prospects for a Unified Lebanon." *Current History* 83 (1984).

Schenker, Hillel, ed. *After Lebanon: the Israeli-Palestinian Connection*. New York: Pilgrim, 1983.

Schiff, Zeev, and Ehud Ya'ari. *Israel's Lebanon War*. NewYork: Simon and Schuster, 1984.

Shaker, Fouad E. *Fire over Lebanon: Country in Crisis*. Hicksville, NY: Exposition, 1976.

Shapiro, William. *Lebanon*. New York: Watts, 1984.

Sharārah, Waḍḍāḥ. *Ḥurūb Al-Istitbā‘* (Wars of Followership). Beirut: Dār Aṭ-Ṭalī‘ah, 1979.

———. *As-Silm Al-Ahlī Al-Bārid* (Civil Cold War). Beirut: Ma'had Al-Inmā' Al-'Arabī, 1980.

Shemesh, Moshe. "The Lebanon's Crisis, 1975–1985: A Reassessment." *The Jerusalem Quarterly,* No. 37 (1986): 77–94.

Sloan, Thomas. "Dyadic Linkage Politics in Lebanon." *Journal of Peace Science* 3 (1978): 147–158.

Snider, Lewis. "Lebanon: Enduring Myths and Changing Realities." *Middle East Insight* 3 (1984): 34–45.

———. "The Lebanese Forces: Their Origins and Role in Lebanon's Politics." *The Middle East Journal* 38 (1984): 1–33.

Starr, Joyce. *Does the United States Have a Long Term Policy on Lebanon?* Washington, D.C.: Center for Strategic and International Studies, n.d.

———. "Lebanese Reconstruction: American Interests and Prospects." *Middle East Insight* 2 (1983).

Starr, Paul. "Ethnic Categories and Identification in Lebanon." *Urban Life* 7 (1978): 111–142.

Stiefbold, Annette E. "Lebanon, Syria, and the Crisis of Soviet Policy in the Middle East." *Air University Review* 28 (1977): 62–70.

Stoakes, Frank. "The Supervigilantes: The Lebanese Kataeb Party as Builder, Surrogate, and Defender of the State," *Middle Eastern Studies* 11 (1975): 215–236.

———. "The Civil War in Lebanon." *World Today* 32 (1976): 8–17.

Stork, Joe. "Report from Lebanon." *MERIP Reports* 13 (1983).

Sullivan, William. "What the Shias Want." *Anti-Defamation League Bulletin* 40 (1984).

Timerman, Jacob. *The Longest War: Israel in Lebanon.* New York: Knopf, 1982.

Tucker, Robert W. "Lebanon: the Case for the War." *Commentary* 74 (1982): 30.

Vatikiotis, P. J. "The Crisis in Lebanon: a Local Historical Perspective." *World Today* 40 (1984): 85–92.

Verrier, June. *Israel's Lebanon War and Its Aftermath.* Basic Paper 11. Canberra: Department of Parliamentary Library, 1982.

Vocke, Harald. *The Lebanese War: Its Origins and Political Dimensions.* London: Hurst, 1978.

Wagner, Donald. "Lebanon: An American's View." *Race & Class* 24 (1983): 401–410.

Waines, David. "Civil War in Lebanon: the Anatomy of a Crisis." *International Perspectives* (Jan.-Feb. 1976): 14–20.

Weinberger, Naomi. "Peacekeeping Options in Lebanon." *The Middle East Journal* 37 (1983): 341–369.

Wiseman, Henry. "Lebanon: the Latest Example of UN Peacekeeping Action." *International Perspectives* (Jan.-Feb.1979): 3–7.

Witty, Cathie. *Mediation and Society: Conflict Management in Lebanon.* New York: Academic, 1980.
Yaniv, Avner. *Dilemmas of Security: Politics, Strategy, and the Israeli Experience in Lebanon.* New York: Oxford University Press, 1987.
Zamir, Meir. "The Lebanese Presidential Election of 1970 and their Impact on the Civil War of 1975–76." *Middle Eastern Studies* 16 (1980): 49–70.
———. "Smaller and Greater Lebanon: The Squaring of a Circle?" *Jerusalem Quarterly,* No. 23 (1982): 34–53.
———. "Politics and Violence in Lebanon." *Jerusalem Quarterly,* No. 25 (1982): 3–26.

Personal Accounts, Memoirs, and Biographical Dictionaries

'Allām, 'Alī. *Dalīl An-Nā'ib Al-Lubnānī* (Guide to the Lebanese Deputy). Beirut: 3A, 1993.
Ball, George. *Error and Betrayal in Lebanon: An Analysis of Israel's Invasion of Lebanon and Its Implications for US-Israeli Relations.* Washington, D.C.: Foundation for Middle East Peace, 1984.
Bickers, William. *Harem Surgeon.* Richmond, VA: Whittet and Shepperson, 1976.
Brown, Dean. *Lebanon: A Mission of Conciliation.* Washington, DC: The Middle East Institute, 1976.
Catroux, (General) Georges. *Dans la Bataille de la Méditerranée.* Paris: Julliard, 1949.
———. *Deux missions en Moyen-Orient.* Paris: Plon, 1958.
Chamoun, Camille. *Crise au Moyen-Orient.* Paris: Gallimard, 1963.
———. *Crise au Liban.* Beirut: 1977.
———. *Mémoires et souvenirs.* Beirut: Catholic Press, 1979.
Dayrī, Ilyās. *Man Yaṣna' Ar-Ra'īs* (Who Makes the President). Beirut: Al-Mu'assasah Al-Jāmi'iyyah, 1982.
De Gaulle, Charles. *Mémoire de Guerre.* Paris: Plon, 1956.
Editions PUBLITEC, ed. *Who's Who in Lebanon.* Beirut: Editions PUBLITEC, 1964–.
Etinoff, Nedko. *Thirty Years in Lebanon and the Middle East.* Beirut: privately published, 1968.
Gemayel, Amine. *Peace and Unity.* Gerrards Cross, Buckinghamshire: C. Smythe, 1984.
———. *L'Offense et Le Pardon.* Paris: Gallimard, 1988.
Gemayel, Maurice. *Pensée, Action et Realisation de Maurice Gemayel: Le Pari Libanais.* Beirut: Dār An-Nahār, 1970.
Guys, Henri. *Beyrout et le Liban: relation d'un séjour de plusieurs années dans ce pays.* Paris, 1850.
Helou, Charles. *Mémoires, 1964–1965.* Araya: Catholic Press, 1984.

———. *Liban: remords du monde*. Paris: Cariscript, 1987.
Hogg, James. *News from Lebanon: Lady Hester Stanhope's Autograph Letter to Michael Bruce*. Salzburg: Universität Salzburg Institut für Anglistik und Amerikanistik, 1988.
Al-Khūrī, Bishārah. *Haqā'iq Lubnāniyyah* (Lebanese Truths). Beirut: Awrāq Lubnāniyyah, 1961.
Leary, Lewis Gaston. *Syria, the Land of Lebanon*. New York: MacBride, 1913.
McGilvary, Margaret. *The Dawn of a New Era in Syria*. New York: Fleming H. Revell, 1920.
Murphy, Robert. *Diplomat Among Warriors*. Garden City, NY: Doubleday, 1964.
Napier, Charles. *The War in Syria*. 2 vols. London, 1842.
d'Orleans, Louis Philippe Albert. *Damas et le Liban: extraits du journal d'un voyage en Syrie au printemps de 1860*. London, 1861.
Pearse, Richard. *Three Years in the Levant*. New York: Macmillan, 1949.
Pharaon, Henri. *Au Service du Liban et son Unité*. Beirut: Le Jour, 1959.
Puaux, Gabriel. *Deux Années au Levant*. Paris: Hachette, 1952.
Rabin, Yitzhak. *The Rabin Memoirs*. Boston: Little, Brown, 1979.
Rizq, Rizq. *Rashīd Karāmī*. Beirut: Mukhtārāt, 1987?.
Ṣāghiyyah, Ḥāzim. *Mawārinah Min Lubnān* (Maronites from Lebanon). Beirut: Al-Markaz Al-'Arabī Li Al-Ma'lūmāt, 1988.
Salem, Elie. *Violence and Diplomacy in Lebanon: The Troubled Years, 1982–1988*. London: I. B. Tauris, 1995.
Spears, Sir Edward. *Fulfilment of a Mission: Syria and Lebanon, 1941–1944*. London: Leo Cooper, 1977.
Stewart, Desmond. *Turmoil in Beirut: A Personal Account*. London: Wingate, 1958.
Ṣulḥ, Sāmī. *Mudhakkirāt* (Memoirs). Beirut: Maktabat Al-Fikr Al-'Arabī, 1960.
Thayer, Charles. *Diplomat*. New York: Harper, 1959.
Tueni, Ghassan. *Une Guerre pour les autres*. Paris: Editions Lettes, 1985.
Yermiya, Dov. *My War Diary: Lebanon, June 5-July 1 1982*. Boston: South End, 1983.

Culture and Literature

Abdel-Nour, Jabbour. *Étude sur la poésie dialectale au Liban*. Beirut: Lebanese University, 1966.
Abou, Selim. *Le Bilinguisme Arabe-Français au Liban*. Paris: Presses Universitaires, 1962.
Adnan, Etel. *Sitt Marie Rose*. Paris: Edition des femmes, 1978.

Ammoun, Charles Daoud. *Cèdre mon héritage*. Beirut: Imprimerie Le Réveil, 1968.

Awwad, T. Y., *Death in Beirut*. London: Heinemann, 1976.

Benoit, Pierre. *La chatelaine du Liban*. Paris: Albin Michel, 1924.

Buheiry, Marwan, ed. *The Splender of Lebanon: Eighteenth- and Nineteenth-century Artists and Travellers*. Delmar, NY: Caravan, 1978.

Chami, Gladys. *Devinettes libanaises*. Beirut: privately published, 1972.

Chamoun, Mounir. "Problèmes de la famille au Liban." *Travaux et Jours,* no. 25 (1967): 13–40.

———. *Les superstitions au Liban: aspects psycho-sociologiques*. Beirut: Dar el-Mashreq, 1973.

Chehab, Maurice. "Le coustume au Liban." *Bulletin du Musée de Beyrouth* 6 (1946): 47–79.

Cooke, Miriam. *War's Other Voices: Women Writers on the Lebanese Civil War*. New York: Cambridge University Press, 1987.

Durtal, Jean. *Said Akl: un grand poète libanais*. Paris: Nouvelles Editions Latines, 1970.

Evans, Louella. *Lebanon: Portrait of a People*. Beirut: Dar el-Mashreq, 1967.

Fāḍil, Jihād. *Al-Adab Al-Ḥadīth fī Lubnān: Naḍhrah Mughāyirah* (Modern Literature in Lebanon: An Alternative View). London: Riad El-Rayyes, 1996.

Farrūkh, 'Umar. *Difā'an 'An Al-'Ilm, Difā'an 'An Al-Waṭan* (In Defense of Education, In Defense of the Nation). Beirut: Beirut Arab University, 1977.

Feghali, Michel. *Textes libanais: contes, légendes, coustumes populaires du Liban et de Syrie*. Paris: Maisonneuve, 1935.

———. *Proverbes et dictons syro-libanais*. Paris: Institut d'Ethnologie, 1938.

Frayha, Anis. *Modern Lebanese Proverbs Collected at Ras el-Matn*. 2 vols. Oriental Series nos. 25–26. Beirut: American University of Beirut, Faculty of Arts and Sciences, 1953.

Gibran, Khalil. *The Prophet*. New York: Knopf, 1923.

Hawi, Khalil. *Khalil Gibran: His Background, Character, and Works*. Oriental Series 41. Beirut: American University of Beirut, Faculty of Arts and Sciences, 1963.

Hilu, Virginia. *Beloved Prophet: The Love Letters of Gibran and Mary Haskell and Her Private Journal*. New York: Knopf, 1972.

Huxley, Aldous. *Adonis and the Alphabet, and Other Essays*. London: Chatto and Windus, 1975.

Ibrāhīm, Emily Fāris. *Adibāt Lubnāniyyāt* (Lebanese Women Writers). Beirut: Dār Al-Rīḥānī, 1964.

Izzard, Ralph, and Molly Izzard. *A Walk in the Mountains*. New York: MacKay, 1959.

Jabr, Jamīl. *Lubnān Fī Rawā'i' Aqlāmihi* (Lebanon through the Magnificence of Its Pens). Beirut: Al-Maṭba'ah Al-Kāthūlīkiyyah, 1964.

Kerner, Susanne, ed. *Oxarchaeology of Jordan, Palestine, Syria, Lebanon, and Egypt*. Amman: Al-Kutba, 1990–1994.

Khalaf, Saher. *Littérature libanaise de langue française*. Ottawa: Editions Naaman, 1974.

Khāṭir, Laḥd. *Al-'Ādāt wa-t-Taqālīd Al-Lubnāniyyah* (Lebanese Customs and Traditions). Beirut: Maktab Ad-Dirasāt Al-'Ilmiyyah, 1977.

Khawam, Rene S. *Contes et légendes du Liban*. Paris: F. Nathan, 1952.

Khayat, M. K., and M. C. Keatinge. *Lebanon: Land of the Cedars*. Beirut: Khayats, 1960.

Khāzin, William al-, and Nabīh Ilyān. *Kutub Wa Udabā'* (Books and Writers). Beirut: Al-Maktabah Al-'Aṣriyyah, 1970.

Lahoud, Rachid. *La Littérature libanaise de langue française*. Beirut: Imprimerie Catholique, 1945.

Matthews, R. D., and Matta Akrawi. *Education in Arab Countries of the Near East*. Washington, D.C.: American Council on Education, 1949.

Najm, Muhammad Yusuf. *Fiction in Modern Arabic Literature, In Lebanon Down to the First World War*. Cairo: 1952.

Ristelhueber, Rene. *Les Traditions Françaises au Liban*. Paris: Alcan, 1925.

Shihadeh, Emile S. *Culture and Administrative Behavior in Lebanon*. Beirut: Khayats, 1963.

Ward, P. *Touring Lebanon*. London: Faber and Faber, 1971.

Economy

Armstrong, Lincoln. "A Socio-Economic Poll in Beirut, Lebanon." *Public Opinion Quarterly* 23 (1959): 18–27.

Asseily, Antoine Edouard. *Central Banking in Lebanon*. Beirut: Khayats, 1967.

Azhari, Naaman. *L'évolution du système économique libanais, ou la fin du laisser-faire*. Paris: Librairie Générale de Droit et de Jurisprudence, 1970.

Barkai, Haim. "Reflections on the Economic Cost of the Lebanon War." *The Jerusalem Quarterly*, No. 37 (1986): 95–106.

Buheiry, Marwan. *Beirut's Role in the Political Economy of the French Mandate*. Oxford: Centre for Lebanese Studies, 1986.

Churchill, Charles W. *The City of Beirut: A Socio-Economic Survey*. Beirut: Dār Al-Kitāb, 1954.

Corm, George. *Politique économique et planification au Liban 1953–1963*. Beirut: Imprimerie Universelle, 1964.

Couland, Jacques. *Le Mouvement syndical au Liban (1919–1946): son évolution pendant le mandat français de l'occupation à l'evacuation et au code du travail*. Paris: Editions Sociales, 1970.

European Economic Community. *Cooperation between the European Community and the Lebanese Republic: Collected Acts*. Brussels: Secretariat of the Council of the European Communities, 1980–.

Fuleihan, Joseph. *Economic Analysis of the Production of Oranges and Bananas in Damour and South Lebanon*. Beirut: American University of Beirut's Faculty of Agricultural Sciences, American University of Beirut, 1965.

Gates, Carolyn. *The Historical Role of Political Economy in the Development of Modern Lebanon*. Oxford: Centre for Lebanese Studies, 1989.

Gibb, Sir Alexander. *The Economic Development of Lebanon*. London: 1948.

Greene, Brook, and Hafiz Farhat. *The Feed-livestock of Lebanon with Projection to 1976*. Beirut: American University of Beirut's Faculty of Agricultural Sciences, American University of Beirut, 1973.

Hajjar, Sami, ed. *The Middle East: From Transition to Development*. Leiden: Brill, 1985.

Himadeh, Said. *The Fiscal System of Lebanon*. Beirut: Khayat, 1961.

———, ed. *The Economic Organization of Syria*. Beirut: American University of Beirut, 1936.

Iskandar, Marwan, and Elias Baroudi. *Social Security for Lebanon: An Economic Study*. Beirut: Dār Aṭ-Ṭalī'ah, 1962.

———. *The Lebanese Economy in 1981–1982*. Beirut: Middle East Economic Consultants, 1983.

Kampe, Ronald. *The Agricultural Economy of Lebanon*. Washington, D.C.: Department of Agriculture, 1965.

Kanovsky, Eliyahu. "The Economy of Lebanon: Post-war Prospects." *Middle East Review* 16 (1983–84): 28–37.

Kfoury, Philippe Daher. *The Future of Our Country: Reflections Addressed to the Lebanese People*. Beirut: St. Paul's, 1954.

Khalaf, Nadim. *Economic Implications of the Size of Nations; With Special Reference to Lebanon*. Leiden: Brill, 1971.

———. "The Response of the Lebanese Labour Force to Economic Dislocation." *Middle Eastern Studies* 18 (1982): 300–310.

el-Khazen, Farid. "The Lebanese Economy after a Decade of Turmoil 1975–1985." *American-Arab Affairs* 12 (1985): 72–84.

———. "Can Lebanon's Economy Recover?" *Middle East Executive Reports* 9 (1986).

Makdisi, Samir. "An Appraisal of Lebanon's Postwar Economic Development and a Look to the Future." *The Middle East Journal* 31 (1977): 267–280.

———. "Flexible Exchange Rate Policy in an Open Developing Economy: the Lebanese Experience, 1950–74." *World Development* 6 (1978): 991–1003.

Mallat, Raymond. *The Economic Challenge: A Master Plan*. Prepared for and in collaboration with Camille Chamoun. Louaize, Lebanon: Notre Dame University, 1988.

———. *Economic Dislocation and Recovery in Lebanon*. Washington, D.C.: International Monetary Fund, 1995.

Mills, Arthur E. *Private Enterprise in Lebanon*. Beirut: American University of Beirut, 1959.

Murray, George. *Lebanon: The New Future; an Economic and Social Survey*. Beirut: Thomson-Rizk, 1974.

Roberts, John. "Lebanon—Pinning Its Hopes of Revival on Entrepreneurs." *Middle East Economic Digest* 26 (1982).

Saidi, Nasser. *Economic Consequences of the War in Lebanon*. Oxford: Centre for Lebanese Studies, 1986.

Sayigh, Yusuf. *Entrepreneurs of Lebanon*. Cambridge: Harvard University Press, 1962.

Shehadi, Nadim, and Bridget Harney, eds. *Politics and the Economy in Lebanon*. Oxford: Centre for Lebanese Studies, 1989.

Toksoz, Mina. *The Lebanon Conflict: Political Shifts, Regional Impact, and Economic Outlook*. London: Economist, 1986.

Ward, Gordon Hugh. *Economic Analysis of Poultry Production in Lebanon*. Beirut: American University of Beirut's Faculty of Agricultural Sciences, 1962.

Yabrūdī, 'Abduh. *Wāqi' Al-Iqtiṣād fī Lubnān* (The Reality of the Economy in Lebanon). Beirut: Bayt Al-Mustaqbal, 1986.

Zeinaty, Afif. "Le syndicalisme libanais est-il en crise?" *Travaux et Jours* (Lebanon), No. 24 (1967): 41–53.

Society and Sects

Abu-Izzeddin, Halim Said, ed. *Lebanon and Its Provinces: A Study by the Governors of the Five Provinces*. Beirut: Khayats, 1963.

Accad, F. E. "Le Protestantisme contemporain au Liban." *Travaux et Jours* (Lebanon), No. 22 (1967): 17–26.

Alamuddin, Nura, and Paul Starr. *Crucial Bonds: Marriage among the Druze*. Delmar, NY: Caravan, 1980.

Aouad, Ibrahim. "Des biens wakfs au Liban." In *Mélanges à la mémoire de Paul Huvelin*. Paris: Sirey, 1938.

Al-A'war, Sajī'. *Al-Aḥwāl Ash-Shakṣiyyah Ad-Durziyyah* (Druze Personal Status Laws). Beirut, 1983.

Barakat, Halim. "Social and Political Integration in Lebanon: A Case of Social Mosaic." *Middle East Journal* (Summer 1973).

Bashir, Iskandar. *Civil Service Reforms in Lebanon*. Beirut: American University of Beirut, 1977.

Beirut College for Women, ed. *Cultural Resources in Lebanon*. Beirut: Libraire du Liban, 1969.

———. *Beirut: Crossroads of Cultures*. Beirut: Librairie du Liban, 1970.

———. *Social and Moral Issues of Children and Youth in Lebanon*. Beirut: Beirut University College's Institute for Women's Studies in the Arab World, 1981.

Betts, Robert Brenton. *Christians in the Arab East: A Political Study*. Athens: Lycabettus, 1975.

Blakemore, William. "The Religious Realities of the Lebanese War." *Christian Century* 93 (1976): 832–837.

Bushakra, Mary Winifred. *I Married an Arab*. New York: Day, 1951.

Campbell, Robert. "The Friday Holiday Question in Lebanon." CENAM Report. In *Tension in Middle Eastern Society*. Vol. 1. Beirut: Dar el-Mashreq, 1973.

Chamie, Joseph. "Religious Groups in Lebanon: A Descriptive Investigation." *International Journal of Middle East Studies*. No. 2 (1980).

———. *Religion and Fertility*. New York: Cambridge University Press, 1981.

Christopher, John. *Lebanon: Yesterday and Today*. New York: Holt, Rinehart, 1966.

Courbage, Youssef and Philippe Fargues. *La situation démographique au Liban*. Beirut: Lebanese University, 1973.

Crow, Ralph. "Religious Sectarianism in the Lebanese Political System." *Journal of Politics,* No. 24 (1963).

Damas, Andre de. *Souvenirs du Mont Liban*. 2 vols. Lyons, 1870.

Deeb, Marius. *Militant Islamic Movements in Lebanon: Origins, Social Basis, and Ideology*. Washington, D.C.: Georgetown University's Center for Contemporary Arab Studies, 1986.

Denoeux, Guilain. *Urban Unrest in the Middle East: A Comparative Study of Informal Networks in Egypt, Iran, and Lebanon*. Albany: SUNY Press, 1993.

Farsoun, Samih. "Family Structure and Society in Modern Lebanon." In *People and Cultures of the Middle East,* vol. 2, ed. Louise Sweet. New York: Natural History Press, 1970.

Fawaz, Leila, ed. *State and Society in Lebanon*. Oxford: Centre for Lebanese Studies, 1991.

Feghali, Michel. *La famille maronite au Liban*. Paris: Maisonneuve, 1936.

Fuller, Anne. *Bouarij: Portrait of a Lebanese Muslim Village*. Cambridge: Harvard University, Center for Middle East Studies, 1966.

Goudard, Joseph. *Lebanon: the Land and the Lady*. Trans. Eugene P. Burns. Beirut: Catholic Press, 1966.

Gulick, John. *Social Structure and Culture Change in a Lebanese Village*. New York: Viking, 1955.
———. *Tripoli: A Modern Arab City*. Cambridge: Harvard University Press, 1967.
Harfouche, Jamal Karam. *Social Structure of Low-Income Families in Lebanon*. Beirut: Khayats, 1965.
———. *Infant Health in Lebanon: Customs and Taboos*. Beirut: Khayat, 1965.
Harik, Judith. *The Public and Social Services of the Lebanese Militias*. Oxford: Centre for Lebanese Studies, 1994.
Ḥatab, Zuhayr. *Taṭawwur Bunā Al-Usrah Al-'Arabiyyah* (Development of the Structures of the Arab Family). Beirut: Ma'had Al-Inmā' Al-'Arabī, 1976.
Jennett, Christine, and Randal Stewart, eds. *Politics of the Future: The Role of Social Movements*. South Melbourne: Macmillan, 1989.
Joly, Gertrude. "The Woman of Lebanon." *Journal of the Royal Central Asian Society* 38 (1951): 177–184.
Joseph, Su'ad, and Barbara Pillsbury, eds. *Muslim-Christian Conflicts: Economic, Political, and Social Origins*. Boulder, CO: Westview, 1978.
Khaṭīb, Ḥanīfah al-. *Tārīkh Taṭawwur Al-Ḥarakah An-Nisā'iyyah* (History of the Evolution of the Feminist Movement). Beirut: Dār Al-Ḥadāthah, 1974.
Makarem, Sami. *The Druze Faith*. Delmar, NY: Caravan, 1974.
Mughayzil, Lur. *Al-Mar'ah Fī At-Tashrī' Al-Lubnānī* (Woman in Lebanese Laws). Beirut: Beirut University College, 1985.
Naff, Alixa. *A Social History of Zahle: The Principal Market Town in Nineteenth-century Lebanon*. 1972.
Nasr, Salim. "Conflit Libanais et resstructuration de l'espace urbain de Beyrouth." In *Politiques urbaines au Machreq et au Magreb*. Ed. J. Mettral. Lyons: Presses universitaires de Lyons, 1984.
Ostrovitz, Nina Landfield. "Who Are the Druze?" *World Affairs* 146 (1983–84): 272–276.
Prothro, Edwin Terry. *Child Rearing in the Lebanon*. Middle Eastern Monograph 8. Cambridge: Harvard University Press, 1961.
Randal, Jonathan. "The Christians of Lebanon: Lebanese Strife Sours Maronites." *Middle East Review* 9 (1976): 13–15.
Rīḥānī, Amīn. *Qalb Lubnān* (Heart of Lebanon). Beirut: Dār Al-Kitāb, 1975.
Saadah, Safiyah. *The Social Structure of Lebanon: Democracy or Servitude?* Beirut: Dar An-Nahar, 1993.
Safa, Elie. *L'Emigration libanaise*. Beirut: St. Joseph University, 1960.
Tabbara, Lina Mikdadi. *Survival in Beirut: A Diary of Civil War*. Trans. Nadia Hijab. London: Onyx, 1979.

Toubi, Jamal. "Social Dynamics in War-Torn Lebanon." *The Jerusalem Quarterly,* No. 17 (1980): 83–109.

Touma, Toufic. *Un Village de montagne au Liban.* Paris: Mouton, 1958.

Witty, Cathie. *Mediation and Society: Conflict Management in Lebanon.* New York: Academic, 1980.

Yaukey, David. *Fertility Differences in a Modernizing Country: A Survey of Lebanese Couples.* Princeton: Princeton University Press, 1961.

Zurayk, Huda, and Haroutune Armenian. *Beirut 1984: A Population and Health Profile.* Beirut: American University of Beirut, 1984.

Bibliographical Sources

American University of Beirut. *A Selected and Annotated Bibliography of Economic Literature on the Arab Countries of the Middle East.* 2 vols. Beirut: American University of Beirut, Economic Research Institute, 1954–67.

Arad, V. *The Geology of Lebanon: Bibliography, 1772–1984.* Comp. V. Arad and A. Ehrlich. Jerusalem: Ministry of Energy and Infrastructure, Geological Survey, 1985.

Avnimelech, Moshe A. *Bibliography of Levant Geology: Including Cyprus, Hatay, Israel, Jordania, Lebanon, Sinai, and Syria.* Jerusalem: Israel Program for Scientific Translations, 1965–69.

Banque de Syrie et du Liban. *Catalogue de la bibliόthèque de la Banque de Syrie et du Liban, juin 1948.* Paris: Banque de Syrie et du Liban, 1948.

Bevis, Richard W. *Bibliotheca Cisorientalia: An Annotated Checklist of Early English Travel Books on the Near and Middle East.* Boston: G. K. Hall, 1973.

Burke, Jean. *An Annotated Bibliography of Books and Periodicals in English Dealing with Human Relations in the Arab States of the Middle East, with Special Emphasis on Modern Times (1945–54).* Beirut: American University of Beirut, 1956.

Centre for the Study of the Modern Arab World. *Arab Culture and Society in Change: A Partially Annotated Bibliography of Books and Articles in English, French, German, and Italian.* Beirut: Dar el-Mashreq, 1973.

Cheikho, Louis. *Catalogue raisonné des manuscripts historiques de la Bibliothèque orientale de l'Université St. Joseph.* 6 pts. Beirut: St. Joseph University, Mélanges de la Faculté Orientale, 1913–1929.

Dagher, Joseph As'ad. *L'Orient dans la littérature française d'après guerre 1919–1933.* Beirut: Angelil, 1937.

Dār Al-Kutub Al-Miṣriyyah. *A Bibliography of Works about Lebanon.* Cairo: National Library, Reference Department, 1960.

Dodd, Stuart Carter. *A Post-War Bibliography of the Near Eastern Mandates 1919–1930: Presented in Eight Fascicules by Languages.* 8 vols. Beirut: American University of Beirut Press, 1933–36.

Ettinghausen, Richard. *A Selected and Annotated Bibliography of Books and Periodicals in Western Languages Dealing with the Near and Middle East: With Special Emphasis on Medieval and Modern Times.* Washington, D.C.: The Middle East Institute, 1954.

Field, Henry. *Near East Travel Bibliography.* Cuernavaca: 1947.

———. *Bibliography on Southwestern Asia.* 7 vols. Coral Gables: University of Miami Press, 1953–64.

———. *List of Documents Microfilmed 1941–1955.* Coconut Grove, FL: 1956.

Grimes, Annie. *An Annotated Bibliography on the Climate of Lebanon.* Washington, D.C.: 1961.

Hopwood, Derek, ed. *The Middle East and Islam: A Bibliographical Introduction.* Zug, Switzerland: Interdocumentation, 1972.

Howard, Harry. *The Middle East: A Selected Bibliography of Recent Works, 1960–1971.* Washington, D.C.: The Middle East Institute, 1972.

International Committee for Social Science Documentation. *Retrospective Bibliography of Social Science Works Published in the Middle East: U.A.R., Iraq, Jordan, Lebanon, 1945–1955.* Cairo: UNESCO, Middle East Cooperation Office, 1959.

Khairallah, Shereen. *Lebanon.* World Bibliographical Series. Oxford, UK: Clio, 1979.

Khalife, Ignace Abdo. *Catalogue raisonné des manuscrits de la Bibliothèque orientale de l'Université St. Joseph.* Beirut: Catholic Press, 1951–52.

———. *Catalogue raisonné des manuscrits de la bibliothèque de la résidence patriarcale maronite.* Beirut: Ministry of Tourism, Department of Antiquities, 1973.

Labaki, George. *The Lebanon Crisis, 1975–1985: A Bibliography.* College Park, MD: University of Maryland, Center for International Development and Conflict Management, 1986.

Lebanon, Embassy of. *Bibliography about Lebanon.* Washington, D.C.: Embassy of Lebanon, 1970.

Ljunggren, Florence, and Mohammed Hamdy. *Annotated Guide to Journals Dealing with the Middle East and North Africa.* Cairo: American University of Cairo Press, 1964.

Maouad, Ibrahim. *Bibliographie des auteurs libanais de langue française.* Beirut: UNESCO, 1948.

Masson, Paul. *Eléments d'une bibliographie française de la Syrie: géographie, ethnographie, histoire, archéologie, langues, littératures, religion.* Marseilles: Borlatier, 1919.

Moyer, Kenyon, ed. *From Iran to Morocco, from Turkey to the Sudan: A Selected and Annotated Bibliography of North Africa and the Near and Middle East.* New York: Missionary Research Library, 1957.

Patai, Raphael. *Jordan, Lebanon, and Syria: An Annotated Bibliography*. New Haven, CT: HRAF, 1957.
Philips, Jill M. *Archaeology of the Collective East: Greece, Asia Minor, Egypt, Lebanon, Mesopotamia, Syria, Palestine: An Annotated Bibliography*. New York: Gordon, 1977.
Sadaka, Linda. *The Civil War in Lebanon, 1875–1976: A Bibliographical Guide*. Beirut: American University of Beirut, 1982.
Salame, Therese. *Bibliographie des études et rapports disponibles dans l'administration libanaise*. Beirut: Ministere du Plan, 1972.
Sharabi, Hisham. *A Handbook of the Contemporary Middle East: Sectional Introductions with Annotated Bibliographies*. Washington, D.C.: Georgetown University, 1956.
Tamim, Suha. *A Bibliography of AUB Faculty Publications 1866–1966*. Beirut: American University of Beirut, 1966.
UNICEF. *Near East and North Africa: An Annotated List of Materials for Children*. New York: U.N. Committee for UNICEF, Information Center on Children's Cultures, 1970.
Universite Saint-Joseph. *Bibliographie de l'Université St. Joseph de Beyrouth: 75 ans de travaux littéraires et scientifiques*. Beirut: Bibliotheque Orientale, 1951.
University of London, School of Oriental and African Studies. *A Cumulation of a Selected and Annotated Bibliography of Economic Literature on the Arab-Speaking Countries of the Middle East 1938–1960*. Boston, MA: G. K. Hall, 1967.
U.S. Weather Bureau. *An Annotated Bibliography on Climatic Maps of Lebanon*. Washington, D.C.: Government Printing Office, 1960.
Wright, L. C. *The Middle East: An Annotated Guide to Source Material*. Chicago: American Library Association, 1966.

Encyclopedias

Bustānī, Fu'ād Afrām. *Dā'irat Al-Ma'ārif* (The Encyclopedia). 14 vols. Beirut: 1956–.
Lebanese Republic. *Dā'irat Ma'ārif Ash-Sharq* (Encyclopedia of the East). 2 vols. Dhūq Muṣbiḥ: GAMA, 1985.
Riḥānā, Sāmī. *Mawsū'at at-Turāth Al-Qarawī* (Encyclopedia of Rural Heritage). Beirut: Nobles, 1993.
Tachau, Frank, ed. *Political Parties of the Middle East and North Africa*. Westport, CT: Greenwood, 1994.

Documentary and Chronological Anthologies

Browne, Walter. *The Political History of Lebanon, 1920–1950*. Salisbury, NC: Documentary Publications, 1976.

———. *Lebanon's Struggle for Independence*. Salisbury, NC: Documentary Publications, 1980.

Dīb, Yūsuf. *Al-Yawmiyyāt Al-Lubnāniyyah* (Lebanese Diaries). Beirut: Fihrist, 1986.

IDREL, ed. *Dhākirat Lubnān* (Memory of Lebanon). Beirut: IDREL, 1993, 1994.

Ismā'īl, Munīr, and 'Ādil Ismā'īl. *Tārīkh Lubnān Al-Ḥadīth: Al-Wathā'iq Ad-Diblumāsiyyah* (The Modern History of Lebanon: Diplomatic Documents). Beirut: Dār An-Nashr Li-s-Siyāsah Wa-t-Tārīkh, 1990.

Karam, George Adib. *La Question du Liban (1918–1920): Sources Historiques*. Beirut: Editions Almanhal, 1983.

Khuwayrī, Antoine. *Ḥawādith Lubnān* (Events of Lebanon). 11 volumes. Beirut: Dār Al-Abjadiyyah, 1976–82.

Khuwayrī, Joslene, ed. *Yawmiyyāt* (Diaries). Junyah: Al-Maṭba'ah Al-Būlusiyyah, 1995, 1996.

Journals

The Beirut Review. Published since 1991 by the Beirut-based Center for Policy Studies.

Panorama de l'actualité. A quarterly (in English, French, and Arabic) on Lebanese affairs and the Middle East conflict. 1977–87.

About the Author

As'ad AbuKhalil was born in Tyre, Lebanon, in 1960. He received his bachelor's and master's degrees in political science from the American University of Beirut. He earned his Ph.D. in comparative government from Georgetown University in Washington, D.C. He has taught Middle East politics at Georgetown University, Tufts University, Randolph-Macon Woman's College, Colorado College, and George Washington University. He was a scholar-in-residence at the Middle East Institute in 1992–93.

He is currently Associate Professor of political science at California State University, Stanislaus, and research associate at the Center for Middle Eastern Studies at the University of California, Berkeley. His articles in English, Arabic, and German on Middle East political and social issues have appeared in *The Oxford Encyclopedia of Islam, The Encyclopedia of the Modern Middle East, Middle East Journal, Feminist Issues, The Nation, Middle Eastern Studies, The Beirut Review, The World and I, The Muslim World, Al-Majal, Arab Studies Quarterly, Arab Studies Journal, Inamo Beiträge, Harvard International Review, Third World Quarterly,* and in various books and publications.